Queen Victoria's Wars

This is a new history of Britain's imperial wars during the nineteenth century. Including chapters on wars fought in the hills, on the veldt, in the dense forests, and along the coast, it discusses wars waged in China, Burma, Afghanistan, and India/Pakistan; New Zealand; and West, East, and South Africa. Leading military historians from around the world situate the individual conflict in the larger context of British domestic history and British foreign policy/grand strategy and examine the background of the conflict, the war aims, the outbreak of the war, the forces and technology employed, a narrative of the war, details about one specific battle, and the aftermath of the war. Beginning with the Indian Rebellion and ending with the South African War, this book enables readers to see the global impact of British imperialism, the function of the army in the service of British political goals, and the evolution of military technology.

Stephen M. Miller is Professor of History at the University of Maine. He is the author of *George White and the Victorian Army in India and Africa* (2020), *Volunteers on the Veld* (2007), and *Lord Methuen and the British Army* (1999), and editor of *Soldiers and Settlers in Africa, 1850–1918* (2009).

Queen Victoria's Wars
British Military Campaigns, 1857–1902

Edited by
Stephen M. Miller
University of Maine

CAMBRIDGE
UNIVERSITY PRESS

University Printing House, Cambridge CB2 8BS, United Kingdom

One Liberty Plaza, 20th Floor, New York, NY 10006, USA

477 Williamstown Road, Port Melbourne, VIC 3207, Australia

314–321, 3rd Floor, Plot 3, Splendor Forum, Jasola District Centre, New Delhi – 110025, India

79 Anson Road, #06-04/06, Singapore 079906

Cambridge University Press is part of the University of Cambridge.

It furthers the University's mission by disseminating knowledge in the pursuit of education, learning, and research at the highest international levels of excellence.

www.cambridge.org
Information on this title: www.cambridge.org/9781108490122
DOI: 10.1017/9781108785020

© Cambridge University Press 2021

This publication is in copyright. Subject to statutory exception and to the provisions of relevant collective licensing agreements, no reproduction of any part may take place without the written permission of Cambridge University Press.

First published 2021

Printed in the United Kingdom by TJ Books Limited, Padstow Cornwall

A catalogue record for this publication is available from the British Library.

ISBN 978-1-108-49012-2 Hardback

Cambridge University Press has no responsibility for the persistence or accuracy of URLs for external or third-party internet websites referred to in this publication and does not guarantee that any content on such websites is, or will remain, accurate or appropriate.

Contents

List of Maps		*page* vii
List of Contributors		viii
Acknowledgements		xii
1	Introduction STEPHEN M. MILLER	1
2	The Indian Rebellion, 1857–1858 DOUGLAS M. PEERS	8
3	Punitive Expeditions in China, 1857–1860 BRUCE COLLINS	40
4	The Expedition to Abyssinia, 1867–1868 CHRISTOPHER BRICE	62
5	The New Zealand Wars, 1845–1872 JOHN CRAWFORD	83
6	The Third Anglo-Asante War, 1873–1874 RYAN PATTERSON	106
7	The Second Afghan War, 1878–1880 RODNEY ATWOOD	126
8	The Anglo-Zulu War, 1879 IAN KNIGHT	146
9	The First Anglo-Boer War, 1880–1881 JOHN LABAND	167
10	Egypt and the Sudan, 1881–1885 ROB JOHNSON	187
11	The Third Anglo-Burmese War and the Pacification of Burma, 1885–1895 IAN F. W. BECKETT	220

12	The Tirah Campaign, 1897–1898 SAMEETAH AGHA	240
13	Reconquest of the Sudan, 1896–1898 EDWARD M. SPIERS	260
14	The South African War, 1899–1902 STEPHEN M. MILLER	281
15	Conclusion STEPHEN M. MILLER	308
	Index	312

Maps

2.1	The Indian Rebellion, 1857–1858	*page* 14
3.1	Eastern China, c. 1860	44
4.1	Abyssinia, 1867–1868	64
5.1	New Zealand Wars	89
6.1	Third Anglo-Asante War, 1873–1874	109
7.1	Afghanistan and North-West Frontier, c. 1879	129
8.1	The Anglo-Zulu War, 1879	148
9.1	The First Anglo-Boer War, 1880–1881	172
10.1	Egypt and the Sudan, 1882–1885	189
11.1	Burma, 1885–1895	223
12.1	The North-West Frontier of British India, c. 1900	244
13.1	Reconquest of the Sudan, 1896–1898	262
14.1	The South African War, 1899–1902	286

Contributors

SAMEETAH AGHA is Associate Professor of Modern World History at Pratt Institute, Brooklyn, New York. Her teaching and research areas include: imperialism and colonialism, British empire, military history, and colonial warfare and resistance with an emphasis on South Asia and Afghanistan. She has published several articles and essays on these topics and is most recently the author of *The Limits of Empire: Sub-imperialism and Pukhtun Resistance in the North-West Frontier* (2020).

RODNEY ATWOOD read history at McMaster University, Hamilton, Ontario (BA Hons) and Churchill College, Cambridge (PhD). Between those two periods of study, he served in the Royal Tank Regiment. He is the author of *The Hessians: Mercenaries from Hessen-Kassel in the American War of Independence* (1980), of three books on Field Marshal Lord Roberts including a biography, and an account of the life of General Lord Rawlinson.

IAN F. W. BECKETT retired as Professor of Military History at the University of Kent in 2015. A fellow of the Royal Historical Society, he has held chairs in both the United Kingdom and the United States, and was Chairman of the Council of the UK Army Records Society from 2001 to 2014. Internationally known for his work on the British army, his publications include *Rorke's Drift and Isandlwana* (2019); *A British Profession of Arms: The Politics of Command in the Late Victorian Army* (2018); and *Wolseley and Ashanti: The Asante War Journal and Correspondence of Major General Sir Garnet Wolseley, 1873–1874* (2009).

CHRISTOPHER BRICE, PhD, is a British independent scholar, lecturer, and member of the Victorian Military Society. He is the author of two books, *The Thinking Man's Soldier* (2012), a biography of General Sir Henry Brackenbury, and *Brave as a Lion* (2015), a biography of Field Marshal Hugh Gough. He is also working on three other books, one of which is a history of the Abyssinian Campaign of 1867–68. Alongside this he acts for the publisher Helion & Co Ltd as a series editor for their 1815–1914 series entitled *From Musket to Maxim*.

BRUCE COLLINS published books and articles on antebellum America before working on British power projection. His recent work includes *War and Empire: The Expansion of Britain, 1790–1830* (2010), 'Defining Victory in Victorian Warfare, 1860–1882', *Journal of Military History* (2013), and *Wellington and the Siege of San Sebastian, 1813* (2017). He is currently writing about the British counterinsurgency and the Indian Uprising of 1857. He has taught at the University of Glasgow and was Professor of International History at the University of Buckingham 1988–96. Following appointments as a dean, he was Professor of Modern History at Sheffield Hallam University from 2004 until his retirement in 2020.

JOHN CRAWFORD is the New Zealand Defence Force Historian and has written on many aspects of the history of the New Zealand Armed Forces and defence policy. Currently he is working on a book about New Zealand's campaigns against the Ottoman Empire during the First World War. His recent publications include: *Phenomenal and Wicked: Attrition and Reinforcement in the New Zealand Expeditionary Force at Gallipoli*, co-authored with Matthew Buck (2020) and *Tutu Te Puehu: New Perspectives on the New Zealand Wars*, co-edited with Ian McGibbon (2018). He is Chairman of the New Zealand Military History Committee.

ROB JOHNSON is Director of the Changing Character of War research centre at the University of Oxford, and a senior research fellow of Pembroke College. A former army officer, he specializes in the history of war, strategic leadership, and operational developments. His area of specialism is the Middle East and Arabic-speaking world, but also aspects of colonial and anti-colonial warfare. He is the author of several books, including *The Great War in the Middle East* (2016) and *True to Their Salt: Indigenous Forces in Western Armed Forces* (2017). He has recently authored a study of Lawrence of Arabia's ideas on war (2019).

IAN KNIGHT studied Afro-Caribbean history at the University of Kent. He has specialized in the study of the Anglo-Zulu War for forty years and has written widely on the subject. In 2000, he served as the historical adviser to the exploratory archaeological dig on the iSandlwana battlefield. He has appeared in a number of television documentaries on the subject and is an honorary research associate of the KwaZulu-Natal Museum. He has advised on a number of museum exhibitions, lectures on Anglo-Zulu history, and leads tours of the battlefields.

JOHN LABAND is Professor Emeritus of History, Wilfrid Laurier University, Canada, and a research associate in the Department of History, Stellenbosch University, South Africa. He is also a Life Member of Clare Hall, University of Cambridge, England, and a fellow of the University of KwaZulu-Natal, South Africa. He specializes in the history of the Zulu kingdom and in colonial wars in Africa. Among his recent books are *The Assassination of King Shaka* (2017), *The Land Wars: The Dispossession of the Khoisan and AmaXhosa in the Cape Colony* (2020), and *The Eight Zulu Kings from Shaka to Goodwill Zwelithini* (2018).

STEPHEN M. MILLER is Adelaide C. and Alan L. Bird Professor and Chair of the Department of History at the University of Maine. He is the author of *Lord Methuen and the British Army* (1999), *Volunteers on the Veld: Britain's Citizen-Soldiers and the South African War* (2007), and *George White and the Victorian Army in India and Africa* (2020), and editor of *Soldiers and Settlers in Africa, 1850–1918* (2009). He has contributed chapters to several books and has published articles in a number of journals, including the *Journal of Military History*, *Journal of British Studies*, *War in History*, and *War and Society*. He is a fellow of the Royal Historical Society.

RYAN PATTERSON, PhD, studies the British Empire and imperial culture with a particular emphasis on the professional and public engagement with nineteenth-century colonial and imperial small wars. His current work is an exploration of the methods and rationale by which new technologies were assessed and incorporated into the British military system, a process highly influenced by prevailing social and cultural movements at the heart of Victorian society. He is currently a contract instructor and research associate in history at Carleton University.

DOUGLAS M. PEERS is Professor of History at the University of Waterloo. He is the author of *Between Mars and Mammon: Colonial Armies and the Garrison State in Early-Nineteenth Century India* (1995), *India under Colonial Rule, 1700–1885* (2006), and, with Nandini Gooptu, co-edited *India and the British Empire* (2012), a companion volume for the *Oxford History of the British Empire*. He has published more than twenty-five articles and chapters on nineteenth-century India, focusing on the military and its influence on the evolution of the colonial state. He is currently writing a study of war and the making of modern South Asia.

EDWARD M. SPIERS is an emeritus professor at the University of Leeds. Among his twenty books are an edited work, *The Sudan: A Reconquest Reappraised* (1998); *The Scottish Soldier and Empire, 1854–1902* (2006); a co-edited volume, *A Military History of Scotland* (2012), which won the Saltire Prize and Templar Medal; and a trilogy on *Letters from the Sieges of Ladysmith, Kimberley and Mafeking* (2010, 2013, and 2019). He has also written six books on chemical and biological warfare.

Acknowledgements

Editing this book was a pleasure from start to finish. Douglas M. Peers, Bruce Collins, Christopher Brice, John Crawford, Ryan Patterson, Rodney Atwood, Ian Knight, John Laband, Rob Johnson, Ian F. W. Beckett, Sameetah Agha, and Edward M. Spiers have all been wonderful contributors. Their work is exceptional, they did not get upset with my meddling, and they met all the deadlines. I especially want to thank Ian Beckett for connecting me with many of the other contributors and offering important collegial support; John Laband for commenting on drafts of the introduction and for other assistance; and, Rob Johnson for reading drafts of the introduction and conclusion and helping me think about the structure of the book. Michael Watson and Emily Sharp have been extremely helpful at Cambridge University Press and their two anonymous reviewers offered critical insight into the project. Douglas M. Peers would like to thank the staff of the British Library and, in particular, what was once called the India Office Library and Records for more than thirty years of assistance and encouragement. Christopher Brice would like to thank George Anderson and Helion & Co Ltd for the use of the map which accompanies his chapter. John Crawford would like to thank Matthew Buck for reading his draft and making helpful suggestions. Ryan Patterson would like to acknowledge Professors Jeremy Black and Richard Noakes. Rodney Atwood would like to acknowledge Peter Boyden and Keith Surridge, who read a draft of the chapter, the gracious permission of H. M. The Queen for use of the 2nd Duke of Cambridge's papers in the Royal Archives, Windsor, the National Library of Wales for the Hills-Johns papers, the British Library Board for use of the India Office papers, and the National Army Museum for use of the Roberts, Haines and Charles Gough papers. Ian Knight would like to thank John Laband, for his advice and collaboration over the years; Paul Marais and Eric Boswell, for exploring rural KwaZulu Natal with him; and Isandlwana Lodge, whose hospitality he has enjoyed at the end of many a weary day tramping over the battlefields. Rob Johnson would like to acknowledge the National Army Museum, London, and the Bodleian

Library, Oxford. Ian F. W. Beckett would like to acknowledge Her Majesty's Stationery Office for quotation from the Crown copyright material in The National Archives, the Trustees of the British Library for material in the Asia, Pacific and Africa Collection (formerly the Oriental and India Office Collection), and the National Army Museum. Edward M. Spiers would like to acknowledge Hatfield House Muniments, The National Archives, the National Army Museum, Sudan Archive, University of Durham, Liddell Hart Centre for Military Archives, King's College London, Museum of Lincolnshire Life, National Library of Scotland, National Records of Scotland, and West Sussex Record Office. I would like to give special thanks to Peter Harrington at the Anne S. K. Brown Military Collection, Brown University Library, for providing the image for the book's cover and Martin Conte for indexing the book.

On a personal note, I would like to thank all those in the Department of History and the College of Liberal Arts and Sciences at the University of Maine for providing a supportive and vibrant intellectual home. This remains as true today during the global pandemic as it did twenty years ago when I arrived. I would also like to acknowledge the librarians at Fogler Library, University of Maine, The National Archives, and, the Wiltshire and Swindon History Centre. Two exceptional historians and people who helped shape my career sadly passed away recently. Bruce Vandervort, who served for many years as the editor of *The Journal of Military History* and contributed to my first edited collection, was kind enough to welcome me into the fold of military historians. Edmund Wehrle, Emeritus Professor at the University of Connecticut, mentored me during my time in graduate school at Storrs. Finally, I wish to thank my two sons, David and Max, K. M., N. M., and the late W. M. for getting me out of the house on walks, and my wife, Jessica, for her love and support.

1 Introduction

Stephen M. Miller

It was over fifty years ago that Brian Bond published his edited collection entitled *Victorian Military Campaigns*, a volume which brought together several of the leading military historians of the day to write about Great Britain's imperial wars of the nineteenth century. At the time, as Bond indicated in his introduction, the scholarship on the subject was quite limited and what existed was often deeply flawed. Historians were only starting to utilize the public archives and, of those, few were interested in military history. Some of the literature was excellent, but most writers of military history remained content writing hagiographies of great generals or recounting the narratives of great wars. Much of the work lacked political context and overlooked the 'enemy' which the British forces had to overcome, and often arguments could not be disentangled from 'imperialist assumptions'.[1] In a brief, yet significant attempt, Bond's contributors, as they had intended, made great inroads in expanding the body of literature and influencing scholars for years to come.

As a result, the scholarship of Victorian military campaigns has grown tremendously since the late 1960s. Political institutions and their relationship with the military have been examined as have important factors related to war and society. The tools of the social and cultural historian have been employed with great efficacy to unlock much of what we now know about the impact of class, race, and gender on the military. Historians are just as likely to study the impact of the regimental system on morale as they are the press, music hall, or volunteer associations. Although there are still some accounts written by journalists and others which make little or no attempt to connect to the available modern historiography and ground themselves firmly in the historical record, no serious historian today would forego a visit to the archives. Indeed, non-English language sources are increasingly seen as vital to any thorough investigation of British imperial history. English-language works

---

[1] Brian Bond (ed.), *Victorian Military Campaigns* (London: Hutchinson & Co., 1967), 3.

may still dominate the field, and the focus of study still leans towards the British experience, but the literature which presents the African, Asian or, in the case of New Zealand, the Māori experience, has grown dramatically as well. As an example of how much things have changed, the major work of reference which Bond mentioned in his introduction, Sir John Fortescue's thirteen-volume *History of the British Army*, heavy on operational detail and light on analysis, is not cited once by any of the contributors to this volume. The last volume of Fortescue's work, which overlaps with some of the period this book explores, may remain an important source for some investigations of the British military, notably how the history of the British army was viewed at the end of the nineteenth century, but its contribution to the study of Victorian imperial wars has been far overshadowed by more modern works.

British imperial conflicts, or 'small wars' as Colonel C. E. Callwell labelled them in his similarly titled work, are too many and too varied to cover in any detail in a single volume. Callwell himself, who wrote the first systematic study of these types of wars in 1896, was not interested in providing his readers with narratives of all these conflicts. He was writing a handbook to instruct officers who might encounter a great variety of conditions, adversaries, weapons, and tactics. By examining what these campaigns shared in common as well as how they differed, he was trying to show how campaigns could be won and lost. Callwell identified three types of small wars: (1) campaigns of conquest and annexation, (2) the suppressions of insurrection and lawlessness, and (3) campaigns to wipe out an insult or avenge a wrong or to overthrow a dangerous enemy.[2] It is important to note, however, that a campaign labelled as one type of small war could easily turn into a different type depending on political decisions and military expediency. Sometimes, these decisions were made in London, but as Bond noted, Victorian generals in the field were regularly granted great independence,[3] not just in overseeing military strategy but dictating peace terms and determining factors which could change the political future of the colony, territory, or annexed state.

Much of *Small Wars* focused on conflicts between Europeans and those who Callwell labelled pejoratively as 'half-civilized' or 'savage' who were 'deficient in courage and provided with poor weapons' and who shunned decisive action.[4] Callwell attempted to provide his readers with instructions of how to defeat this type of enemy whether it be

---

[2] C. E. Callwell, *Small Wars: Their Principles and Practice*, 3rd ed. (London: HMSO, 1906; Reprint, Lincoln: University of Nebraska Press, 1996), 25–28.
[3] Bond (ed.), *Victorian Military Campaigns*, 20.   [4] Callwell, *Small Wars*, 31–32.

through the seizure of his capital, the capture of a recognized political leader, or the destruction of his crops and livestock. The selection of the objective was often determined by the cause of the campaign and the perceived political structure of the enemy. In determining the appropriate tactics to utilize in the campaign, Callwell looked at environmental factors and discussed hill and bush warfare, as well as the principles of employing tactical expedients such as the square, the laager, and the zeriba to their maximum effect. He also had to consider the advantages which the breechloading rifle as well as new types of smokeless propellants and other advancements in artillery provided European countries over most of their overseas enemies which resulted in a profound technology gap which only began to shrink, in some cases where western technology could be imported, in the 1890s.

Early twenty-first-century conflict in the Middle East and Central Asia has generated a renewed interest in asymmetrical warfare and Callwell's observations. Naturally, a number of articles have appeared in the similarly entitled journal *Small Wars & Insurgencies*, but references to Callwell and small wars have appeared in all of the leading military history journals, including *The Journal of Military History*, *War & Society* and *War and History*.[5] Although many of the chapters in this volume do not specifically mention him by name, the authors were all keenly aware of Callwell's attempt to essentially codify the European, mostly British, experience of warfare overseas in the second half of the nineteenth century despite the great diversity of these imperial campaigns. All three types of small wars are discussed in the following chapters as are the environmental factors, the objective of the campaigns, and the political and social organization of the enemy. Callwell often ignored, rushed to assumptions, or did not understand the latter, and Bond's book was much more interested in looking at British institutions and British generals than in conducting detailed investigations of the armies, strategies, and war aims they had to counter. Organizational strength, however, was extremely important in determining how effectively the enemy could respond in wartime.

---

[5] See, for example, Alexander Morrison, '"The extraordinary successes which the Russians have achieved" – The Conquest of Central Asia in Callwell's Small Wars', *Small Wars & Insurgencies* 30, 4–5 (2019): 913–36; Daniel Whittingham, '"Savage warfare": C. E. Callwell, the roots of counter-insurgency, and the nineteenth century context', *Small Wars & Insurgencies* 23, 4–5 (2012): 591–607; and, David Martin Jones and M. L. R. Smith, 'Myth and the small war tradition: Reassessing the discourse of British counter-insurgency', *Small Wars & Insurgencies* 24, 3 (2013): 436–64. Also see, Daniel Whittingham, *Charles E. Callwell and the British Way of Warfare* (Cambridge: Cambridge University Press, 2020).

Politics at home frequently determined the timing of a small war, the objective, and the overall military response. It could also shape the aftermath of a successful campaign. Conservative, Liberal, and Whig governments alike engaged in small wars. At times, a change of government during a campaign could produce a significant impact on its direction. Commanding officers overnight could become hobbled by the civilian War Office or could take action prematurely out of fear of being recalled or anticipation of being pressured to end a war. All of the chapters in this volume, discuss how political actions at home could profoundly affect small wars overseas. They also examine the role of local politics.

The impetus for many of the military campaigns launched by Britain came from overseas and were instigated by the 'men on the spot'.[6] Military force could, as mentioned above, avenge a wrong or restore order, or perhaps allow for the better movement of trade or interrupt a monopoly, for example, which primarily benefited local actors. The location, local factors, and the type of conflict could also determine whether the British effort would rely on local auxiliaries and/or volunteers or use them to supplement British troops. But often campaigns were launched with foreign policy in mind. Transportation and communication networks had to be protected; vulnerable frontiers had to be safeguarded. Fears of Russian intrigue in Central Asia, French challenges to the Nile and Indochina, and a potential German–Boer alliance in Southern Africa all directly or indirectly produced military activity which had far-reaching consequences. The contributors have addressed, when relevant, issues of foreign policy and security both at home and overseas.

The contributors have also paid close attention to what Daniel R. Headrick referred to in 1981 as the 'progress and power of industrial technology' and its linkages to Europe's rapid conquest of Africa and Asia during the Age of New Imperialism.[7] 'The Tools of Empire', whether they came in the form of technological innovation or invention which opened up an arms gap or led to advances in communication and transportation, at times, gave Great Britain a decisive advantage in some of these conflicts. The following chapters discuss, when relevant, how the British Army utilized new technologies to overcome both the enemy and

---

[6] See Ronald Robinson and John Gallagher with Alice Denny, *Africa and the Victorians*, 2nd ed. (London: Macmillan, 1981); and Alexander Schölch, 'The "men on the spot" and the English occupation of Egypt in 1882', *The Historical Journal* 19, 3 (1976): 773–85.

[7] Daniel R. Headrick, *The Tools of Empire: Technology and European Imperialism in the Nineteenth Century* (New York: Oxford University Press, 1981), 3.

environmental factors, as well as address what technologies their opponents were able to employ.

In his delightfully crafted 1972 account, *Queen Victoria's Little Wars*, the popular historian Byron Farwell mentioned as many as sixty campaigns the Victorian army took part in during the second part of the nineteenth century and tried to detail almost half of them in thirty dedicated chapters.[8] The scope of this work is not as ambitious but nevertheless presents thirteen imperial conflicts dating chronologically between the Indian Rebellion of 1857–58 and the South African War, 1899–1902. By limiting the number of expeditions considered, the authors have been able to examine each case in greater detail. Each chapter includes discussions of the origins of the conflict, its outbreak, the armies employed by both sides, the war aims, the role of technology, the function of the Royal Navy, when pertinent, and the aftermath. In addition, each chapter includes an up-to-date historiographical discussion and provides further reading. A brief narrative of each conflict is included as is, in most cases, an examination of a typical battle during the campaign.

As mentioned before, this book does not include discussions of every small war Great Britain engaged in during the period under examination. It has included the most significant, in terms of numbers and cost, and has attempted to provide a good cross section, including wars of imperial conquest, campaigns of pacification, and punitive expeditions. By including wars in North, South, East, and West Africa; South, Central, and East Asia; and in New Zealand, it has demonstrated the regional, topographical, and climatic diversity highlighting the organizational difficulties and challenges which Great Britain had to overcome. Beginning with the Indian Rebellion and ending with the South African War, it also enables readers to see the impact of changing military and military-purposed technology on strategy and tactics during this fifty-year period. Whereas the Bond volume omitted both the Indian Rebellion and the South African War, a thorough understanding of each is absolutely indispensable to an examination of imperial small wars.

Douglas Peers' investigation of the Indian Rebellion starts off this collection of essays. India was such a vital component of the British empire that its security, both domestic and foreign, was paramount and had to be protected at all costs. In large numbers, British forces, along with Sikhs from the Punjab and Gurkhas from nearby Nepal, were

---

[8] Byron Farwell, *Queen Victoria's Little Wars* (New York: W. W. Norton & Company, 1972). Also see Philip J. Haythornthwaite, *The Colonial Wars Source Book* (London: Arms and Armour, 1995).

required to preserve Britain's rule in India when challenged in 1857 by a variety of forces, including many mutinous sepoys in the Bengal Army. Britain continued to maintain a large European and Indian force throughout its rule which was utilized at home and overseas in several small wars. Whether the British government or the Governor-General/ Viceroy practiced a forward policy or one of 'masterly inactivity', force was regularly utilized to further strategic and economic ambitions. In the case of Afghanistan, as Rodney Atwood shows in Chapter 7, the goal of the small war was not annexation but to ensure influence on the frontier. When the war ended, the troops returned to their peacetime activities. In the case of Upper Burma, however, as Ian F. W. Beckett demonstrates in Chapter 11, many years of pacification were required after the rapid seizure of Mandalay, the overthrow of the ruling family, and annexation. The expedition to Tirah in 1897 – launched in part to pacify the Afridi and the Orakzais and to restore British prestige, as Sameetah Agha argues in Chapter 12 – did little to change British policies on the frontier.

Bruce Collins looks at Britain's punitive expeditions to China between 1857 and 1860 in Chapter 3. Although there were certainly strategic issues at stake, mostly concerning other western powers, the British government asserted that wrongs had to be avenged and commercial practices had to be protected and augmented. Although not driven by economic factors but solely by the need to maintain prestige, Christopher Brice, in Chapter 4, looks at the unique conflict in Abyssinia in the 1860s and the success the British achieved against both Tewodros II and nature. As Callwell wrote, 'small wars are, generally speaking, campaigns rather against nature than against hostile armies'.[9] In Chapter 6, which addresses the Third Anglo-Asante War, Ryan Patterson similarly asserts it was the local environment which presented such great challenges to Sir Garnet Wolseley's expedition. The British forces had to overcome supply problems caused by distance and lack of roads, disease, and combat in dense forests. In Chapter 5, John Crawford investigates the New Zealand Wars, a series of conflicts lasting more than forty years, waged between Māori and the British armed forces and British (Pākehā) settlers primarily over land rights, which proved disastrous for the Māori.

Many of Great Britain's most formidable opponents during the period of investigation proved to be in northern and southern Africa. In Chapter 10, Rob Johnson details two small wars. The first, the Egyptian Campaign of 1881–82, secured the safety of the newly built Suez Canal and ensured British indirect control in Cairo. The second,

---

[9] Callwell, *Small Wars*, 57.

which proved much more difficult, and resulted in the failure of relieving Khartoum in time to save Charles Gordon, was the war in the Sudan against Mahdist forces. Edward M. Spiers continues the story of the British in the Sudan in Chapter 13. Sir H. H. Kitchener's successful reconquest would restore British prestige and add to his own growing reputation. In Chapter 8, Ian Knight discusses the Anglo-Zulu War of 1879, the result of a mixture of political, strategic, and economic concerns, which included, arguably, the greatest defeat the British suffered in battle in their many small wars. But if the British fully restored their prestige after the Battle of iSandlwana by winning the war, it was challenged again only two years later and 100 miles away at Majuba Hill. John Laband explores the First Anglo-Boer War, what Callwell identified as 'operations of regular armies against irregular, or comparatively speaking irregular forces' in Chapter 9.[10] Those same irregular forces were put to a much greater test twenty years later when British forces, eventually numbering upwards of half a million, faced off against the Transvaal and Orange Free State commandos in a terrible campaign which devastated the land, and led to the deaths of more than 25,000 white, primarily, children, and perhaps 20,000 Africans in concentration camps. In the final chapter, Stephen M. Miller discusses the South African War, 1899–1902.

[10] Ibid., 21.

2 The Indian Rebellion, 1857–1858

Douglas M. Peers

Background

The uprising known variously as the Indian Mutiny, the Indian Rebellion, the First War of Indian Independence, the Sepoy War, or even the Soldiers' Revolution has been the subject of hundreds of books, articles, and pamphlets.[1] Others have turned to the Urdu expression, *ghadar*, which translated means outburst, mayhem, rebellion, riot, or disturbance,[2] in an effort to encapsulate what consisted of a loosely connected series of events involving military mutinies, civil unrest, economic protests, religious revivals, and efforts at restoring dethroned aristocrats. Mutiny was for a long time the most common term, particularly amongst the British. But mutiny is a very limiting term: it was not only sepoys who challenged British rule – peasant cultivators, their landlords (*zamindars* and *taluqdars*), and many religious figures also participated. Others joined in at the prospect of plunder or settling old scores. Benjamin Disraeli aptly observed that 'the people of India were only waiting for an occasion and a pretext'.[3] By the end of July 1857, three months after the first regiments had risen against their officers, only thirteen of the seventy-four Bengal Native Infantry Regiments were still in existence, the rest having mutinied or been disarmed and disbanded, often with considerable loss of life. All ten regular cavalry regiments had mutinied, and ten of the eighteen irregular cavalry regiments had mutinied or been disbanded. In other words, more than two thirds of the native portion of the Bengal Army had either disappeared or taken up arms

---

[1] Updated spellings have been used as far as possible except in instances where either the quote is from a contemporary source, the term was part of official nomenclature used at the time, or the changes are so recent that many readers may not be aware of the difference. 'Native' is used when necessary to prevent confusion when trying to identify or differentiate between individuals or units of Indian rather than European heritage, e.g. native regiments or native officers.

[2] Mahmood Farooqui (ed.), *Besieged 1857: Voices from Delhi* (New Delhi: Penguin, 2010), 394.

[3] Eric Stokes, *The Peasant Armed* (Oxford: Oxford University Press, 1986), 13.

against their one-time masters. There were isolated outbreaks of violence elsewhere with smaller mutinies breaking out as far east as Chittagong and Dhaka and in various stations of the Bombay Presidency including Karachi, Satara, and Kolhapur, as well as in Hyderabad and a few stations of the Madras Presidency. Even the French in their enclave at Pondicherry were sufficiently worried to request protection.[4] Contemporaries feared and not without some justification that India might be lost to the British. Henry Norman, the Assistant Adjutant General of the Bengal Army, observed just how quickly colonial rule had collapsed, and wrote to his wife that 'We did not meet one single cart, or any sign of trade. Everywhere the dak bungalows, turnpikes, police stations and telegraph lines had been destroyed. Ten months before I had travelled along the road witnessing every sign of good government and prosperity'.[5]

These uprisings have been attributed to a Muslim conspiracy, a Hindu Brahmin plot, Christianization, not enough Christianization, modernization, not enough modernization, resurgence of tradition, and peasant discontent. Militarily, the rebels often displayed determination, commitment, and ingenuity. But the lack of an overall strategic plan, their failure to break out of the Doab (the lands lying between the Jumna and the Ganges) and ignite other areas, and their difficulties fighting large scale pitched battles against the British ultimately led to their defeat. For their part, British forces tended to best the rebels when they faced them in an open battle, but whatever advantages the British possessed were often neutralized in the bitter and bloody street fighting necessary to retake cities and towns.

A distinguishing feature of these conflicts was the savagery and destructiveness exhibited by nearly all participants. The sheer scale of the crisis and extent to which colonial authority nearly disappeared caught the British by surprise. Shock produced demands for revenge, creating what became in many respects a race war. It was also an early example of a total war, at least in terms of the extent to which distinctions between military and civilians disappeared, which accounts in part for the brutality. Arthur Peppin, a private trader in Calcutta, wrote in June 1857 that 'the fright continues strong as ever', and went on to justify the violence unleashed as it was 'more than a hatred of people to people,

---

[4] Lord Clarendon to Vernon Smith, 29 Sept 1857, MSS Eur F231/23, India Office Library and Records, British Library (IOLR).
[5] William Lee-Warner, *Memoirs of Field Marshal Sir Henry Wylie Norman* (London: Smith, Elder and Co., 1908), 176.

but of race to race'.[6] Race and religion were often used interchangeably: hence a war on heathens was synonymous with a war on natives who were described and marked by their skin colour. And while the dominant narrative at the time stressed British courage in the face of adversity and the perfidy of their Indian subjects, there were some who acknowledged with regret that revenge had become an end in itself. William Howard Russell, the Crimean War correspondent from the *Times* who was dispatched to India, lamented that 'All these kinds of vindictive, unchristian, Indian tortures, such as sewing Mahomedans in pig-skins, smearing them with pork-fat before execution, and burning their bodies, and forcing Hindoos to defile themselves, are disgraceful, and ultimately recoil on ourselves. They are spiritual and mental tortures to which we have no right to resort, and which we dare not perpetrate in the face of Europe'.[7]

Most commentaries on the Mutiny have framed their discussions in terms of a colonial dichotomy pitting what is British against what is Indian, a convention which ironically has been perpetuated by nationalist narratives. But on closer scrutiny one finds many parallels between the colonial forces and their rebel opponents, including recourse to religion and a readiness to use terror and brutality not only on combatants but on civilians at large. Would-be martyrs were found on both sides as were appeals to be doing the work of God. The British were tempted to read religion into everything, and to try and characterize rebel actions and thinking within tight religious parameters. Religion also shaped the actions of British soldiers. At Lucknow, Henry Norman found that some sailors who were serving with the relieving force had taken some 24-pounder shot and used it to smash some glass and marble at Shah Najaf; they declared that they 'did not intend to stand any of their idolatry'.[8] And in Delhi, a British soldier nicknamed 'Quaker Wallace' bayonetted mutineers while chanting the 116th psalm.[9]

In practice, religion proved to be far more malleable than what colonial narratives have typically assumed. It was never as simple as a fight between one religion and another, nor was religion in and of itself an all-determining force even though British explanation at the time tended to fixate on religion, and particularly what they saw as a Muslim conspiracy. Rebel proclamations which spoke of Hindu–Muslim unity, and

---

[6] Arthur Peppin, 22 June 1857, MSS Eur C488, IOLR.
[7] William Howard Russell, *My Diary in India, in the Year 1858–9*, 4th ed. (London: Routledge Warne and Routledge, 1860), ii, 46.
[8] Lee-Warner, *Memoirs*, 187.
[9] William Dalrymple, 'Religious rhetoric in the Delhi Uprising', in Sabyasachi Bhattacharya (ed.), *Rethinking 1857* (New Delhi: Orient BlackSwan, 2007), 35.

orders prohibiting the slaughter of cattle, existed alongside episodes of communal violence such as the murder of Muslim butchers by high caste sepoys. As Nile Green has written, 'Muslims and their religion were at times less the enemies of empire than its assistants ... [religion] was capable of assisting or resisting imperial agendas, lending mechanisms of loyalty no less than rebellion'.[10] Religion provided a language and a framework around which resistance could be articulated and directed, but was not the all determining force upon Indians that contemporary sources often assumed. Instead, religion provided the participants with a vocabulary, an identity, and a rationale for what was happening.

★ ★ ★ ★

Few events in Indian or Imperial history have generated the number of publications as has the Indian Mutiny of 1857, arguably it was the subject of more literary works than any other conflict in the nineteenth century.[11] Yet while there is no shortage of British official and unofficial, published and unpublished sources from which to work, the same cannot be said for vernacular sources. A large trove of ten thousand plus documents which comprise the Mutiny papers at the National Archives of India have been recently mined by a number of scholars, notably William Dalrymple and Mahmood Farooqui.[12] But the literature remains handicapped by a paucity of first-hand accounts from sepoy participants. *From Sepoy to Subedar*, first published in 1873, is the one autobiography purportedly left by an Indian soldier in the nineteenth century, but its authenticity is open to question. If Sita Ram did exist, it is likely that the life described by him was rewritten and repackaged to make it more palatable to a British audience still seeking to understand the Rebellion in a way that did not call core beliefs into question.[13] Notably, it charts the declining discipline and morale in the Army and is nostalgic for an earlier era marked by mutual respect and comprehensibility between Indian sepoy and British officer. Kaushik Roy's translation from Bengali of the memoirs of Durgadas Bandopadhyay provides a welcome and unique perspective, albeit an after-the-fact retrospective from a middle-class

---

[10] Nile Green, *Islam and the Army in Colonial India* (Cambridge: Cambridge University Press, 2009), x–xi.
[11] Gautam Chakravarty, *The Indian Mutiny and the British Imagination* (Cambridge: Cambridge University Press, 2005), 3.
[12] Farooqui (ed.), *Besieged 1857*, 396; William Dalrymple, *The Last Mughal: The Fall of a Dynasty, Delhi, 1857* (London: Bloomsbury, 2006).
[13] Sita Ram, *From Sepoy to Subedar: Being the Life and Adventures of Subedar Sita Ram, a Native Officer of the Bengal Army Written and Related by Himself* (London: Macmillan, 1970).

Bengali military clerk employed by and loyal to the British who served with the 8th Bengal Irregular Cavalry, a regiment which mutinied at Bareilly in May 1857.[14]

A key foundation for much of what has been written on 1857–58 is the multi-volume history of the Indian Rebellion initiated and written in part by Sir J. W. Kaye, and which was later revised and extended by Colonel G. B. Malleson. The wide range of sources which fed into this history and its narrative form gave it immediacy and an authenticity that consolidated its reputation. Kaye, unusual for the time, acknowledged that it was more than simply a mutiny of discontented soldiers and argued that efforts to westernize India were largely to blame. Malleson was less interested in probing the deeper causes, particularly within the wider population, and instead used his history to prove British racial superiority.

The hundredth anniversary of the Rebellion not surprisingly resulted in a proliferation of histories and, of these, S. N. Sen's *Eighteen Fifty-Seven* stands out for its thoughtful and careful reassessment. Somewhat surprisingly given that it was produced at the behest of a government keen to frame 1857 within a national narrative, Sen found no evidence to sustain the argument, stretching back through the Hindutva ideologue V. D. Savarkar to Karl Marx, that 1857–58 was the First War of Indian Independence.[15] He concluded that it was primarily a military mutiny, driven largely by the grievances of the Company's sepoys, though it drew its 'strength from the widespread disaffection among the civilian population'.[16] The connection between the military and wider society was further tested by Eric Stokes in *Peasant Armed* which concluded that 'in a real sense the revolt was essentially the revolt of a peasant army breaking loose from its foreign masters'.[17] Stokes's work has been extended and complemented by more regionally focused studies by Rudrangshu Mukherjee on Awadh and Tapti Roy on Bundelkhand.[18]

The recent study of the military dimensions of 1857–58 by Saul David has pushed back against the soldier-as-peasant model, arguing that it was ultimately a massive mutiny by what were in effect mercenary troops

---

[14] Kaushik Roy (ed.), *1857 Uprising: A Tale of an Indian Warrior* (London: Anthem, 2008).

[15] Vinayak Damodar Savarkar, *The Indian War of Independence of 1857* ([London]: [s.n.], 1909).

[16] S. N. Sen, *Eighteen Fifty-Seven* (Delhi: Ministry of Information and Broadcasting, 1957), 405.

[17] Stokes, *The Peasant Armed*, 14.

[18] Rudrangshu Mukherjee, *Awadh in Revolt, 1857–1858: A Study in Popular Resistance* (Delhi: Oxford University Press, 1984); Tapti Roy, *The Politics of a Popular Uprising: Bundelkhand in 1857* (Delhi: Oxford University Press, 1994).

against their foreign master.[19] Kaushik Roy and Sabyasachi Dasgupta have given the sepoys a fresh examination, and while not denying their roots within peasant society, they have come down somewhere between Stokes and David, arguing persuasively that sepoys are much more than simply peasants in uniform.[20] Military service imbued within them a strong corporate identity and encouraged wider perspectives than would have been the case if they were merely armed peasants. The power of rumour and the manner in which violence became a means in and of itself for both sides during the rebellion is explored in recent writings by Kim Wagner.[21]

Outbreak of War

Barely a year before the Rebellion broke, Henry Lawrence, British Commissioner to the recently annexed Kingdom of Awadh, warned that 'Those who have watched events, or have studied Indian Military History, can distinctly trace almost all past murmurs and mutinies, we might indeed say every one, to some error or omission, trivial or great, of our own'.[22] There were clear signs of discontent in the Bengal Army, less so in the other Presidency armies, and, in particular, there were growing protests amongst the sepoys over a new cartridge which would accompany the new Enfield rifle. Loading the rifle required the soldier or sepoy to bite open a greased cartridge, the grease necessary to make pushing the ball down the barrel easier. The grease was initially made of cow and pig fat, defiling to both Hindus and Muslims. This was quickly changed to beeswax and linseed oil and the government sought to reassure sepoys that no offence had been intended. The damage, however, was done. Rumours circulated that the British were deliberately using pig and cow fat to violate the sepoys' religions. Charles Canning, Governor-General of India (1856–62), observed that 'The men it seems have no objection to use the cartridge on their own, but dread the taunts of their comrades after they have rejoined', and went on to concede that 'on the matter of the grease the govt was to some degree in the wrong, not having taken all

---

[19] Saul David, *The Indian Mutiny, 1857* (London: Viking, 2002).
[20] Kaushik Roy, 'Combat, combat motivation and the construction of identities: A case study,' in Gavin Rand and Crispin Bates (eds.), *Mutiny at the Margins: New Perspectives on the Indian Uprising of 1857*, vol. 4, *Military Aspects of the Indian Uprising* (New Delhi: Sage, 2013), '24–40; Sabyasachi Dasgupta, *In Defence of Honour and Justice: Sepoy Rebellions in the Nineteenth Century* (New Delhi: Primus, 2015).
[21] Most notably, Kim A. Wagner, *The Skull of Alum Bheg: The Life and Death of a Rebel of 1857* (Oxford: Oxford University Press, 2018).
[22] Henry Lawrence, 'The Indian Army', *Calcutta Review* 26 (1856): 206.

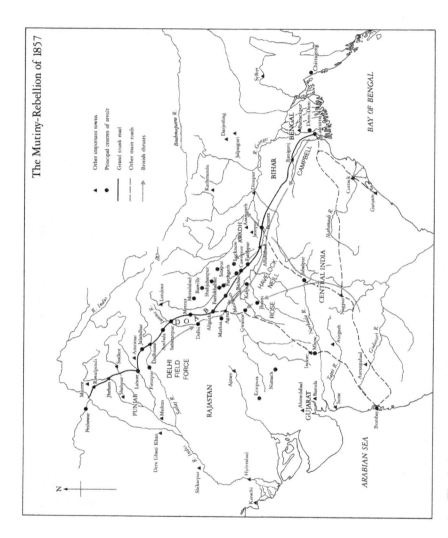

Map 2.1 The Indian Rebellion, 1857–1858.
National Portrait Gallery, London

the precautions that might have been taken to exclude objectionable ingredients'.[23] When approached by J. W. Kaye for his opinion on the issue of the cartridge, the Muslim educationalist and political leader, Sir Syed Ahmad Khan reported that 'Almost all the sepoys had unanimously resolved never to bite the cartridge [and] had the sepoys at Meerut been given an alternative to biting the cartridge, or could have resigned the service, they would have done so and there would not have been a mutiny'.[24]

Matters reached a crescendo in February 1857 when sepoys in the 19th Bengal Native Infantry stationed at Berhampur refused to use the new cartridge. Orders were issued that they were to be marched down to Barrackpur where they would be disarmed and disbanded. A month later, Mangal Pandey, a sepoy in the 34th Bengal Native Infantry attacked and tried to kill two officers at Barrackpur. That he did so in public and that no sepoys tried to stop him illustrates how much discipline had broken down. Pandey was tried and executed.[25] So too was Issuree Pandy, a jemadar from his regiment, who was charged with failing to arrest and stop Mangal Pandey and for preventing others from doing so.[26] The army, increasingly mindful of just how extensive the alarm was over the new cartridges, coupled these punitive acts with reassurances that there was no plan of interfering with their religion. But such efforts were to no avail for greased cartridges were only a catalyst. The precarious discipline of the Bengal Army, the sepoys' propensity to turn to mutiny as a collective protest, and the presence across North India of many dispossessed and discontented communities created a particularly explosive environment.

The Bengal Army had a uniquely hybrid military culture, one which combined British drill and organization with a respect bordering on obsession for Indian cultural practices and religious customs. The infantry mainly recruited from the middle ranking, but higher caste agricultural communities of eastern Awadh and western Bihar, communities which had historically sought to supplement agricultural incomes with military service.[27] The cavalry drew more heavily from Muslim

---

[23] Charles Canning to General Anson, 4 April 1857, MSS Eur F699/1/1/4/2 #14, IOLR.
[24] Syed Ahmad Khan to J. W. Kaye, 14 Dec 1869, Mutiny Papers of Sir J. W. Kaye, H/MISC/725 (33), 1011–16.
[25] General Order, 18 April 1857, L/MIL/17/2/306, p. 285, IOLR.
[26] General Order, 21 April 1857, L/MIL/17/2/306, p. 296, IOLR.
[27] Dirk H. A. Kolff, *Naukar, Rajput, and Sepoy: The Ethnohistory of the Military Labour Market of Hindustan, 1450–1850* (Cambridge: Cambridge University Press, 1990) and Seema Alavi, *The Sepoys and the Company: Tradition and Transition in Northern India, 1770–1830* (Delhi: Oxford University Press, 1995).

communities in Rohilkhand and further west including Pathans and Punjabi Muslims. British officers in Bengal took pride in what they saw as more martial and respectable soldiers and encouraged their sepoys to maintain their religious practices.[28] This led to a strong corporate culture, one which was also self reproducing as Bengal sepoys were given regular furloughs so they could visit their families where they were expected to return with new recruits. In Madras, sepoys were recruited from a wider range of communities, making their military service a vehicle for upward mobility. Bombay drew heavily upon the same areas and communities as the Bengal Army, but the Bombay Army made far less accommodation for religious and caste customs and practices. Consequently, while individual acts of dissent and indiscipline could and did occur in any of the presidency armies, collective acts were much more likely in the Bengal army due to its much stronger corporate identity, an identity which the British officers had done much to encourage out of their respect for what they understood as the caste and religious rites expected by their recruits.[29]

Given the sepoys' strong sense of corporate identify, the Indian Army was frequently beset by collective protest, some of which had been violently suppressed such as the mutiny of the 47th Bengal Native Infantry at Barrackpur in 1824. But prior to 1857, such breakdowns had usually been contained within the unit where they arose and there was little evidence that they commanded much attention or support from civil society. The situation was different in 1857. Much of Indian society was on edge, and nowhere was this more evident than in what was then Awadh and the North Western Provinces, the region that was not coincidentally the major recruiting ground of the Bengal Army. Military training and service did give sepoys a unique corporate identity, but they could never be fully isolated and consequently were exposed to the fears and grievances of the communities from whence they came. As George Clerk, one of the most experienced and insightful administrators in the region, noted, the 'sepoy is, at all times, the exponent of the feelings of the fraternity there – and chiefly the agricultural classes and castes'.[30]

---

[28] Douglas M. Peers, 'Army discipline, military cultures, and state formation in colonial India, ca. 1780–1860', in Huw Bowen, Elizabeth Mancke, and John Reid (eds.), *Britain's Oceanic Empire: Atlantic and Indian Ocean World, c.1550–1850* (Cambridge: Cambridge University Press, 2012), 282–308.

[29] Dasgupta, *In Defence of Honour and Justice*, 75; Douglas M. Peers, '"The habitual nobility of being": British officers and the social construction of the Bengal Army in the early 19th century', *Modern Asian Studies* 25 (1991): 545–69.

[30] George Clerk, Commonplace Book, MSS Eur D538/6, ff. 17–18, IOLR.

It was widely believed with justification that morale within the Bengal Army was rapidly deteriorating. Military service was seen as no longer providing the status and benefits it had once conferred. Opportunities for advancement were limited as promotion from the sepoy ranks to native officer was determined by seniority and there were just not enough vacancies. Salaries for sepoys had remained unchanged for more than half a century. With inflation outpacing salaries, any additional perquisites or benefits took on an added importance. *Batta* (field pay) was one entitlement. Efforts to curb military expenditure had led to constraints being placed on where and when it would be paid, further threatening to weaken the sepoys' material condition as well as their sense of status. The same was true of making overseas service voluntary in Bengal but not in the other presidencies. This was due to the recognition that overseas service was considered to be polluting, necessitating expensive purification rituals upon the sepoy's return to recover their status. The General Enlistment Act of 1856 put an end to this by dictating that all sepoys who joined the Bengal Army in the future would be liable for service anywhere they were ordered. For many sepoys, this was further proof that the Army was deliberately trying to weaken if not destroy their identity as high caste warriors. The deteriorating situation was compounded by what many viewed as the regrettable alienation of European officers from their sepoys.[31] In addition to the growing estrangement caused by the increasing insularity of the European community in India, ambitious European officers became more inclined to seek postings elsewhere, either in military administration or in civil and political positions where they could expect better pay and promotion prospects.

Revolt spread most quickly in those areas where colonial rule was in its earliest and most disruptive phase. Traditional elites were losing out and there were relatively few groups or individuals who had come to benefit. Economic turmoil and social upheaval accompanied the political transition. This was very noticeable in Central India and the Gangetic plains, which included the North Western Provinces and Awadh, where peasant farmers and small landholders faced growing tax demands from an increasingly alien administration. Nomadic and marginalized communities also found their lives increasingly constrained by the colonial state. Moreover, while it would be anachronistic to try and frame much of this reaction against colonialism as a form of nationalism, given that the nation had yet to be defined, there were nevertheless several cultural

---

[31] 'The past and the present of the Sepoy Army', *The Friend of India* (23 July 1857): 703–04.

and intellectual currents which transcended religion, language, and caste/class, and served to bind people together.[32]

Much of the turmoil in North India can be attributed to actions taken during the governor-generalship of Lord Dalhousie (1848–56). A keen modernizer, and in general unimpressed by Indian society and culture, he actively promoted the introduction of railways and telegraphs, and pushed for western education and greater commercialization of Indian agriculture. He was impatient with Indian customs and traditions and actively sought where possible to replace princely rule and the landed classes. He instituted the doctrine of lapse which negated the longstanding practice in Indian kingdoms of the ruler having the option of adopting his heir. States which lacked a biological male heir were deemed to lapse to the British, enabling the British to seize control of a number of key Indian states. A number of rulers who were affected, including the Rani of Jhansi and Nana Sahib, would become rebel leaders in 1857.

Dalhousie also ordered the annexation of Awadh (known then as Oude or Oudh) on the grounds that it was being misruled. Annexation accelerated the imposition of private property rights, and with that key land-controlling segments of rural society (known as *taluqdars*) lost significant rights in land which was the basis of their prosperity and status. In a posthumously published article, Henry Lawrence described the very volatile composition of Awadh as he found it in 1856–57: 'Oude has long been the Alsatia of India. In that province were to be met, even more than at Hyderabad or at Lahore, the Afreedee and Durukzye of the Khyber, the Belooch of Khelat, and the Wazaree of the Sulimani range. There also congregated the idle, the dissipated, and the disaffected of every Native state in India'.[33]

In early 1857, sepoys from disbanded regiments heading home to their villages in eastern Awadh and western Bihar helped spread discontent and provided a key vector for the circulation of rumours and information. Anxieties were heightened by reports that the British were grinding bones into flour and throwing pig and cattle carcasses into wells in a calculated effort to cause Indians to lose their caste and religion. While there was no basis for many of these rumours, some British actions understandably triggered alarms. At Fatepur, the local judge translated and posted the ten commandments in his courthouse. He was an early victim of the rebels, shot by a crowd that reportedly carried the Koran before them. A translation from Urdu of a printed circular published at Bareilly

---

[32] Rajat Kanta Ray, *The Felt Community: Commonality and Mentality before the Emergence of Indian Nationalism* (New Delhi: Oxford University Press, 2002), 353–60.

[33] Henry Lawrence, 'Army reform', *Calcutta Review* 27 (1858): 110.

stressed that the 'English are destroyers of faith' and declared that 'We all know now that if these English stay in Hindustan they will kill everyone and spoil the faith' and offered in a gesture of solidarity that Muslims will commit to ending cow slaughter if Hindus join them.[34] Even in the army there were some officers, General Hugh Wheeler at Kanpur among them, who sought religious discussions with their sepoys in the hopes of securing converts.[35]

British and Rebel Forces

At least initially, there was more in common than uncommon between the two sides. As one contemporary noted, 'The reality was both armies facing each other belonged to the same government and had been trained by the same British officers'.[36] Moreover, despite the many sepoy regiments that disappeared because of mutinies, the British still relied heavily on Indian troops, a combination of those that had remained loyal together with recruits from newly taken territories, Sikhs from the Punjab in particular, as well as Gurkha levies provided by the King of Nepal. In terms of training, and at least initially in terms of weaponry, there was more in common between the rebel forces and the British than might appear. Small arms were similar though more British than sepoy regiments had been given Enfields.

In 1857, the East India Company had under its control some 36,000 British soldiers, 257,000 Indian regulars, and 54,000 irregulars. Of the regular forces, 24,000 European and 136,000 native troops were in Bengal. But they were very unevenly distributed, with the bulk of the European troops concentrated in the recently-conquered Punjab and along the ever-turbulent northwest frontier. Between Calcutta and Delhi, a densely populated area swept by the Rebellion, there were only five European regiments, of which two were in Calcutta, leaving one each for Lucknow, Dinapur, and Agra. Twelve European regiments were posted to the west of Delhi, and these would become a vital reservoir from which the British could draw once they were confident that they had a good grip on the Punjab. In the Punjab, while individual regiments of the Bengal Army either mutinied or came close to it, the colonial infrastructure was not so dangerously exposed. There, the British could count

---

[34] 'The Shastras and the obligation to fight the treacherous firangis', in Farooqui (ed.), *Besieged 1857* (pamphlet published in Bareilly, undated), 23–25.
[35] Charles Canning to General Anson, 10 April 1857, MSS Eur F699/1/1/4/2 (15), IOLR.
[36] Zahir Dehlvi, *Dastan-E-Ghadar: The Tale of the Mutiny*, trans. Rana Safvi (New Delhi: Penguin Books, 2017), 110.

upon larger numbers of European troops to subdue any signs of discontent in any native infantry or cavalry posted to the province. The British were also assisted by the lack of any clear popular identification with or empathy in the Punjab for sepoys in the Bengal Army. The local population instead remembered the *purbiyahs* (roughly translates as 'easterners', a term used to describe the sepoys of the East India Company) as the force which had only recently conquered them. In fact, the British found there was enthusiastic take-up to their calls for volunteers to join units being sent down to Delhi and the Doab.

Initially, however, British authorities in the Punjab were only willing to dispatch four regiments to deal with the mutinies breaking out between Delhi and Allahabad. But once authorities had addressed their security concerns over native infantry regiments stationed there – partly through disarming and disbanding, partly through brutal suppression of discontent – more Europeans were released for service. Native infantry regiments in the Punjab and northwest frontier which were broken up were replaced by locally raised levies of Sikhs and Punjabi Muslims. They recruited enough to garrison the Punjab and provide fresh units to strengthen the British columns attempting to restore order between Delhi and Lucknow. Over time, the British were able to grow and deploy their manpower effectively. The rebels, however, failed to expand either their numbers or their area of operation.

The British also benefitted from the relative stability of the Bombay and Madras armies. While there were undeniable signs of discontent in those armies, and some prosecutions for mutiny, they remained largely loyal throughout. Not loyal enough to allow them to be deployed in large numbers against the rebels, but sufficiently reliable that the British could redeploy some Europeans from these presidencies to Bengal. To these would be added European troops returning from the recent expedition to Persia as well as troops diverted to India who were intended for China (see Chapter 3).

Yet despite all this shuffling of troops, there was for the first several critical months a shortage of European troops in the areas most affected by the uprising, which was a key point of vulnerability. As late as the end of July, there were only 1,500 Europeans at Delhi and another 1,000 marching on Lucknow.[37] Although the strength of the Indian establishment listed 40,000 European soldiers, this figure is misleading as so many were tied up in the Punjab and Calcutta, or were serving in the other presidencies.

[37] Stokes, *The Peasant Armed*, 29.

As far as the rebels are concerned, while the numbers of men under arms is impressive if difficult to calculate, they were not necessarily formed into effective fighting units. They also suffered from deficiencies in leadership. When regiments mutinied, only rarely did they do so in a unified and coordinated manner. More typically, the regiment would disintegrate. Some mutineers would head off to join other rebels, still others would fade away in the hopes of making it back to their villages, and there were often some sepoys or native officers who remained loyal to the British. The evidence suggests that native officers rarely led or instigated regimental mutinies though it is clear that many were well aware of the discontent brewing amongst the sepoys.[38] Once mutinies had broken out, some native officers did step in to provide leadership. But there are many cases of native officers from mutinied regiments remaining with their European officers, and there were a good number who slipped back to their villages. British military policy and practice deliberately ensured that Indian officers were denied the opportunity to gain experience of commanding and coordinating larger bodies of men; the highest rank an Indian could aspire to was Subedar-Major and such officers exercised command over no more than 100 men. This constraint would become evident in the military operations where rebel sepoys and officers proved themselves adept at small-scale operations, particularly holding a defensive position, but had difficulties maneuvering in larger formations.

The Indian landed classes were also split. Some actively took up arms against the British, others came out in support of the British, while still others stayed on the sidelines. At Bithur, near Kanpur, Nana Sahib, the successor to the last peshwa or prime minister of the Marathas, took advantage of the breakdown of authority to announce the re-establishment of the Maratha Empire. He was angered not only by the British failure to acknowledge his ancestral titles, but also by their recent decision in 1853 to deprive him of the *jagir* (land grant) that financially and symbolically confirmed his status. Notable among those who rallied to the promise of a restored Maratha Confederacy was the Rani of Jhansi who joined on behalf of her son. She was the young widow of the Raja of Jhansi, a small Maratha state, who had died without male issue in 1853. Under the terms of the doctrine of lapse, Dalhousie declared that the territory was now under direct British rule. The Rani of Jhansi unsuccessfully pleaded her son's case as the adopted heir. The imposition of direct British rule had increased British presence in the region, and in the

---

[38] Ibid., 56

summer of 1857 the landed classes and much of the peasantry broke into revolt and secured Jhansi. But even those who did come out in support of the British did not necessarily do so with the support of their people. Shinde of Gwalior offered his troops to the British; however, many of them had other ideas and chose instead to join the Rani of Jhansi. One officer wrote to his wife that 'The hatred of the native population now to the English is something extraordinary, three days after the town being in our possession, two officers went into the magazine and a native quietly put a match in and blew them up in sight of several officers outside who cut him down'.[39] In Awadh in general, and Lucknow in particular, the British faced what can best be called a popular uprising for much of the population openly sided with and supported the rebels.

The British, however, had a definite edge at the start and had access to more resources, both in India and further afield. They were able to pay their soldiers and suppliers on time whereas the rebels were often short of cash – and, in the case of Delhi, this partly explains not only the frequent desertions which affected rebel formations but also the widespread looting committed by the rebels. This in turn weakened the support they could call upon from the local population. In time, the British were able to bring in fresh troops from outside India and ensured that they were well-armed and supplied. Heavy artillery needed to retake North Indian cities and dislodge rebels from forts was within reach.

Strategy and War Aims

The overarching goal of the British was to re-establish authority both within their army and in the many districts where colonial authority had been snuffed out. For the rebels, aims and goals were less clear cut. There was no overarching leadership, nor a clear plan, nor even a shared vision of what the future could entail. Some rebels fought to restore previous regimes, whether this was the Mughal court in Delhi, the Nawab in Awadh, or the Maratha peshwa. Other rebels fought in defence of their religion while there were those who fought to settle old scores. Some fought for loot. Rebels had attacked jails and released the prisoners inside. It is estimated that upwards of 23,000 prisoners were freed.[40] And a good number of rebels fought because they had no choice. The British practice of collective discipline, by which whole regiments could be punished for the acts of a few, sometimes with death, meant that the

---

[39] Brigadier M. W. Smith to Charlotte Smith, April 1858, MSS Eur C590, IOLR.
[40] Clare Anderson, *The Indian Uprising of 1857–8: Prisons, Prisoners and Rebellion* (London; New York: Anthem Press, 2007), 2.

decision by a few sepoys to murder their officers in effect associated all of their colleagues with the act of mutiny.

With the exception of Tantia Tope, most of the rebel leaders lacked military acumen. However, the same can be said for many British generals in this war, thereby suggesting that leadership was not the major difference between the two sides. The rebels' failure to break out of north central India was in the long run their biggest handicap as it allowed the British to concentrate their forces for maximum impact. The rebels did not march on Calcutta or Bombay, the key ports that were vital to the British. The rebels were ultimately vulnerable to a three-pronged attack as the British could march troops from Bengal, from the Punjab, and from Central India. Delhi arguably became a sheet anchor that ultimately slowed down and contained the revolt. The rebel decision to try and hold Delhi 'was to deprive rebellion of its expansive proclivities'.[41] The rebels' decision to fight a defensive action at Delhi, rather than use Delhi as a springboard for attacks elsewhere, coupled with the British not losing their grip on Allahabad, meant that a slender line of communications was maintained between Calcutta and the Punjab. Communications, some supplies, but most importantly, troops could be moved through the Gangetic heartland.

The major challenge for the British was that the bulk of the troops whose loyalty could be counted upon, namely the Europeans, were not well-distributed for an internal conflict. Instead, most of the European cavalry, infantry, and artillery was pushed up towards the north-west frontier. While this would in time allow the British to disarm and disband native infantry regiments in the Punjab more easily and secure the region, it meant that there were few troops in the area where civil and military grievances converged to create the greatest opposition to the British, namely Awadh and the territories lying between Delhi and Allahabad. Widespread panic among Europeans and Eurasians forced the government to retain more troops in Calcutta and other downriver stations than they might have otherwise. The disarming of three sepoy regiments at Dinapur at the end of July had been a disaster – many sepoys melted away taking their arms with them. Canning was in particular worried about the possibility of a wider Muslim rebellion breaking out, and to that end overruled the Commander-in-Chief's recommendations that more troops be directed to the attacks into Awadh.[42] Moreover, moving reinforcements proved to be a challenge. To move troops as

---

[41] Stokes, *The Peasant Armed*, 49.
[42] Patrick Grant, Commander-in-Chief of the Madras Army, was brought to Calcutta to serve as acting Commander-in-Chief between the death of General George Anson on

expeditiously as possible, they had to be broken down into manageable packets: in the words of Lady Canning, the wife of the Governor-General, it was akin to 'sending reinforcements in teaspoonfuls'.[43] Consequently, they could not be easily used as fighting units as they moved upcountry in such small formations. Furthermore, their presence was often sufficient to cause alarm but insufficient to restore authority.

The Course of the War

The tenth of May is often identified as the start of the Rebellion. On that day, troops at Meerut mutinied and proceeded to march on nearby Delhi. As early as 24 April, it was clear to European officers there that the new cartridge was causing a great deal of unrest. Only five of ninety *sowars* of the 3rd Bengal Light Cavalry accepted the new cartridge. The remaining eighty-five were tried for mutiny and sentenced to ten years hard labour and to dishonourable discharge. The situation deteriorated still further when sepoys in the 20th Bengal Native Infantry began to shout at their officers. An officer who went to speak with them was shot dead and soon sepoys in the 11th Bengal Native Infantry joined in the tumult. Europeans and their property came under attack. The local police force disintegrated and crowds began to pillage the cantonment. The eighty-five prisoners from the 3rd Cavalry were rescued by their colleagues, and most of the mutineers set off for Delhi, forty miles away.

Within a couple of weeks, mutinies had broken out at many stations of the Bengal Army. The security situation deteriorated still further as rebels attacked and forcibly opened up many of the jails in the area. In most areas, the police openly sided with the rebels.[44] Martial law was proclaimed, and British officers in command of divisions, brigades, and even stations were given extraordinary powers to convene courts martial and try any soldier or follower, and to carry out the sentence immediately, even death sentences.[45] This legislation, which came to be called the Hanging Act, eventually extended to the prosecution of anyone except British-born individuals for so-called heinous offences in the areas affected by the revolt, namely Bengal, Awadh, Punjab, and the North

27 May 1857 and the arrival of Sir Colin Campbell in mid-August 1857. Charles Canning to Patrick Grant, 6 June 1857, MSS Eur F699/1/1/4/2, IOLR.
[43] Ibid., 22.
[44] Narrative of Events Attending the Outbreak of Disturbances and the Restoration of Authority in the Agra Division in 1857–58, L/MIL/17/2/493, IOLR.
[45] General Order, 16 June 1857, L/MIL/17/2/306, p. 382, IOLR; General Order, 14 May 1857, L/MIL/17/2/306, p. 336, IOLR; and, General Order, 6 June 1857, L/MIL/17/2/306, pp. 375–76, IOLR.

Western Provinces. It was in effect a licence to kill and it is telling that no sepoys were tried by general courts martial in 1858.[46] Sepoys were instead tried through this expedited process, one which did not leave records, and was not subject to approval and appeal.

Much of the military operations tended to cluster around the major centres of Delhi, Lucknow, and Kanpur, plus a more mobile front which developed following an uprising at Jhansi. In Delhi and Lucknow, resistance to the British tended to converge around the remnants of the old Mughal order. Elsewhere, and in particular to the south and southeast, princes and aristocratic families who had been dispossessed by the doctrine of lapse became rallying points for discontent. Delhi provided the rebels with a rallying point, and in the person of the Mughal Emperor, a figurehead around which they could unite. The poet and courtier, Zahir Dehvli, reported that the mutineers pressed Bahadur Shah, the Mughal Emperor, to assume command, declaring that the 'British want to destroy our faith and religion and convert the whole of Hindustan to Christianity'.[47] Bahadur Shah eventually agreed. While there is no evidence that he had prior knowledge of the mutinies, it would be a mistake to see him as powerless in the face of the rebels. His decision to host a *durbar* (public gathering), have coins issued in his name, as well as the letters he wrote to many of the landed elites in areas outside Delhi requesting troops and money, suggests a willingness on his part to fulfill at least some of the expectations hoisted upon him. Yet events in Delhi over the several days following the arrival of the Meerut mutineers reveal just how fluid was the situation. Some sepoys rallied at first to their British officers and helped to defend them from mutineers. As British resistance began to falter, with Europeans either being killed or forced to flee, many of those sepoys who had initially sided with the British either fled or joined the rebels.

The fall of Kanpur and the massacres that occurred there would come to have an impact on the British far in excess of the military importance of this action.[48] Kanpur was one of the larger cantonments, strategically located on the Ganges between Calcutta and Delhi. In 1857, there were approximately three thousand sepoys at the station, but critically there were relatively few European troops. Wheeler, an experienced sepoy

---

[46] There are no sepoy trials listed in the two volumes of General Orders for 1858, L/MIL/ 17/2/307, pts 1 and 2, IOLR.

[47] Dehlvi, *Dastan-E-Ghadar*, 57.

[48] Rudrangshu Mukherjee, '"Satan let loose upon Earth": The Kanpur Massacres in India in the Revolt of 1857', *Past and Present* 128 (1990): 92–116. See also Barbara English and Rudrangshu Mukherjee, 'Debate: The Kanpur Massacres in India in the Revolt of 1857', *Past and Present* 142 (1994): 169–89.

commander, had initially downplayed the threat of rebellion, confident that discontent would remain confined to a few badly-led regiments. The scale of the uprising, however, became more apparent as European refugees descended on the city, eventually creating a community of about 1,000 Europeans of whom 300 were from the military. He remained upbeat, assuming that his own troops would remain steady, at least until relief had arrived from Calcutta. Eventually, he was persuaded to make some defensive preparations and ordered that a trench be dug around two ageing barracks. In hindsight, this was a bad decision – it was not sufficient to repel an attack but was sufficient to convince sepoys that they were now the enemy. British officers on 4 June 1857, alarmed at the gathering sepoys, opened fire. European properties were torched and then the rebels left the city, intent on joining their colleagues in Delhi. However, as they passed through Bithur, they joined up with Nana Sahib and returned to besiege Kanpur. It is still not clear just how culpable was Nana Sahib and whether he stepped in and took command on his own initiative or whether, like the Mughal Emperor, he was, at least initially, pressured to take command. Although the recent decision to strip him of his pension and standing had deeply offended him, he had historically been on good terms with the British and even offered at the outset of the rebellion to send some of his armed retainers to post guard at the treasury and other offices.

Three weeks of shelling, sniper fire, and shortages of food and water (the one well within the British lines was in a dangerously exposed position), during the hottest month of the year, reduced British numbers by a quarter. Wheeler accepted Nana Sahib's offer of safe passage to Allahabad if they surrendered. As they boarded boats for the trip downriver, rebels opened fire. It is still not clear whether this was a deliberately planned massacre. Only four of the British men attacked at the boats would survive. By all accounts, there was widespread participation in the attack on the European men at the river, but rebel sepoys refused to attack the women and children. Reports of the ad hoc executions being committed by forces under Colonel James Neill who was leading the relief column to Kanpur fanned the fury of the crowd. Neill, with psychopathic fury, allowed and even encouraged his troops to murder Indians indiscriminately, burning villages, and, in one case hanging a number of small boys who 'had flaunted the rebel colours and gone about beating tom-toms'.[49] The 125 women and children were sent off

---

[49] Andrew Ward, 'The house of the ladies: Cawnpore', in Rosie Llewellyn-Jones (ed.), *The Uprising of 1857* (Allahabad: Alkazi Collection in association with Mapin Publishing, 2017): 128.

to the Bibighar (translated as the Ladies House or the House of the Ladies) where they were joined by some European women and children from Fatehgarh who sought shelter in Kanpur. It is estimated that as many as 200 women and children died in Kanpur, with most being slaughtered and thrown down the well on 15 July, just two days before the British recaptured Kanpur. They were murdered by no more than five individuals, two of whom were butchers by trade, who were specifically recruited for the task.

The British recapture of Kanpur unleashed an orgy of violence directed indiscriminately against any Indian in the vicinity. Neill ordered prisoners to lick the blood-stained floor and walls of the Bibighar before they were executed. In a very deliberate and conscious inversion of Hindu and Muslim death rites, he ordered that the bodies of executed Muslims be burned and Hindus be buried.[50] *The Times* declared that 'Extraordinary crimes require extraordinary penalties ... we must make a signal example of the men who have offered these affronts upon it'.[51] Six months later, Russell observed along the route linking Allahabad with Kanpur and Lucknow that 'wherever a bit of white could be found it was covered with the writings of men of the various detachments passing up towards Cawnpore. "Revenge your slaughtered countrywomen!" "To —— with the bloody sepoys." Rough sketches of men hanging from trees and gallows, and various eulogiums of particular regiments'.[52]

Having recaptured Kanpur, the columns under Major-General Henry Havelock and Neill set off for Lucknow. The annexation of Awadh the previous year created a huge unemployment problem in Lucknow as courtiers, civil servants, and the state's own soldiers found themselves out of work and often with their pay deeply in arrears and their pensions in jeopardy. At one time, the King of Awadh had forces totaling nearly 60,000 soldiers and officers; of these, less than half were taken up by the British to staff the military and police units they raised to garrison Awadh. The remainder were demobilized, often taking their weapons with them, creating a large pool of armed, angry, and trained fighters.

While trouble had been building up in Lucknow for some time, a flashpoint was reached in early May 1857 when recruits into a recently raised unit, the 7th Oudh Irregular Infantry, insisted that they would not touch the cartridges which were to be distributed along with the new Enfield rifles. The British Commissioner, Henry Lawrence, met the troops, arrested fifty, and disarmed the rest. Sepoys retaliated and torched the cantonment, and some set off to Delhi. Others rallied around

---

[50] Ibid., 131.　　[51] *The Times*, 28 Aug 1857, 6.　　[52] Russell, *Diary*, vol.1, 144.

Begum Hazrat Mahal, one of the deposed ruler's wives who declared her son, aged twelve, to be Nawab and had Bahadur Shah confirm it. Expecting further attacks, Lawrence began to fortify the Residency. He had limited resources at hand: troops from the 32nd Regiment, which was understrength due to casualties and disease; two companies of Bengal artillery; some Sikhs who had been taken on following the disbandment of some local units; plus some troops of questionable loyalty from the Oude Irregular Force.

The relief column under Havelock, which had been joined by troops under Major-General James Outram who had recently returned from the Persian expedition, managed to break through in late September, but with only 2,800 troops it was not enough to break the siege or even extricate the garrison. Instead, the column could only reinforce those holed up in the Residency compound and await a larger force, which under General Colin Campbell, the newly appointed Commander-in-Chief, India, arrived in November. Numbering 4,500 troops, including a detachment of naval gunners, the column was strong enough to battle through to the garrison and extricate them. Casualties were however steep due to the large and well-entrenched rebel force, especially in their strongpoints at Shah Najaf and Sikanderbagh, which required the use of 8-inch naval guns firing at point-blank range to dislodge. The relief of Lucknow also required extensive mining and counter-mining. Outram recounted that 'I am aware of no parallel to our series of mines in modern war: twenty-one shafts, aggregating 200 feet in depth, and 3291 feet of gallery have been executed. The enemy advanced twenty mines against the palaces and outposts; of these they exploded three, which caused us loss of life, and two which did no injury; seven have been blown in; and out of seven others the enemy have been driven, and their galleries taken possession of by our miners'.[53] Campbell managed the tricky extrication of a large garrison under the cover of night and by distracting the rebels with an artillery barrage that led them to fear a further British attack.

Campbell was criticized for his decision to withdraw from Lucknow, leaving only a covering force of 4,000 under Outram at Alambagh until such time as he could mobilize a large enough force to return. But as events at Delhi had shown, securing control over a dense patchwork of streets and alleys controlled by a resolute and determined enemy required time, troops, and artillery. Campbell did not have enough of any of these to guarantee success. It was also a form of warfare for which the British troops were not trained and many of their officers were wary

---

[53] James Outram, *Lieut.-General Sir James Outram's Campaign in India, 1857–1858, Comprising General Orders and Despatches* (London: Smith, Elder and Co., 1860), 47.

of urban warfare, knowing just how much it strained the discipline of their troops. And the situation was even more daunting in Lucknow where the rebels could count upon a much higher degree of popular support than that enjoyed by their counterparts in Delhi. There were in Lucknow, according to some intelligence sources, as many as 120,000 armed rebels and upwards of 131 guns. These were carefully dug in and the defenders could count upon well prepared positions throughout the city.

By December, with Delhi in British hands, and Bengal and Bihar largely quiet, the focus for the British was on the restoration of authority in Awadh. Both Canning and Campbell recognized just how critical it was to regain control over this region. However, Campbell's concerns that urban warfare would overly tax his troops and incur the risk of having to withdraw led him to try and persuade Canning to defer any attack until later in 1858 when the onset of the cooler weather in November would create better conditions and also give him time to amass resources and troops. He calculated that he would need at least 30,000 troops to do it with any guarantee of success. Canning, however, pushed him to attack sooner, insisting that as long as Lucknow held out, rebels would still believe that there was a chance that the British could be overthrown.

Three columns began their assault on Lucknow in February 1858, totaling 31,000 troops including 12,000 Gurkhas. It was a careful and methodical attack, drawing on the lessons from Delhi, and for which Campbell was praised by Russell: 'Sir Colin relies on his artillery and will not waste life in street fighting'.[54] Mortars were particularly important in reducing enemy strongpoints. Of the 10,432 rounds fired, more than half, or 6,241 were fired by the 10-inch, 8-inch, and 5.5-inch mortars.[55] Street fighting tested the discipline of the British troops, and looting and pillaging were common. Russell reported at the Kaiserbagh that the 'men are wild with fury and lust of gold – literally drunk with plunder'.[56] But unlike Delhi, British troops do not appear to have hesitated or threatened to disobey orders. Begum Hazrat Mahal and her followers were driven from the city and fled north into the border region with Nepal. While she was never captured, her forces were broken by hunger and disease, and by attacks from British columns sent in pursuit, and she would eventually die in 1879.

[54] Russell, *Diary*, vol. 1, 211.
[55] Brigadier Sir R. Napier, Report on the Engineering Operations at the Siege of Lucknow in March 1858, L/MIL/17/2/500, pp. 3–5.
[56] Russell, *Diary*, vol.1, 333.

The reconquest of Central India was largely entrusted to a force assembled in the Bombay Presidency and sent from Mhow under Major-General Hugh Rose. The plan was to march northwards and squeeze any rebel forces up against Campbell and British forces operating along the Jumna. Rose laid siege to Jhansi in March 1858, which drew Tantia Tope southwards. An indecisive battle followed, after which Tantia Tope and the Rani of Jhansi launched a surprise attack on Gwalior, which they were able to capture. However, by 20 June, Gwalior was back in British hands and this marked the last major battle of the Rebellion. To some, Rose's campaign was militarily the most successful and the most admired, for 'In roughly five months, Rose had marched 550 miles, fought eight major engagements and taken three of the strongest fortresses in India, much of this at the height of the Indian hot weather'.[57] Tantia Tope's lightly-equipped forces, however, eluded Rose and Tope remained at large until the spring of 1859. His capture in April and swift execution in effect marked the end of the war.

One of the biggest challenges facing Canning and Campbell throughout these operations was to dampen demands for revenge and ensure that law and order was restored as soon as possible. They recognized that brutality was not only driving some who were undecided into the rebel camp, but that the long-term stability of the British in India had to be fashioned out of something more substantial and durable than fear. Canning, with the support of Queen Victoria, the British government, and importantly William Howard Russell, who served as an embedded journalist with Campbell's headquarters for *The Times*, successfully argued against the demolition of the *Jama Masjid*, or Great Mosque in Delhi. Canning wrote that 'I am quite opposed to touching the Jumma Musjid which is a religious building, because I will do nothing which will stamp this rebellion as being in the estimate of the British Government and people a religious one'.[58] He also pushed for pardons and for normal legal processes to be restored as soon as possible. Such efforts, however, brought down on him a lot of wrath. He was derisorily nicknamed 'Clemency Canning' and he was widely lambasted in such venues as *Punch*.

---

[57] Brian Robson, 'The unknown general: A reassessment of Sir Hugh Rose'. *Journal of the Society for Army Historical Research* 75, 302 (1997): 103.

[58] Canning to Vernon Smith, 25 Nov 1857, MSS Eur F231/11, IOLR. See also Douglas M. Peers, '"The blind, brutal, British public's bestial thirst for blood": Archive, memory and W.H. Russell's (re)making of the Indian Mutiny,' in Gavin Rand and Kaushik Roy (eds.), *Culture, Conflict, and the Military in Colonial South Asia* (London: Routledge, 2017), 104–30.

Anatomy of a Battle: Delhi

The battle for Delhi, in the words of Eric Stokes, 'embodied the sepoy war par excellence'. It had the largest concentration of sepoys, giving the rebels the advantage of numbers, training, and a higher degree of cohesion than they enjoyed elsewhere.[59] Moreover, the rebel sepoys were joined by thousands of other fighters. But the rebels were handicapped by the lack of a clear chain of command. The Mughal Emperor, around whom the rebels had initially rallied, found that his orders and requests went ignored. His son, Mirza Mughal, whom he named Commander-in-Chief, did not fare any better. Leaders of the larger rebel bands jealously guarded their autonomy while the sepoys preferred their own internal arrangements, consisting of committees and councils. In late June, the rebel sepoys formed a Court of Mutineers set up around six representatives from the military, with two each from the cavalry, infantry, and artillery, and four civilians, which was intended to oversee and coordinate military operations.[60]

The number of rebels would continue to grow. By the end of June, a contemporary estimated that there were more than 12,000 sepoys in the city. Of these, a large detachment from Nimach consisting of sepoys from four regiments of native infantry, one cavalry regiment, and one troop of horse artillery. Another group arrived from Bareilly under the command of Muhammed Bakht Khan, a one-time Subedar-Major in the Company's horse artillery, who looted the Bareilly Treasury before marching on Delhi. He held on to these funds rather than turn them over, and this gave him the ability to ensure his troops were regularly paid. These additional troops were to prove a mixed blessing – they bolstered the defense of the city and proved to be well-trained and functioned effectively as independent units. But they increased the strain on the city's resources. Joining too were large numbers of Muslim volunteers. This group of largely untrained but religiously inspired insurgents, estimated at 7,000 and known as *ghazis,* heightened conflict within the city as they were not only not susceptible to military discipline but were often accused of plundering the city's inhabitants. The fact that the city held out for so long was testimony not only to the skill and determination of many of its defenders but also to the leadership and administrative structures that were brought into play. The police in particular proved to be essential, for it was through them that supplies and

---

[59] Stokes, *The Peasant Armed*, 68.
[60] 'Constitution of the court of mutineers and its rules and regulations', in Mahmood Farooqui (ed.), *Besieged 1857: Voices from Delhi* (New Delhi: Penguin, 2010), 56–58.

resources could be secured. Even the lunatic asylum remained in operation. But, unlike other urban centres such as Lucknow, Jhansi, Bareilly, or Kanpur, the rebels in Delhi could not depend upon much popular support. Nor was there much support forthcoming from surrounding towns and villages. Looting and pillage became commonplace as the rebel leadership found itself hard-pressed to feed and to pay all the troops and volunteers who had gathered. Rebel numbers peaked in late July with an estimated 100,000 ex-sepoys having congregated in Delhi, but over the course of the summer many melted away as food and ammunition ran out. By early September, there could have been as few as twenty-five or thirty thousand sepoys remaining with perhaps as many *ghazis* again.

The British forces who managed to escape Delhi regrouped on a ridge which was about a kilometer north of the city. In the words of Henry Norman, 'We had from the first no choice as to the front of attack, our position on the north side being the only one from which we could possibly keep up our communications with the Punjab' and the river on their left gave the British some security from attack from that direction.[61] The British forces were largely left alone in the critical early days and eventually they were reinforced when joined by remnants of the British garrisons at Ambala and Meerut. More troops arrived from the Punjab but not in numbers sufficient to allow them to try and retake Delhi. By the end of July, the British forces at Delhi numbered only 5,000. Brigaduer-General Archdale Wilson, commander of the Delhi Field Force, only managed to secure more replacements by threatening British authorities in the Punjab that he would have to lift the siege of Delhi and fall back on Karnal. In early September, a siege train arrived from Ferozepur with fifteen 24-pounder and twenty 18-pounder guns plus howitzers, mortars, and plenty of ammunition. Such firepower was necessary to deal with a well-fortified city, one which ironically had been strengthened by the British over the past decade: its walls were up to 12 feet thick at their base and 24 feet high and they were fronted by a ditch that was 16 feet deep and 20 feet wide.

The rebels had mounted a number of forays over the summer months that were intended to dislodge the British from the Ridge. Rebel commanders however were not used to maneuvering large formations and they were forced back, but not before inflicting some losses on the British. The bigger strategic error on the part of the rebels was not using Delhi as a base from which to launch raids more deeply into surrounding territories. Had they done so, the British would likely have had to pull back from Delhi.

---

[61] Lee-Warner, *Memoirs*, 144.

By mid-September, British gunfire and mining had weakened the northern stretch of the city wall sufficiently to allow an attack. Kashmir Gate was breached on 14 September and troops poured through a narrow gap into the city. Some made it as far as the Jama Masjid, but the narrow, twisting lanes and determined resistance by rebel sepoys and ghazis threw the attacking columns into confusion. By the end of the day, the British had a precarious grip on a stretch of the city wall from Water Gate to Kabuli Gate but at the cost of 1,200 casualties. Yet none of the columns, which comprised European, Sikh, and Gurkha troops, had secured their second objectives, which would have given them control over the Jama Masjid and the main routes leading to the Red Fort. The British were in a difficult situation and some feared that they might have to retreat. Their base camp was understrength and dangerously exposed; troops within the city had lost momentum; discipline was breaking down with soldiers refusing orders; and much of the surrounding countryside was still in rebel hands. Looting and pillaging became common, and orders that civilians, particularly women and children, were to be spared went unheeded. Large stocks of beer and spirits were found by the British soldiers near the breach at Kashmir Gate, leading some to think this was a deliberate ploy on the part of the rebels.[62] The British commander complained to his wife that 'our men have a great dislike of street fighting. They do not see their enemy, who on the tops of houses and under cover, and get a panic and will not advance'.[63] Had the rebels counterattacked in force, the British might have been routed. Tactics had to be improvised: infantry squads sent forward into the streets with field pieces and light mortars to knock down buildings in which rebel snipers were hiding. It was not until 20 September, a week later, before the British controlled the city and the Red Fort at its centre. Bahadur Shah was captured the following day along with two of his sons; the latter would be murdered a day later by Major William Hodson, the British intelligence chief at Delhi, and their bodies publicly displayed. Norman, the Adjutant General of the Delhi Field Force, concluded that 'Hodson shot them because he believed they deserved death, and was apprehensive if he brought them in alive their lives might be spared'.[64]

The capture of Delhi took a total force of nearly ten thousand British and Indian soldiers and a further three thousand troops from their allies. That one third of the soldiers and one half of the officers in the six regiments assigned to the final assault became casualties illustrates just how fiercely the rebels resisted. Most contemporary writers and many

---

[62] Ibid., 156.   [63] Stokes, *The Peasant Armed*, 98.   [64] Lee-Warner, *Memoirs*, 169–70.

subsequent commentators have depicted the retaking of Delhi as an impressive victory, a triumphalist narrative and testimony to the fighting qualities and grim determination of the British. Such a picture not only fails to credit the many Indian troops who fought alongside them but also conveniently skates over just how badly the British stumbled once they punctured the walls, and it ignores the violence, rape, arson and looting which followed. One could argue that it was less a case of the British winning Delhi and more the rebels losing the city. It certainly meets the definition of a pyrrhic victory for the principle objective, the capture or death of the rebel sepoys, was largely unattained. Instead, much of the blood spilled in Delhi was that of civilians who were targeted by the British and their allies. Thousands were killed or executed with little effort to assign guilt and many more were driven from the city. George Wagentrieber, the editor of the *Delhi Gazette*, gleefully reported to his readers that 'Hanging is, I am happy to say, the order of the day here'.[65] Many British officers and civilians readily believed rumours that rebels had sexually assaulted European women before killing them (a charge proved false by a subsequent inquiry commission), and so it was not surprising that little was done to protect the women of Delhi despite orders from the British commander that women and children were to be spared.[66]

The Role of Technology and the Royal Navy

Because the sepoys and soldiers involved in the fighting came out of the same military organization, technological differences, at least at first, were not that great or significant. The one exception was the Enfield rifles, which had been more widely distributed amongst the British, and were used by them more frequently than was the case with the sepoys. In open warfare, the Enfield rifles with their greater range and accuracy gave the British an edge. However, as Rose's central Indian force discovered, the intense heat of campaigning in the summer caused Enfields to jam.[67] But in the close conditions of street fighting in Delhi and Lucknow, the

---

[65] Dalrymple, *Last Mughal*, 403.
[66] Memorandum on the enquiries made by the desire of the GG into the number of European women having been dishonoured during the late mutiny, Mutiny Papers of Sir J. W. Kaye, H/MISC/725 pt. II, pp. 633–50, IOLR; See also Russell's unpublished comments on British soldiers after the retaking of Lucknow. William Howard Russell, diary entry for 26 March 1858, Russell Diary, vol. 3, Russell Papers, News International Record Office.
[67] T. A. Heathcote, *Mutiny and Insurgency in India 1857–1858: The British Army in a Bloody Civil War* (London: Pen and Sword, 2007), 190.

Enfield rifle was of limited value and instead the British had to resort to the bayonet to clear out the rebels, and in such conditions technological differences were of little importance. It is also worth noting that despite the protests that initially greeted the cartridges associated with the Enfield rifles, rebel sepoys who did have access to them were often willing to use them.

Lacking access to the arsenals available to the British, the rebels had to make do with what they could scrounge. The Delhi Armoury, when it fell into their hands, yielded 8,000 muskets and nearly one million cartridges.[68] Matchlocks were also put to use despite being slow, cumbersome, and of very limited value in the rains. But the workmanship of locally-made weapons impressed the British. Rebels made use of the destroyed telegraph lines, turning the wire into slugs for their muskets and burning the wooden poles as firewood.[69] Some particularly ingenious sepoys even tried to fashion cannons out of some metal poles. In his notes for a speech he gave, Corporal Joseph Porter noted that rebels were running out of guns, so they improvised. They used iron sockets that were used to protect telegraph poles from white ants, tied them to poles, filled them with powder and chopped pieces of telegraph wire as shrapnel.[70] A greater challenge to the rebels was the fact that they did not have access to heavy artillery or siege trains. Here, the Royal Navy indirectly played an important role as crews and large-calibre cannon from two frigates became part of the siege train that retook Lucknow.

Modern transportation and communication technology were especially critical for the British. The telegraph allowed for resources to be identified and ordered to India in a more timely manner, while steamships and railways hastened their actual deployment. The rebels were well aware of the value of telegraphs and not surprisingly telegraph lines and poles were frequently targeted. It was estimated that rebels had ripped up 760 miles of telegraph line. It was reported, perhaps apocryphally, that a 'sepoy, waiting to be hanged, pointing to the overhead telegraph line, exclaimed "that is the accursed wire that strangled us"'.[71] Yet, there were major flaws in the telegraph which meant that

---

[68] Kaushik Roy, 'Structural anatomy of the rebel forces during the Great Mutiny of 1857–58: Equipment, logistics and recruitment reconsidered', in Bhattacharya (ed.), *Rethinking 1857*, 292.

[69] P. V. Luke, 'Early history of the telegraph in India', *Journal of the Institute of Electrical Engineers* 20 (1891): 111.

[70] Corporal Joseph Porter, 1857, MSS Eur B273, IOLR.

[71] Deep Kanta Lahiri-Choudhury, 'Communication, information, and identity during the uprising of 1857', in Subhas Ranjan Chakraborty (ed.), *Uprisings of 1857: Perspectives and Peripheries* (Kolkata: Asiatic Society, 2009), 96–97.

for operational command and control, it was not as important as it was later claimed. There were several occasions when it was critical, but day-to-day communication was largely through traditional channels and indigenous networks where the British did not enjoy any advantage, and in fact were often at a disadvantage. An important limitation on telegraphs was that they had been designed to connect the interior with the port cities. They had not been developed as a local network linking together the various stations and outposts in India.

Aftermath

The end of the Rebellion signaled the end of the East India Company as authority was transferred to the British government. It also marked the end of the Mughal Dynasty as Bahadur Shah was tried, deposed, and sent into exile in Rangoon. An amnesty was issued by Canning to all those who mutinied but who had not committed murder, though he recognized the difficulty in ascertaining who was guilty of what.[72] The Royal Proclamation of 1858 provided a pardon for most sepoys who had deserted and taken up arms against the British provided that they took up peaceful pursuits and returned to their villages.

The end of the Company also meant the end of the East India Company's Army – it too was transferred to the British government though not without controversy. The Company's European regiments were absorbed into the British army. A great number of them refused to acknowledge the transfer in what contemporaries came to call the White Mutiny. In the end, a number of soldiers were tried, one was executed, but the government quietly backed off and let the soldiers take their discharge if they wished.[73] The many casualties caused by disease and the generally poor health of so many soldiers, coming on the heels of all the Crimea scandals, triggered the launch of an official enquiry.[74] And fears about the loyalty of Indian sepoys would permeate the post-Mutiny army. Changes to recruitment practices were made to lessen dependence on the high caste sepoys who were held responsible, and attention shifted to those troops seen to be both more reliable and warlike, particularly Sikhs and Gurkhas who became the model, martial races in the

---

[72] Canning to General John Low, 15 Feb 1858, MSS Eur D1082, IOLR.
[73] Peter Stanley, *White Mutiny: British Military Culture in India* (London: Hurst, 1998), 222–23.
[74] Report of the Commissioners Appointed to Enquire into the Sanitary State of the Army in India, London, 1863, L/PARL/2/145, IOLR.

post-mutiny army. Further changes to the army would come on the heels of the report of the Peel Commission which had been struck in the aftermath of the Indian Rebellion to provide guidance on any future military force in India.[75] Attention was paid to ensuring that the ratio of European to Indian troops was kept closer than it had been in the past, and it became a deliberate policy to ensure that Indian troops were never as well armed as were their British counterparts. In effect, this meant that the Indian Army's equipment was often a generation behind that of the British Army. Such measures, intended to hobble Indian troops in case they rose again, did however compromise the Indian's Army's fighting effectiveness and its ability to be used as part of a wider imperial force. The sheer size of the Indian Army, and its location, rendered it an excellent reservoir of trained troops which could be used to support imperial efforts throughout Africa and Asia. But the combination of deliberately imposed constraints upon its effectiveness, as well as its battlefield experience consisting largely of small-scale punitive campaigns, so-called Small Wars, meant that it was ill-equipped to handle the demands of modern industrial war.

The kinds of social, economic, and political transformations envisaged by Dalhousie and others like him, and which had informed decisions before 1857, had become discredited. India, for many, was not ready for modernization. Instead, British policies and attitudes became more conservative and cautious.[76] The landed classes, derided by Dalhousie, were now looked to as vital partners in the Empire. George Trevelyan, writing soon after the Rebellion had ended, concluded that 'Cantonments and arsenals, field batteries, and breaching batteries seemed more essential to the government of the country than courts of law, normal schools, and agricultural exhibitions'.[77] Security obsessions also shaped urban planning. Lucknow was re-organized and re-structured – two-fifths of the old city was knocked down. In its place came a city set up in a grid with much more clearly demarcated European and Indian areas.[78] Similar measures were taken in Delhi to impose order on the cityscape.

---

[75] Report of the Commissioners Appointed to Inquire into the Organization of the Indian Army, Together with the Minutes of Evidence and Appendix [Peel Commission], L/MIL/17/5/1622, IOLR.
[76] Thomas R. Metcalf, *Ideologies of the Raj: The New Cambridge History of India*, III, 4 (Cambridge: Cambridge University Press, 1994).
[77] G. O. Trevelyan, *The Competition Wallah* (London: Macmillan, 1866), 302.
[78] Veena Talwar Oldenburg, *The Making of Colonial Lucknow, 1856–1877* (Princeton: Princeton University Press, 1984), xix.

Imperial policy and practice in the aftermath of the Rebellion reveal an obsession with security and stability and a proclivity to brutally suppress any sign of popular protest which would last until the end of the Raj. This preoccupation with security is perhaps best appreciated in the symbolic weight which the British attached to the persons and places of 1857–58, for just before midnight on the day that India and Pakistan were to be made independent in 1947, the GOC Eastern Command, Sir Francis Tuker, was given secret orders to send a detachment of troops to Lucknow where it was to take down the Union Jack that had been flying there since 1858. It was the only place in the Empire where the flag flew continuously. This small force also destroyed the flagstaff, thereby preventing the feared desecration of one of the more potent symbols of British rule.[79] Workmen were also sent on a hush-hush mission to dismantle the statue at Kanpur in memory of the women and children who had died there.

It is however clear that the poignancy of such sites has largely disappeared for the British. Few people in the United Kingdom today would be able to identify any of the military worthies who are celebrated with statues at Trafalgar Square. One Mayor even boasted of his ignorance of them. In India, on the other hand, the events of 1857–58 continue to excite comment and commemoration. In 2007, British tourists who had gone to Meerut as part of a 150th anniversary tour were pelted with stones.[80] Near to where the angel statue at Kanpur had stood is now a statue to Tantia Tope, and the memorial park was renamed Nana Rao in honour of Nana Sahib.[81] There are no less than three memorials to Mangal Pandey at Barrackpur. The new galleries at the Red Fort that were opened in 2019 focus less on the Mughals who built the Red Fort and more on rebels and independence fighters who can be placed in a lineage stretching back to 1857–58. And at the Victoria Memorial in Kolkata, recently renovated galleries that were just opened in January 2020 contain Tantia Tope's coat and a lock of his hair. It is clear that the events of 1857–58 will continue to resonate in India, no matter how much they have faded from view in Britain.

---

[79] Stokes, *The Peasant Armed*, 2.
[80] 'Protests force India War grave visitors to end tour', *Guardian*, 27 Sept 2007, www.theguardian.com/world/2007/sep/27/india.uknews4.
[81] Manu Goswami, '"Englishness" on the imperial circuit: Mutiny tours in colonial South Asia', *Journal of Historical Sociology* 9 (1996): 5484; Stephen Heathorn. 'Angel of empire: The Cawnpore Memorial Well as a British site of imperial remembrance', *Journal of Colonialism and Colonial History* 8 (2007). http://muse.jhu.edu/journals/journal_of_colonialism_and_colonial_history/v008/8.3heathorn.html.

Further Reading

Bhattacharya, Sabyasachi (ed.) *Rethinking 1857*. New Delhi: Orient BlackSwan, 2007.
Chakravarty, Gautam. *The Indian Mutiny and the British Imagination*. Cambridge: Cambridge University Press, 2005.
Dalrymple, William. *The Last Mughal: The Fall of a Dynasty, Delhi, 1857*. London: Bloomsbury, 2006.
Dasgupta, Sabyasachi. *In Defence of Honour and Justice: Sepoy Rebellions in the Nineteenth Century*. New Delhi: Primus, 2015.
David, Saul. *The Indian Mutiny, 1857*. London: Viking, 2002.
Dehlvi, Zahir. *Dastan-E-Ghadar: The Tale of the Mutiny*. Trans. Rana Safvi. New Delhi: Penguin Books, 2017.
Farooqui, Mahmood (ed.) *Besieged 1857: Voices from Delhi*. New Delhi: Penguin, 2010.
Kaye, John William, and G. B. Malleson. *Kaye's and Malleson's History of the Indian Mutiny of 1857–1858*. 6 vols. London: Longman, Green, 1897–98.
Llewellyn-Jones, Rosie (ed.) *The Uprising of 1857*. Ahmedabad: Alkazi Collection of Photography in association with Mapin Publishing, 2017.
Mukherjee, Rudrangshu. *Awadh in Revolt, 1857–1858: A Study in Popular Resistance*. Delhi: Oxford University Press, 1984.
Rand, Gavin, and Crispin Bates (eds.) *Mutiny at the Margins: New Perspectives on the Indian Uprising of 1857. Volume 4: Military Aspects*. New Delhi: Sage, 2013.
Roy, Kaushik (ed.) *1857 Uprising: A Tale of an Indian Warrior*. London: Anthem, 2008.
Roy, Tapti. *The Politics of a Popular Uprising: Bundelkhand in 1857*. Delhi: Oxford University Press, 1994.
Sen, S. N. *Eighteen Fifty-Seven*. Delhi: Ministry of Information and Broadcasting, 1957.
Stanley, Peter. *White Mutiny: British Military Culture in India*. London: Hurst, 1998.
Stokes, Eric. *The Peasant Armed*. Oxford: Oxford University Press, 1986.
Wagner, K. A. *The Skull of Alum Bheg: The Life and Death of a Rebel of 1857*. Oxford: Oxford University Press, 2018.

3 Punitive Expeditions in China, 1857–1860

Bruce Collins

Background

The sequence of events leading to conflict in China was relatively straightforward. From October 1856 to January 1858, a series of confrontations occurred at Canton (Guangzhou),[1] China's principal commercial port. These arose from the British need to export opium into China, from the protection given by the Royal Navy to trading vessels owned by Chinese residents in the British colony of Hong Kong (acquired in 1842), and from growing demands that foreign traders should be allowed to enter the walled, old city of Canton and not be constricted to the suburbs assigned to them along the Canton River. Strong-willed British and Chinese officials clashed over commercial practices, future development, and the local balance of power. This led to violence in Canton in October 1856 and the despatch of a small expeditionary force in the spring of 1857. The British, with French participation, attacked the walled city on 28–29 December 1857 and set up an administration with Chinese local officials early in 1858. The British maintained a substantial garrison at Canton, which was sixty miles from the coast and Hong Kong, for over three years.

The dispute at Canton highlighted a broader clash between foreign powers and the Chinese government. Great Britain, France, Russia and the United States wanted direct diplomatic representation at, and thus access to, the imperial court in Beijing. The Chinese sought to keep foreigners at arm's length, confining them to designated areas and conducting official business with them through commissioners in the regions, as at Canton. The violent clashes at Canton were immediately followed by Western pressure on the imperial court to recalibrate its conduct of foreign policy. In May–June 1858, June 1859, and August 1860, Western forces entered or attempted to enter the Peiho (Hai) River

---

[1] Since virtually all existing works adopt the older forms, Anglicized names will be used with modern Chinese transliterations noted.

and advance to Tientsin (Tianjin) in order to negotiate a new diplomatic relationship with China. The level of fighting increased each year until a Franco-British force pushed on beyond Tientsin to Beijing in 1860 and secured the Western powers' political objectives.

★ ★ ★ ★ ★

This prolonged confrontation involving three separate punitive expeditions has been studied from five perspectives. First, the struggle has been examined as an episode in economic imperialism. From 1757 to 1842, China officially permitted foreign trade only through Canton. The first so-called Opium War opened up four more designated ports from 1842. During the period 1849–58, an annual average of 5.83% of all British imports, overwhelmingly tea and silk, came from China. But Britain exported little in return; imports from China during 1854–58 were worth, per year, four and a half times on average the value of British exports to China. This yawning trade gap was filled by exports of opium from British-controlled India. The trade in opium was illegal but condoned by Chinese officials. J. Y. Wong shows that the British government in 1856 planned a small military expedition to force the Chinese to open their markets to British exports beyond the five treaty ports of 1842, and to legalize the opium trade. This trade, in Wong's impressive analysis, was vital to Britain's international system of payments far beyond commercial links with China. Events in Canton in 1856 merely helped the prime minister, Lord Palmerston, secure electoral backing for his policies.[2]

A second approach stresses the struggle for British diplomatic recognition. The high commissioner sent out to negotiate a new trade relationship, the Earl of Elgin, privately deplored 'commercial ruffianism',[3] reminding British merchants in Shanghai in March 1858 'that they must exert themselves and not trust to cannon if they intend to get a market in China'. They still had to compete with 'a population the most universally and laboriously manufacturing of any on earth'.[4] But Elgin was fully committed to Lord Palmerston's diplomatic objectives. The prime minister, who served throughout this period, except between February

---

[2] J. Y. Wong, *Deadly Dreams: Opium, Imperialism, and the Arrow War (1856–1860) in China* (Cambridge: Cambridge University Press, 1998), 336, 338, 342.

[3] O. Checkland, 'Bruce, James, eighth earl of Elgin and twelfth earl of Kincardine (1811–1863), Governor-in-Chief of British North America and Viceroy of India', *Oxford Dictionary of National Biography*, accessed 9 December 2019, www.oxforddnb.com/view/10.1093/ref:odnb/9780198614128.001.0001/odnb-9780198614128-e-3737.

[4] Theodore Walrond (ed.), *Letters and Journals of James, Eighth Earl of Elgin* (London: John Murray, 1872), 239–40, 304–05.

1858 and June 1859, had long defended British 'rights' abroad and supported British officials overseas in vigorously upholding such 'rights'.[5] Elgin's success in forwarding British demands resulted in part because the confrontation with Britain eventually helped shift power within the Chinese government. In Masataka Banno's interpretation, a peace party within the court recognized, by early 1861, that Britain and France had no territorial ambitions in China and that the regime faced more serious challenges from the Taiping rebellion in the south, the Niens in the north, and Russian expansion from the north.[6] These threats to the regime seemed far more serious than the stirrings of Western economic imperialism.

A third approach highlights longer-term consequences. Harry Gelber concludes a detailed synthesis by stressing that the interventions contributed to the development and celebration of Britain's global projection of power. The conflict also weakened the Chinese regime and was used later to blame foreign interventions for the ills suffered by China from the early nineteenth to the mid-twentieth centuries.[7] A fourth approach, which there is insufficient space to consider here, emphasizes the moral dimensions of a dispute sparked by the trade in opium and the cultural implications of the British response to the Chinese. For some contemporaries, however, the political defence of British 'rights' overseas outweighed their revulsion against the opium trade, as Lord Shaftesbury, one of the Victorians' leading humanitarian reformers, demonstrated in his support for Palmerston.[8]

Finally, military accounts have typically assessed the campaigns of 1857–60 positively. In 1875, Captain Henry Knollys, editing the journals of the expedition's commanding officer, concluded that 'It is scarcely too much to say that the China War of 1860 may be considered the most successful and best carried out of England's "little wars," if, indeed, the latter term be not a misnomer'. Although the campaign was expensive, it opened China to British trade, benefitted the 'civilised world' in protecting Westerners from Chinese 'oppression and barbarous outrages',

---

[5] David Steele, 'Temple, Henry John, third Viscount Palmerston (1784–1865), prime minister', *Oxford Dictionary of National Biography*, accessed 9 December 2019, www.oxforddnb.com/view/10.1093/ref:odnb/9780198614128.001.0001/odnb-9780198614128-e-27112.

[6] M. Banno, *China and the West, 1858–1861. The Origins of the Tsungli Yamen* (Cambridge: Harvard University Press, 1964), 220–23.

[7] Harry Gelber, *Battle for Beijing, 1858–1860. Franco-British Conflict in China* (Basingstoke: Palgrave Macmillan, 2016), 191–93; John Selby, 'The Third China War,' in Brian Bond (ed.), *Victorian Military Campaigns*, New ed. (London: Tom Donovan, 1994), 71–104.

[8] Geoffrey B. A. M. Finlayson, *The Seventh Earl of Shaftesbury 1801–1885* (London: Eyre and Methuen, 1981), 445–47.

destroyed the Chinese belief in their superiority over Europeans, and secured international diplomatic access to Beijing.[9] John Fortescue, in 1929, viewed it as 'a well-managed little expedition' marred mainly by delays caused by the French, who, lacking the British experience of small wars over the previous 150 years, 'did not understand that description of work, and were, therefore, except on the actual field of action, an encumbrance'.[10] In 1967, John Selby agreed that the French slowed progress, but otherwise the intervention 'achieved what it set out to do ... without any real hitch'. Despite the heterogeneous forces involved, the campaign of 1860 'must surely rank as one of the most successful small wars ever conducted by Britain'.[11] The fine study by Gerald Graham, focused on the Royal Navy's role, stressed that the expeditions could not rely on British supremacy on the high seas to secure the government's objectives.[12]

Outbreak of War

The conflict consisted of four punitive British expeditions directed against China's two most heavily populated cities, Beijing and Canton. Troops were despatched from Britain in the spring of 1857 to press for compensation for the destruction of the foreign trading quarter at Canton in late 1856 and for the seizure of the small, British-flagged *Arrow*, and to gain diplomatic access to Beijing. However, the Indian Uprising (see Chapter 2) in May 1857 diverted British troops to India and intervention was confined to a naval action on the river system near Canton in June 1857. This destroyed the bulk of a Chinese navy consisting of craft useful only for riverine and coastal operations.[13] By December 1857, sufficient forces, although fewer than requested by the army commanders, were available at Hong Kong to attack and seize Canton. About six miles in circumference, the old, walled city in 1860 contained perhaps 600,000 people, plus 100,000 in suburbs along the riverfront.[14] After its capture, Elgin proceeded north and arrived

---

[9] Henry Knollys, *Incidents in the China War of 1860 Compiled from the Private Journals of General Sir Hope Grant* (Edinburgh and London: William Blackwood and Sons, 1875), 224–25.
[10] John Fortescue, *A History of the British Army*, 13 vols. (London: Macmillan, 1900–1930), vol. 8, 406–08, 420–22,
[11] Selby, 'The Third China War, 1860', 76, 79–80, 92, 103.
[12] Gerald S. Graham, *The China Station: War and Diplomacy 1830–1860* (Oxford: Clarendon Press, 1978), 419.
[13] Graham, *The China Station*, 316–17.
[14] Jules Picard, *État Général des Forces Militaires et Maritimes de la Chine* (Paris: J. Corréard, 1860), 498–500.

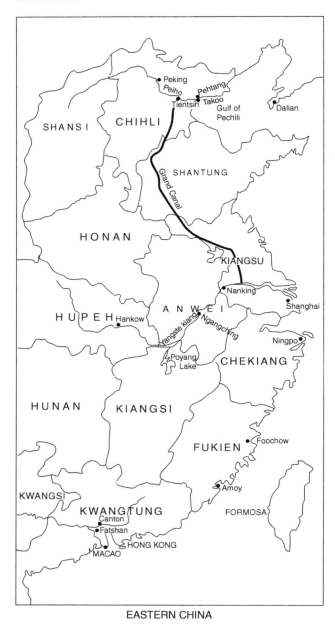

Map 3.1 Eastern China, c. 1860.
Redrawn and adapted from D. Bonner-Smith and E. W. R. Lumby (eds.), *The Second China War 1856–1860* (London: Navy Records Society, 1854)

offshore from the Peiho estuary, approximately 1,600 miles from Hong Kong, in April 1858. The Taku (Dagu) forts, guarding the entry to the Peiho River were attacked and easily taken on 20 May. Elgin proceeded up-river to Tientsin and negotiated a treaty in June which apparently settled the dispute. But when the British attempted to ratify the treaty of Tientsin by going to Beijing in June 1859, the Chinese blocked their entry at the reinforced Taku forts and destroyed British gun-boats. This triggered a more formidable campaign in 1860.

British and Chinese Forces

If the strategy pursued by the British was relatively straightforward, securing the necessary military resources proved more challenging. When the Governor of Hong Kong, Sir John Bowring, requested troops from India in late 1856, Lord Canning, the Governor-General of India, could spare only 500 Indian sepoys stationed at the Straits Settlement, explaining in February 1857 that he was overstretched by an expedition to Persia.[15] The total number of troops assigned to China eventually rose from 1,095 in March 1857 to 4,792 a year later. But the demand in India for British troops meant that 44% of those land forces in early 1858 were supplied by the Royal Marines and 23% by Indians. As the pressure in India eased, so the Indian army's contribution in China rose to 2,121 men (40% of the total force) in March 1859, and, in the wake of the second campaign, to 4,727 out of 11,806 land forces in March 1861. The Royal Marines' contribution more than halved between March 1858 and March 1860.[16] The total naval force for the East Indies and China fleet, including marines, was 10,428 in March 1858, at the height of the first campaign, and 7,464 in June 1860, as preparations for the second peaked.[17] The deployment of fewer than 5,000 Indian troops from 210,000 Indian rank and file and 8,000 British troops from the UK army of about 150,000 men was not numerically demanding, but troop deployment was never straightforward.

The French government contributed fewer troops, stipulating in 1860 that the British contingent be limited to 10,000 so as not to outnumber them significantly. In fact, the British exceeded their target, explaining that the government in India when sending troops in 1860 was

---

[15] Graham, *The China Station*, 310–13.
[16] Great Britain. Parliament. House of Commons. Returns of the Number and Descriptions of Troops of all Arms at the Different Stations in China..., 1862, 138, XXXII, 289.
[17] D. Bonner-Smith and E. W. R. Lumby (eds.), *The Second China War 1856–1860* (Navy Records Society, 1954), xxii.

unaware of the cap and arguing that troops dispersed in garrisons should be excluded from it. As of 15 April 1860, the French Expeditionary force at Shanghai consisted of about 7,332 soldiers and 300 support personnel.[18]

Manpower was plentiful in China, whose population was estimated at between 300 and 360 million. One Chinese estimate suggests that over 800,000 soldiers were available in the early 1840s during the first so-called Opium War. These forces were divided between eight imperial Banner brigades, totalling about 200,000 men, and the locally-raised Green Standard troops, totalling perhaps 600,000 men. They were distributed in the eighteen provinces and widely dispersed in small units, came under civilian officials' control and orders, and engaged in policing rather than military duties. Re-deployment proved slow in the campaign of 1842, since long-distance roads were poor and incapable of taking large numbers of men at any one time. The British were quicker in conveying troops from India to south China than the Chinese were in sending reinforcements from more distant provinces to the Canton area.[19] One British expert in 1857 stressed that the Chinese were 'essentially un-warlike, and have no taste for war, or any employment that has even the semblance of it. They look upon war as an idle and profitless employment'.[20]

British assessments were informed by Thomas Wade's study of the Chinese military published in 1851 and expanded in a French translation in 1860. Wade arrived in China in 1842, became a prominent official at Hong Kong, and served the British envoys throughout 1857–61. He concluded that a weak command system and atrophied decision-making created a 'large and useless army'. The Banner units fulfilled ceremonial, patrolling, and guard duties. Well-drilled in archery, the troops were recruited by hereditary succession, tended to be confined from generation to generation to particular garrisons, and were dominated by Tartars. The imperial government failed to grasp the lessons of the war of 1840–42, blaming shortcomings on individual commanders and ignoring recommendations to improve organization, ethos, equipment, and training. Wade argued that the Bannermen might provide the nucleus of an army if they were regularly paid. The lack of a strong

---

[18] Knollys, *Incidents*, 27–28, 30–32.
[19] Mao Haijian, *The Qing Empire and the Opium War. The Collapse of the Heavenly Dynasty*, trans. Joseph Lawson, Reprint (Cambridge: Cambridge University Press, 2016), 46–47, 49, 55–56.
[20] J. Crawfurd, 'On China and the Chinese', *Journal of the United Service Institute* I (London, 1858): 56. The text is an extended report of a talk by Crawfurd.

military ethos resulted from China's unique position among major states in facing no challenging external competitors or enemies for thousands of years.[21] Modern research stresses that muskets were typically obsolete, gunpowder was expensive and of variable quality, artillery guns were often antique or, if relatively new, were made of inferior materials to uneven dimensions.[22]

Wade described the Green Standard troops as long-service, Chinese (not Tartar) volunteers, whose numbers were inflated by officers embezzling non-existent soldiers' pay. According to Chinese reports, they were unskilled in 'cannon, musket, sword or spear', so poorly paid and so misused by their officers that only 'vagabonds' would enlist.[23] The mass risings during the Taiping Rebellion of 1851–64 led to the formation of provincial militias, who may have totalled 300,000 men. But their effectiveness depended on individual commanders and they did not gel with the regular forces which, dispersed in numerous garrisons, tended anyway to concentrate on their varied, prescribed functions.[24] The imperial court remained confident that while Westerners, and especially the British, were unassailable on the high seas and coastal sea lanes, they would struggle on land against China's overwhelming cavalry numbers. This approach proved ill-founded; the dynasty, as Wade stressed, 'has shown a most unlettered confidence in strong bodies of horse and foot'.[25]

War Aims

The Chinese aimed to uphold their own definition of international relations, in which the Chinese empire transcended barbarian states. The imperial court was divided between those who accepted conflict and those who sought a settlement. Officials at Beijing denied Western demands in 1857–58 and became more anti-foreign after the first allied capture of the Taku forts in May 1858. They were further emboldened by the victory gained at the forts in June 1859 and remained in the ascendant until August 1860.[26] They naturally refused any liability for the incidents which led to confrontation in 1856 and reaffirmed their

---

[21] Thomas Wade, *The Chinese Army* (Canton: Chinese Repository, 1851), 10, 20, 23, 32, 45, 50, 126–28, 130.
[22] Haijian, *The Qing Empire*, 27–31, 212–13. [23] Wade, *The Chinese Army*, 130–31.
[24] Edward L. Dreyer, *China at War 1901–1949* (London and New York: Longman, 1995), 10–13; Raymond Bourgerie and Pierre Lesouef, *Palikao (1860) Le Sac du Palais d'Été et la prise de Pékin* (Paris: Economica, 1995), 74–76.
[25] Wade, *The Chinese Army*, 130. [26] Banno, *China and the West*, 66–67, 88, 238–43

right to delegate the conduct of relations with foreign powers to provincial officials.

British aims were clear-cut in April 1857: to obtain reparations for British subjects and those under British protection for a range of losses at Canton and to ensure that the treaty ports, especially Canton, fulfilled their treaty obligations. If such issues were resolved, Elgin was instructed to seek the right of foreign powers to appoint representatives at Beijing with access to the highest officials. The British government also wanted 'access to cities on the great rivers' for British trade and ships 'from all ports of the Chinese empire without distinction' to be allowed to trade at Hong Kong.[27]

The British government pressed for a speedy resolution. Sidney Herbert, Secretary of State for War, informed Sir Hope Grant of that imperative when the general was chosen to command in China, in November 1859. In April 1860, Herbert, in lifting his earlier injunction against advancing to Beijing, added that 'we could not winter there, and we should have to leave almost immediately after our arrival'. Pressure for a speedy outcome arose, as Herbert acknowledged in May 1860, from the fact that 'the war is not popular here'. In July, he informed Grant that the funding for the expedition aroused 'a good deal of dissatisfaction from all parties in the House of Commons'. He argued that 'the country was keen for war' in 1856–57, when 'we were in the wrong', whereas the country 'is now weary of the expense and unsatisfactory results, and ready for any means of escape from the difficulty'. In October, the minister repeated his hope that the campaign would deliver 'a good and speedy result'. In December, he informed the general that 'A protraction of the war, with its enormous expenditure, will, I fear, meet a doubtful reception in Parliament'.[28] The men on the ground were given clear objectives.

Course of the War

The conflict was not in any modern sense a war, but the logistical challenges of mounting these expeditions were considerable. Operations against Beijing depended on linking the base at Hong Kong with the Peiho River, which accessed the imperial capital, some 1,600 miles away, using staging points, notably the island of Chusan (Zhoushan), the merchant quarter at Shanghai, and the forward base established at Talien (Dalian).

---

[27] Bonner-Smith and Lumby, *The Second China War*, 195, 211, 213.
[28] Knollys, *Incidents*, 140, 145, 148, 151–53, 158.

The campaign depended upon close co-operation with some of the Chinese. First, the British recruited plentiful local labour. Hong Kong's population in 1855 of 72,607, among whom 70,651 were Chinese, proved a useful source of labour and also, with 1,813 vessels totalling 612,875 tons, a source of shipping.[29] General labourers to man the boats were readily hired for two months' pay in advance. Some 400-500 labourers, supported by Chinese physicians, were apparently recruited in Hong Kong for every UK regiment despatched to the campaign.[30] One estimate put the total raised at between 3,000 and 4,000. Their duties extended to carrying ammunition to troops in battle and carrying the wounded from the battlefield.[31]

Second, local supplies were readily obtained. At Talien in 1860, British forces were well supplied by the population of a 'fertile, well wooded, and cultivated' hinterland. At Tientsin in early September 1860, merchants and townsmen furnished 'large supplies of sheep, oxen, vegetables, fruit, and blocks of ice' to the newly arrived allies. The Peiho valley impressed British participants with its rich agricultural productiveness and the eagerness with which local farmers and merchants traded with the allies. By early October 1860, the British were running 200 boats on the Peiho south of Beijing, operated by 800 locals; they were mainly shallow-draft salt boats very readily hired at generous rates.[32]

Campaigning remained intensely localized. In May 1857, J. Crawfurd, who had served widely in South-East Asia, accurately framed the confrontation:

We are at open war with Canton; but the other four ports have not entered into the quarrel, and our trade with them goes on only the more briskly that there is no trade at all with the sister port. Even when we attack, capture, and occupy Canton, which we must do, its capture and occupation will have no sensible effect upon the Imperial Government. The other ports will take no heed, and we shall want neither tea nor raw silk.[33]

Responding to the crisis at Canton proved controversial. Rear Admiral Sir Michael Seymour, commanding the East Indies and China fleet, argued for punishing Canton for the violent incidents of 1856. But Elgin contended that an effective assertion of British power required

---

[29] Picard, *État Général*, 511–12, 520.
[30] D. F. Rennie, *The British Arms in North China and Japan* (London: John Murray, 1864), 12, 14, 21–22, 122.
[31] Rennie, *The British Arms*, 122–23.
[32] Knollys, *Incidents*, 48, 104; Rennie, *The British Arms*, 130–31, 134, 138, 173; His Widow [Victoria Hamilton Goodenough] (ed.), *Journal of Commodore Goodenough* (London: Henry S. King, 1876), 46–47.
[33] Crawfurd, 'On China and the Chinese', 51–58.

British control of the hinterland beyond the river port, an objective which the commander of British military forces, Major-General Thomas Ashburnham, insisted was beyond the capacity of his limited manpower. Elgin wanted initially to prioritize pressure on Beijing. But Seymour and others persuaded him that negotiations with the imperial government would fail if the British could not even control Canton.[34]

Although the Chinese had ample notice of the attack on 28–29 December 1857, the British escaladed Canton's walls with limited losses. The defenders concentrated their forces where no direct attack occurred and perhaps had no heart for the fight. The bulk of the operation fell to the Royal Navy's 1,550 men, who sustained thirty-nine casualties in fighting and seventeen in an accidental explosion. Compared with the levels of resistance offered by Indian cities during the Uprising there in 1857–58, Canton was feebly defended. The British seized Commissioner Ye, their main antagonist at Canton, and exiled him to India, although the Chinese government reduced this action's impact by dismissing Ye for incompetence. More significantly, the British, recognizing that they had far too few troops to advance inland, maintained the existing local and regional administrations.

Elgin regretted the action against Canton. He confided in his diary in October 1857, before the assault:

I do not think that the naval actions here have really done anything towards solving our questions, and perhaps they may have been injurious, in so far as they have enabled the Government and the Press to take up the tone that we could settle our affairs without troops. All these partial measures increase the confidence of the Chinese in themselves, and confirm them in the opinion that we cannot meet them on land. They have never denied our superiority by sea.

He concluded that a naval attack alone would result in a 'great deal of massacre and bloodshed' without influencing the Chinese government.[35] On the day of the bombardment, he noted that 'I hate the whole thing so much, that I cannot trust myself to write about it'. Although he later remarked that less damage was done to the city than had seemed likely, he ruminated in May 1858 that 'crowds of women and children' had been 'the victims of the bombardment of Canton'.[36]

The seizure of Canton failed, as Elgin predicted, to unblock the diplomatic impasse which the intervention was intended to resolve. Elgin therefore sailed north, reaching the Peiho estuary on 14 April, to

---

[34] Bonner-Smith and Lumby, *The Second China War*, 196, 208–14; Graham, *The China Station*, 325–26, 332–34.
[35] Walrond, *Letters and Journals*, 204–05.   [36] Ibid., 214–15, 248.

force negotiations with imperial officials. But moving from the estuary of the Peiho up-river to Tientsin, where meetings would be held, required both river transport and armed protection from the Royal Navy. Rear Admiral Seymour continued to concentrate on the Canton River, wearing down his gun-boats in transport duties. He had promised Elgin eighteen gun-boats by March and had delivered only two by early May.[37]

Elgin blamed Seymour for failing to support the government's strategic requirements. On 23 April, he noted a missed opportunity to exert political pressure by intercepting junks carrying grain to the capital along the Peiho; he had only one gun-boat capable of crossing the Peiho bar, plus a despatch boat 'lightened for the purpose'. On 29 April, Elgin, appropriately aboard HMS *Furious*, wrote angrily to the Foreign Secretary of the delay in providing gun-boats for operations on the Peiho River and on 9 May repeated that his mission was being undermined by the lack of appropriate naval support. Since his arrival twenty-six days earlier, an average of fifty junks a day, 'laden with supplies for Pekin', had crossed the Peiho's bar, offering an open target for naval action to apply pressure on the Chinese government.[38]

Once a flotilla was assembled, the British easily attacked and took the Taku forts on 20 May and advanced upon Tientsin, where in June, a treaty was agreed to which met British and French demands and opened another eleven ports to foreign trade. Implementation, however, proved challenging. Elgin, in February 1860, stated that he would have pressed on to Beijing after concluding the Treaty of Tientsin had troops not been required for Canton.[39] The military demands for holding Canton and policing the surrounding countryside continued to be relatively high.[40] In March 1858, 4,126 of the 4,792 troops deployed to China, excluding Royal Navy personnel, were at Canton; in March 1859 some 3889 out of 5,124 were; in March 1860 the total was 4,586 out of 6,325.[41] The bulk of the military forces were based a long way from the Peiho where pressure on the regime needed to be strongest.

Instead, little pressure was applied from June 1858 to June 1859. When British and French envoys sought access to the imperial court in 1859, they were instructed to await the arrival of Chinese plenipotentiaries at Shanghai. The new British envoy, Frederick Bruce, Elgin's younger brother, insisted on securing direct access and summoned

---

[37] Graham, *The China Station*, 343, 345, 355.
[38] Bonner-Smith and Lumby, *The Second China War*, 313, 318, 323.
[39] Banno, *China and the West*, 68.   [40] Graham, *The China Station*, 362–63.
[41] Returns of the Number and Descriptions of Troops, 289.

a small contingent to force the entry to the Peiho and accompany him to Beijing.

Rear Admiral Sir James Hope reached the Gulf of Pechili (Bo Hai) on 17 June 1859. On 25–26 June, Hope's flotilla of nine vessels, with two more in reserve, attempted to enter the Peiho river and a small force spearheaded by Royal Marines attempted to take the Taku forts commanding the river mouth. Four craft were disabled or sunk during the attempt, although one was later recovered. The flotilla suffered 118 killed and wounded (including the rear admiral and two captains). A force of 600 marines, sappers, and sailors attacked the fort on land but only about fifty reached its walls, and casualties amounted to 316.[42] This humiliating reverse could scarcely be overlooked, especially by Lord Palmerston, who returned to the premiership in July 1859. A new and far more powerful expedition was authorized for 1860.

Sir Hope Grant, having held an active command during the Indian Uprising in 1858, reached Hong Kong on 13 March 1860. The advance on his prime objective, the Taku forts, began on 12 August. The intervening five months were used to assemble and re-position a small army from Hong Kong to within marching range of the forts. The first staging post was the island of Chusan, one of China's most important strategic positions, commanding access to major rivers, the imperial Grand Canal, and important east coast cities.[43] The final staging-post was the large bay at Talien (Dalian) near the entry of the Gulf of Pechili and about 220 miles by sea from the Peiho estuary.

By 9 July 1860, the British force at Talien consisted of 6,285 British and 2,218 Punjabi infantrymen, 1,565 Royal Artillerymen and 235 Royal Engineers, and 288 men of the British military train supported by 428 men from the Madras (Chennai) mountain train, sappers, and miners. There were few cavalrymen, with only 198 from Britain and 825 from India.[44] This force could not confront legions of mounted Tartar Banner Troops on their own terms but would rely instead on its artillery contingent. The specially formed Chinese Coolie Corps supplied 278 men, while thousands of labourers were hired on short-term contracts from whom, according to the official return, an estimated 1,290 sailed with the expedition to the mainland on 26 July.[45] On 1 August, 2,000 troops, equally divided between the two allies,

---

[42] Bonner-Smith and Lumby, *The Second China War*, 390–97; Graham, *The China Station*, 375.
[43] Picard, *État Général*, 501–02.   [44] Knollys, *Incidents*, 49–50.
[45] Swinhoe, *Narrative*, 52.

spearheaded the landing at the shallow estuary of the Pehtang (Beitang) River. Their first task was to cross 'at least two miles of mud'.[46]

The landing place itself had proved controversial. Charles Cousin-Montauban, the French commander, initially proposed, independently of the British, to take the Taku forts from the south and therefore to land south of the Peiho River, not at Pehtang to its north. Grant believed that Montauban could not subdue the forts from the south and insisted 'with all the force in my power' that Montauban agree to advance from Pehtang.[47]

Once the landing positions were consolidated, the march through marshy terrain towards the Taku forts began on 12 August. A series of manoeuvres, involving flanking and frontal field artillery fire, kept the Tartar cavalry at a distance from the causeway used by the allies and drove them back upon the Taku forts, where they posed far less of a threat than if they had withdrawn into open country to the north-west. Artillery also proved decisive when, on 14 August, the allies took Tangku (Tanggu), at the cost of only fifteen wounded, with the aid of thirty-six guns which were advanced in stages to within 350 yards of the defences.[48] The nearest Taku fort lay four miles from Tangku. The forts' capture on 21 August was the campaign's military culminating point. (See the 'Anatomy of a Battle: The Taku Forts' section.)

The capture of the Taku forts led to a truce accompanied by tentative diplomatic probes and an allied advance to Tientsin. When talks broke off, the advance continued. By 16 September, at the half-way point between Tientsin and Beijing, the allies assembled about 3,840 British and 1,200 French soldiers.[49] This force encountered a Chinese army covering a front of three miles on 18 September at Changkiwan. The Chinese position was turned by a French, flanking attack and was outgunned in an artillery duel. The Chinese 'had not apparently the power of moving their guns' and, so Grant claimed, lost eighty guns in a two-hour engagement. It is possible that the Chinese had not expected an allied advance that day. Allegedly inflicting 'at least' 2,000 casualties on 20,000–25,000 Chinese, the allies suffered 51 casualties.[50] On 21 September, artillery fire held off Tartar horsemen, reportedly 10,000 to 12,000 in strength at Tongzhou, about fifteen miles from Beijing, at an important canal crossing. Montauban then stormed and

---

[46] Knollys, *Incidents*, 53.   [47] Ibid., 41, 45, 48, 63–64.
[48] Swinhoe, *Narrative*, 86–94, 97–98, 102–06.
[49] Knollys does not provide manpower for the engineers, artillery, or cavalry; I extrapolate from his figures on the forces present in June. Knollys, *Incidents*, 29, 105.
[50] Swinhoe, *Narrative*, 236–37; Knollys, *Incidents*, 111–14; Gelber, *Battle for Beijing*, 145.

took the Palikao bridge against a rear-guard action staged by the Manchu Imperial Guard in the campaigns' most celebrated French action.

The British established a new camp outside Tongzhou. Captain Roderick Dew RN, commanding the river transport, secured boats to bring supplies about thirty miles up-river and used local river barges to transfer them to this camp. According to Swinhoe, the town's governor was 'informed that if he made no hostile demonstrations against us, his city would be spared, and the people protected, and he accordingly showed his good will by instructing the townspeople to open a market on the stone bridge', despite the presence of, apparently, tens of thousands of Tartar light cavalrymen in the surrounding area.[51]

The allied army halted from 21 September to 5 October while diplomatic exchanges took place and finally advanced to Beijing where further negotiations concerned, among other issues, the release of British prisoners, whose return was completed on 17 October. Some prisoners had died after being tortured. Grant and Elgin quickly decided that the imperial Summer Palace would be destroyed in retribution. Grant had already set 1 November as his deadline for withdrawal before the worst of the winter set in. On 18 October, he justified this measure as one directed at the government, not Beijing's population, and at the place where British prisoners had suffered violence. Elgin saw no viable alternative punishments.[52]

Throughout 18 and 19 October, some 4,515 officers and men of the 1st Division, supported by 300 Royal Engineers plus cavalry units, destroyed all buildings in the Summer Palace gardens, which covered 857 acres or well over one square mile, and neighbouring villages.[53] If the French deplored this as vandalism comparable to the burning of ancient Alexandria, the sack of Rome, and Louis XIV's devastation of the Palatinate, Elgin viewed the action as necessary to achieving the objective privately emphasized in April 1860: 'a speedy settlement, on reasonable terms – as good terms as possible; but let the settlement be speedy. This, I think, is the fixed idea of all'.[54] Such punitive actions mirrored village-burning practised in 'colonial' campaigning, especially where battlefield resolutions proved elusive. The commander of the 1st Division, Major-General Sir John Michel, had commanded the Malwa Field Force during the Indian Mutiny-Rebellion, and he and Grant were familiar with the

---

[51] Swinhoe, *Narrative*, 264–65, 269.
[52] Gelber, *Battle for Beijing*, 149–52, 154; Knollys, *Incidents*, 203–04; Swinhoe, *Narrative*, 319–20, 323–30.
[53] James L. Hevia, *English Lessons: The Pedagogy of Imperialism in Nineteenth-Century China*. (Durham and London: Duke University Press, 2003), 107–08.
[54] Bourgerie and Lesouef, *Palikao*, 125; Walrond, *Letters and Journals*, 317.

destruction of insurgent villages.[55] In Cape Colony, he had crushed Xhosa opposition to British frontier expansion by extensive village burning and seizing cattle stocks when, in 1851–52, Xhosa warriors could not be pinned down in formal fighting.[56]

Anatomy of a Battle: The Taku Forts

The critical objective in August 1860, as it had been in May 1858 and June 1859, was the cluster of the five Taku forts commanding the entrance to the Peiho River. According to Robert Swinhoe, an official in the Consular Service, Grant wanted 'merely to get possession of the forts' commanding the entry 'with as little loss as possible'. Montauban wished to cross the river and assault the Great South Fort. Grant objected that troops having crossed the Peiho by a bridge of boats would suffer 'very serious' losses inflicted by flanking fire from the northernmost fort. Although success on the south bank would have blocked the Tartars' line of retreat towards Tientsin and forced them to surrender or fight their way out, Swinhoe argued that 'Our object was not to subdue the country, but merely to open a way for negotiations with its government' while suffering few casualties. 'Such were the thoughts and expressions current at the time throughout the army'.[57] On 16 August, Elgin pressed Grant to capture the Taku forts as soon as possible, since he did not wish to respond to a Chinese offer of a ceasefire until the river was open to the allies.[58] Yet, as late as 20 August, Montauban continued to press the southern option and agreed to an attack on the three north bank forts only under formal protest. Grant wanted 'the forts to fall speedily and with little loss' to the allies because he needed to accomplish much 'before the end of the season'.[59]

The Upper North Fort selected for attack was about two miles from the British camp. At 5.00 a.m. on 21 August, the Chinese opened fire on the allied positions from the Great North Fort, about 1,300 yards from the Upper Fort. The allies responded with a three-hour bombardment from forty-seven guns. Heavy guns suppressed the Great South Fort, while lighter guns at Tangku countered enemy fire from an entrenchment on the south bank. The main focus, from variously placed batteries

---

[55] H. M. Chichester and R. Stearn, 'Michel, Sir John (1804–1886), army officer', *Oxford Dictionary of National Biography*, accessed 9 December 2019, www.oxforddnb.com/view/10.1093/ref:odnb/9780198614128.001.0001/odnb-9780198614128-e-18649.
[56] Noel Mostert, *Frontiers: The Epic of South Africa's Creation and the Tragedy of the Xhosa People* (London: Jonathan Cape, 1992), 1107, 1110, 1121, 1124–25, 1128–29, 1150.
[57] Swinhoe, *Narrative*, 121–23.   [58] Knollys, *Incidents*, 72–73.
[59] Knollys, *Incidents*, 76–77, 80–86.

including two 32-pounders, was the Upper North Fort. Eight allied gun-boats were positioned at the mouth of the Peiho to fire on the southern forts.[60]

The Upper North Fort's powder magazine was hit, exploding with great force at 6.30 a.m. Field guns were then advanced to within 500 yards of the walls. By trial and error, two howitzers were dragged to within 50 yards of a gate and blew out a narrow gap. Allied contingents competed to enter the fort first, with some escalading the walls. The British contingent of about 2,500 men lost seventeen men killed and 184 officers and men wounded. The other four forts, with 600 guns, then surrendered, once the population and their property were guaranteed protection. Swinhoe reported 130 French casualties in its 1,000-strong assaulting party and insisted that the Chinese losses across the Taku forts 'could not have been less than 2,000' with corpses strewn 'everywhere'.[61] As with field artillery, the Chinese guns proved very difficult to manoeuvre. The majority of guns in the forts pointed to the river and the coast, from which direction the attacks of 1858 and 1859 had come.[62] With access to the Peiho River secured, the allies advanced up-river to Tientsin by 23 August, establishing a forward base there for their forces and diplomatic representatives.

Classic failings in assaulting fortifications recurred, despite a wealth of precedents. The allies found it difficult to cross the fort's ditches. 'Some of our men swam across the ditch' after sailors were shot down in trying to place pontoons upon it. The French forced labourers up to their necks in a ditch's water to support horizontal scaling-ladders on their hands and shoulders as soldiers trod across them. When breaches were attacked, they were typically well-defended and men reaching the tops of them were assailed by swords and spears. Breakthroughs occurred at small breaches or by sheer chance, as when Captain Anson cut the ropes of a drawbridge he came upon under the walls. Bourgerie and Lesouef likened the assault to medieval warfare, with troops clambering up ladders set against the ramparts.[63]

The Role of Technology and the Royal Navy

The major technological innovations of the 1850s affected transport, communications, and weaponry. China possessed no railways or

---

[60] Swinhoe, *Narrative*, 129–30.
[61] Swinhoe, *Narrative*, 130–33, 136–37; Knollys, *Incidents*, 86–92.
[62] Graham, *The China Station*, 400.
[63] Knollys, *Incidents*, 87–88; Bourgerie and Lesouef, *Palikao*, 86.

telegraph systems and the allies did not improvize makeshift infrastructure, as occurred in Abyssinia in 1867–68 when the British constructed a railway line.[64] But two technological advances, neither of which had been adopted by the Chinese, were relevant. Although they were not novel, steamboats played a significant role in allied operations. More innovatively, the breech-loading Armstrong gun appeared for the first time on campaign. The Armstrong's increased speed of reloading and range enhanced the allies' ability to disperse large formations of light cavalry. Reports on its use, though indicating some defects, encouraged Herbert to describe it in 1861 as 'at this moment the best gun in the world'.[65] The impact of technology needs, however, to be contextualized.

The Royal Navy's larger warships were of limited use in the fighting. Canton was about sixty miles from the sea. Some 1,554 naval personnel were assigned to assaulting the city in December 1857, but the majority of the warships involved had crews of between forty-five and seventy-five in strength. When the campaign swung north, large warships could approach no closer than 'several miles' – the flagship in April 1860 had to anchor eight and half miles from shore - from the mouth of the Peiho because the coastal waters of the Gulf of Pechili were too shallow. Even smaller craft encountered difficulties on the Peiho. The bar at the mouth of the Peiho was 400 yards long and 150 yards wide and could not be crossed by a vessel drawing over eleven feet and six inches of water at high tide. To put that in context, HMS *Calcutta*, the flagship, of eighty guns, drew twenty-five feet of water. Meanwhile, in the gulf the 'weather is often so boisterous and the swell so high vessels cannot discharge their cargo for several days together'.[66]

Transporting soldiers from Hong Kong to Talien Bay and then to the Peiho in 1860 depended on British superiority on the open seas, but it also required large numbers of Chinese junks. The latter were plentifully available. Some estimates reported that 3,000 junks crewed by 100,000 Chinese were engaged in the coastal trade.[67] The main British force used 200 transports in 1860, of which 120 were hired.[68]

The allies' objective on the Peiho was Tientsin. This busy river port was strategically positioned at the northern head of the Grand Canal from the Yangtsi River, a vital route for supplying Beijing, notably with grain. It was also a centre for the internal trade in salt, produced under

---

[64] China No 4 (1864) Commercial Reports ... for the Year 1862, 1864, 3302, LXIII, 362, Command Papers.
[65] Hansard, House of Lords Debates, vol. 161, 14 February 1861.
[66] Picard, *État Général*, 498; Bonner-Smith and Lumby, *The Second China War*, 268–69, 317; China No 4 (1864) Commercial Reports, 336–37, Command Papers.
[67] Banno, *China and the West*, 71.   [68] Graham, *The China Station*, 385.

strict government license. Its mercantile community was amply supplied with boats.[69] This was crucial because the Peiho above Tientsin became even shallower, incapable of taking vessels drawing 10 or 11 feet.[70] By early October 1860, any further advance to Beijing depended on boats mostly designed for the salt trade. The British readily hired, at 2 dollars per day, about 200 boats, manned by 800 locals and supervised by 200 sailors.[71]

The need for local river craft was underscored by the problems sometimes faced by larger, more sophisticated vessels. An early instance occurred in on 1 June 1857, when the steamer *Hong Kong* grounded twice in leading an advance along the Fatshun River and other tributaries of the Canton River. Men and guns had to be transferred to smaller craft.[72] In June 1858, Commander Goodenough noted that it took four days to cover the sixty miles up the Peiho from its estuary to Tientsin. This was partly because the river was new to the allies and 'very winding', but also because 'the French ships were frequently aground'.[73] Even in peacetime, the Peiho 'owing to its insignificant depth of water and tortuous course, is extremely difficult of navigation'.[74] On 1 August 1860, Goodenough grounded his ship almost immediately after entering the Pehtang River, partly by 'not keeping a stricter look out' and partly because 'I was rather jockeyed by another despatch-vessel on to the bank'.[75] En route to Tientsin, the steamship *Leven* grounded and spent a night stuck in the shallows. Later that day, 25 August 1860, at least three craft went aground on a narrow stretch farther up-river. A 'crowd of villagers vigorously' assisted French sailors in re-floating their gun-boat, while the *Leven* stuck once more. It was pulled free with the aid of 'plenty of volunteers' among the watching crowds.[76] The arrival of the siege guns for the final advance on Beijing was delayed to 29 September by the Peiho's shallow waters and the work of Madras sappers in cutting channels in the river.[77]

As for field artillery, the British demonstrated during the Indian Uprising that the range and mobility of light guns were critical in dispersing enemy concentrations, especially of cavalry, and minimizing British casualties. Non-Western armies failed to deploy their artillery equally flexibly. In the encounter with thousands of Tartar cavalrymen on

[69] China No 4 (1864) Commercial Reports, 337, 345–46, Command Papers.
[70] Graham, *The China Station*, 400–01.   [71] *Journal of Commodore Goodenough*, 46.
[72] Bonner-Smith, *The Second China War*, 202–03.
[73] *Journal of Commodore Goodenough*, 33.
[74] China No 4 (1864) Commercial Reports, 336, Command Papers.
[75] *Journal of Commodore Goodenough*, 44.   [76] Rennie, *The British Arms*, 128–32.
[77] Knollys, *Incidents*, 122.

12 August 1860, Swinhoe, an eye-witness, singled out the role played by the British artillery and especially the Armstrong guns.[78] This advance on Sinho, when Armstrong guns first entered active service, 'inaugurated a new epoch in artillery', according to Surgeon Rennie.[79] Although Rennie later found little evidence of damage or casualties inflicted by the Armstrongs and rejected reports on their contribution to victory as wholly fanciful, he overlooked their impact in dispersing large concentrations of the enemy.[80] There were problems with the time-fuses and with the breech-pieces, which came loose when not tightened firmly in the heat of action.[81] But field artillery in general broke opponents' morale as much as it killed or severely wounded them.

The British fully understood the Chinese imperial forces' deficiencies in weaponry, organization, motivation, and command. While naval strength, high morale, and overall technical superiority gave the allies distinct advantages, success also depended upon the extensive mobilization of local manpower and resources, frequent improvization, and the flexible use of artillery both against fortified defences and in the open field.

Aftermath

Claims for the long-term effects of these interventions are open to question. The expeditions' impact on China was dwarfed by the devastation caused by the Taiping rebellion. Beginning in 1851, the uprising threatened Beijing in 1853, provoked local military mobilizations by imperial officials from 1856, and lasted to 1864, by which time it had caused at least twenty million deaths.[82] The uprising weakened the imperial government and made European interventions, which Beijing defined as a fourth-order challenge, possible. Subsequent reform was a reaction to the Taiping insurgency and the real lesson from 1857–60, the need to transform the army, was not grasped until 1901.[83]

As the allies desired, the Chinese established a separate ministry to deal with foreign affairs. The British gained greater control over the customs service, vital since the indemnity of about £2,500,000 imposed upon China was paid as a proportion of the annual customs revenue. Allied forces remained at Tientsin, important for customs collection,

---

[78] Swinhoe, *Narrative*, 93.   [79] Rennie, *The British Arms*, 88.
[80] Ibid., 103–04, 124–25.   [81] Knollys, *Incidents*, 157.
[82] Jurgen Osterhammel, *The Transformation of the World*, trans. Patrick Camiller (Princeton and Oxford: Princeton University Press, 2014), 547–49.
[83] Dreyer, *China at War*, 15.

until 1862 and at the Taku forts until 1865.[84] On the commercial front, the coastal region was opened to Western trade. The Anglo-Chinese trade gap narrowed as exports from Britain increased, but only gradually as British dependence on exporting opium from India declined in relative terms. As Elgin predicted, there was no transformative boom in British exporting to China.[85] In military terms, not much was learned. The use of Punjabi forces indicated Britain's robust recovery in India after the challenges of the Uprising. But the scale of the deployment, amounting to fewer than 5,000 troops from Indian armies totalling 210,000 other ranks in early 1860, was hardly dramatic. The medical service was, in relative terms, far larger than the support provided in the Crimea and sickness was reduced from the levels suffered in China in 1840–42 and in the Crimea.[86] The tactics used against fortifications were unsophisticated and the neutralization of the extremely numerous Tartar cavalry, the bedrock of Chinese strategy, resulted from light artillery tactics frequently applied in India. The adaptability of the Royal Navy underpinned the interventions, but British warships faced no meaningful opposition from the Chinese. Progress up the Peiho was slow and essentially unopposed once the Taku forts were taken.

Franco-British relations were not markedly improved. Elgin repeatedly viewed the French alliance in China as a hindrance.[87] British 'public opinion' remained volatile when faced with French naval rearmament. In 1859–60, Palmerston's government focused primarily and warily on French policy during the protracted crisis in Italy. But freer trade, so insistent an objective in China and the subject of a treaty with France in 1860, remained in Palmerston's eyes a vital goal in international relations.[88]

Further Reading

Banno, Masataka. *China and the West, 1858–1861: The Origins of the Tsungli Yamen*. Cambridge: Harvard University Press, 1964.
Gelber, Harry. *Battle for Beijing, 1858–1860: Franco-British Conflict in China*. Basingstoke: Palgrave Macmillan, 2016.

---

[84] Banno, *China and the West*, 232–33, 240–44.
[85] P. J. Cain and A. G. Hopkins, *British Imperialism, 1688–2000*, 2nd ed. (Harlow: Longman, 2002), 362–68.
[86] Lieutenant General Sir Neil Cantlie, *A History of the Army Medical Department*, 2 vols. (Edinburgh: Churchill Livingstone, 1974), vol. 1, 477–81; II, 250–54.
[87] Walrond, *Letters and Journals*, 337, 344.
[88] C. I. Hamilton, *Anglo-French Naval Rivalry 1840–1870* (Oxford: Clarendon Press, 1993), 78–85; David Brown, *Palmerston: A Biography* (New Haven and London: Yale University Press, 2010), 435–50.

Graham, Gerald. *The China Station: War and Diplomacy, 1830–1860*. Oxford: Clarendon, 1978.
Haijian, Mao. *The Qing Empire and the Opium War: The Collapse of the Heavenly Dynasty*. Trans. Joseph Lawson, Reprint. Cambridge: Cambridge University Press, 2016.
Hevia, James L. *English Lessons: The Pedagogy of Imperialism in Nineteenth-Century China*. Durham and London: Duke University Press, 2003.
Selby, John. 'The Third China War, 1860'. In Brian Bond (ed.) *Victorian Military Campaigns*. London: Tom Donovan 1994.
Walrond, Theodore (ed.) *Letters and Journals of James, Eighth Earl of Elgin*. London: John Murray, 1872.
Wong, J. Y. *Deadly Dreams: Opium, Imperialism, and the Arrow War (1856–1860) in China*. Cambridge: Cambridge University Press, 1998.

4   The Expedition to Abyssinia, 1867–1868

Christopher Brice

Background

Abyssinia was a feudal society, in reality a loose confederation. Although there was one Emperor, rulers of large areas often styled themselves as *Negus*, or King. At the same time there were the *Ras*, or Princes, who ruled large tribal areas. For many centuries, Abyssinia had been isolated from the wider world. In 1520, this isolation briefly came to an end when a Portuguese envoy visited. Despite the attempts to build some sort of diplomatic alliance, the Abyssinian Negus was only interested in Portuguese muskets and swivel guns. Under threats from their Muslim neighbours, it was understandable that Abyssinia was interested in buying weapons from potential Christian allies.

The desire to improve their fighting technology continued into the nineteenth century. In 1848, Kassa, a young Abyssinian Chief led a force of 20,000 men against the isolated and undermanned, Egyptian-controlled fortress at Dabarki. Despite their overwhelming numerical superiority, the Abyssinians suffered large casualties due to the training and superior weaponry of the Egyptians. The young Chief is alleged to have remarked, 'The Egyptians are no braver than us, but they have the discipline of the West'.[1] Kassa, who would become better known as Tewodros II, became obsessed with acquiring modern weaponry and technology.

Tewodros II, often anglicized as Theodore, was a complex, albeit unstable ruler, once described as a 'combination of robber-chieftain, idealist and madman'.[2] He was certainly ambitious, for himself and for his people. His people, however, often failed to share his ambition. His attempts to modernize the country only received reluctant support.

---

[1] John P. Dunn, *Khedives Ismail's Army* (Abingdon: Routledge, 2005), 129.
[2] D. G. Chandler, 'The expedition to Abyssinia 1867–68', in Brian Bond (ed.), *Victorian Military Campaigns* (London: Hutchinson & Co, 1967), 111. The question of Tewodros' mental instability is debatable. See Phillip Curtin, *Disease and the Empire* (Cambridge: Cambridge University Press, 1998); and, Frederick Myatt, *The March to Magdala* (London: Leo Cooper, 1970).

Tewodros dreamed of a great Coptic Christian Empire with himself at the centre, and of ultimately leading a 'crusade' to liberate Jerusalem. Modernization, or westernization, was essential to this plan.

By the late 1840s, Tewodros has risen to great importance in Abyssinia. While the Emperor was technically the ruler of Abyssinia, in reality he had little real power. The de facto power lay in the hands of Ras Ali II of Yejju. Tewodros's emergence challenged Ali's power, and clashes were inevitable. As a peace offering, Ali II's daughter, Tewabech, was given to Tewodros in marriage. Peace, however, was temporary and Tewodros displayed his military ability in a number of daring attacks, some at night. When the decisive battle came, at Ayshal in June 1853, it was Tewodros who triumphed. In Ethiopian history, Tewodros's victory marks the end of the Era of Princes, *Zemene Mesafint*, in which the country was divided and the Emperor had little authority. Almost two years later, in March 1855, Tewodros declared himself Emperor. Although there was still unrest in the Empire, this was the most united it had been for almost two centuries.

★ ★ ★ ★ ★

The British expedition to Abyssinia generated plenty of literature. A very good introductory text to the campaign is David G. Chandler's 'The Expedition to Abyssinia 1867–68', in Brian Bond's edited, *Victorian Military Campaigns*. Books such as Darrell Bates, *The Abyssinian Difficulty* and Fredrick Hyatt, *The March to Magdala* appeared at either end of the 1970s, giving good accounts of the overall conflict. Of more modern books, few have dealt with the campaign itself. Philip Marsden's *The Barefoot Emperor* is an interesting historical account of Tewodros.

Shortly after the campaign a number of very useful books were published. The two-volume history prepared by Major Trevenen Holland and Captain Henry Hozier, *Record of the Expedition to Abyssinia*, is rich in detail. Captain Hozier also wrote a separate account of the campaign entitled, *The British Expedition to Abyssinia*. A number of diaries and journals from people involved in the campaign were published, including W. W. Scott's *Letters from Abyssinia during the Campaign of 1868*, and William Simpson's *Diary of a Journey to Abyssinia 1868*. Perhaps the most interesting account is that of Colonel Robert Phayre entitled, *Abyssinian Expedition: official journal of the reconnoitring party of the British force in Abyssinia*. An interesting account of the 'ordeal' of the 'European' captives can be found in *Narrative of Captivity in Abyssinia with Some Account of the Late Emperor Theodore, His Country and People*, by Dr Henri Blanc. Accounts of Tewodros vary in quality. Sven Rubenson's *King of Kings: Tewodros of Ethiopia* is one of the best.

64 Christopher Brice

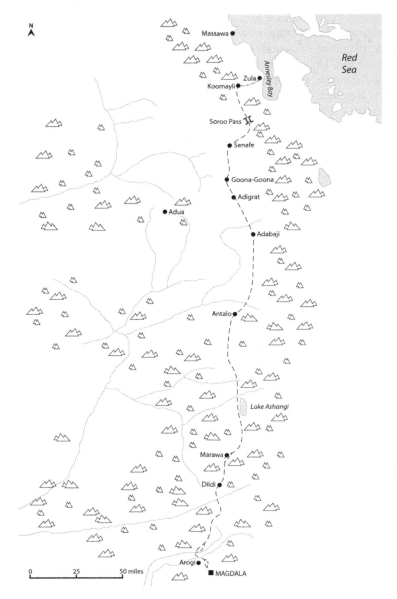

Map 4.1 Abyssinia, 1867–1868.
Map drawn by George Anderson for Helion & Co Ltd

Unfortunately, no modern biography of Robert Napier, the British commander of the expedition, exists. The only major work on Napier remains the biography written by his son who also edited and published Napier's private papers. It would be wrong not to recognize the numerous articles and books written by the late Richard Pankhurst, who died in 2017. His excellent knowledge of the field and his first-hand experience of Ethiopia made his work all the more interesting.

Outbreak of War

By the early 1860s, much of the Abyssinian Empire was in revolt against Tewodros. This was largely due to resentment of his dictatorial rule and his modernization schemes. The personal ambition of many Rases was also at play. Although the assertion by Phillip Curtin that 'Whatever else the British expedition might [have] done, it did not drive Tewodros from power. He had already lost it on his own', might be exaggerated, it is clear that Tewodros's authority was far from secure.[3] His response to these many challenges was becoming more brutal. Mass executions were reported, and, in 1866, after supressing a revolt in the rich city of Gondar, Tewodros looted and ransacked the city and then burnt much of it including the majority of its churches.[4]

The British Empire's relationship with Abyssinia was limited. Indeed, when writing of relations between the two nations, J. R. Hooker referred to normal relations as 'the Foreign Office ceased to regard it unless under compulsion'.[5] The British consul, Walter Plowden, who held that position from 1848 until 1860, was not even resident in Abyssinia but in the Egyptian-held coastal town of Massawa. Often seen as a calming and beneficial force, Plowden has also been criticized for getting involved in matters that did not concern him. Tewodros appreciated his council, and also the role he could play in enabling Tewodros's ambitions. For Tewodros, the British represented an opportunity to advance his empire technologically, particularly in terms of weaponry. Plowden probably did not have as much influence as another Englishman, John Bell. Bell virtually became an 'Abyssinian', married a local woman, purchased considerable land, and fought alongside Tewodros. Bell became Tewodros's closest adviser on matters both public and private.

---

[3] Curtin, *Disease and the Empire*, 36–37.
[4] Darrell Bates, *The Abyssinian Difficulty* (Oxford: Oxford University Press, 1979), 119.
[5] J. R. Hooker, 'The Foreign Office and the "Abyssinia Captives"', *Journal of African History* 11, 2 (1961): 245.

In March 1860, Plowden was murdered by one of Tewodros's rivals. The murder affected Tewodros badly, and he ordered mass executions in the area where it had taken place; the action was also a response to the open defiance of his authority.[6] The news of Plowden's death did not reach Great Britain until May. Lord Palmerston, the British Prime Minister, saw no need to send a replacement for Plowden immediately, and it was not until 1862, that Captain Charles Cameron arrived at Tewodros's court. Cameron's tenure started poorly. Tewodros had been confused by gifts sent from the Government of India, without either a covering note or envoy. He was also insulted that Cameron brought with him a letter from 'Mr Russell', the Foreign Secretary, rather than the Queen.[7] He felt aggrieved that the letter had come from a 'servant' and not from a fellow 'monarch'. Tewodros clashed with several European missionaries, particularly Rev Henry Stearn, who attempted to introduce more 'conventional' Christianity into Abyssinia.

The immediate origins of the war, however, lie elsewhere. In February 1862, Tewodros sent a letter of thanks and friendship, and a request for technical assistance to Queen Victoria. Due to Foreign Office oversight, no reply or even an acknowledgment was returned. Already suspicious of the British, and in an agitated and paranoid state, Tewodros started to imagine plots. The British had urged him not to wage war on his Egyptian neighbours or to take any action against the town of Massawa. The British were most interested in protecting the Red Sea route to India and feared that actions in this area could disrupt stability. Cameron would often, on instruction from the Foreign Office, spend a lot of time in Muslim areas adjacent to Tewodros's territory. Tewodros, however, saw this as proof of a growing Anglo-Muslim plot against him. The situation was not helped when an assistant for Cameron arrived at his capital, without the long-anticipated reply from Queen Victoria.

Paranoid and furious over the perceived insult, Tewodros imprisoned Cameron and his staff. It is clear from the beginning that Tewodros intended to use them as bargaining chips. Over the following months, most of the Europeans and their allies in Abyssinia were also imprisoned. Only those craftsmen manufacturing his weapons of war were allowed limited freedom.

It took some time for news of the imprisonment of Cameron to reach London. Initially there was little concern; it was viewed as a

---

[6] The exact date of Plowden's murder is unknown. It partly depends upon which version of his death one believes. The earliest date given is 13 March 1860, but it may have been as late as the first week of April.

[7] The British were not the only ones to make this 'mistake'. The French envoy also carried a note from the Foreign Minister rather than Emperor Napoleon III.

misunderstanding based on a Foreign Office oversight. To solve that problem, Lord John Russell had the Queen write a response to Tewodros's letter and it was entrusted to Hormuzd Rassam, who served on the staff of the British Political Officer at Aden. An archaeologist of some note, Rassam had also conducted political negotiations in the Arabia peninsula. Rassam arrived at Massawa on 23 July 1864. He spent over a year waiting for Tewodros' permission to enter Abyssinia, and it was not until October 1865 that Rassam, and his party including Blanc and Lieutenant W. F. Prideaux, were allowed to travel. On 22 January 1866, Rassam reached Tewodros' camp at Damot and was able to present the letter from Queen Victoria (incidentally dated 26 May 1864), along with a number of gifts. Initially matters went well, and the prisoners were released and joined Rassam. However, as they attempted to leave, Tewodros changed his mind and had them all arrested. Tewodros, increasingly desperate and with much of the countryside hostile to him, retreated with his captives, eventually to his mountain fortress at Magdala.

The condition of the captives varied. Some, especially the missionaries, were cruelly tortured, and Cameron spent two years literally in chains during his captivity. At other times, conditions were not as bad. They were allowed servants, could write letters, and were given goodly amounts of food.[8] Yet, as David Chandler wrote, 'the knowledge that their future was dependent on the unpredictable whims of a half-demented tyrant imposed a grave mental strain upon one and all'.[9]

Tewodros knew the value of his hostages, which was partly why he moved them to the security of Magdala. He attempted to use his hostages in order to secure the technical assistance he wanted from the British. Tewodros chose Martin Flad as his emissary. On 10 July 1866, Flad reached London. The new Conservative government of Lord Derby was now placed in a difficult position. The Palmerston and Russell governments had clearly underestimated Tewodros. Tewodros's letter, delivered by Flad, had thanked the Queen for the gifts received and stated that further donations, particularly in the form of machinery and skilled workmen, would be gratefully received as well. In a separate letter addressed to the Foreign Secretary, Tewodros was more open and specific.[10] Tewodros was blackmailing the British Empire.

---

[8] There is a story that the former captives found the food of the expeditionary force to be worse in quality and quantity that they had enjoyed in captivity! Frederick Myatt, *The March to Magdala* (London: Leo Cooper, 1970), 153.
[9] Chandler, *The Expedition to Abyssinia*, 114.
[10] Included in his list of requests were: two gunsmiths, an artillery officer, an iron founder capable of building a foundry and furnace, one or two boatbuilders, a wheel-wright, a small blast steam engine for the foundry, a turning bench with necessary tools, a distilling

The initial reaction of the Derby cabinet was to work with Tewodros and directed Colonel William Merewether, the British Resident at Aden, to try to find the people and the items he required. Merewether was largely successful in his efforts. He noted that the cost would be at least £3,500, but likely more once all the machinery had been manufactured. Merewether pointedly remarked that although 'The sum may appear large', it would be 'small compared to the cost of a campaign in such a country as Abyssinia'.[11]

Having initially considered giving in to Tewodros's blackmail, the British soon changed their minds. New reports from Abyssinia indicated that the conditions of the captives were worsening and the fact that they had been moved to Magdala was found alarming. It was also reported that a 'trial' of Cameron and others had taken place in which it was clear that Tewodros believed Britain and the Ottoman Empire were conspiring against him. Reports of the construction of a railway from Suakin to Kassala, which could allow for the rapid movement of Egyptian troops into Abyssinia seemed to confirm his fears. In London, it was becoming clear that the military option might be the only one that could resolve the situation. British prestige, as much as the lives of the hostages, was now at risk. Surprisingly, it was the Liberal press and politicians who were demanding decisive action from the Conservative government. Before committing fully, Derby initially decided to return Flad with a strong letter from Her Majesty expressing displeasure and asking for the immediate release of the hostages. No threats were made, however, other than the withholding of the 'gifts' and workmen he had 'requested'.

Flad arrived at Massawa with the letter in October 1866. Merewether and his party of men and materials arrived a month later to find Flad still there. This seemed a clear indication that Tewodros was losing further power and authority in Abyssinia by the day. Flad was unable to travel due to the 'disturbed state' of the two possible routes he could use. Instead, he despatched a couple of messengers with copies of the Queen's letter. Eventually one got through to Tewodros. At first, Tewodros was delighted that his scheme seemed to have worked. He knew through his spies that the equipment and workmen had arrived, and that Merewether was with them. Tewodros hoped that he could induce Merewether to come to Magdala with the equipment and workmen. Merewether's reputation was known and Tewodros

---

machine, machinery for the production of gun caps, a good telescope, a good supply of gunpowder and gun-caps, along with various, shotguns, carpets, silks, tumblers, goblets, pistols, swords, and other 'European curiosities'.
[11] Bates, *The Abyssinian Difficulty*, 77.

appreciated the appeal of so notable a hostage. Merewether was not going to fall into this trap.[12]

The British government was under much pressure to act but remained reluctant to commit to a military expedition. It was decided in April 1867 that another letter should be written, this time urging Tewodros to immediately release the hostages or face the consequences. At the same time, a 'bazaar rumour' was started in Massawa suggesting that a military expedition was already being planned. As a result, it was decided that enquiries into a military expedition had to be made. A political game of 'pass the parcel' now ensued as the request for enquiries was passed around Whitehall and India before finally arriving in the hands of the Commander-in-Chief of the Bombay Army, Lieutenant-General Sir Robert Napier, as the nearest British military command capable of carrying out the expedition.

Robert Napier born in Colombo, Ceylon (Sri Lanka) on 6 December 1810, was an experienced commander. The son of a soldier, he attended Addiscombe and Chatham before being commissioned Lieutenant in the Bengal Sappers and Miners (later the Bengal Engineers). His early career in India was largely spent in civil and military engineering projects, where two systems of construction, namely the Napier system of flood defences, and the Napier system for cantonments, were part of his legacy. He had also seen much active service in small wars, including the Anglo-Sikh Wars, the Indian Rebellion (see Chapter 2), and the Second Anglo-China War (see Chapter 3). From 1861 to 1865, Napier was the Military Member of the Governor General's Council, and he briefly served as acting Viceroy. Although Napier took reasonability for the enquiries, his Quartermaster-General, Colonel Robert Phayre, an officer of a great deal of practical experience, did the majority of the work. The starting point for their preparations was to examine the supplies and equipment used during the Persian campaign of 1856–57 and the China Expedition of 1860. Phayre and Napier worked with speed and by the 29 July, their answers had reached London.[13]

In order to defeat Tewodros, it was determined that a force of about 12,000 combat troops, backed by a much larger force of labourers and camp followers, would be required. It would take about three to four months to ready such a force providing initial preparations could start immediately. Napier added that given the rainy season in Abyssinia, it was essential that the operation was ready to go no later than January so

---

[12] Ibid., 80–81.
[13] Napier's biographer states that Napier became aware of this on 12 July rather than 10 July. Most other sources recognize the 10th however.

that it could be finished by June when the rains set in. At least 10,000 pack animals would also be required for transportation. The troops would all need to be equipped with tents, waterproofs sheets, and blankets. They also needed as much information, maps, and intelligence as possible on Abyssinia to be gathered and sent to them.[14]

While British preparations had begun, in early August 1867, one of the messengers who had taken the 'final' letter to Tewodros, returned to Massawa and reported that after waiting ten days and receiving no reply, he was dismissed. It was therefore decided that an expedition was inevitable. On 15 August, Napier was offered command of the expedition, which he accepted. Four days later, the Cabinet gave its approval for an expedition to free the captives. Two days after that, Benjamin Disraeli, the Chancellor of the Exchequer, secured from the House of Commons a commitment of £2 million to support the expedition.

British and Abyssinian Forces

The actual size of the army and the number of men Tewodros could call upon is unknown. He had lost much of his authority and support and at best, his forces amounted to no more than 10,000 men. Every man possessed a firearm, about half of which were relatively modern. These were a mixture of doubled barrel shotguns and muskets, using percussion caps. The older weapons were flintlock and matchlock muskets. In addition to a firearm, every man also carried more traditional weapons such as a sword, spear, and shield. In theory, Tewodros also possessed an impressive artillery train. Exact figures are hard to come by. Since thirty-eight guns were later captured at the fortress at Magdala, it is conceivable that he had as many as fifty guns.[15] His artillery varied dramatically in size from 6-pounders to five 24-pounders and even three 56-pounders. He also possessed at least ten mortars of varying sizes, most notably amongst them was the five-ton mortar he had named 'Sebastopol'.[16] The sheer weight and size of Sebastopol required 800 men to drag it on ropes. Tewodros had very few pack animals.

---

[14] Trevenen Holland and Henry Hozier, *Record of the Expedition to Abyssinia*, 2 vols. (London: HMSO, 1870), I, 155–62. This is Napier's report. The official report of the Government of India is found on pages 162–64. Both reports were submitted to London.

[15] Holland and Hozier, *Record of the Expedition to Abyssinia*, vol. 2, 59.

[16] The alternative spelling of Sevastopol is sometimes used. Although generally believed to be a five-ton mortar, it has also been recorded as being over seven tons. A replicable of the mortar is found sitting on a plinth of a busy roundabout in modern day Addis Ababa.

The British army used in the Abyssinian expedition was in fact largely Indian in composition. Of the five regiments of cavalry deployed only one, the 3rd Dragoon Guards, was British. The other four, the 10th Bengal Lancers, the 12th Bengal Lancers, the 3rd Bombay Light Cavalry, and the 3rd Regiment of Scinde Horse, were all Indian, with the former two from the army of the Bengal Presidency, and the latter two from the army of the Bombay Presidency. Of the fourteen battalions of infantry, four were from the British Army, two from the Bengal Army, and eight were from the Bombay Army. Of the six batteries of artillery all were Royal Artillery, except for one company of the 25th Mountain Battery of the Bombay Army.[17] Of the eight companies of engineers, only one was from the British army, with four coming from the Bombay Army, and three from the Madras Army.

The British were in the midst of changing their main service weapon. The muzzle-loading Enfield 1853 rifle was slowly being replaced with a breech-loading rifle. The latter were far easier to use, maintain, quicker-firing, and had proved their worth in continental warfare. The British solution was the Snider-Enfield, which added the Snider breech-loading mechanism to the existing Enfield rifle. For what was considered a stopgap solution, it produced a surprisingly good weapon. The Snider-Enfield was used by all British infantry in the expedition. Consequently 4,000 Snider rifles and 1,000 Snider Carbines, along with 2,500,000 rounds of ammunition, were despatched from Bombay. A further 2,420,000 rounds were kept in Alexandria in reserve.[18]

Since the Rebellion, it had been decided to keep the Indian troops a technological step behind their British counterparts. Thus, they were still armed with muzzle-loading smooth bore muskets. In late 1867, Napier asked permission of the Indian authorities to arm the Indian troops with the Enfield rifles that his British troops had given up for Sniders. In a telegram dated 21 January 1868, the Viceroy of India consented.[19] In post-mutiny India, the granting of such a request was taken very seriously.

Supporting the 13,088 combat troops were an army of camp followers, British, Indian, Chinese, and locals. Exact numbers are hard to come by, but a strength of around 20,000 to 30,000 men at any one time is realistic. A 'cooly' or 'Kahar' corps was raised in India and amounted

---

[17] There were also two rocket batteries provided by the Royal Navy.
[18] Holland and Hozier, *Record of the Expedition to Abyssinia*, vol. 1, 198.
[19] Ibid., vol. 1, 199. This was not carried through until after the Battle of Magdala and the return march.

to 1,943 men.[20] Their specific role was to support the army in lifting and carrying, equipment, stores, and wounded men. A large number of animals were required to support the expedition as well. 2,538 horses (excluding cavalry and artillery horses), 17,943 mules and ponies, 5,735 camels, 1,759 donkeys, 8,075 bullocks, and 44 elephants were all landed on the coast.[21]

The logistical element of conveying all the men, material, and animals from Britain, India, and Egypt, made this expedition a huge undertaking. That it was achieved successfully says much about the preparations. This was a far cry from the logistical system, which a little over ten years earlier had all but collapsed under the strain of the Crimea War.

Strategy and War Aims

As spelt out by the British government, their war aims were to release the hostages. It was also understood that there would have to be reprisals against Tewodros. A proclamation, approved by Napier, was issued before the campaign stating that 'no injury was intended to the peoples of Abyssinia, who might remain quietly in their homes'.[22] This was an attempt to make clear that Tewodros and his supporters were being targeted, not the Abyssinian people. The expedition was not carried out for benevolent reasons. Nor was it undertaken to achieve any sort of territorial aggrandizement or the enlargement of the empire. The addition of such an area as Abyssinia would only make sense if the region was viewed as prosperous or potentially economically advantageous. Prior to the construction of the Suez Canal, the strategic value of Abyssinia was considered limited. In addition, occupation would require a large military presence and the construction of fortresses, cantonments, roads, railways, and general infrastructure. It would also have required arrangement with the Egyptians/Ottomans to purchase the coastline. Simply put, holding Abyssinia was not worth the money and effort required.

---

[20] The term 'cooly' or 'coolie' holds negative connotations and is considered a racial slur. At the time, even though it was used as a generic term to refer to unskilled labourers, it still carried with it a derogatory inference. The British applied it to Chinese, Indian, African, and South-East Asian laborers. Holland and Hozier, *Record of the Expedition to Abyssinia*, vol. 2, 436–39.

[21] The figures are the official returns for shipping. A figure of 8,000 camels used by the expedition is often quoted, but this probably includes animals purchased locally, for which records are limited. Holland and Hozier, *Record of the Expedition to Abyssinia*, vol. 1, 234.

[22] Holland and Hozier, *Record of the Expedition to Abyssinia*, vol. 1, 331.

Tewodros's aims are unclear. He had been playing a dangerous game. For a while, it had worked to work, and his hostages had seemed to be worth taking. Having reckoned on the inability of the British to mount an expedition, his underestimation of the British put him in a very difficult position. The retreat to his mountain fortress of Magdala was probably his best, if not only, option. Initially, he hoped that the arrival of the British would unite his people against the invader, but this did not materialize. Indeed, at times, his rivals colluded with the British. Once the British landed, he could only hope that the expeditionary force would be unable to reach Magdala in any condition to fight. He knew that a journey of 400 miles through a largely inhospitable landscape would not be easy.

The Course of the War

The initial British force arrived off the coast of Massawa on 1 October 1867 commanded by Colonel Merewether and consisting of about 400 men. After surveying the coastline, it was decided that Massawa was not adequately suited to serve as a base of operations. As a result, Merewether sailed along the coast to Annesley Bay. On the western side, near the small village of Zula, a new site was chosen. There was no infrastructure, but the bay was calm and there was a supply of fresh water nearby, and more could be found in the mountains only 13 miles away. Plans were already in place to pump water down from the mountains to the bay, and large quantities of copper pipping, water pumps, and the latest water-boring technology were shipped to Zula. Scouting of the area and the nearby interior was commenced. The terrain was found, however, to be inhospitable, and the arid dry heat brought with it the promise of disease. Colonel Phayre, Quartermaster-General, decided that the Koomayli Pass offered the best route through the mountains into the highlands of Abyssinia and along the route to Magdala.

Much would need to be done before the main force arrived. The first thing was to construct a pier over 700 yards in length,[23] so that shipping could land men and materials directly. In due course, roads and even a small railway would assist the movement of men and materials.[24] On 21 October, the advance guard of the expeditionary force arrived, mostly consisting of sappers and engineers who started the work of building the infrastructure required. Within months, a fully operation port was up and

---

[23] The pier ended up being closer to 900 yards in length and could typically accommodate more than one ship at a time. Chandler, 'The expedition to Abyssinia', 125.
[24] Technically it was a tram way, but the term railway is used in most accounts.

running. By early December, the pier was operational. A remarkable feature at the end of the pier was a water condenser, which turned seawater into drinkable water. In addition, a railway was constructed that would run from the pier to twelve miles in land. By mid-December the force was starting to gather at Zula. Two-thousand British and 5,000 Indian troops had landed, along with 5,000 mules, 956 carts, 926 bullocks, and 956 carts, along with over 5,000 tons of supplies.[25] Things were not perfect, and many problems were encountered, but the fact that so much had been achieved in barely two months was remarkable.

On 2 January 1868, Napier landed at Zula. He ordered the expansion of the camp in order to prevent disease. He also set about correcting the deficiencies in supplies, particularly food, and improved the allocation of equipment to the Indian troops, ordering 15,000 pair of boots and woollen socks and 15,000 blankets.[26] Despite this, by the end of January, Napier was disappointed with the speed of preparations. Napier was under pressure to get the expedition completed as soon as possible, certainly before the start of the rainy season in June/July. He not only had to think of the journey to Magdala but also the return journey. The prospect of making the return during the rainy season, or being trapped nearby Magdala until it passed, was not appealing. The difficulty of moving supplies through the Koomayli pass to the forward base Senafe (Senafay) would certainly slow things up. Napier introduced greater supervision, at all levels, and continued a process of replacing local labour with Indian labour, the latter proving far more effective.

Napier had to balance speed of movement with attention to detail. The potential for disaster was large. The longer he waited the more danger there was to the hostages, and that caused by the seasons. Yet Napier knew that to move without preparations would be fatal. He needed to have a strong supply line. Living off the land was not a viable option, even in terms of firewood, fodder, and water. Without a strong supply depot at Senafe, Napier would be taking a great risk. Those in Whitehall and India who urged a 'quick dash' to rescue the captives failed to understand the situation. His greatest supporter in the need to be adequately prepared was the Duke of Cambridge, the Commander-in-Chief of British Forces.[27]

Napier expected Tewodros to resist the expedition. He would therefore need all his artillery to match Tewodros. This added to the transport

---

[25] Chandler, 'The expedition to Abyssinia', 125.   [26] Ibid., 126–27.
[27] See in particular, H. D. Napier, *Field Marshal Lord Napier of Magdala: A Memoir by His Son* (London: Edwin Arnold & Co, 1927), chapters XII and XIII.

burden, but Napier solved the logistical problems by using elephants. These problems, in all their forms, would likely have overwhelmed a lesser man than Napier. Instead, he came up with a plan to advance on Magdala with a force of 5,000 troops and the necessary support. The 1st Division, commanded by Major-General Sir Charles Staveley, would form the main advance. The 2nd Division, under Major-General G. Malcolm, would in effect guard his depots and his ever-extending supply lines.

On 25 January 1868, the British force, stretching some seven miles, began its march towards Magdala. Progress was initially good, and by 29 January, the advance guard had reached Adigrat some thirty-five miles from the forward base at Senafe. By 6 February, much of the force had reached Adigrat where a two-week halt was deemed necessary as Napier had become concerned that his force was too stretched out. It was a sensible decision, but given the pressure on Napier, it was a brave one. Even the Duke of Cambridge was becoming anxious and wrote to him urging the use of flying columns, but Napier knew this was not practical as the problem of supply would still have existed.[28] The advance guard reached Antalo, 200 miles inland, on 14 February. The further the British force got from the coast the slower progressed as transport animals and porters felt the strain. Napier tried his best to reduce the size of the column by shedding the number of non-combatants and the amount of kit carried.

On 2 March, Napier again ordered a lengthy halt to allow men and animals to recover. By 20 March, the column was still 100 miles from Magdala, yet he called for another rest. The strain was beginning to show on all concerned. Some of the 33rd (First Yorkshire West Riding) Regiment of Foot, leading the advance of the column, displayed ill-discipline. Napier handled the situation by removing them from pride of place, from the advance, and replacing them with the 4th (King's Own) Regiment of Foot. It had the desired effect and the ill-discipline ceased.[29]

On 8 April, the expedition arrived within twelve miles of Magdala. As the British prepared for the final push, Tewodros also got ready for the assault. How realistic he was about victory is unknown but nevertheless, he made an impassioned plea to his remaining five to eight thousand men. He outnumbered the British and still had all his artillery intact. He was concerned about the discipline of his troops and certainly would

---

[28] Robert Napier, *Letters of Field Marshal Lord Napier of Magdala*, ed. H.D Napier (London: Jarrold & Sons, 1936), 15.
[29] Chandler, 'The expedition to Abyssinia', 134–35.

have thought about the battle against the Egyptians at Debarki twenty years earlier.

The Battle of Arogee (or Arogi) on 10 April 1868 was never intended by Napier. At daybreak, Staveley led the advanced guard, preceded by Phayre and 800 sappers and miners. The march took them down into a ravine before they ascended the hills. It proved a very difficult and demanding climb. Phayre sent back an ambiguous message that led Staveley and Napier to believe that he held the head of the valley and that the road would be easily passable for the baggage train and guns. Thus, Napier ordered Stavely to advance with a guard of only 100 men of 4th Foot. Realising the potential hazards to the baggage train, Napier ordered the remainder of the 4th, who were having a well-earned rest, to advance quickly to protect it. Almost at the moment they started to move, Abyssinian artillery fire landed amongst them. This was shortly followed by a large body of Abyssinian warriors, maybe 5,000 in number, who rushed at the British. The 4th, however, were able to reach the top of the slope and commence firing on the enemy. The rapid fire of the Snider proved vital. On the left of the battlefield, the Punjab Pioneers held the edge of the ravine, supported by a naval rocket brigade. During the attack, Brevet Lieutenant-Colonel L. W. Penn arrived to support them with his six 7-pounder mountain guns. The Punjab Pioneers showed great discipline and skill in handling their old smoothbore muskets and bayonets. Here, the fighting was at its fiercest, much of it hand to hand. The attack on the baggage train was halted by the 100 men of the 4th Foot, where again the rapid fire of the Snider was key. The Abyssinians were finally driven from the battlefield by British artillery, and a bayonet charge led by the 4th Foot. For their part, the Abyssinian artillery had played little role after the opening salvo. The battle had lasted three hours. Despite great bravery, the Abyssinians were decisively beaten. The discipline of British and Indian troops, the rapid fire of the Snider, and the effective deployment and handling of the artillery were the decisive factors. Even caught by surprise, the technological superiority of the British had won the day. Abyssinian casualties were calculated at 700 dead and 1,200 wounded. British figures were twenty wounded, two of them fatally. Of the 5,000 men who sallied forth against the British, barely 600 are thought to have returned to Magdala, with many deserting.[30]

Tewodros had witnessed the battle from the plateau where his artillery was positioned, entrusting command of the attack to Fitaurari Gabri,

---

[30] Holland and Hozier, *Record of the Expedition to Abyssinia*, vol. 1, 37–38; Bates, *The Abyssinian Difficulty*, 185.

who was killed in the engagement. Thinking he was only attacking the baggage train, Tewodros had sensed a cheap victory. The losses, and the clear technological superiority of the British, convinced him he was doomed. Sending for the British envoy, Rassam, Tewodros attempted to negotiate his way out of the impending disaster. What amounted to a letter of surrender was delivered to Napier. The British general, however, found himself in a difficult position. The political aim of the expedition had been to release the hostages. This could be achieved without further force. However, the various Abyssinians who had supported his force, or at least had not worked against his advance, had done so in the belief that Tewodros would be overthrown. Napier's reply explicitly demanded the release of the hostages, but only implicitly asked for the surrender of Tewodros and his family. Tewodros refused to surrender. Although some of his chiefs argued that the time had come to kill the hostages, wiser council prevailed, knowing that doing so would unleash the full furry of the British.

In despair, Tewodros attempted suicide but the pistol failed to go off. Realising that all was lost, Tewodros agreed to release the prisoners.[31] He hoped that this would appease Napier and that the British would withdrawal as a result. However, Napier elected not to withdraw as he saw that British honour had to be restored by punishing Tewodros. With a force still at Tewodros's disposal, Napier also considered how a British retreat would impact other Abyssinians. He decided that he had to attack and destroy Magdala. Preparations were made for an assault, and the cavalry were deployed to prevent Tewodros from escaping.

Anatomy of a Battle: Magdala

On 13 April 1868, British forces attacked Magdala. Its natural defences made this a potentially formidably task. The only access to the mountain fortress was a narrow, twisting pathway. The defences themselves included two large gates with stones piled behind them, a small barbican flanked by stone walls, and wooden stockades twelve feet high, topped with thorn bushes creating a natural type of barbed wire. Seventy feet further on were similar defences guarding the final entrance to the Magdala plateau. Tewodros only had a couple of hundred men left, plus a few light guns. His defences could not stand up to sustained artillery fire, but bringing the guns into play would be easier said than done because of the topography.

---

[31] Just over half were released on 11 April, the remainder on 12 April.

Napier had no alternative but to conduct a frontal attack along the causeway. To cover it, the rocket brigade and the twelve 7-pounder mountain guns were deployed on a lower slope about 1,300 yards away from the fortress. At 1.00 p.m., the artillery bombardment commenced, but had relatively little effect. Two companies of the 33rd Foot in skirmish order led the assault, which commenced at 4.00 p.m. Their task was to supress enemy fire and cover the advance of the 10th Company of Royal Engineers and a company of the Madras Sappers and Miners. They carried scaling ladders, picks, crowbars, and charges of powder to blow the gates. The remaining six companies of the 33rd followed them to make the assault. The 45th (Nottinghamshire) (Sherwood Foresters), having only joined the expedition on 8 April, were first reserve to follow up the attack made by the 33rd. The remainder of the force stood by to assist if required.

The assault went well until the advancing troops reached the gate. There they found that the fuses for the powder charges had been left behind, and that the scaling ladders had all been destroyed. Improvising, two Irish soldiers of the 33rd Foot found a slightly shorter part of the wooden palisade. Private James Bergin managed to knock the thorns from the top using his bayonet. He then pushed Drummer Michael Magner to the top of the wall. From there, Magner helped Bergin to climb up and then assisted other soldiers as well, while Bergin laid down covering fire. All this was done under continual heavy fire. The Abyssinians fled towards the second line of defences, and the gates were opened. Bergin led a party of men forward to keep them open, while another party fought its way down to the main gate and allowed the remainder of the assaulting force to enter Magdala. Bergin and Magner were both later awarded with the Victoria Cross for their actions.

Magdala fortress had fallen. British losses were fifteen wounded. Resistance ended with the news that Tewodros was dead, having committed suicide. The prisoners were free, and British honour had been restored. Napier did not stay long at Magdala. After destroying the fortress and its remaining guns, he ordered the immediate return to the coast. By 17 April, the British had completely abandoned Magdala. As they returned, they destroyed much of the infrastructure they had built along the way. Some of the guns, older muskets, ammunition, and gunpowder were presented to the Chiefs who had assisted in the advance. Sadly, and rather inevitably, this led to a further round of internal fighting.

By 2 June, the British expeditionary force was back at Zula and preparing to sail. Over 13,000 animals were either sold or given away, and 15,000 were taken away. The entire camp was dismantled. By the time the last ship sailed on the 19 June, there was little left behind. The stone pier, largely stripped, and various scars on the landscape were all that remained of a once-large British port and camp on the Red Sea coast of Africa.

The Role of Technology

The latest technology proved vital to the success of an operation in such an inhospitable location and climate. In addition to modern breech-loading rifles and artillery, the use of steam shipping, railways, telegraph, and other modern technology important for communication and transport, proved significant to British success. The role of the Royal Navy as well as the force of mercantile marine provided by the British and Indian governments helped provide the life blood of the expeditionary force. One of the more interesting pieces of technology was the use of limelights to illuminate the countryside around the various camps. This precaution was taken due to Tewodros's reputation for night attacks.

In no place did new technology play a more important role than in providing a supply of fresh drinking water. For all the animals, horses, mules, donkeys, camels, bullock, and elephants, the total requirement for water was between 150,000 and 200,000 gallons a day.[32] Each man was allowed one and a half gallons a day, and with upwards of 40,000 troops, laborers, and camp followers, that amounted to about 60,000 gallons. Therefore, the estimated total requirement for the force was approximately 200,000 to 260,000 gallons a day. The shipping in the harbour produced between 50,000 and 96,000 gallons a day from their condensers. The two land-based condensers could produce just over 12,000 gallons a day.[33] One hundred Norton tube wells, were shipped over from the United States, and proved highly effective. They could bore in to all but the hardest rocks and boulders. Added to this was the Bastier chain pump which could lift to the surface 120 gallons a minute from a depth of 270 feet. At the same time, pumps and miles of copper piping helped to bring water from the mountains to Zula. At the start of the expedition, before the freshwater-producing techniques were up and running, many animals died from lack of water. Once the technology was in full flow, however, the force could be kept adequately supplied.

---

[32] All the figures are estimates based on the daily demands. As the force kept changing in size it is difficult to be more accurate. Holland and Hozier, *Record of the Expedition to Abyssinia*, vol. 2, 284–300, 343–44.

[33] Three further condensers were sent for but did not arrive until after the campaign was over.

The expedition was also the first British campaign to include a great number of scientists and technical advisers including official geographers, archaeologists, zoologists, meteorologists, and photographers who both recorded what they experienced and brought with them technical knowledge to assist the expedition.

Aftermath

In Abyssinia, the fall of Tewodros led to further bloodshed as his death created a large political void. Numerous competing forces fought for control of Abyssinia. Men like Wagshum Gobazey, Kassai, and Menelik challenged each other for supremacy; all three would become Emperor at some point. Napier's decision to reward Abyssinians who assisted his expedition with arms and ammunition aggravated the problem. However, Britain was not the only European country bringing weapons to Abyssinia. France and Russia sold guns to warring factions as well. Indeed, while the British withdrew from Abyssinia, other powers started to move into the wider region. Egypt expanded its control along the Red Sea coast and moved in land from Massawa, and France and Italy ventured into neighbouring Somaliland.

In 1889, Menelik became Emperor and finally brought political stability to Abyssinia. Throughout his rule he consolidated power and expanded his domain. His rule is perhaps best remembered internationally for the First Italo-Ethiopian War 1895–96, and the crushing defeat he handed the Italians at the Battle of Adowa. At Adowa, an Italian force of just under 15,000 men suffered casualties of approximately 6,000 killed, 1,700 wounded, and 3,000 captured.[34] The Italians had taken the Abyssinians lightly, with the Italian Prime Minister, Francesco Crispi, remarking shortly before the battle that the Italians would achieve in a shorter time, and at a far lesser cost, more than the British had in 1868.[35] Overconfidence was not the only problem. They also suffered from poor lines of supply and communication, and did not take advantage of modern technology. As David Chandler remarked, Adowa showed 'What might have happened had a less capable and thorough soldier (than Napier) been in command'.[36]

In Great Britain, the Abyssinian expedition was hailed as a great success. Throughout the whole nine months of operations, only 34 men

---

[34] Figures vary somewhat, but the following from Chandler seems reasonable. Chandler, 'The expedition to Abyssinia', 153.
[35] Negussay Ayele, 'Adawa 1896: Who was Civilized and who was Savage?' in Paulos Milkias and Getachew Metaferia (eds.), *The Battle of Adawa: Reflections on Ethiopia's Historic Victory against European Colonialism* (New York: Algora Publishing, 2005), 164.
[36] Chandler, 'The expedition to Abyssinia', 153.

had died and 333 were either wounded or got sick, a remarkably low figure that says much about the meticulous planning and the work of the medical services. Individual honours were bestowed, particularly upon Napier who was raised to the peerage as Baron Napier of Magdala, made a GCB and GCSI, as well as given a pension of £2,000 a year, a vote of thanks of both houses of Parliament, and the freedom of the cities of London and Edinburgh, along with other honors. Napier was lauded as one of the finest soldiers of his generation, and it was no surprise when in April 1870, he was appointed Commander-in-Chief, India. In 1878, with the possibility of war with Russia at hand, Napier was called from the semi-retirement of the Gibraltar command to potentially lead a British force into war.

The celebration of the British achievement in Abyssinia was slightly curtailed once the enormous cost of the expedition was revealed. Parliament had voted to cover the costs of the war totalling £2 million until the end of 1867. After that, it was thought that £600,000 a month would be sufficient. However, the final figure was £8,600,000 which far exceeded the planned amount. As a consequence, the income tax had to be raised to meet the cost. There had been mismanagement and perhaps even some corruption which was not Napier's fault.[37] But most of the British public failed to appreciate what Napier had achieved. He had a port and infrastructure built from scratch, requiring a huge amount of equipment, animals, and men, and sailed a force hundreds of miles, marched it over 400 miles to Magdala, and then defeated the enemy.

As for future involvement in Abyssinia, the British did not appoint a new consul at Massawa. In a minute to Lord Stanley, the Foreign Secretary, by James Murray Undersecretary of State at the Colonial Office, it was stated succinctly that 'the appointment had involved us in complications which it was most desirable for the future to avoid'..[38]

Further Reading

Bates, Darrell. *The Abyssinian Difficulty*. Oxford: Oxford University Press, 1979.
Blanc, Henry. *A Narrative of Captivity in Abyssinia*. London: Smith Elder, 1868.
Chandler, D. G. 'The expedition to Abyssinia 1867–8'. In Brian Bond (ed.) *Victorian Military Campaigns*. London: Hutchinson & Co, 1967.
Curtin, Phillip D. *Disease and Empire: The Health of European Troops in the Conquest of Africa*. Cambridge: Cambridge University Press, 1998.

---

[37] It is said that 4,000 mules at Bombay were 'lost'. How this could happen without corruption has never successfully been explained.
[38] Bates, *The Abyssinian Difficulty*, 218.

Holland, Trevenen and Hozier, Henry. *Record of the Expedition to Abyssinia*. 2 vols. London: HMSO, 1870.

Hozier, Henry. *The British Expedition to Abyssinia*. London: Macmillan & Co, 1869.

Marsden, Phillip. *The Barefoot Emperor: An Ethiopian Tragedy*. London: Harper Collins, 2007.

Myatt, Frederick. *The March to Magdala*. London: Leo Cooper, 1970.

Napier, H. D. *Field Marshal Lord Napier of Magdala: A Memoir by His Son*. London: Edwin Arnold & Co, 1927.

Rubenson, Sven. *King of Kings: Tewodros of Ethiopia* Addis Ababa: Haile Selassie, 1966.

5   The New Zealand Wars, 1845–1872

John Crawford

Background

The wars between Māori and the British armed forces and British (Pākehā) settlers that raged across much of New Zealand's North Island in the mid-nineteenth century remain the most divisive and controversial chapter in New Zealand's history. Pākehā land hunger, sense of racial superiority, and Māori resolve to retain control of their land were at the heart of these conflicts. Also important was a determination among Māori to defend the right to control their own affairs. They believed this right had been guaranteed in the Treaty of Waitangi, under which New Zealand became a British colony in 1840.[1]

Traditionally Māori society was organized into *iwi* (tribes) and *hapu* (lineage groups). Warfare was a significant part of Māori life, but increased greatly in scale and ferocity after the introduction of firearms to New Zealand. Māori quickly became adept at the use of small arms and also made limited use of artillery. The design of their *pā* (fortified strongholds) was radically changed to provide protection against musket fire and to maximize the effectiveness of defensive fire. Between 1807 and 1839, the Musket Wars saw casualties, displacement of population, and changes in tribal boundaries on an unprecedented scale. The introduction of European diseases and the Musket Wars led to a sharp fall in the Māori population from about 100,000 in 1769 to about 60,000 in 1858; by which time the Pākehā population had reached a similar level. All these developments facilitated British colonization.[2]

Relations between Pākehā and Māori were, from the outset, marked by occasional outbreaks of violence usually prompted by cross-cultural

---

[1] Vincent O'Malley, *The New Zealand Wars Ngā Pakanga o Aotearoa* (Wellington: Bridget Williams Books, 2019), 9–28.

[2] Ron Crosby, *The Musket Wars, a history of inter-iwi conflict 1806–45* (Auckland: Reed, 1999), 17–24, 367–77; O'Malley, *New Zealand Wars*, 24; Elsdon Best, *The Pa Māori* (Wellington: Whitcombe and Tombs, 1927), 365–75.

misunderstandings, disputes, or particular crimes or slights.[3] The topography of New Zealand's North Island, where the great majority of Māori lived, favoured Māori resistance. Most of the island was densely forested; there were large areas of rugged hill country and many, mostly unnavigable, rivers. The small British settlements, scattered around the coast, generally had little cleared land around them and were all vulnerable to attack from the Māori-controlled hinterland.[4]

* * * * *

Articles and books about the New Zealand Wars by Pākehā participants and observers began to appear while fighting was still underway. In the 1920s, James Cowan's detailed government-sponsored work, *The New Zealand Wars*, was published. It remains an essential source for serious study of the New Zealand Wars. In 1986, James Belich's, influential *The New Zealand Wars and the Victorian Interpretation of Racial Conflict* appeared. Although substantial aspects of Belich's analysis have been brought into question, his central argument that the nature and success of Māori resistance had not been properly recognized, has been accepted by most New Zealand historians. The two most important books to appear in more recent years about the wars are Māori historian Danny Keenan's *Wars Without End: The Land Wars in Nineteenth Century New Zealand*, which emphasizes the central importance of the control of land as the cause of the wars; and Vincent O'Malley's meticulous *The Great War for New Zealand: Waikato 1800–2000*.

Outbreak of War

Although conflict about the ownership of land and the exercise of authority lay at the heart of the New Zealand Wars, each conflict was triggered by particular issues. The first of the conflicts, the Northern War of 1845–46 was primarily caused by the anger of Ngā Puhi chief, Hone Heke, and his ally, Te Ruki Kawiti, at the economic losses caused by the transfer of the capital from Kororāreka (now Russell) in their territory to Auckland, and by concern that the colonial authorities were usurping powers guaranteed to them under the Treaty of Waitangi. Hōne Heke and Kawiti expressed their unhappiness by felling the flagpole at Kororāreka, a powerful symbol of authority, three times in 1844–45.

---

[3] Crosby, *Musket Wars*, 280–81.
[4] Charles Pasley, 'The War in New Zealand', *Journal of the Royal United Services Institute* 6, 5 (1863): 569–72, 583–84.

Hōne Heke did not have the support of all his tribe. During the Northern War some Ngā Puhi hapu took a neutral stance while others led by Tāmati Wāka Nene fought with the British forces.[5]

British and Pākehā, and Māori Forces

Māori warriors were part-time soldiers, who spent more of the year tending to their crops than they did fighting. The forces that fought the British included some female warriors (*wāhine toa*) and all able-bodied members of a tribe would, when required, be involved in such key tasks as building defences. Because of the small size of the Māori population and the limited number of tribes that took up arms, the number of warriors opposing the British and Pākehā forces in any engagement varied from less than 100 to only about 2,000. They were led by chiefs who were generally experienced, capable warriors and good tacticians. Even the most highly ranked chiefs, however, could not demand unquestioning obedience from other chiefs. As a result, major Māori forces were always coalitions in which key decisions were subject to debate, and there was always the possibility that some iwi or hapu would decline to accept a particular course of action.[6] In engagements in the open, such as at Puketutu in May 1845, the individual martial skills of Māori were generally no match for highly disciplined British infantry. Throughout the New Zealand Wars, Māori relied heavily on pā to compensate for their limited numbers and other weaknesses.[7]

The design of pā developed considerably during the New Zealand Wars. Some pā were constructed to defend areas of economic or other importance, others as bases for operations, but some were placed in favourable defensive positions in the hope that the British would unsuccessfully attack them and incur significant losses for no good purpose. The Māori strongholds of Ōhaeawai and Ruapekapeka in the Northern War were the first artillery pā encountered by the British. These pā were fully enclosed by stockades that included salients and deep, well-traversed firing trenches and strong anti-artillery bunkers. When available, Māori incorporated artillery, generally old ships' guns, into their defences. During the Taranaki War of 1860–61 there were significant advances in pā design. At Waireka (Kaipopo), a new style of low-profile

---

[5] O'Malley, *New Zealand Wars*, 42–45.   [6] Ibid., 18–22.
[7] Pasley, 'War', 589–90; James Belich, *The New Zealand Wars and the Victorian Interpretation of Racial Conflict* (Auckland: Auckland University Press, 1986), 43–44, 49; Cliff Simons, *Soldiers, Scouts and Spies: A Military History of the New Zealand Wars 1845–1864* (Auckland: Massey University Press, 2019), 42–43.

pā appeared that relied for its strength on a complex of concealed rifle pits and trenches, and incorporated only a weak fence primarily intended to slow an attacker and to mask the defences. Such pā were difficult targets for artillery. At Puketakauere in June 1860, Māori made good use of outlying, concealed rifle pits near the pā from which attackers could be engage and defeated even before they reached the main defences. The final stages of the war saw the Māori construct complex barrier pā consisting of rifle pits, trenches, bunkers, and stockaded strong points designed to defend areas of particular importance. These pā faced towards the expected direction of attack and generally had their flanks protected by swamps or other obstacles. They were not enclosed and had escape and support routes. All of these developments were seen during the Waikato War and the Tauranga Campaign. Te Kooti was not a skilled pā builder; Tītokowaru, however, was. His pā were small but of advanced design. He made especially good use of hidden, outlying positions that turned areas around his pā into killing zones.[8]

The New Zealand Wars were significant undertakings for the British Army which required a total of fourteen regiments serving in New Zealand between 1843 and 1870. In addition to the British and local forces, an East India Company's ship and a small detachment of the company's artillerymen took part in the Northern War, and the colony of Victoria's only warship was involved in the Taranaki War.[9] In New Zealand, as in other colonial campaigns, the success of the British forces was founded on robust logistics.[10] Britain was fortunate that it had bases in Australia and was able to call upon the resources of the Australian colonies, which throughout the wars were an important source of manpower, supplies, and to a lesser extent equipment for the British and colonial forces.[11]

---

[8] Robert Carey, *Narrative of the Late War in New Zealand* (London: Richard Bentley, 1863), 88–89; Best, *Pa Māori*, 392–409; Nigel Prickett, 'Pākehā and Māori fortifications in Taranaki, 1860–1881: Form and purpose,' in Kelvin Day (ed.), *Contested Ground Te Whenua I Tohea: the Taranaki Wars 1860–1881*, (Wellington: Huia, 2010), 81–102; Peter Cooke, *Won by the Spade: How the Royal New Zealand Engineers Built a Nation* (Dunedin: Exisle, 2019), 26–36; Belich, *Wars*, 241–45, 251–52, 267–72.
[9] James Cowan, *The New Zealand Wars: A History of the Māori Campaigns and the Pioneering Period*, 3rd ed., vol. 1 (Wellington: Government Printer, 1983), 75, 182; Ian F. W. Beckett, 'The Victorian army, Māori and the conduct of small wars,' in John Crawford and Ian McGibbon (eds.), *Tutu Te Puehu: New Perspectives on the New Zealand Wars*, (Wellington: Steele Roberts, 2018), 470–88.
[10] Simons, *Soldiers, Scouts and Spies*, 44–45.
[11] Jeff Hopkins-Weise, 'The role of the Australian colonies in New Zealand's wars of the 1840s and 1860s', in *Tutu Te Puehu*, 433–45.

Until the withdrawal of British forces from active operations, the Royal Navy played a significant part in the New Zealand Wars. The ability to quickly move men and supplies to and around New Zealand was central to the success of British and later colonial operations. During the wars the Royal Navy maintained, with considerable difficulty, blockades to prevent hostile Māori from receiving arms and other supplies. Naval brigades fought as infantry in most of the major actions in the Northern War, in Taranaki, in the Waikato and at Tauranga. Naval guns and gunners also fought on land. In 1864 the Admiralty expressed its displeasure at what it saw as the excessive employment of Royal Navy personnel on land during operations in New Zealand. The Royal Navy had a particularly important role in the invasion of the Waikato, which was supported by four warships. Naval personnel commanded and manned gun-boats, barges, and other craft deployed on the Waikato River. Royal Navy officers had overall command of this vitally important flotilla.[12]

Several different kinds of locally-raised forces were involved in the New Zealand Wars. After the outbreak of the Northern War in 1845, the New Zealand Militia was established. Virtually all male, non-Māori, British subjects between the ages of 18 and 60 were liable for service. Volunteer militia service companies saw action in the later stages of the Northern War and in the fighting around Wellington in 1846. The new Militia Act of 1858 provided for the formation of volunteer corps who elected their own officers and had more flexible terms of service. Volunteers and the militia were used extensively in the Taranaki War and in the early stages of the Waikato War. In late 1863, about 1,650 militiamen and volunteers were actively involved in the Waikato War. At this time, there were in total 9,600 militiamen and volunteers in the North Island; more than one in seven of the Pākehā population. Militia and volunteer units had a much more limited role in the later stages of the New Zealand Wars.[13]

In 1863, the New Zealand government began recruiting, principally in Australia and the South Island, the Waikato Militia and the Taranaki Military Settlers. In total, 5,397 men served in the Waikato Militia, which played a substantial part in the later stages of the Waikato War. The approximately 800-strong Taranaki Military Settlers also saw a

---

[12] Peter Dennerly, 'The Navy in the Northern War: New Zealand 1845–46,' and Denis Fairfax, 'Hobbling to the front: The Royal Navy in the Waikato and Tauranga campaigns 1863–64,' in *Tutu Te Puehu*, 57–84, 194–222.

[13] Peter Cooke and John Crawford, *The Territorials: The History of the Territorial and Volunteer Forces of New Zealand* (Auckland: HarperCollins, 2011), 13–73.

significant amount of action. The personnel of both forces and the smaller Hawke's Bay Military Settlers, which was formed in 1864, were after completing their period of service, eligible for grants of confiscated Māori land.[14]

Two small, highly effective regular units, the mounted Colonial Defence Force and the Forest Rangers, were also raised by the colony's government in 1863. The Forest Rangers were an elite unit that specialized in fighting Māori war parties in the dense bush that covered most of the North Island. The colonial government also raised other smaller, shorter-lived regular units.[15]

During the fighting in the 1840s, British forces were armed with percussion muskets. By the 1860s, these had been replaced by the Pattern 1853 Enfield rifle. The colonial forces also made extensive use of Enfield rifles and the breach-loading Callisher and Terry carbine. The British forces in New Zealand employed a range of guns, howitzers, and mortars which were supplemented by revolutionary rifled Armstrong guns beginning in 1861. Although Māori continued to use traditional weapons, their most widely-used close-quarter weapon was the iron tomahawk. Māori employed a variety of firearms, including captured Enfield rifles and flintlock and percussion muskets, but their most favoured weapon was the double-barrelled percussion shotgun (*tūpara*). Māori considered that under New Zealand conditions the tūpara's firepower outweighed its inaccuracy and short range.[16]

The Course of the War: The Northern War

In the early hours of 11 March 1845, Heke and Kawiti launched a carefully planned attack on the British forces at Kororāreka. Their principal objective was to once again fell the town's flagpole. After muddled fighting, their 450-strong force got the better of the approximately 300 defenders, who consisted of British troops, Royal Navy sailors, and

---

[14] Ian McGibbon (ed.), 'Military settlers', in *The Oxford Companion to New Zealand Military History* (Auckland: Oxford University Press, 2000), 325–27.
[15] Cowan, *The New Zealand Wars*, vol. 1, 265–72; 'Colonial Defence Force', in *Oxford Companion*, 103–04; John Crawford, 'This unlucky colony: The New Zealand government and the military crisis of 1868', in *Tutu Te Puehu*, 321–25.
[16] Tim Ryan, 'The Māori warrior and British soldier', in *Contested Ground*, 105–23; Pasley, 'War', 583–85; Matthew Wright, *Two Peoples, One Land: the New Zealand Wars* (Auckland: Reed, 2006), 90–91, 123–25; Richard Taylor, 'The strategy of war: The Taranaki War and the development of Māori and British strategy,' in *Contested Ground*, 57.

The New Zealand Wars, 1845–1872

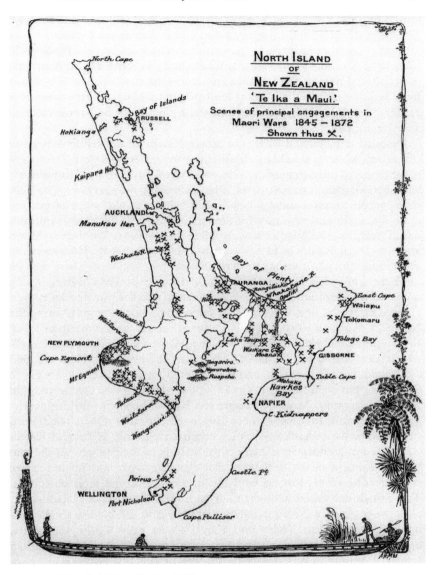

Map 5.1 New Zealand Wars
Note: When this map was prepared in the 1920s for James Cowan's *The New Zealand Wars and the Pioneering Period*, the conflicts in New Zealand between 1845 and 1872 were generally called the 'Maori Wars'. More recently other names including the 'Anglo-Maori Wars' and the 'Land Wars' have had periods of popularity, but since the 1980s the 'New Zealand Wars' has become almost universally accepted as an appropriate name for these conflicts.
Alexander Turnbull Library, Wellington New Zealand

armed settlers. Kororāreka was evacuated, it was then looted and burned. The defenders lost about twenty killed and Māori about thirteen.[17]

After receiving reinforcements, British forces went on the offensive. In June 1845, Colonel Henry Despard, who had just arrived from Australia, established a base at the Waimate mission station where his 600-strong force was joined by allied Māori led by Tāmati Wāka Nene. A few days earlier Nene had wounded and inflicted a significant defeat on Heke at Te Ahuahu pā.[18]

Despard then moved inland to attack Kawiti's formidable new pā at Ōhaeawai, which was held by about 100 warriors. A week-long bombardment of the pā did no significant damage. On 1 July, Despard impulsively launched an assault on Ōhaeawai after a sortie by the garrison. The 220-man combined naval and military assault column could not penetrate the main stockade and was met by devastating fire. Within a few minutes nearly forty of the attackers were killed and seventy wounded; Māori losses were minimal. On 11 July, it was discovered that Kawiti's men had abandoned the pā. It was then demolished.[19]

There was a lull in operations until the end of 1845 during which unsuccessful negotiations were undertaken to end the war. In December, George Grey, the new Governor, ordered an all-out attempt to bring the Northern War to a close. Colonel Despard set out with more than 1,100 British personnel and hundreds of allied Māori against Ruapekapeka pā, which was located south-east of Ōhaeawai. The new pā, which was held by Kawiti and Heke with about 500 men, was similar in design to Ōhaeawai, but even stronger. On 11 January 1846, it was discovered that the pā was empty. Most of its garrison had withdrawn into the nearby forest, probably to escape the heavy bombardment the pā had been subjected to for several days. After confused fighting, Heke and Kawiti succeeded in withdrawing safely with the bulk of their forces. At the end of the month a peace deal was struck ending what was an indecisive conflict. The rebels lost no land but had not achieved their objectives. The British had failed to assert their authority in the Bay of Islands.[20]

Between April and August 1846, disputed land sales led to small-scale fighting in the Hutt Valley and Kāpiti Coast near Wellington at the bottom of the North Island. The outcome of this low-level conflict around Wellington was the establishment of effective government control over a wider area around the settlement. Both the Wellington fighting and skirmishing around the settlement of Wanganui during 1847,

---

[17] Belich, *Wars*, 29–41. [18] O'Malley, *New Zealand Wars*, 49; Belich, *Wars*, 45–47.
[19] Best, *Pa Māori*, 392–95; Cowan, *New Zealand Wars*, vol. 1, 49–72; Belich, *Wars*, 47–57.
[20] Belich, *Wars*, 58–70.

120 miles to the north, again illustrated the differences within and between iwi, which would see Māori repeatedly pitted against each other in the New Zealand Wars.[21]

The Course of the War: The Taranaki War

During the 1850s, the majority of North-Island Māori became increasingly reluctant to sell land to Pākehā. At the heart of this development was the pan-tribal *Kīngitanga* (Māori king) movement based in the Waikato. The Kīngitanga's support was based on the Waikato and surrounding areas, but important tribes north of Auckland and to the east and south of the North Island remained aloof for a variety of reasons. The Governor and the colonial government established after New Zealand was granted self-government in 1853 came to regard the Kīngitanga as a challenge to British sovereignty.[22]

A much-disputed sale of a small block of land at Waitara, near the settlement of New Plymouth in Taranaki, led to violence amongst local Māori. In March 1860, war broke out when British troops clashed with Māori opposed to the sale. Several Taranaki tribes were engaged in the war, the most important of which was Te Ātiawa. Warriors outside Taranaki, most importantly Kīngitanga supporters from the Waikato, also took part in the war. The strength of the Māori forces fighting in the war fluctuated but was always under a 1,000. Initially, Colonel C.E Gold, the British commander in Taranaki, had fewer than 500 troops available, and most British forces were tied down defending New Plymouth and a few outposts. By late June 1860, British forces in Taranaki had grown to some 1,200 troops and Royal Navy personnel supported by nearly 600 militia and volunteers.[23]

Most fighting took place in the semi-open land around New Plymouth and the forest margin. Māori hemmed in the British forces with a large number of pā from which they conducted raids that drove the Pākehā settlers from their land and into the town. In part, their operations were designed to provoke the British into risky attacks on strong pā. New Plymouth became overcrowded and unsanitary conditions lead to serious outbreaks of disease. A successful British attack on a pā at Waireka

---

[21] Wright, *Two Peoples*, 65–80.
[22] Vincent O'Malley, *The Great War for New Zealand: Waikato 1800–2000* (Wellington: Bridget Williams Books, 2016), 88–96.
[23] Pasley, 'War', 569–70; Carey, '*Narrative*', 17–18; Danny Keenan, *Wars without End: The Land Wars in Nineteenth Century New Zealand* (Auckland: Penguin, 2009), 160–93; Cowan, *New Zealand Wars*, vol. 1, 158–70; Belich, *Wars*, 81–84.

on the coast south-west of New Plymouth on 28 March had no impact on the difficult situation facing the settlers and British forces. On 27 June, a 350-strong British force undertaking an ill-conceived attack on a pā at Puketākauere near Waitara was ambushed and decisively defeated, suffering more than sixty casualties including thirty dead.[24]

The commander of British forces in the Australasian colonies, Major-General Thomas Pratt, arrived in Taranaki early in August with additional troops and took over command. Pratt embarked upon a well-thought-out strategy. He was determined to avoid costly defeats that might have encouraged additional iwi to take up arms. From an early stage, Pratt decided to rely on the techniques of siege warfare to deal with pā rather than direct assault. Pratt also arranged the evacuation of more women and children from New Plymouth, improving conditions in the town and reducing the amount of food required by the civilian population. He improved New Plymouth's defences and abandoned outposts of little value. These steps meant he could employ more than 1,400 men in offensive operations by early September. Pratt also enhanced his force's logistical support. These steps all supported his intention to apply continuous pressure on Māori, inflicting losses on them that they could not readily make good and keeping them from attending to their crops.[25]

In the early spring of 1860, British columns destroyed crops and villages, captured livestock, and besieged several pā that were abandoned by their defenders before they could be assaulted. In November, two British columns surprised a Kīngitanga war party developing an old pā at Māhoetahi and destroyed it, inflicting more than 100 casualties. At the end of 1860, Pratt embarked on a major campaign against the chain of barrier pā protecting Te Ātiawa's heartland in the elevated country south of Waitara. Pratt first established a strong base of operations and then began sapping towards the major Māori position at Huirangi, periodically constructing redoubts to secure his advance. Māori responded vigorously by attempting to outflank the saps and making a determined but unsuccessful and costly assault on the most advanced redoubt late in January. They were then obliged to abandon Huirangi and withdraw to the last of their fortresses, Te Arei. By mid-March, Pratt had constructed eight redoubts and advanced his double sap to within 250 feet of the Māori stronghold. Te Ātiawa were well aware of the difficult position they were in. Worn down by the increasing toll of the war, they agreed on

---

[24] Carey, *Narrative*, 88–90: Cowan, *New Zealand Wars*, vol. 1, 171–89; Wright, *Two Peoples*, 94–101.

[25] Carey, *Narrative*, 91–93; Pasley, 'War', 573, 590; Taylor, 'Strategy', 70–71; Wright, *Two Peoples*, 101.

a ceasefire and then signed a peace agreement recognizing the authority of the Governor.[26]

The Course of the War: The Waikato War

George Grey, who returned to New Zealand for a second term as governor late in 1861, agreed with his predecessor that in order to bring real peace to Taranaki and break the power of those Māori tribes who opposed land sales, it would be necessary to invade and occupy the Kīngitanga's Waikato heartland. Over the next eighteen months Grey, with the support of the colonial government, pursued a policy that had two elements: a drive to isolate and undermine the position of the Māori King through political and administrative initiatives; and preparations for war.[27]

Lieutenant-General Duncan Cameron, who had replaced Pratt in March 1861, from the outset recognized that sound logistics were essential if an invasion of the Waikato was to succeed. Intelligence gathering quickly identified that the most favourable invasion route was an advance up the Waikato River and its navigable tributary, the Waipā. Between January 1862 and July 1863 the Great South Road, an all-weather road, and New Zealand's first telegraph line were constructed running south from Auckland to the boundary with Kīngitanga territory near the Waikato River. To provide the necessary logistical support for the invasion, the Commissariat Transport Corps was established in mid-1861. It and a specialist water transport unit established in 1863 played a critical role in the Waikato invasion.[28]

Grey successfully pressed the Colonial Office for additional forces. In July 1863, there were fewer than 4,000 regular troops in the province of Auckland, but by March 1864 the strength of the British forces was 14,000, including 9000 British Army and Royal Navy personnel. To oppose this substantial force the Kīngitanga could muster, at best, about 2,000 warriors, although the total number of Māori warriors who took some part in the fighting was substantially more than this.[29] The British preparations for war did not escape the eyes of the Kīngitanga leaders. They responded by seeking support from tribes outside the Waikato,

---

[26] Pasley, 'War', 576, 585; Cowan, *New Zealand Wars*, vol. 1, 190–220; Wright, *Two Peoples*, 94, 101–10.
[27] O'Malley, *Great War*, 149–69.
[28] Richard Taylor, *Logistic Operations in the Waikato War, 1863–64* (Trentham: Military Studies Institute, 2005), 5–9, 14–16.
[29] O'Malley, *Great War*, 215–28.

accumulating reserves of essential supplies and by beginning work on formidable pā designed to block any advance up the Waikato River.[30]

In May, skirmishing broke out in Taranaki as a result of provocative action ordered by Grey. The Governor used Kīngitanga involvement in the Taranaki conflict, its independent stance, and dubious reports of Kīngitanga plans for attacks on Auckland, as justifications for an invasion of the movement's territory. Early on 12 July 1863, British forces invaded Kīngitanga territory. An ultimatum by Governor Grey to Kingitanga chiefs that demanded they accept the establishment of military posts in their territory, although dated before the invasion, was not issued until a few days later. It was carefully crafted to portray Grey's aggressive policy as a defensive one, forced upon him by the threat posed by the Kīngitanga.[31]

Five days after the beginning of the invasion, Cameron's forces defeated a small Māori contingent constructing defences at Koheroa, south of the Queen's Redoubt, which was at the end of the Great South Road. The main British effort at this time was preparing for their advance up the Waikato River towards the heartland of the Kīngitanga. This task was complicated by an effective Māori guerrilla campaign targeting settlers and British transport, and patrols in South Auckland around the Great South Road. At the end of September, Māori abandoned this campaign, probably because they wished to concentrate their forces on the defence of their barrier pā at Meremere on the Waikato River.[32]

By late October, Cameron had accumulated enough supplies, personnel, and boats to begin his advance up the Waikato River to Meremere. Of particular importance was the arrival of the *Pioneer*, an armoured paddlewheel gun-boat that had been rapidly designed and built in Sydney. The Māori defences at Meremere were formidable, but crucially, the few old ship's guns emplaced there, lacked the fire power to prevent British vessels moving upstream and outflanking the defences. This the British forces did in a well-executed operation on 31 October, landing a substantial force six miles further up the river. After the failure of an attack on the force upstream of their positions, Māori abandoned Meremere and withdrew about twelve miles up-river to their second line of defences at Rangiriri.[33]

---

[30] Wright, *Two Peoples*, 116; Taylor, *Logistic*, 11–12.
[31] O'Malley, *Great War*, 192–211.
[32] Cowan, *New Zealand Wars*, vol. 1, 251–307; Belich, *Wars*, 133–41; O'Malley, *Great War*, 230–42.
[33] O'Malley, *Great War*, 242–45.

The barrier pā at Rangiriri was more than a half of a mile in length and stretched across a low ridge running from the Waikato River in the west to Lake Waikare in the east. The defences centred on wide, parallel ditches approximately 8.8 to 13.7 feet deep separated by an entrenched parapet and included salients and bunkers. At the centre of the position was a small, strongly built redoubt. Near the river bank the defences turned and ran further south to guard against an attack from the Waikato River. The position included other features including well-sited, outlying concealed rifle pits. Because no palisades were used and the ground was low lying, the full extent and strength of the position was not obvious.[34]

Cameron wished to destroy the Māori garrison at Rangiriri rather than allowing it to flee. He decided, therefore, that he would attack Rangiriri from the north with most of his force, and at the same time use his control of the river to land a sizeable body of troops immediately behind the Māori position to assist in the assault and cut off their retreat. On 20 November Cameron led an 860-strong force south from Meremere, which included 375 men of the 65th Regiment and smaller contingents from other regiments. A flotilla of boats and barges carrying 331 men from the 40th Regiment sailed up the Waikato at the same time. For a variety of reasons, most importantly the demands of the planting season, the Kīngitanga were only able to assemble a force of about 400 to hold Rangiriri. Cameron reached Rangiriri with his main force and flotilla on the afternoon of 21 November. At around 3.30 p.m., Cameron ordered the landing of the troops behind the main position, but strong winds and currents prevented this. The attack was postponed and for the next hour and a half Rangiriri was bombarded. At about 5.00 p.m., Cameron decided he could wait no longer and ordered his force to attack. The main thrust was made by the 65th Regiment towards the Māori positions near the Waikato River. Though it was met by heavy fire, the 65th Regiment managed to enter the main Māori position. They then drove east along the parapet until they reached the central redoubt, which they unsuccessfully attempted to seize. At the same time another element of the regiment pushed south clearing the fortifications facing the Waikato River. They were joined in this task by the first elements of the 40th Regiment, which had finally managed to land.

Following the failure of his initial efforts to seize the central redoubt, Cameron committed two companies from his reserve and renewed the assault. This attack also failed as did later ill-considered efforts by a contingent of thirty-six Royal Artillery gunners and a 90-strong party

---

[34] Cowan, *New Zealand Wars*, vol. 1, 321–29; Belich, *Wars*, 142–44; O'Malley, *Great War*, 248–50.

from the naval brigade that formed part of Cameron's forces. It seems inexplicable that Cameron should have thought that attacks by such small forces would succeed against a formidable entrenchment held by a much stronger force that had already repelled assaults by his infantry. Although significant losses had been inflicted on Māori, including more than forty dead, British losses were severe: forty-seven dead or mortally wounded and eighty-five wounded. During the night, the Māori evacuated their wounded and the majority of the surviving members of the garrison across Lake Waikare.[35]

Early the next morning, a white flag appeared above the Kīngitanga position. Why the Māori did this is unclear, but they certainly did not intend to merely surrender. While a government interpreter was preparing to talk to the leaders of the garrison, British troops entered the redoubt, exchanged greetings with Māori and then demanded that the 183 occupants of the redoubt, which included a few women, surrender their weapons and leave the redoubt as prisoners. The defeat at Rangiriri with the loss of more than 200 men, including several prominent chiefs, was a major setback to Māori resistance.[36] Māori peace overtures after the battle did not elicit a clear or positive response from Governor Grey.[37]

The British forces continued their advance up the Waikato and on 6 December occupied Ngāruawāhia, the Māori King's capital. A few days earlier the New Zealand Settlements Act was passed. It contained sweeping powers to confiscate Māori land.[38]

The British forces moved up the Waipā river valley in January 1864 to threaten the productive agricultural lands that were vital to the Kīngitanga's economy. To guard this area, at the direction of Rewi Maniapoto, the Kīngitanga tribes committed tremendous resources – moving more than 12,000 tonnes of earth – to building at Pāterangi and nearby the most formidable and extensive barrier pā ever constructed. It was held by a garrison of nearly 2,000 warriors.[39]

Cameron realised that a direct assault on Pāterangi would be both costly and risky. Instead, with the help of Māori guides, on the night of 20 February 1864, his forces quietly slipped pass the defences. Cameron then attacked the village of Rangiaowhia, a crucial supply base for the defenders of Pāterangi. In the chaotic fighting that followed a number of

---

[35] Cowan, *New Zealand Wars*, vol. 1, 326–35; Belich, *Wars*, 142–52; O'Malley, *Great War*, 250–54, 277.
[36] 'Further particulars of the battle of Rangiriri', *Taranaki Herald*, 5 December 1863, 2; Belich, *Wars*, 152–55; O'Malley, *Great War*, 254–59.
[37] O'Malley, *Great War*, 261–70.   [38] Ibid., 407–25.
[39] Cowan, *New Zealand Wars*, vol. 1, 336–46; Cooke, *Spade*, 33–34.

Māori non-combatants were killed. Exactly how many is unclear, but the assault on Rangiaowhia remains a highly controversial incident in the New Zealand Wars.[40]

The British advance and capture of Rangiaowhia fatally undermined the Māori position, forcing them to abandon Pāterangi. The bulk of the Kīngitanga force withdrew to the east, but a small faction, including Rewi Maniapoto, decided to construct a new pā at Ōrākau, south of Rangiaowhia. The site of the pā was poorly chosen. It was soon discovered and surrounded by British forces. On 2 April Cameron offered the garrison the chance to surrender honourably. One of the chiefs in the pā replied with the famous words: '*Ka whawhai tonu mātou, ake ake, ake!*' (We shall fight on for ever, and ever and ever!) Later in the day the 300 occupants of the pā including women and children audaciously broke out through a small gap in the British positions. The British and colonial troops pursued the Māori, killing about half of them.[41]

The siege and breakout from Ōrākau proved to be the last major action in the Waikato War. Although the Kīngitanga had been defeated, but not destroyed, Cameron had achieved his principal objectives. British attention shifted to establishing military settlers on the large area of the Waikato that had been confiscated and operations elsewhere in the North Island. The Kīngitanga retained control of the land beyond the Puniu River, which became the de facto border between British-controlled New Zealand and what came to be known as the 'King Country'. Until 1881, when the Kīngitanga came to terms with the New Zealand government, the King Country was virtually an independent state.[42]

The Course of the War: The Tauranga Campaign

Late in January 1864, a small British expedition was landed at Tauranga in the Bay of Plenty to disrupt the flow of supplies to the Kīngitanga in the Waikato. Local Māori responded by building a pā, known as Gate Pā, near the British camp and challenging them to attack. In April, Cameron arrived in Tauranga with his reserves boosting the British force's strength to more than 1,600 men and decided to go on the offensive.[43]

On 27 April, Cameron began to move troops and guns towards Gate Pā. During the night of 28/29 April, 700 men of the 68th Regiment moved through the swamp and took up positions south of Gate Pā to

---
[40] Wright, *Two Peoples*, 130–34; O'Malley, *Great War*, 291–304.
[41] O'Malley, *Great War*, 316–35; Wright, *Two Peoples*, 136–41.
[42] O'Malley, *Great War*, 315–89.
[43] Cowan, *New Zealand Wars*, vol. 1, 421–25; Wright, *Two Peoples*, 141–43.

act as a blocking force. The pā was a narrow barrier defence built along a low ridge between two areas of swamp. It was held by about 240 warriors. Early on 29 April the British began to subject Gate Pā to the heaviest bombardment ever seen in the New Zealand Wars. The bombardment was, however, of limited effectiveness, with many shells from the Armstrong guns missing their target or failing to explode in the soft ground.[44]

By 4.00 p.m., a significant breach had been opened in the western corner of the pā and Cameron ordered an assault by 150 sailors and marines, and 150 men from the 43rd Regiment. The British assault column entered the pā, but lost cohesion because of the particularly heavy casualties amongst officers and confusion caused by the complex nature of its interior defences. After brutal fighting the soldiers and sailors fled. British losses were substantial: ten officers and twenty-one other ranks killed and seventy-six wounded. Māori lost about twenty dead. They succeeded in evacuating the pā once night fell. Cameron's conduct of the operation is open to serious question. He underestimated the strength of the pā and overestimated the effectiveness of his bombardment.[45]

The British defeat at Gate Pā was avenged on 21 June when a strong British column found about 500 Māori who had begun building a new pā at Te Ranga, a mile and a half south of Gate Pā. The British immediately attacked, killing more than 100 Māori. This was a heavy blow to Tauranga Māori and a local peace treaty was concluded in August 1864.[46]

The Course of the War: Pāi Mārire Tītokowaru and Te Kooti

After the end of the Tauranga campaign, the New Zealand Wars entered a new phase that increasingly pitted colonial troops and allied Māori against comparatively small groups of Māori in small-scale, often ruthless campaigns. Central to the first part of this phase was the new Māori faith, Pāi Mārire (Good and Peaceful), or Hauhau, founded by Te Ua Haumēne in 1862. The new religion had pronounced messianic and millenarian characteristics. Pāi Mārire attracted many followers, especially in the areas worst affected by war. Pākehā regarded its followers as

---

[44] John M. Gates, 'James Belich and the modern Māori Pa: Revisionist history revised', *War and Society* 19 (2001): 56–61; Cowan, *New Zealand Wars*, vol. 1, 421–26; Wright, *Two Peoples*, 144–46.
[45] Cowan, *New Zealand Wars*, vol. 1, 426–33; Belich, *Wars*, 178–88; Gates, 'Revisionist history', 63–64.
[46] Cowan, *New Zealand Wars*, vol. 1, 435–39; Belich, *Wars*, 188–96.

dangerous fanatics and many Māori were also opposed to it because of the threat it posed to chiefly authority and tribal autonomy.[47]

Between mid-1864 and mid-1865, Pāi Mārire supporters were involved in small-scale military actions in Taranaki, near the Whanganui River, in the Bay of Plenty, and on the east coast of the North Island. These actions, especially the murder of the missionary Carl Vőlkner at Ōpotiki, caused much anger and concern, but militarily they were generally unsophisticated and unsuccessful.[48]

By 1865, Cameron was disillusioned with Governor Grey and the colonial government's desire for further military operations. He wrote to Grey complaining about 'this miserable war for the profit and gratification of the Colony'.[49] Cameron resigned and in August 1865 was replaced by Major-General Trevor Chute, who did not share his scruples. From 1864, British and colonial troops in Taranaki had increasingly used 'bush scouring' tactics in which lightly-equipped but well-supplied small columns attacked Māori villages and agricultural assets in a successful drive to cower Māori communities and to severely damage their ability to resist. Bush scouring was only feasible when there were no substantial Māori forces in an area. Between December 1865 and February 1866, Chute led the most famous bush scouring expedition through densely forested parts of Taranaki that no British force had previously penetrated. Chute's column devastated Māori communities in the area, many of which were not supporters of Pāi Mārire. Chute left the colony in August 1867 having carried out what were to be the last active operations by the British Army in the New Zealand Wars.[50]

Changes in British policy towards funding military forces in self-governing colonies, and growing concerns about the cost of operations in New Zealand and the objectives being pursued, led to the withdrawal of eight regiments between 1865 and 1867. One regiment remained until 1870, but in a purely garrison role. The New Zealand government responded with the 'self-reliant policy' under which it took full control of policy towards Māori, and the colonial forces became wholly responsible for internal security. The central problem facing the New Zealand government in implementing the new policy was that it could only with great difficulty pay for adequate defence forces.[51]

---

[47] Belich, *Wars*, 203–05; O'Malley, *New Zealand Wars*, 151.
[48] Wright, *Two Peoples*, 160–67; Cowan, *New Zealand Wars*, vol. 2, 1–29.
[49] Cameron to Grey, 28 January 1865, 1865, A-4, 6, Appendix to the Journal of the House of Representatives (AJHR).
[50] O'Malley, *New Zealand Wars*, 162–68; Taylor, 'Strategy', 75–77.
[51] B. J. Dalton, *War and Politics in New Zealand 1855–1870* (Sydney: Sydney University Press, 1967), 206–59.

From 1865, colonial forces, except when they were operating with British forces, were under the direct control of the government in Auckland. In mid-1866, the local regular forces had an effective strength of 1,612.[52] The existing regular colonial military forces were disbanded in July 1867. Many personnel from these forces transferred to their smaller replacement, the New Zealand Armed Constabulary, a paramilitary police force, which was to an extent modelled on the Royal Irish Constabulary. The Armed Constabulary, which had a strength of 600, lacked the capacity to deal with any significant renewal of Māori resistance.[53]

In 1867 the minor Ngāti Ruanui chief Riwha Tītokowaru, a former Methodist and Pāi Mārire convert, led a well-conceived campaign of passive resistance against the survey of confiscated land in South Taranaki. Tītokowaru was a charismatic leader who developed his own religious beliefs. Throughout his adult life he alternated between acting as a peacemaker and a highly effective military leader. In mid-1868, Tītokowaru turned to war, killing settlers and attacking the garrison of a half-completed redoubt.[54]

Just as this new war in South Taranaki broke out, on the east coast of the North Island another major threat emerged. In 1866, without any proper legal process, captured Pāi Mārire supporters and some others suspected of disloyalty were exiled to the Chatham Islands, 500 miles east of New Zealand. Amongst this group was Te Kooti Arikirangi Te Turuki, who while imprisoned on the Chatham Islands founded the Ringatū church. The new faith, like Pāi Mārire and Tītokowaru's teachings, was a syncretic blend of Christian and traditional Māori beliefs. It quickly won over the vast majority of the prisoners on the Chatham Islands. On 3 July 1868, Te Kooti and nearly 300 of his followers seized a supply ship and used it to return to the east coast. Over the next few weeks, they defeated the weak colonial forces that attempted to prevent them from moving into the rugged interior.[55]

Tītokowaru was correctly regarded as the more serious threat to the colony, and the government concentrated its rapidly expanding forces

---

[52] Return showing the present effective state of the colonial forces', 1866, A5, AJHR; Dalton, *Politics*, 251; Cooke and Crawford, *Territorials*, 62–75.

[53] Richard Hill, *The Colonial Frontier Tamed: New Zealand Policing in Transition, 1867–1886: The History of Policing in New Zealand*, vol. 2 (Wellington: Historical Branch Department of Internal Affairs, 1989), 1–17; Crawford, 'Unlucky colony', 310–13.

[54] Belich, *Wars*, 235–41; Carl Bradley, 'Syncretic religion and war leadership: Titokowaru, peace and violence in Southern Taranaki,' in *Tutu Te Puehu*, 337–57.

[55] Bronwyn Elsmore, *Mana from Heaven: A Century of Māori Prophets in New Zealand* (Auckland: Reed, 1999), 168–83, 196–209; Judith Binney, *Redemption Songs: A Life of Te Kooti Arikirangi Te Turuki* (Auckland: Auckland University Press, 1995), 63–118.

including a completely militarized Armed Constabulary against him. After receiving reinforcements from elsewhere in the colony, Lieutenant-Colonel Thomas McDonnell attacked Tītokowaru's base in the dense Taranaki bush, the village of Te Ngutu o te Manu. On 7 September 1868, McDonnell's force of 360 men, including 110 allied Māori, was ambushed at the village by Tītokowaru's sixty warriors. They let the colonial forces enter the clearing in which the village stood and then opened fire from concealed positions. The colonial troops retreated having suffered heavy losses, including twenty-four dead. After this disaster McDonnell was replaced by Lieutenant-Colonel George Whitmore, a former British Army officer who set about tightening discipline and reorganising his force. As well as taking military initiatives to respond to the crisis, the colonial government successfully stepped up its efforts to gather intelligence and dissuade other iwi from joining the uprising. Early in November, Whitmore led a force of more than 500 colonial troops and allied Māori in an attack on Tītokowaru's new pā at Moturoa, which was held by about 200 warriors. The pā was much stronger and more complex that it at first appeared. Whitmore's force was repulsed and then harried as it retreated, suffering nearly forty casualties. As in the earlier engagements, Tītokowaru's losses were trifling.[56]

A few days later, on the east coast, Te Kooti and a picked force carried out a carefully coordinated night-time attack on settlers in Poverty Bay. In total, sixty Pākehā and local Māori were killed. This attack, which became known as the Poverty Bay Massacre, caused outrage and alarm across the colony. The government responded by going on the defensive in South Taranaki and sending Whitmore and the bulk of its striking force to the east coast. Whitmore's force and allied Māori pursued and then besieged Te Kooti's force, which had occupied an old pā at Ngātapa. On the night of 4/5 January 1869, however, Te Kooti and most of his followers escaped down a cliff at the rear of the pā. They were pursued by allied Māori, mainly Ngāti Porou under their formidable leader Rāpata Wahawaha. More than fifty of Te Kooti's followers were killed during the siege or pursuit and about a further 140 captured, most of whom were summarily executed.[57]

After the fall of Ngātapa, Whitmore's forces returned to Taranaki and prepared to attack Tītokowaru's strong new pā at Tauranga-ika. At the beginning of February, the colonial forces began a siege of the pā, but shortly afterwards they discovered that it had been abandoned.

---

[56] Cowan, *New Zealand Wars*, vol. 2, 202–21, 244–52 Belich, *Wars*, 239–52; Crawford, 'Unlucky colony', 317–27.
[57] Binney, *Songs*, 120–47; Cowan, *New Zealand Wars*, vol. 2, 263–82.

Rather than simply retreating, Tītokowaru's force fell apart, for reasons that remain unclear. The colonial forces began an unsuccessful pursuit of Tītokowaru's and his increasingly small band of supporters. He later became one of the leaders of the renowned pacifist community at Parihaka.[58]

Following the collapse of Tītokowaru's force, Whitmore and most of his troops returned to the east coast where Te Kooti remained active. In May 1869 some 1,300 colonial troops and allied Māori invaded the isolated and extremely mountainous Urewera country in an unsuccessful attempt to destroy Te Kooti and his followers. The government then decided to use only picked forces of allied Māori with some Pākehā officers in offensive operations against Te Kooti. Over the next two years Te Kooti's position steadily worsened. In May 1872, he managed to escape into the King Country where he was given sanctuary, bringing the New Zealand Wars to an end. Te Kooti renounced violence, was pardoned in 1883, and spent the rest of his life as the leader of the Ringatū church.[59]

Aftermath

The strength of Māori resistance led to the existence of the King Country and other smaller autonomous zones in the post-wars period. These areas had a major, long-term role in the survival of Māori society and culture. Nonetheless, the New Zealand Wars were a disaster for Māori. Huge areas of their land in the North Island were confiscated by the government, including much that belonged to tribes that had taken no part in the wars. Māori were impoverished, their numbers declined precipitously, and they despaired of the future.[60] The wars directly claimed the lives of an estimated 2,000 Māori who fought against the Crown and 250 allied Māori. British and colonial forces had 560 killed. These are not large figures, but when you consider that the Māori population of the North Island in the 1860s was about 50,000 and the Pākehā population about 40,000, it is apparent that proportionately casualties were substantial. The level of mobilization amongst Māori and Pākehā was also high.[61] British Army personnel generally had great respect for Māori, who they regarded as perhaps the most

---

[58] Belich, *Wars*, 268–75, 307.
[59] Binney, *Songs*, 310–15; Ron Crosby, *Kūpapa: The Bitter Legacy of Māori Alliance with the Crown* (Auckland: Penguin, 2015), 368–450.
[60] Belich, *Wars*, 305–07.
[61] David Green, *Battlefields of the New Zealand Wars: A Visitor's Guide* (Auckland: Penguin, 2010), 12–16.

formidable indigenous forces they had faced.[62] In the later phases of the wars, however, the killing of civilians, mutilation of bodies, ritual cannibalism, and other acts of extreme violence led to a much more bitter conflict.[63]

Before 1840, Māori were well organized for war and get rid of inter-tribal warfare was endemic. This meant that in some respects they were well prepared to resist British forces, but it also meant that the kind of general rising most feared by British and colonial authorities was extremely unlikely. Crucially, some important tribes chose to ally themselves with the British, albeit in pursuit of their own interests. Warriors from these tribes, who were generally known as kūpapa, played a vital role in the crushing of Māori armed resistance.

Traditional Māori warfare was essentially a seasonal activity governed by the demands of agriculture for manpower. In order to combat a European army, Māori needed to maintain their strength in the field for longer periods, but were never able to properly develop the kind of inter-tribal supply and manpower networks that would have made this possible.[64] The adoption by Māori of a predominantly pā-based strategy of resistance was fully consistent with pre-colonial warfare in New Zealand and with Māori culture that placed great importance on maintaining a presence on land in order to uphold a tribe's mana (status) and rights to particular territory.[65] These cultural imperatives shaping Māori strategy were set out clearly by a wounded Māori prisoner in 1865. When asked by Lieutenant-General Sir Duncan Cameron why his group had engaged a much larger British force, he replied: 'What would you have us do? This is our village, these are our plantations. Men are not fit to live if they are not brave enough to defend their own homes'.[66]

Some contemporary and more recent commentators on the New Zealand Wars have suggested that a Māori strategy that relied predominantly on guerrilla tactics would have been more militarily effective.[67] Cultural considerations also seem to have played a key part here, at least, in the decision by Māori not to make a concerted effort to interdict the long, and rather vulnerable British supply lines during the Waikato

---

[62] Pasley, 'War', 583, John Fortescue, *A History of the British Army*, vol. 13 (London: Macmillan, 1930), 516.
[63] L. H. Barber, 'Military strategies against the Hauhau', *Defence Force Journal* 37 (1982): 24–32; Crawford, 'Unlucky colony', 315.
[64] Taylor, 'Strategy', 60–62   [65] Keenan, *Without End*, 18–19, 22–23.
[66] Morgan S. Grace, *A Sketch of the New Zealand War* (London: Horace Marshall and Son, 1899), 130.
[67] Pasley, 'War', 564; Fortescue, *British Army*, vol. 13, 488–89.

War.[68] The successes enjoyed by Tītokowaru and Te Kooti suggest that a guerrilla-based strategy that incorporated the use of pā as traps and bases for operations would have posed formidable difficulties for the British and colonial forces. Widespread guerrilla warfare and the resulting British countermeasures would have increased the proportion of civilian casualties in the wars causing more animosity between Pākehā and Māori.[69] The adoption of a primarily pā-based strategy meant that a high proportion of casualties were amongst combatants. This, the proven Māori capacity for armed resistance, and the fact that many Māori had fought for the British, partly accounts for race relations in New Zealand during the late-nineteenth and early- twentieth centuries being as good as they were.[70]

Further Reading

Belich, James. *The New Zealand Wars and the Victorian Interpretation of Racial Conflict*. Auckland: Auckland University Press, 1986.
Binney, Judith. *Redemption Songs: A Life of Te Kooti Arikirangi Te Turuki*. Auckland: Auckland University Press, 1995.
Cowan, James. *The New Zealand Wars: A History of the Maori Campaigns and the Pioneering Period*, 3rd ed., 2 vols, Wellington: Government Printer, 1983.
Crawford, John and McGibbon, Ian (eds). *Tutu Te Puehu: New Perspectives on the New Zealand Wars*. Wellington: Steele Roberts, 2018.
Crosby, Ron. *Kūpapa: The Bitter Legacy of Māori Alliance with the Crown*. Auckland: Penguin, 2015.
Dalton, B. J. *War and Politics in New Zealand 1855–1870*. Sydney: Sydney University Press, 1967.
Day, Kelvin (ed.) *Contested Ground Te Whenua I Tohea: the Taranaki Wars 1860–1881*. Wellington: Huia, 2010.
Glen, Frank. *Australians at War in New Zealand*. Christchurch: Wilsonscott, 2011.
Green, David. *Battlefields of the New Zealand Wars: A Visitor's Guide*. Auckland: Penguin, 2010.
Keenan, Danny. *Wars without End: The Land Wars in Nineteenth Century New Zealand*. Auckland: Penguin, 2009.
O'Malley, Vincent. *The Great War for New Zealand: Waikato 1800–2000*. Wellington: Bridget Williams Books, 2016.

---

[68] G. F. von Tempsky, Memoranda of the New Zealand Campaign in 1863 and 1864, MS-copy-micro-0168, pp. 93–94, Alexander Turnbull Library (ATL).; J. E. Gorst, *The Māori King*, 2nd ed. (Hamilton: Paul's Book Arcade, 1959), 403; Taylor, *Logistic*, 12–14.
[69] 'The intended massacre at Coromandel', *New Zealand Herald*, 10 April 1865, 4; Taylor, 'Strategy', 63–66.
[70] Belich, *Wars*, 308–10.

The New Zealand Wars Ngā Pākanga o Aotearoa. Wellington: Bridget Williams Books, 2019.

Simons, Cliff. *Soldiers, Scouts and Spies: A Military History of the New Zealand Wars 1845–1864.* Auckland: Massey University Press, 2019.

Wright, Matthew. *Two Peoples, One Land: The New Zealand Wars.* Auckland: Reed, 2006.

6 The Third Anglo-Asante War, 1873–1874

Ryan Patterson

Background

Great Britain's presence in West Africa dates back to the seventeenth century but its influence had long been limited to a scattering of coastal enclaves centering on Cape Coast Castle.[1] British administrators claimed a geographically and legally nebulous protectorate over the Fante (Fanti or Fantee in contemporary British sources), Assin, Akyem, Akwapim, Denkyira, and Wassa peoples that lived in the forty to fifty miles from the coast of the Gulf of Guinea to the Pra River. To the north of the Pra lay the Asante Empire (Ashanti or Ashantee in contemporary British sources).[2]

The first *Asantehene* (King) had established the kingdom at the beginning of the eighteenth century. Fueled by the lucrative trade in slaves, ivory, palm oil, and gold, the Asante Empire was economically successful, administratively centralized, militarily powerful, and geographically vast, encompassing much of modern-day Ghana, Togo, Benin, and Ivory Coast.

Thomas Bowdich had established formal political and commercial relations with the Asante in 1817.[3] Though often trading partners, British and Asante interests periodically clashed, with violent flashpoints in 1807, 1823–31 (First Anglo-Asante War), 1853, and 1863–64 (Second Anglo-Asante War). Disputes generally revolved around competing or misunderstood claims of sovereignty over the protectorate nations. The Asante demanded tribute from subject peoples and expected the British to return any fugitives who escaped into the

---

[1] Andrew Porter, 'Introduction', in Andrew Porter and Wm. Roger Louis (ed.) *The Oxford History of the British Empire: Volume III: The Nineteenth Century* (Oxford: Oxford University Press, 1999), 14.

[2] Ian Beckett (ed.), *Wolseley and Ashanti: The Asante War Journal and Correspondence of Major General Sir Garnet Wolseley 1873–1874* (Stroud, Gloucestershire: History Press for the Army Records Society, 2009), 3, 6.

[3] T. Edward Bowdich, *Mission from Cape Coast Castle to Ashantee, with a Statistical Account of That Kingdom and Geographical Notices of Other Parts of the Interior of Africa* (London: John Murray, 1819), 5–13.

protectorate. In the 1824 conflict, a small expedition led by the British Governor of Sierra Leone, Sir Charles McCarthy, was defeated and the Governor himself was beheaded.[4]

In the last campaign, a British force marched inland to the Pra River just in time for the onset of the rainy season. Disease enveloped them and killed so many soldiers that Conservative MP and former Secretary of State for War, Lieutenant-General Jonathan Peel, compared the disaster to the Crimean War.[5] Lord Palmerston, the British Prime Minister, took sharp criticism; the Liberals narrowly evaded a dissolution of Parliament; and Edward Cardwell, then Colonial Secretary, ordered that British troops would never again be deployed to the deadly Gold Coast climate.[6]

Cape Coast Castle was left under the protection of a small force of West India Regiment soldiers and Hausa and Fante armed police. However, certain commercial and administrative circles never lost interest in Asante as part of a growing desire to 'open up' the African interior to trade. Explorers and administrators such as Thomas Bowditch (1817), Joseph Dupuis (1820), William Hutton (1821), John Beecham (1841), Richard Burton (1863), and Winwood Reade (1868) had shown that small groups of Europeans could sojourn into the territory. Due to a dearth of reliable information at the War Office Topographical and Statistical Department, planning for the 1873 expedition would come to rely heavily on their dated accounts.[7] T. C. McCaskie was thus correct to describe the Third Anglo-Asante War as the 'first serious British military venture into the tropical African interior'.[8] It represented a significant change in British policy and marked an important step towards the Scramble for Africa.

★ ★ ★ ★ ★

A literary cannon on the history of the 1873–4 Asante war began to take shape very quickly after its conclusion.[9] Five professional newspaper correspondents accompanied the British expedition, four of whom

---

[4] Beckett, *Wolseley and Ashanti*, 4.
[5] Henry Brackenbury and G. L. Huyshe, *Fanti and Ashanti: Three Papers Read on Board the S. S. Ambriz on the Voyage to the Gold Coast* (London: William Blackwood and Sons, 1873), 34; House of Common Debates, 17 June 1864, vol. 175, col. 2008.
[6] House of Common Debates, 17 June 1864, vol. 175, col. 1962–3; Cardwell to Gov. Pine, 23 June 1864, Parliamentary Papers: 'Accounts and Papers' (1873), XLIX, 864–5.
[7] Charles Wilson, *Notes to Accompany Itinerary from Cape Coast Castle to Coomassie* (London: Topographical and Statistical Department, War Office, 1873), 1; 'The Medical officers and the Late War', *The Lancet* 103, 2641 (11 April 1874), 521.
[8] T. C. McCaskie, 'Cultural encounters: Britain and Africa in the nineteenth century', in *The Oxford History of the British Empire*, 676.
[9] See 'Further Reading' section for some of this section's references.

would go on to publish books about the campaign.[10] Five British officers also moonlighted as 'military correspondents' for newspapers and five officers published book-length accounts.[11]

Modern scholarly engagement with the war began with an article by W. D. McIntyre and A. Lloyd's, *The Drums of Kumasi: The Story of the Ashanti Wars*.[12] J. Keegan and L. Maxwell provided chapter-length accounts in B. Bond's *Victorian Military Campaigns*, and *The Ashanti Ring: Sir Garnet Wolseley's Campaigns 1870–1882* respectively.[13] R. Edgerton's, *The Fall of the Asante Empire: The Hundred-Year War for Africa's Gold Coast* assessed the war as part of a chain of conflicts leading to Asante's colonization.

More recent histories of the conflict have all come from contributors to this volume. Edward Spiers brought his expertise in both military and press history to bear on chapter-length accounts in *The Victorian Soldier in Africa* and *The Scottish Soldier and Empire, 1854–1902*, the latter focused on the 42nd Highlanders.[14] In his biography, *Evelyn Wood VC: Pillar of Empire*, Stephen Manning followed Wood through this early-career campaign where he commanded a native regiment.[15]

Historians are now fortunate to have Ian Beckett's invaluable resource, *Wolseley and Ashanti: The Asante War Journal and Correspondence of Major General Sir Garnet Wolseley 1873–1874*. Gathering sources from a range of public and private archives, this collection features edited transcriptions from Wolseley's diary (particularly valued in light of the man's eccentric penmanship), private letters to his wife, and both ingoing and outgoing official reports and dispatches. What makes this work more than a collection of sources is Beckett's insightful analysis throughout,

---

[10] Frederick Boyle, *Through Fanteeland to Coomassie: A Diary of the Ashantee Expedition* (London: Chapman and Hall, 1874).

[11] Henry Brackenbury, *The Ashanti War, A Narrative: Prepared from the Official Documents by Permission of Major-General Sir Garnet Wolseley* (London: William Blackwood and Sons, 1874); W. T. Dooner, *Jottings En Route to Coomassie* (London: W. Mitchell & Co., 1874); Capt. E. Rogers, *Campaigning in Western Africa and the Ashantee Invasion* (London: W. Mitchell & Co., 1874); W. F. Butler, *Akim-Foo: The History of a Failure*, 3rd ed. (London: Sampson Low, Marston, Low, & Searle, 1875).

[12] W. D. McIntyre, 'British policy in West Africa: The Ashanti Expedition of 1873–4', *The Historical Journal* 5, 1 (1962): 40; Alan Lloyd, *The Drums of Kumasi: The Story of the Ashanti Wars* (London: Longmans Green and Co., 1964).

[13] John Keegan, 'The Ashanti campaign 1873–4,' in Brian Bond (ed.), *Victorian Military Campaigns* (London: Hutchinson & Co, 1967); Leigh Maxwell, *The Ashanti Ring: Sir Garnet Wolseley's Campaigns 1870–1882* (London: Leo Cooper, 1985).

[14] Edward Spiers, *The Victorian Soldier in Africa* (Manchester University Press, Manchester, 2004); Edward Spiers, *The Scottish Soldier and Empire, 1854–1902* (Edinburgh: Edinburgh University Press, 2006).

[15] Stephen Manning, *Evelyn Wood VC: Pillar of Empire* (Barnsley: Pen & Sword Military, 2007).

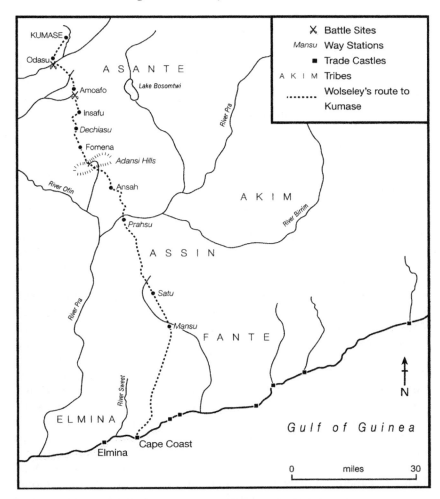

Map 6.1 Third Anglo-Asante War, 1873–1874.
Edinburgh University Press Limited

rooted in a mastery of the wider context.[16] My own article, '"To form a correct estimate of their nothingness when compared with it": British exhibitions of military technology in the Abyssinian and Ashanti expeditions', considered the importance of technological spectacle to British expedition culture in the domestic press and the field itself.

[16] Beckett, *Wolseley and Ashanti*.

Outbreak of War

The immediate origins of the Third Anglo-Asante War arose in 1867 when the British and Dutch began negotiations to trade their coastal forts to better consolidate their Gold Coast territories. Meanwhile, in the Asante capital of Kumase (Coomassie in contemporary British sources), Asantehene Kwaku Dua Panin died and was succeeded by Kofi Karikari. A man of about thirty, Karikari was less politically moderate and more psychologically mercurial than his predecessor. He represented an imperial faction that desired the reassertion and possible expansion of Asante boundaries and claims. In 1869, he took a Swiss missionary and a German missionary family hostage.

The Asante had long claimed a right of tribute (or rent) over the Dutch-controlled port of Elmina, and Dutch officials had always paid this rent. When Elmina passed from Dutch to British administration in April 1872, British officials did not recognize the Asante claim and the payments stopped. The Asante had never considered their grievances from the Second Anglo-Asante War as settled – the loss of Elmina's tribute added a fresh insult – and Karikari worried that the Anglo-Dutch trades might combine several of his former subjects with the Fante against him. In December 1872, he ordered his army to invade the British Protectorate, reassert Asante suzerainty over Elmina, and demonstrate dominance over the Fante.[17] Under the command of Amankwatia, the main army of somewhere between 30,000 and 40,000 men crossed the Pra River in January and scattered the Fante and Hausa armed police forces who attempted to stop them. In April they took the town of Dunwka and were poised to move in on Cape Coast itself.

The first British reinforcement to arrive was a flotilla of seven ships under Captain Edmund Fremantle RN. Fremantle made for Elmina, and on 13 June landed 110 Royal Marines along with some 1st West India Regiment soldiers and sailors commanded by Brevet Colonel Francis Festing. Festing attempted to disarm the largely hostile Elmina population, triggering enough resistance that Fremantle's ships bombarded the town. Festing's composite force then repelled an attack by 3,000 Asante troops, killing a number of important chiefs in the action.[18]

In London, the Colonial and War Offices considered their options. Four companies of the 1st West India Regiment in Barbados were sent to reinforce the Cape Coast garrison but would not arrive until July. After the battle at Elmina, 200 additional Marines were despatched and

---

[17] Ibid., 7–11.   [18] Spiers, *The Victorian Soldier in Africa*, 20–21.

officials began to discuss sending a full Army expedition from England. They brought in Brevet Colonel Sir Garnet Wolseley, who began his own plans for a possible campaign in the early summer. On 13 August, Wolseley was appointed the Administrator and Commander-in-Chief on the Gold Coast, making him both the civil and the military authority. He was instructed to personally select thirty-six officers for a special service mission to recruit and train a native force of Fante and other protectorate nations for a retaliatory attack on Asante territory. They floated the notion that if this proved to be impossible with native levies alone, the government would consider sending the next three battalions due for overseas service. A separate, smaller expedition was also sent under Commander John Glover and six special service officers, with orders to similarly recruit the tribes around the Volta River some 150 miles to the east of Cape Coast.[19]

British and Asante Forces

The Asante Empire did not have a formal standing army. Fighting men were maintained as part of a regional quota system and called up when needed. The Asantehene demanded contingents from subject tribes as well and, all told, could expect to raise between 60,000 and 80,000 armed men. The main army commanded by Amankwatia numbered closer to 40,000 and stood a half-day's march from Cape Coast.[20] By the 1860s, Birmingham exported from 100,000 to 150,000 guns to Africa each year, a large part of which went to the Gold Coast.[21] There was a thriving gun trade into Asante, and the Empire's substantial military power in the region was based entirely upon musket infantry. The quality of Asante's firearms and powder was generally poor, but their tactics mitigated this by focusing on ambushes and envelopments, using the thick undergrowth to get as close as possible to an enemy before firing.

As the youngest man ever promoted to Lieutenant-Colonel in the British Army, Wolseley was a rising star of the 'Imperial School' of officers focused on the peculiarities of colonial expeditions. He was considered a radical in some officer circles for his intellectual tendency and vocal support of military reform. Wolseley had just turned forty when he was given command of the expedition under the local rank of Major-General.

[19] Beckett, *Wolseley and Ashanti*, 13–15, 31.   [20] Ibid., 4, 93.
[21] Daniel R. Headrick, *The Tools of Empire: Technology and European Imperialism in the Nineteenth Century* (Oxford: Oxford University Press, 1981), 106.

The Asante expedition was a key event in Wolseley's cultivation of an inner circle of handpicked officers. He began maintaining a list during his command of the 1870 Red River Expedition, first adding Redvers Buller and William Butler. In 1873, he asked Buller to lead his intelligence department and Butler to recruit an allied nation against the Asante. By the end of the campaign, the 'Wolseley Ring' of officers would become widely known as the 'Ashanti Ring', or the 'mutual admiration society'. The ring had a profound and lasting effect on Britain's presence in Africa, going on to direct military policy during the height of imperial conquest through to the end of the century.[22]

Since first moving across the Atlantic in 1819, the 2nd West India Regiment had formed the backbone of British West African defence, supported by units of African armed police such as the Hausa.[23] The garrison had, however, been reduced and neglected over the preceding decade. Soon after he arrived at Cape Coast, Wolseley urgently requested that the 1st West India Regiment from Barbados join the few battalions that were despatched at the outset of the conflict. They would arrive in December.[24] After his subsequent request for European battalions, in November 1873 the War Office informed Wolseley that the 2nd Rifle Brigade, the 23rd Fusiliers (Royal Welsh Fusiliers), and the 42nd Highlanders (Black Watch) would also arrive at Cape Coast in early December.

Since taking office in December 1868, Gladstone's Secretary of State for War, Edward T. Cardwell, had implemented a comprehensive reform of army organization and administration.[25] Cardwell's abolition of commission purchase and his introduction of short-term service enlistment were highly controversial among the largely conservative officer corps, and also the subject serious debate in the press.[26] Success in Asante might allow Cardwell's supporters (Wolseley foremost among them) to claim that the reforms had created an effective and efficient military force, ready to tackle colonial conflict anywhere it might arise.[27] As a matter of fact, Wolseley's troops were long-term enlistment soldiers of

---

[22] Ian F. W. Beckett, 'Manipulating the "modern curse of armies": Wolseley, the press, and the Ashanti War, 1873–1874,' in Stephen M. Miller (ed.), *Soldiers and Settlers in Africa, 1850–1918* (Leiden: Koninklijke Brill, 2009), 221-2.
[23] S. C. Ukpabi, 'West Indian troops and the defense of British West Africa in the nineteenth century', *African Studies Review* 17, 1 (Apr 1974): 133.
[24] Wolseley to Cambridge, 9 October, Cambridge MSS, RA VIC/ADD E/1/7203.
[25] Edward M. Spiers, *The Late Victorian Army 1868–1902* (Manchester: Manchester University Press, 1992), 2.
[26] Sir Robert Biddulph, *Lord Cardwell at the War Office* (London: John Murray, 1904), 224.
[27] McIntyre, *British Policy in West Africa*, 40.

the old system and the officers had, with very few exceptions, purchased their commissions.

Wolseley challenged regimental tradition by re-equipping all the expedition soldiers in a custom uniform designed specifically for jungle conditions.[28] Officers wore canvas-covered cork helmets, grey homespun (light tweed) Norfolk jackets, and shooting boots with gaiters. The troops wore light Indian helmets, grey smock-frocks, trousers, and long boots.[29] Wolseley even forced the 42nd Highlanders to abandon their kilts for the new trousers.[30] The West Indians, Marines, and Naval Brigade sailors wore their regular uniforms. The officers carried revolvers and all ranks carried the Elcho sword bayonet. Top-heavy and machete-like, it had a cutting edge to hack through underbrush and a saw-edged back to remove branches and trees.

Soon after he arrived on the coast, Wolseley summoned the Fante Kings and Chiefs and insisted that they provide levies of soldiers to act in their own defence.[31] These formed the core of the first of two native levies under Lieutenant-Colonel H. Evelyn Wood and Major Baker Russell. Wood's Regiment was made up of Fante from Cape Coast, but also men from the Bonny River and Susu, who refused to fight with anything but swords and were issued naval cutlasses. Russell's Regiment was made up of a backbone of Hausa with contingents from Sierra Leone, the coastal town of Mumford, and several other locales.[32] Wolseley's artillery officer, Captain Arthur Rait, trained a force of Hausa gunners to man the expedition's two 7-pounder breech-loading Armstrong cannons, Hale rocket tubes, and the first two Gatling guns ever deployed by the Army.[33] It was truly a 'composite force'.

The overall plan was for four separate columns to attack Asante from different directions. Wolseley sent Captain Butler to the Western Akyem and Captains Dalrymple and Moore to the Wassaw, instructing them to induce their hosts to invade Asante territory.[34] As discussed earlier, Glover left in August to recruit the Volta tribes. The War Office indicated that these allied nations were intended to 'protect his flanks and act

---

[28] Precis of the Ashanti Expedition, Intelligence Department, Horse Guards, War Office, 13 April 1874, WO 147/27, p.15, The National Archives (TNA).
[29] 'The Ashantee War, uniform for the soldiers of the expedition', *Illustrated London News*, 18 October 1873, 365.
[30] Precis of the Ashanti Expedition, Intelligence Department, Horse Guards, War Office, 13 April 1874, WO 147/27, p. 15, TNA.
[31] Cambridge MSS, RA VIC/AD E/1/7201; Cambridge MSS, RA VIC/ADD E/1/7203.
[32] Beckett, *Wolseley and Ashanti*, 98–99.
[33] Brackenbury, *The Ashanti War, A Narrative*, 255.
[34] Wolseley Journal, Sunday 18 January, WO 147/4, TNA.

as decoys to keep the Ashanti disorganized'.[35] The decoy columns would never substantially materialize, leading Butler to title his campaign narrative, *Akim-Foo: The History of a Failure*.[36]

It was well known that draft animals could not survive in West Africa. Asante sat squarely in the West African tsetse fly belt, its armies could provide no cavalry.[37] While veterinary disease was certainly an issue, before long the officers realized that this had been overblown. One hundred and fifty mules were belatedly sent, but the campaign was so quick that they made little impact, save for allowing Wolseley the dignity of riding into Kumase.[38] The entire transport system thus relied on human carriers from the protectorate nations. Carriers were paid and fed, but they were recruited by offering per-capita rewards to their Chiefs. Many volunteered, but many more were coerced or, as transport problems slowed Wolseley's advance, outright rounded up.[39]

Strategy and War Aims

Britain's military objectives would be modest, almost tentative. William Gladstone's Liberal Party had a majority in Parliament and his Colonial Secretary, the Earl of Kimberly, was set against any increase in Britain's presence on the Gold Coast. Cardwell's comprehensive instructions directed Wolseley to force Karikari to release the captive missionaries, withdraw his army from the protectorate, guarantee its future territorial security, and renounce any claims of tribute from British-controlled areas. Wolseley was also instructed to encourage trade with Asante and discourage the practice of human sacrifice if at all possible.[40]

Karikari's war aims expanded during the conflict as his ambitions were bolstered by early successes and upheld by a court tendency to sugarcoat any news that got back to him. Originally asserting his claim to Elmina when the invasion began in January, by April he also claimed the Akyem, Assin, and Denkyira territories.[41] This aggression served his domestic and regional objectives. A successful raid south would affirm the

---

[35] Precis of the Ashanti Expedition, Intelligence Department, Horse Guards, War Office, 13 April 1874, WO 147/27, p. 41, TNA.
[36] Butler, *Akim-Foo*.
[37] William Beinart and Lotte Hughes, *Environment and Empire*, ed. Roger Louis (Oxford: Oxford University Press, 2007), 188.
[38] Beckett, *Wolseley and Ashanti*, 37.
[39] Bodleian, Alison MSS, MS. Eng. lett. C. 450; WO 147/3, 147/4, TNA.
[40] Kimberly to Wolseley, 10 September 1873, CO 879/6, BPP, Cmd. 8901, pp. 143–44, TNA.
[41] Beckett, *Wolseley and Ashanti*, 11.

Asantehene as a strong ruler able to inspire fear among Asante's many regional enemies and stand up to the Europeans.

West Africa encompassed a wide range of the most dangerous tropical diseases, making any expedition a serious concern for medical and military professionals alike.[42] Disease posed such a threat to British soldiers, claimed *The Lancet*, that 'the expedition may ... be likened to the march of a force under fire'.[43] While Wolseley was initially sent to employ only locally-recruited troops and the West India Regiments, from early in the planning stage he had decided to request European Army battalions. Conscious that this might be a red flag for the War Office, before leaving he assured the Commander-in-Chief of British forces, the Duke of Cambridge, 'if I possibly can attain the objects in view without landing European soldiers, I shall certainly endeavor to do so, as I am most anxious to avoid exposing the lives of more than are absolutely necessary, to the baneful influences of such a climate'.[44]

After assessing the situation in the protectorate, Wolseley would indeed send a request for British troops, claiming that the Fante were unwilling and unable to fight. Kimberley granted his request, on the clear condition that 'you will not employ this force, especially in the interior, a day longer than the paramount objects of your mission may require. The limit of their employment is fixed by the continuance of the more healthy season'.[45] Cardwell was similarly blunt.[46] The dry season was known to be less dangerous, when attacks of fever were less frequent and less severe.[47] Wolseley would thus have to operate within a limited time window.

The Course of the War

If Wolseley's arrival is taken to signify the start of Britain's formal expedition, the conflict can be described in three phases. The first phase (October to December 1873) was a period of preparation in which

---

[42] 'Confidential Report', Correspondence dealing with the problems of Ashanti, [1874], WO 33/26, p. 2, TNA.; Surgeon-Major Albert Gore, *A Contribution to the Medical History of our West African Campaigns* (London: Baillière, Tindall and Cox, 1876), 1.
[43] 'The Ashantee War', *The Lancet* 102, 2609 (30 Aug 1873), 307.
[44] Wolseley to Field Marshal HRH George, Duke of Cambridge, 3 September 1873, MSS, RA VIC/ADD E/1/7191.
[45] Kimberley to Wolseley, 24 November 1873, CO 879/6, TNA.
[46] Edward Cardwell to Wolseley, 8 September 1873, WO 106/285, TNA; WO 147/27; CO 879/6; CO 96/107; BPP, Cmd. 1891.
[47] W. M. Muir, Ashanti Expedition. Arrangements for Hospital Ship Conveyance of Troops, Sick and Stores, Army Medical Department, Sanitary Branch, 11 Oct 1873, MT 23/38, p. 1, TNA.

Wolseley's primary concerns were transport and recruitment with some notable clashes with Asante forces. The second phase (January 1874) was spent advancing towards and into Asante territory, culminating in the major battle of Amoafo. The third phase (February to March 1874) was marked by several concluding engagements, British victory, and a rapid withdrawal from the region.

When Wolseley and his cadre of officers arrived at Cape Coast, they faced an acute shortage of troops. The West India Regiments and Hausa armed police were spread thin across a series of strongpoints upcountry. Wolseley pressed the protectorate chiefs to provide troops and carriers while Russell, Wood, and Rait formed and trained their native contingents (discussed earlier). Cape Coast was given some reprieve by an outbreak of smallpox in the Asante army. By November, they were pulling out to the north of the Pra but Wolseley lacked the numbers to effectively harass them.

In the early days of the expedition, Wolseley was concerned with the powerful image of 'the bush' among the Asante, his Fante allies, and his own troops. Asante culture held that the bush protected their kingdom, repelling Europeans and removing any advantages which their technology might otherwise afford them.[48] Wolseley needed to disprove this notion if he hoped to convince the protectorate nations to join him. He also wanted to convince a reticent War Office to send the British battalions. A small decisive victory would serve both purposes.

Spreading the false information that Glover needed urgent support on the Volta River to the east, Wolseley loaded a mixed force of 500 troops onto Fremantle's ships in the early morning. In fact, the ships headed west to Elmina.[49] After disembarking, the force conducted a daylong punitive raid through several coastal towns with naval bombardment support. There was a sharp engagement with a larger Asante force. By the end of the day, they had burned several hostile towns, inflicted a defeat on the Asante, and suffered only one killed and twenty-five wounded.[50] Freemantle believed that 'the effect of this operation ... the impression it must make on the natives, both hostile and friendly, is incalculable. We have shown that we are capable of carrying all before us in the densest bush'.[51] Wolseley made the same boast to the War

---

[48] Wolseley to Cambridge, [15–]19 October 1873, Cambridge MSS, RA VIC/ADD E/1/7207.
[49] Wolseley to Colonel William Earle, 25 November 1873, Govt. House: Cape Coast, Hove, Wolseley MSS, Autobiographical Collection.
[50] Wolseley Journal, 15 October, WO 147/3, TNA.
[51] Wolseley, *The Life of King Koffee*, 8.

Office, and also claimed that the Hausa and West Indians had underperformed.[52]

In early November, Amankwatia attacked a small British outpost at the town of Abrakampa with 10,000 Asante soldiers. The defenders had converted a Wesleyan chapel into a loopholed fortress and, critically, cleared the surrounding bush to deny the Asante any cover. The Asante slugs did little damage at range and over a protracted firefight their casualties mounted while the defenders took no losses and minimal wounded.[53]

Wolseley disarmed many of the native levies and deployed them as carriers. This was necessary because of a looming transport crisis that his officers would never completely resolve. It was impossible to recruit enough carriers for the force's needs and desertion among them was widespread. There were also repeated interruptions to the transport system when carriers dropped their loads and fled if they believed Asante were approaching. When the Rifle Brigade and 23rd Fusiliers arrived in mid-December, Wolseley had to send them back out to sea until he could move enough supplies up to the forward camps.[54]

The European battalions and Naval Brigade landed over the first several days of the new year and began moving upcountry a half battalion at a time. The soldiers marched seven miles a day in the comparatively cool early mornings and rested through the midday heat and evening humidity in a chain of camps and depots built by the Royal Engineers over the preceding months. There were eight camps and two hospitals along the seventy-four miles from Cape Coast to the Pra River. The camp on the southern bank of the Pra was a major base built to accommodate 2,000 European troops and 5,000 people in total.[55] Wolseley reached the Pra camp on 2 January as his forces amassed there for the push into Asante territory.[56]

It had become clear that the missions to recruit three decoy columns were not going well. Glover sent word that he could only muster 700 instead of the expected 16,000 men and that he might cross the Pra three weeks behind schedule.[57] Butler did gather a substantial force of Akyem soldiers but they refused to cross the river.[58] Dalrymple and Moore had similar difficulty with the Wassaw.

---

[52] Wolseley to Cambridge, 9 October 1873, Cambridge MSS RA VIC/ADD E/1/7203.
[53] Wolseley to Cambridge, 7 November 1873, Cambridge MSS RA VIC/ADD E/1/7232.
[54] Cambridge MSS, RA VIC/ADD E1/1/7258; WO 147/3, TNA.
[55] Boyle, *Through Fanteeland to Coomassie*, 212–13.
[56] Beckett, *Wolseley and Ashanti*, 300.
[57] Wolseley to Cambridge, 26 December, Cambridge MSS, RA VIC/ADD E/1/7276.
[58] Cambridge MSS, RA VIC/ADD E/1/7286; WO 147/3, TNA.

On 5 January, the engineers completed a 63-yard bridge across the river with a Gatling-armed bridgehead on the north side.[59] Scouts, engineers, and labourers crossed to clear the path and begin building the next set of fortified forward camps (there would be nine north of the Pra). Wolseley and the main body of troops began to cross on 20 January, five days behind schedule.[60]

During the march north, Wolseley and Karikari engaged in an ultimately fruitless diplomatic exchange through both envoys and letters (the Asantehene having one of the captive missionaries to translate the letters). Karikari focused on buying time for his forces to prepare defences while Wolseley held firm to his demand that the King accept the War Office's list of war aims.[61] The Asante did release all the captive missionaries, who arrived at British camps on 12 and 21 January.

The Asante army prepared its main defensive action at the village of Amoafo and awaited Wolseley's approach. The ensuing battle on 31 January 1874 ended in a complete British victory (see 'Anatomy of a Battle: Amoafo' section). After Amoafo, the Asante launched a series of attacks on the supply train in the British rear. Wolseley did not have the necessary supplies or carriers to continue in a regular manner. However, the onset of the rainy season was imminent and he needed to maintain momentum.

The decision was made to leave most of the baggage behind, including the tents, and rush a flying column to Kumase with the men carrying their own reduced provisions. The combined force of 1,611 men left on 2 February and the following night were soaked with rain while sleeping rough.[62] They fought a series of ambushes and counter-attacks, culminating in a final pitched battle at the northern bank of the Oda River during which two of Wolseley's men were killed and he took a direct hit to his cork helmet.

After defeating this last Asante stand, Wolseley sent the 42nd forward to take Kumase, which they did virtually unopposed on 5 February. The Asantehene and his court had fled, leaving no one to sign a treaty of surrender. Wolseley could not afford to wait. The rain had been an ominous sign that the weather was turning against British forces; fresh

---

[59] Major Robert Home, 'Rough Sketch of the Tete-De-Pont at the Prah', Journal of the Engineer Operations on the Gold Coast during the Recent Expedition 64, WO 147/27, TNA.
[60] WO 147/4, TNA.
[61] Wolseley to King Kofi Kakari, Cambridge MSS, RA VIC/ADD E/I/7208, 13 October 1873; Wolseley to King Kofi Kakari, 2 January 1874, CO 879/6, CO 806/2, TNA; Wolseley to King Kofi Kakari, 26 January 1874, CO 879/6, TNA.
[62] WO 147/3, TNA.

thunderstorms again drenched the men in Kumase. Fires also broke out in the capital, possibly set by the Fante prisoners they had released from captivity or by the carriers. When he received word that the newly erected bridge over the Oda River was already under the rising waters, Wolseley ordered a retreat to the coast. Officers oversaw the seizure of treasures from the royal palace before the engineers blew it up with Asante stores of gunpowder. The city was then formally set on fire and the force withdrew while the 42nd maintained a rearguard.[63]

With the British in withdrawal, Karikari had little reason to negotiate. He had suffered a serious defeat but did not need to sign a treaty ratifying that fact until, two days after Wolseley's withdrawal, he learned that a *second* British column was approaching from the southeast. It was Glover, leading a tiny force of Hausa and native levies, arriving just late enough to be in the nick of time. Karikari panicked, dispatching an envoy with a preliminary payment of gold dust to find Wolseley and negotiate the Asante surrender. Glover briefly entered Kumase and left for the coast without incident.[64]

Anatomy of a Battle: Amoafo

The major battle of the war would be fought on the Asante's terms. Amankwatia set up a strong defensive ambush on the path to Kumase, just outside the village of Amoafo, with his main army of 15,000 to 20,000 soldiers deployed in a horseshoe formation on a ridge that overlooked a ravine of dense bush and swampland. The Asante had the high ground, the British would need to descend and then ascend along a single narrow path, and any troops off of the path would be slowed by the terrain and blinded by the vegetation. Envelopment was certain.[65]

Wolseley did at least have the chance to prepare, warned of the ambush by one of Buller's Fante scouts whose report did a tremendous service to the expedition. The plan was to form a large hollow square formation, 2,200 men strong, and advance along the main path straight toward the Asante army. The Highlanders formed the front face, extending 300 yards on either side of the path, along which Captain Rait moved his two 7-pounder Armstrong guns. To the left, Russell's native regiment and half the Naval Brigade formed another face. To the right, Wood's native regiment and the rest of the Naval Brigade formed another. Two rocket troughs were positioned at each of the front corners.

---

[63] Ibid.; Beckett, *Wolseley and Ashanti*, 365; Spiers, *The Victorian Soldier in Africa*, 31.
[64] Beckett, *Wolseley and Ashanti*, 370–71.
[65] WO 147/3, TNA; Hove, Wolseley MSS, W/P 4/7.

The 2nd Rifle Brigade formed the rear face. Wolseley, his staff, and the 23rd Fusiliers in reserve moved in the center of the square. Engineers and teams of laborers were to cut parallel paths on either side of the main path to allow the sides of the square to advance. The baggage, field hospital, and reserve ammunition were left behind, guarded by the West Indians.

Wolseley's square began its advance the morning of 31 January. Once the 42nd, bagpipers playing, had descended into the ravine they were pinned down by a withering semicircle of Asante fire. Visibility was limited to nonexistent in the thick bush, in which the Asante skillfully concealed and waited to fire at close range. This tactic gave the first hours of the battle the feel of an extended rolling ambush against the advancing British.[66] Winwood Reade, the only journalist with the front face of the square, explained that the Highlanders were forced to fire blind: 'in bushfighting great waste, or apparent waste, of ammunition is unavoidable ... The bush should be cleared by volleys whenever there is reason to suspect the enemy is there'.[67] The men of the front face lay flat and crept forward while their commander repeatedly called for additional support.

Once engaged with the enemy, the square began to seriously lose its shape. The left lost contact with the 42nd and had to cut a diagonal path to the right to reconnect. Just as the right similarly began to lose contact with the front, they were pinned to the ground by heavy Asante fire and unable to reconnect the line. Men began to fall out. Captain Buckle was shot through the heart and killed on the left while Lieutenant-Colonel Wood, commander of the right face, was hit by a nail that just missed his heart and had to be carried to the rear.[68] Wolseley sent company after company of the reserve Fusiliers and Rifle Brigade rear to the front.

As the square lost cohesion, groups of Asante soldiers were able to infiltrate into the center and lines of fire tangled. There were several cases of friendly fire where British battalions either mistook each other for Asante or actually did fire at Asante not realizing that their shots were cutting through vegetation toward their comrades beyond. A group of Asante broke through the front-right and came within a hundred yards of Wolseley and his staff.

The 42nd had been operating without artillery support for over two hours as Rait and his men struggled to haul their Armstrong guns

---

[66] 'The Ashantee War', *The Times*, 17 March 1874, 11.
[67] 'Bush-Fighting', *The Broad Arrow*, [n.d.], 'The Ashanti Expedition of 1873-1874: News Cuttings, Correspondence and Extracts from Letters from Hart's Son, Lieut. A. Fitzroy Hart', WO 211/71, no. 17, TNA.
[68] Manning, *Evelyn Wood VC*, 80.

through the swampy lowland. At long last they managed to get one of them up onto a clear section of path from which they could directly support the front line. The gunners fired fifteen rounds of case shot from less than fifty yards away, at which distance the bush provided very little cover for the massed Asante soldiers. The Highlanders charged forward and the Asante centre went into retreat.[69]

On the right, which was still under pressure, Wolseley moved two Rifle Brigade companies to the northeastern flank the Asante position. Two of Wood's companies, including the Susu who fought only with swords, charged in and the Asante pulled back into the bush.[70] The 42nd pushed through the Asante camps and entered Amoafo at midday. There was a scattering of further flank attacks but Wolseley's front was effectively secure by two in the afternoon.

The British rear, however, came under assault during the afternoon as the flanks of the original Asante envelopment formation moved south of Wolseley's force and attacked several minimally defended villages along the road. Sick and wounded men in the field hospitals had to mount vigorous defences, and Wolseley was forced to send back many of the Riflemen and some of the Highlanders to secure the road and defend the baggage route. When Asante attacked the baggage column itself, many carriers dropped their loads and retreated, seriously hampering the supply chain and hindering Wolseley's plan for a quick push to Kumase.[71]

Amankwatia had selected an excellent position to resist the British advance and his soldiers had moved against them very aggressively. Wolseley's defensive square formation, however appealing on paper, did not hold together in the terrain and by midway through the battle all his reserves were engaged and many of his battalions immobilized. In the many little ambushes that took place along the front and sides of the square, Asante soldiers succeeded in getting close to, indeed through, the British line to fire at close range.

Yet, the disparity in firepower between British and Asante forces was so great that as afternoon turned to evening somewhere between 800 and 1,600 Asante lay dead, along with Amankwatia himself, and only four of Wolseley's men had been killed (more would die later of their wounds). The low number of deaths can be pinned squarely on the surprisingly low penetrative power of Asante musket slugs, since 194 of Wolseley's men had in fact been shot. In total, twenty-one officers and 173 other

---

[69] Beckett, *Wolseley and Ashanti*, 309–11.   [70] Manning, *Evelyn Wood VC*, 81.
[71] Wolseley's Journal, 31 January, WO, 147/3, TNA.

ranks were wounded, most of whom were removed back to Cape Coast and out of the campaign. Unsurprisingly, the 42nd sustained the highest casualty rate.[72]

The Role of Technology and the Royal Navy

The campaign was laden with advanced technology. Martini-Henry rifles, light Armstrong cannons, Hale rockets, and telegraph lines played significant roles in Britain's military success, while the more ostentatious Gatling Guns, a failed railway scheme, and steam sappers (traction engines) proved unworkable in the field and were instead used for a series of highly-publicized but only marginally effective demonstrations for Asante envoys and Fante allies.

Festing's Royal Marines were pivotal to the campaign. After Wolseley's arrival, the Naval Brigade was under army command and the naval units highly interspersed with the army. As mentioned earlier, Fremantle's ships provided naval artillery support during both Festing's and Wolseley's attacks at Elmina.

After the outbreak of hostilities, Kimberley and the Colonial Office wanted to halt the sale of arms, ammunition, and gunpowder to the French-linked coastal city Assinie (modern day Ivory Coast), which traded on Asante's behalf.[73] Kimberley tried to apply the 'Customs and Consolidation Act' to that end, but the Law Office took the opinion that it would not stick except in cases of completely banned articles of trade.[74] Frustrated that he could not even stop British traders from selling to an enemy belligerent under existing colonial law, Kimberley contacted Colonel Harley, the Governor of Cape Coast. 'An Ordinance to empower the Administrator to regulate or prohibit the importation and sale of munitions of war' passed the Gold Coast Legislative Council on 29 April 1873.[75] Harley finally imposed a legal blockade on 29 August and Fremantle deployed four of his seven ships to enforce it. With so large a coast to patrol, it was only partially effective, made less so by the fact that it only applied to the stretch under British jurisdiction, thus excluding Assinie.[76] Moreover, following an appeal by the prominent

---

[72] Spiers, *The Victorian Soldier in Africa*, 29.
[73] 'The Ashantee Expedition', *Newcastle Courant*, 31 Oct 1873, 2; Colonial Office to Law Office, Papers Relating to the Ashanti Invasion (Gold Coast) &c, 7 May 1873, CO 879/4, no. 31, TNA.
[74] Law Officers' Opinion, 20 May 1873, CO 879/4, no. 54, TNA; Colonial Office to Commissioners of Customs, 22 May 1873, CO 879/4, no. 61, TNA.
[75] Colonel Harley, C. B., to the Earl of Kimberley, 3 May 1873, CO 879/4, no. 108, TNA.
[76] Brackenbury, *The Ashanti War, A Narrative*, vol. 2, 312.

London-based trading company, F. & A. Swanzy, the Law Office again declared the blockade illegal in November. Freemantle did what he could to maintain the porous and legally-awkward blockade until it was lifted for good in March 1874.[77] Several Swanzy ships were detained.[78] The *Pall Mall Gazette* railed against 'Blockade Running on the Gold Coast'.[79]

Aftermath

The Asante emissary caught up with Wolseley at Fomena and accepted terms on Karikari's behalf. The Treaty of Fomena, signed on 13 February, formalized the complete list of Cardwell's remaining war aims, the missionaries having already been released. The Asantehene renounced his right of client tribute from protectorate nations and any claim on Elmina, accepted free trade and access between the coast and Asante, removed all remaining Asante forces from the protectorate, agreed to prevent human sacrifice, and also to pay an indemnity of 50,000 ounces of gold. Just over one thousand ounces were ever paid.[80]

The only remaining goal was a speedy withdrawal. Wolseley and his staff arrived at Cape Coast on 19 February. After an auction to sell off the loot taken from Kumase, the British forces began to embark for England. Wolseley had been made administrator of the Gold Coast for the course of the operation, however, and someone had to take his place. Four officers were each offered the position at an annual salary of £4,000 yet, Kimberley later recalled, 'one & all replied – "not if we receive £4000 a day!"'[81] Wolseley and much of the Ashanti Ring left for home on 4 March.[82]

Accolades came pouring in. Cambridge issued congratulatory general orders that were widely printed in the newspapers. Queen Victoria granted Wolseley the KCB and reviewed the troops at Windsor Park. Both Houses of Parliament thanked Wolseley, and the Commons voted

---

[77] Sir E. R. Fremantle, *The Navy as I Have Known It, 1849–1899* (London: Cassell and Company, 1904), 208.
[78] Brackenbury, *The Ashanti War, A Narrative*, vol. 2, 311.
[79] 'Blockade Running on the Gold Coast,' *Pall Mall Gazette*, 2 Oct 1873, 8; 'Blockade Running on the Gold Coast', *Pall Mall Gazette*, 3 Oct 1873, 7.
[80] Treaty of Peace between Wolseley and Saibee Enquie, Acting on Behalf of King Kofi Kakari, 13 February 1874, FO 93/6/4, TNA.
[81] John Wodehouse, *The Journal of John Wodehouse, First Earl of Kimberley, 1862–1902*, eds. Angus Hawkins and John Powell (Cambridge: Cambridge University Press, 1997), 287.
[82] TNA, WO 147/3, TNA, CO 96/114.

him a personal grant of £25,000. Almost every officer was promoted, in Wolseley's case to Major-General (backdated to 1868).[83]

The campaign had been economical at a cost of £767,093, with the War Office's share coming in under the original estimate.[84] Sickness rates had actually been quite high, with 43% of the European battalions and 71% of the Wolseley Ring having been invalided out.[85] The death rates due to illness, however, were astonishingly low. Disease killed forty of the British contingent, 1.5% of its total strength.[86] That was a far cry from the disastrous 1863–64 war. Moreover, while many of the soldiers had been wounded, only thirteen of the Europeans and one of the West Indians died from enemy action in the Gold Coast.[87]

The Asante Kingdom was left in chaos. The death toll from disease and combat had been devastating and the utter defeat undermined Karikari's legitimacy. His brother, Mensa Bonsu, overthrew him in October 1874 and the country descended into a long civil war. The former Asantehene was murdered in 1884.[88]

In Britain, the highly publicized success of the expedition opened up political, military, and public opinion to the notion that European armies could manage the threat of disease and venture into the interior of Africa. The public now refused to support a withdrawal from the region, which had seemed a foregone conclusion only a few years earlier.[89] After Wolseley's return, Britain annexed the lands of the Fante Confederacy. The newly founded Gold Coast Colony, proclaimed on 24 July 1874, became the first substantially inland British colony in tropical Africa and came about as a direct result of the Third Anglo-Asante war.[90]

Further Reading

Beckett, Ian F. W. 'Manipulating the "modern curse of armies": Wolseley, the press, and the Ashanti War, 1873–1874.' In Stephen M. Miller (ed.) *Soldiers and Settlers in Africa, 1850–1918*. Leiden: Koninklijke Brill, 2009.

---

[83] John Joseph Crooks (ed.), *Records Relating to the Gold Coast Settlements from 1750 to 1874* (London: Frank Cass, 1973), 533; Beckett, *Wolseley and Ashanti*, 375–76.
[84] Beckett, *Wolseley and Ashanti*, 372   [85] Lloyd, *The Drums of Kumasi*, 150.
[86] Beckett, *Wolseley and Ashanti*, 107; Keegan, *The Ashanti Campaign*, 194–45. E. A. Parkes, *On the Issue of a Spirit Ration during the Ashanti Campaign of 1874* (London: J. & A. Churchill, 1875), 61; Parkes, 'Report on the issue of a spirit ration during the march to Coomassie', *The Lancet* 104, 2660 (22 Aug 1874): 263–67; Gore, *A Contribution to the Medical History of our West African Campaigns*, 1.
[87] Beckett, *Wolseley and Ashanti*, 107.   [88] Ibid., 108, 372–73.
[89] McIntyre, *British Policy in West Africa*, 45.
[90] Foreign Office, *British Foreign and State Papers, 1874–1875* (London: William Ridgway, 1882), vol. LIX, 1194.

Wolseley and Ashanti: The Asante War Journal and Correspondence of Major General Sir Garnet Wolseley 1873–1874. Stroud, Gloucestershire, UK: The History Press for the Army Records Society, 2009.

Brackenbury, Henry. *The Ashanti War, A Narrative: Prepared from the Official Documents by Permission of Major-General Sir Garnet Wolseley*. London: William Blackwood and Sons, 1874.

Butler, William Francis. *Akim-Foo: The History of a Failure*. 3rd ed. London: Sampson Low, Marston, Low, & Searle, 1875.

'Daily News' Special Correspondent [Sir John Frederick Maurice]. *The Ashantee War: A Popular Narrative*. London: Henry S. King & Co., 1874.

Edgerton, Robert B. *The Fall of the Asante Empire: The Hundred-Year War for Africa's Gold Coast*. London: The Free Press, 1995.

Henty, G. A. *The March to Coomassie*. 2nd ed. London: Tinsley Brothers, 1874.

Keegan, John. 'The Ashanti Campaign 1873–74.' In Brian Bond (ed.) *Victorian Military Campaigns*. London: Hutchinson & Co, 1967.

Lloyd, Alan. *The Drums of Kumasi: The Story of the Ashanti Wars*. London: Longmans Green and Co., 1964.

McIntyre, W. D. 'British Policy in West Africa: The Ashanti Expedition of 1873–74'. *The Historical Journal* 5, 1 (1962): 19–46.

Patterson, Ryan. '"To form a correct estimate of their nothingness when compared with it": British exhibitions of military technology in the Abyssinian and Ashanti Expeditions'. *The Journal of Imperial and Commonwealth History* 44, 4 (Aug 2016): 551–72.

Ramseyer, Friedrich and Johannes Kuhne. *Four Years in Ashantee*. New York: Robert Carter & Brothers, 1875.

Reade, Winwood. *The Story of the Ashantee Campaign*. London: Smith, Elder, & Co., 1874.

Stanley, Henry M. *Coomassie and Magdala: The Story of Two British Campaigns in Africa*. London: Sampson Low, Marston, Low & Searle, 1874.

Wolseley, Garnet. *The Story of a Soldier's Life*. New York: Charles Scribner's Sons, 1903.

7 The Second Afghan War, 1878–1880

Rodney Atwood

Background

Fears for Indian security drove British involvement in nineteenth-century Afghanistan. Prior to the Europeans' arrival in the subcontinent, invasions had come from the north. In both wars they waged in the nineteenth century, the British sought 'regime change', not annexation, to ensure a friendly buffer state to India's North-West Frontier. India's British rulers feared that a Russian advance in Central Asia, their influence in Afghanistan and the approach of a hostile army, Russian or Afghan or both, might lead to a rising among India's subject peoples, or even worse, the Sepoy army, as had happened in 1857. This fear was most clearly stated by J. R. Seely in *The Expansion of England*. The fear predated the book's publication in 1883. British opinion was divided on how to meet this threat. Successive Viceroys John Lawrence, Lord Mayo, and Lord Northbrook adopted a policy of 'masterly inactivity'. They argued that India's best defence lay in her geographical setting, 'towering mountain systems, mighty rivers, waterless deserts and warlike tribes'and that any Russian advance was best met by allowing the invader to overextend his strength and communications.[1] When Dost Mohammed, the Afghan Amir during the First Afghan War, 1838–42, died, the British were keen not to be involved in the ensuing civil war, but to recognize Sher Ali, the third son of the Dost's favourite wife, as his successor if he could hold the country together. This he did with help from his son, Yakub. His chief rival, Abdur Rahman, was driven into exile in Samarkand and Sher Ali ruled in Afghanistan for the next decade, 1868–78.[2] In 1869, the British gave Sher Ali a lavish reception at a *durbar* at Ambala, expressing their renewed diplomatic and financial support, as well as providing weapons for his army.[3]

---

[1] Peter Hopkirk, *The Great Game* (London: Oxford University Press, 1990), 6.
[2] Robert Johnson, *The Afghan Way of War* (London: Hurst & Co, 2011), 91–97.
[3] Brian Robson, *The Road to Kabul: The Second Afghan War 1878–1881* (Staplehurst: Spellmount, 1996), 35; Field Marshal Lord Roberts, *Forty-One Years in India* (London: Longmans, 1898), 304–08.

British policy changed with the formation of Disraeli's Conservative Ministry in 1874, which espoused a more active imperial role, in words at least. This encouraged proponents of the 'forward school' to champion an assertive policy towards Afghanistan. The forward school argued that the best defence against Russian advance was to control border states and create cooperative satellites. In Central Asia, Russia was on the march, acquiring Tashkent in 1865, Khojent in 1866, and Bokhara in 1867. The Russian driving force was General Konstantin Kaufman, a veteran of war in the Caucasus, a friend of Alexander II's War Minister Dimitri Milyutin, and a soldier of vision and energy.[4] In 1873, Britain and Russia came to an understanding that the area south of the river Oxus would fall within the British sphere of influence and be ruled by the Afghan Amir. Nonetheless, Kaufman's advance continued to Khiva in 1873 and Kokand in 1876, and he began attacks on Turkmen tribes in Merv. These activities seemed to justify the arguments of the forward school's proponents, including Sir Henry Rawlinson, a veteran of the First Afghan War, a former diplomat, a member of the India Council in London, and the author of *England and Russia in the East* published in 1875.

Sher Ali thought it wise to adopt a warmer policy towards Russia. British fears of Russia encouraging an Indian rising were fed by the translation and publication of the Colonel Terentiev's *Russia and England in the Struggle for the Markets of Central Asia*. The Indian Rebellion had failed in 1857, Terentiev maintained, because the Indians lacked a proper plan and outside support. He wrote, 'Sick to death [of British rule], the natives are now waiting for a physician from the north'. Russian military reforms after the Crimea had emphasized using fast-moving, mounted columns and raising 'people's wars of insurrection'.[5]

The arrival of Disraeli's new Viceroy in 1878 gave the forward school its chance. Lord Lytton had two main tasks: to organize a Durbar to proclaim Queen Victoria *Kaiser-i-Hind* (Empress of India), and to bring a fresh approach to Afghan policy. His first step in the latter was to send

---

[4] The classic account of Central-Asian rivalry is Hopkirk, *The Great Game*; for Russian policy, see David Gillard, *The Struggle for Asia 1828–1914: A Study in British and Russian Imperialism* (London: Methuen, 1977); W. C. Fuller, *Strategy and Power in Russia 1600–1914* (Toronto: Maxwell Macmillan, 1992); Dominic Lieven, *Empire: The Russian Empire and its Rivals from the Sixteenth Century to the Present* (London: Pimlico, 2003); and, Alex Marshall, *The Russian General Staff and Asia 1800–1917* (Abingdon: Routledge, 2006).
[5] Hopkirk, *Great Game*, 363; Adrian Preston, 'Sir Charles MacGregor and the defence of India, 1857–1887', *The Historical Journal* XII, I (1969): 58–77.

troops into Quetta on the route to Afghanistan through the Bolan Pass. To Sher Ali this was a threatening reminder of the British advance to Kabul in 1838–39. Lytton and Disraeli sought to undo Northbrook's rebuff of Sher Ali by offering a defensive treaty with a British representative at Kabul or Herat. The policy might have succeeded had it not been for the Eastern Crisis of 1878 and Lytton's impatience. In the crisis, the Russians threatened Constantinople, and Disraeli dispatched the Mediterranean Fleet to Besika Bay and Indian troops to Malta. This laid the background to the crisis leading to Afghan war.

* * * * *

Contemporary discussion of Britain's second Afghan conflict largely followed the division between the forward school and the proponents of masterly inactivity. Frederick Roberts's autobiography *Forty-One Years in India*, Lady Betty Balfour's account of her father's Viceroyalty and edition of his letters, and Charles Metcalfe MacGregor's official history support the former. Henry Hanna's short volume, *Lord Roberts in War*, found fault with nearly all aspects of Roberts's generalship, although his three-volume history published a few years later in 1899, which found parallels with the first war's disaster and criticized Lytton's policy, paid tribute to some of Roberts's qualities. After the closing victory at Kandahar, Lytton's successor, Lord Ripon, published an official and self-congratulatory *Kandahar Correspondence*, a useful although selective source.

A spate of new writing followed Western involvement in Afghanistan after the destruction of the Twin Towers in New York, in 2001. Many of these books are ignorant of strategic results and picture recent incompetence as mirrored in the past. Better earlier volumes include Tony Heathcote's *Afghan Wars* which emphasized the roles of General Donald Stewart and Roberts as key British participants, and Brian Robson's *The Road to Kabul*, the best modern account, replacing Hanna. Peter Hopkirk's *The Great Game* placed the Afghan Wars in a wider context. William Trousdale's *War in Afghanistan*, which utilized unpublished sections of MacGregor's war diary, gave Roberts's critics more ammunition. Rob Johnson's *The Afghan Way of War* is sympathetic to that side, although dependent on British sources.

The opening of Russian archives following the end of the Cold War provided historians with opportunities to gain new insight into Tsarist policy and re-evaluate British success in Afghanistan. Alex Marshall's *The Russian General Staff and Asia 1800–1917*, Dominic Lieven's *Empire: The Russian Empire and its Rivals from the Sixteenth Century to the Present* and W.C. Fuller's *Strategy and Power in Russia 1600–1914* all offer new insights.

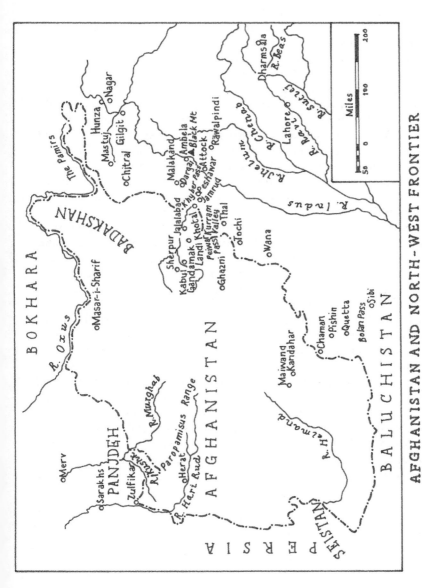

Map 7.1 Afghanistan and North-West Frontier, c. 1879

Outbreak of War

Tsar Alexander II and his ministers supported Kaufman's proposal that, if war broke out with Britain over the Ottoman Empire, a 30,000-strong Russian force would strike against India. To reassure Sher Ali that this policy was not directed against him, Major-General Stolietov, an officer with Asian experience, led a mission to Kabul in late 1878 to inform the Amir where these troops were destined.[6] Stolietov's mission coincided with Sher Ali's refusal of Lytton's application for a British resident at Kabul. Lytton became convinced that that Sher Ali was plotting with the Russians. He could have demanded from St Petersburg Stolietov's withdrawal, as the Congress of Berlin had settled the dispute between the Ottoman Empire and Russia. Instead, he despatched an envoy with an armed escort to present an ultimatum.[7] From this point, Disraeli's ministry was drawn in the Viceroy's wake towards war.

The timing of the ultimatum could not have been worse. The Amir was mourning the death of his favourite son and declared heir, and yielded to the appointment of 'the faithless wretch', his eldest son Yakub, as his successor.[8] The Amir's officer commanding the frontier post on the Khyber Pass, Faiz Mohammed Khan, followed orders to turn back the British envoy, Brigadier-General Neville Chamberlain.[9] Disraeli and Salisbury, bringing 'peace with honour' from the Berlin Conference, found themselves facing an Afghan war. Lytton telegraphed to London his plan. His proposed manifesto would condemn the Amir while at the same time professing friendship to the Afghan people. It would justify sending troops to occupy the Kurram Valley and seize the Khyber Pass. The cabinet agreed to the dispatch of a final ultimatum to the Amir demanding a full apology and acceptance of a British mission at Kabul. Sher Ali's belated answer was deemed inadequate as it contained no apology. Reluctantly, Disraeli's cabinet backed Lytton as he launched what he planned as a limited war.[10]

---

[6] Marshal, *Russian General Staff and Asia*, 135.
[7] Percival Spear, *The Oxford History of Modern India* (Delhi: Oxford University Press, 1965), 252.
[8] 'Abdullah Jan', *The Times* (London), 23 August 1878, 10. He had imprisoned Yakub for four years.
[9] Haines to Duke of Cambridge, 26 Sep 1878, VIC/ADDE/1/8397, Royal Archives, Windsor.
[10] Robson, *Road to Kabul*, 46–52. Roberts outlines the events clearly while placing blame on the Russians and the Amir in *Forty-One Years*, 335, 341–48.

British and Afghan Forces

The British faced a combination of both regular and irregular Afghan troops. In the First Afghan War, popular militias from the hill tribes fought the British. Sher Ali had visited India in 1869 and came away convinced that unless the Afghans modernized their army they would continue to be regarded (in the words of his grandson) 'as ignorant asses that they had always been'.[11] Following steps taken by his father, Dost Mohamed, Sher Ali continued to reform the army, obtaining rifles, ammunition, and other equipment from the British and support from Indian NCOs to train Afghan regulars, a force of 56,000 with 379 guns. The artillery was their strongest arm.[12] Russian Colonel Grodekov, visiting Herat in 1878 ahead of the possible march of Russian columns in the Eastern Crisis, thought Sher Ali's army to be of good quality, but believed the infantry was hampered by drill manuals based on English models, ill-suited to Afghan character.[13] A Russian estimate numbered irregular troops at 140,000. Among them were fanatical Ghilzais, steeled by Islam to give their lives for the Prophet, but usually poorly armed with mediaeval weapons, such as spears, swords, and daggers. Their loyalty was also uncertain. The bulk of the regulars were recruited from Ghilzais and Wardak Pashtuns who had supported Sher Ali in the Civil War. Traditional Afghan methods emphasized using their local knowledge of the harsh terrain and coming out in strength only when the odds favoured them.[14]

The British force, which included British as well as Indian regiments, was armed with superior weaponry. A decade of rapid technological change was reflected in the confidence of Lytton's Chief Military Advisor, Sir George Colley, in the firepower of breach-loading weapons. British and Indian troops were well-trained, and in the Sikh, Gurkha, and Highland battalions fighting spirit was high. Among regiments recruited from border peoples such as Pathans, there were doubtful loyalties, as Major-General Sir Frederick Roberts discovered in his first battle. Some of the 29th Bengal Native Infantry fired warning shots to alert their fellow Muslims of impending attack. Conversely, seventy men of the elite Corps of Guides, also recruited from hill folk, fought to the

---

[11] Quoted T. Barfield, *Afghanistan: A Cultural and Political History* (Princeton: Princeton University Press, 2010), 139.
[12] See Barfield, *Afghanistan* and Johnson, *Afghan Way of War*.
[13] Marshal, *Russian General Staff and Central Asia*, 138.
[14] Hasan Kakar, *Government and Society in Afghanistan: The Reign of Amir Abd'al Rahman Kahn* (Austin: University of Texas Press, 1979), 96.

last man against overwhelming odds in the Bala Hissar (the 'High Fort') at Kabul in September 1879.

British soldiers new to India had to adapt to a harsh climate in which cholera, typhoid, and sometimes pneumonia were rife. British infantry carried the breach-loading, single-shot Martini-Henry, firing a heavy man-stopping round. The Indians' Snider was not as good, however, fearful of a repetition of 1857, the British ensured their Indian soldiers had inferior weapons. Cavalry carried sword, lance, and carbine. Muzzle-loading rifled cannon fired out to 5,000 yards and screw guns carried on mule-back, to 4,000. The British abandoned bright scarlet and 'all were dressed from top to toe in *Khakee*, or mud colour'.

One senior officer thought that fighting with modern rifles 'will be the easiest part of the job' while 'difficulties of communication and climate will be serious'. He added, 'Roberts and Stewart are both competent officers, and when the forces have been put together and Reg[imen]ts are accustomed to one another, and to the new Staff, all will go well'. He did not extend similar approval to Sam Browne, Commander of the Peshawar Valley Field Force of 16,000, striking at the Khyber.[15] Browne's appointment was a political decision to remove him from the Viceroy's Council in favour of Neville Chamberlain.[16]

Lytton's faith in Colley led him to marginalize the Indian Army Commander-in-Chief, Sir Frederick Haines. Mutual mistrust handicapped smooth operations. Another handicap was the Indian famine of 1876–78, which had disastrous effects on the country's ability to support a war logistically.

Wisely, acting on Haines's pleading, Lytton chose a war of limited objectives, occupying the Khyber Pass, Kurram Valley, and Kandahar, to bring about policy or regime-change giving Britain a friendly buffer against the Russians. An advance to Kabul would have tested the Indian Army's supply and transport arrangements to the utmost. The Indian famine had badly affected agriculture, reducing food supplies and animal numbers.

Strategy and War Aims

Sher Ali's strategy had been to keep both empires at arm's length, trapped as he was between the bear and the lion. As war became

---

[15] VIC/ADDE/1/8408, Gen. A.E. Hardinge to Cambridge, Royal Archives, Windsor.
[16] Richard Goldsborough, 'Passed over for "strong political reasons": Sir Frederick Maude and the politics of appointment in the second Afghan War', *Journal of the Society for Army Historical Research (JSAHR)* XC (Autumn, 2012): 158.

imminent, he relied upon regulars to hold the strategic passes, the Khyber, Kurram, and Bolan, and Ghilzai irregulars to raid and harass British communication lines. This strategy failed: the invaders swept aside their Afghan opponents in a matter of weeks. Sher Ali then concentrated his forces in the northern provinces to marry up with the Russians. Russian support, however, was not forthcoming. The death of Sher Ali opened the way for talks at Gandamak. Further fighting resolved into harassing tactics and opposing the British advance to Kabul. Against Roberts outside Kabul in the winter of 1879–1880, the Afghan Commander, Mohammed Jan, was able to launch co-ordinated attacks, but he faced a redoubtable foe. Subsequently, Afghan leaders vied with each other for political power, negotiating with the British where it was to their advantage. Their method of war was favoured by the wild and rugged country, with narrow defiles made for ambush.[17] The Russians observed with interest, but despite British suspicions, they did not intervene.

The British war aim was to secure a compliant Afghan leader who would keep out the Russians and provide a buffer. Lytton should have realized that his invasion was a failure of this policy. Nonetheless, early British successes enabled them to obtain an agreement with Sher Ali's successor, his son Yakub Khan, to send a diplomatic mission to Kabul to enforce their policy. This also failed. However, with Roberts's successful defence of Kabul, emphasis in fighting shifted to Kandahar and to diplomatic endeavours to find a suitable candidate as Amir. Abdur Rahman appeared to be the best choice, but the British had to first deal with his rival, the formidable Ayub Khan. Victory against Ayub by Roberts in battle outside Kandahar allowed the British to withdraw with military prestige restored. The concluding phase of the war followed their departure – the fight between Ayub and Abdur.

The Course of the War

On 21 November 1878, Lytton and Colley launched three attacking columns totalling 36,000 men with 248 guns. As Lieutenant-General Donald Stewart, commanding 12,600 men of the Kandahar Field Force, wrote, this force was too small to occupy Afghanistan or interfere with the country's administration, but it could prevent the Amir making friends 'with people who can damage us', namely the Russians.[18]

---

[17] Johnson, *Afghan Way of War*, 110.
[18] George Robert Elsmie, *Field Marshal Sir Donald Stewart: An Account of his Life* (London: John Murray, 1903), 214.

Stewart advanced through the Bolan Pass and captured Kandahar with scarcely any casualties, but his transport suffered heavily with the loss of 12,000 camels. The smallest column of 6,600 men commanded by Major-General Frederick Roberts secured a spectacular victory in a high-risk operation in the Kurram Valley. The largest force under Lieutenant-General Sir Sam Browne seized the fortress of Ali Masjid at the mouth of the Khyber Pass. Browne's column went on to take Dakka at the west end of the Khyber and then Jalalabad, the capital of the region. On Christmas Eve, news reached India of Sher Ali's flight to Russia and his eldest son Yakub's assumption of authority. Sher Ali had decided on 10 December to travel to Russia to plead with the Tsar for help even though the Russians had already told him by letter to make terms with the British. He was refused entry and died at Balkh on 21 February 1879.

The Viceroy ordered a mission led by Major Louis Cavagnari to negotiate a settlement with Yakub. Cavagnari was an experienced frontier soldier and administrator. He and Yakub negotiated at Gandamak. Inauspiciously, the bleached bones of the remnant of the 44th Regiment of Foot who made their last stand there in 1842 were plainly visible. Negotiation with the British was not popular in Afghanistan. Nonetheless, the Treaty of Gandamak, signed on 26 May 1879, seemed to bring a favourable conclusion to Lytton's war. The new Amir pledged to live 'in perfect peace and friendship' with India and agreed to British control of Afghan foreign policy in return for troops, arms, and money if a foreign power attacked. A British Agent was to reside at Kabul and a telegraph line would run thence to the Kurram. In return for a subsidy of six lakhs (600,000 rupees), the Khyber, Kurram, and Quetta enclaves were 'assigned' to the British as protectorates, rather than 'annexed', suggesting a chance that they could be returned.[19]

With fighting apparently over, Browne's Khyber column was largely disbanded, and Stewart's force ordered to leave Kandahar. Roberts's column was to garrison and administer the Kurram Valley. In mid-July, Cavagnari with an escort of seventy-five men from the Corps of Guides, set forth for Kabul as British representative. Despite his high spirits, foreboding overhung the occasion. In all minds was the fate of Alexander Burnes, the late British envoy, who was murdered at Kabul in 1841. The escort was on constant alert.[20] In London, former Viceroy John Lawrence foretold the worst: 'They will all be killed'.[21]

---

[19] Robson, *Road to Kabul*, 111–13.
[20] Colonel H. B. Hanna, *The Second Afghan War*, vol. 2 (London, Constable & Co, 1899–1910), 345.
[21] Harold Lee, *Brothers in the Raj: The Lives of John and Henry Lawrence* (Karachi: Oxford University Press, 2002), 416.

In early September, Cavagnari and his escort were attacked by overwhelming numbers, six Herati regiments supported by the Kabuli *badmashes* (bandits). After several hours of fierce fighting against impossible odds, Cavagnari and his escort were killed, just as Lawrence had predicted. Only a small party which had been dispatched to cut grass survived. Over 400 of the attackers were dead. The shock of the news reaching Lytton at Simla brought a rapid reply. Roberts was ordered to march with his small force from the Kurram to Kabul, eighty-five miles distant, occupy the capital, find the culprits, and exact imperial vengeance. Stewart reoccupied Kandahar.[22]

Roberts's force was hampered by limited transport, allowing him to move only one section at a time. Nevertheless, he had very capable troops in the hard-fighting Highlanders and Gurkhas. Near the village of Charasiab, en route to Kabul, Roberts again defeated well-entrenched Afghans and occupied the capital. Roberts's father had accompanied an Anglo-Indian army to the region in 1838 and he eagerly anticipated this occasion. He inspected Sherpur outside the city, a great parallelogram of a cantonment, 2,700 yards by 1,100, as yet incomplete. Here the British found most of Yakub's extensive artillery, no less than 214 guns.[23] He visited the Bala Hissar and the Residency where Cavagnari and the Guides had made their last stand. The reporter, Howard Hensman, accompanying the column wrote: '[W]e entered the main court of the Residency, and were soon thoroughly able to appreciate the fate of its defenders ... The whitewashed walls are here and there bespattered with blood ... a desperate struggle had taken place in this room, the blood stains on the floor and walls being clearly discernible'.[24]

At this stage, it appeared Roberts hoped to establish a permanent British presence. This was never realistic. The costs of permanent occupation were too great.[25] The British also discussed partition. This plan too was dropped.

Meanwhile, Roberts with the aid of two judicial commissions, exacted vengeance for the deaths of Cavagnari and the Guides. The hanging of eighty-nine Afghans on two tall gallows outside the city walls

---

[22] Betty Balfour (ed.), *Personal and Literary Letters of Roberts, 1st Earl Lytton*, vol. 2 (London: Constable, 1906), 196.

[23] Roberts Diary 1879, Entries 10th and 11th Oct, National Army Museum; Charles Low, *Major-General Sir Frederick Roberts* (London: W. H. Allen & Co, 1883), 248n; IOL, L/MIL/5/681, nos. 7926 and 7927, British Library.

[24] Durand Papers, Item PP Ms55/21 (Diary 1875–1880), Entry 15 Oct 1879, SOAS; William Trousdale, *The War in Afghanistan: The Personal Diary of Major General Sir Charles Metcalfe Macgregor 1879–1880* (Detroit: Wayne State University Press, 1985), 104; Howard Hensman, *The Afghan War of 1879–1880* (London: W. H. Allen, 1881), 54.

[25] Johnson, *Afghan Way of War*, 27.

exacerbated, but did not originate, hatred of the foreigner. Roberts found it difficult to gather intelligence. Nonetheless in early December, he learnt of a planned assault led by an able Afghan artillery commander, Mahomed Jan. In confused fighting in the valleys outside Kabul, Roberts himself was unhorsed and rescued from untimely death by an Indian *sowar* (cavalryman). He withdrew into Sherpur. There on the early morning of 23 December, his force beat off a mass assault. As Afghan efforts weakened, he ordered four guns escorted by cavalry to leave the cantonment and bring flanking fire onto the attackers. Next morning, Brigadier-General Charles Gough's relieving force arrived, having advanced through a snowy and silent countryside.[26]

With Roberts's successful defence complete, the war slept through winter. In Britain, the conflict was not popular. Liberal opposition found a cause in 'Bulgarian Atrocities' committed by the Turks in 1876. Blunders in Zululand lent further strength to Gladstone's famous Midlothian campaign. Press attacks on Roberts's hangings began in India's English-language newspapers and spread to Britain, making the situation for the Conservatives even worse.[27] In the Commons, MP and military commentator, Charles Dilke, and others questioned discrepancies between Lytton's statements and Roberts's despatches.[28] On Lytton's advice, Roberts prepared counter-arguments. His letter was read by Viscount Cranbrook, Secretary of State for India, in the House of Lords on 13 February, offering 'a short explanation of what has really occurred since we entered Afghanistan last September', justifying martial law and prohibiting firearms 'among a nation of fanatics' and denying that Afghans were 'hanged for the simple fact of their having fought against us'. There was enough truth in the letter to make it plausible. The Lords applauded it with 'loud cheers from both sides of the House'. A *Times* leader declared that the letter 'sets at rest some very painful questions', that it would be 'ridiculous' to complain of the actions of a General exposed to such dangers.[29] The advantage of a good pen enabled the government to survive the immediate storm although difficult questions continued. On 13 December, contrary to Roberts's claim that no one was executed without trial, war correspondent Hensman reported four *Maliks* (Chieftains) and four servants were shot out of hand.[30]

---

[26] Robson, *Road to Kabul*, 164.
[27] Frederic Harrison, *Martial Law in Kabul* (London: Chapman and Hall, 1880), reprinted from the *Fortnightly Review*.
[28] For example, Hansard, Commons Debates, 15 Feb 1880, vol. 251, CC. 1008–09.
[29] Hansard, House of Lords debates, 13 Feb 1880, vol. 250, CC. 579–82; *The Times*, 14 February 1880, 6, 9.
[30] Hanna, *Second Afghan War*, vol. 3, 272–74: Hensman, *Afghan War*, 204.

Roberts's harsh methods caused the Indian government to order Donald Stewart to march from Kandahar to Kabul to take command. Kandahar had been quiet, aided by a good harvest in southern Afghanistan. A British agent, Gholam Hussein Khan, had transferred there as Governor; 'by his wisdom and justice he had become most popular with the Afghans'.[31] The local Wali Sher Ali would eventually succeed as ruler of Kandahar, a plan which Stewart supported.[32] At Kabul, however, there was still no political solution. Rivals for the Amirship, Abdur Rahman, Sher Ali's nephew and pensionary of the Russians, and Ayub Khan, Sher Ali's son and Herati Sirdar, were on the move.[33]

Stewart was unhappy leaving Major-General Primrose behind to command in Kandahar, 'a very poor selection ... neither safe nor strong I fancy', he wrote. Primrose's Bombay troops were new to the region, ignorant of 'ways & methods of dealing with the people'.[34] On 27 March 1880 Stewart mustered 7,249 men, 7,272 followers, and more than 11,000 animals, with six weeks' supplies, and set out through a bleak and empty countryside. The march was carried out under stringent discipline, 'neither troops nor followers allowed to enter a village except when detailed as part of an organised foraging party'. The weather was good, frosty at night, warm and sunny by day, and the roads were reasonably easy. Signs of impending opposition were confirmed on 18 April with intelligence of 9,000 Ghilzais moving on a parallel track ten miles away. The next morning, a patrol sent by Stewart found the Ghilzais's camp deserted. The expected battle, a British victory, occurred at Ahmed Khel later that day (see 'Anatomy of a Battle: Ahmed Khel' section).

Stewart's march continued. Three miles beyond the fortress of Ghazni, 6,000 Afghans reinforced by local inhabitants held the villages Arzu and Shalez, strongly entrenched with a mud and stone wall. Stewart sent 2,800 men to the attack. British artillery could not smash the wall, a feigned retreat failed to draw out the defenders and Stewart brought up reinforcements. Not wishing to face British firepower a second time, the Afghans retreated from the villages. Stewart reported Afghan losses as 500.[35] On 1 May, Stewart

---

[31] Hansard, Lords Debates, Tribute by Napier, 4 Aug 1879, vol. 249, C. 19.
[32] Elsmie, Sir Donald Stewart, Stewart to Wife, 16 March 1880, 315–16.
[33] Major-General C. M. MacGregor, *The Second Afghan War* (Simla and Calcutta: Government Printer, 1885–86), vol. 5, 258; Barfield, *Afghanistan*, 142.
[34] Dolaucothi L3651 and L3653, 7 and 26 March 1880, National Library of Wales, Aberystwyth.
[35] 5 May 1880, IOL, L/MIL/5/683, no. 11,834, British Library; E. F. Chapman, 'Two years under Field-Marshal Sir Donald Stewart in Afghanistan 1878–1880', *Blackwoods Magazine* (1902); Johnson, *Afghan Way of War*, 127–28.

reached the Argandeh Valley where 'Bobs came out to see me, looking very jolly and well'. He entered Kabul the next day and took command.

During the march, news reached the soldiers in Afghanistan of the British election.[36] Results marked a huge swing to the Liberals, who secured a majority of 137. Stewart told his wife a Liberal victory would upset 'everything that is being done here'.[37] Roberts told Colley that he was much upset by press reports of him 'as a murderer'.[38] Early in June, he telegraphed to Lytton for permission to leave Kabul and retire from the campaign, partly for his health: 'I am quite happy with General Stewart but my wish to leave is so strong I trust your Lordship will approve of my doing so'. Lytton replied with sympathy but wisely urged his general 'not to leave your post till close of war ... I feel sure your premature retirement would be generally misinterpreted to your great detriment'.[39] Roberts's friend James Hills, Governor of Kabul during its occupation, also offered encouragement in 'a very cheery letter telling him he must stick to his task till the very end'.[40] Roberts was convinced, fortunately for his future.

In the aftermath of the election, Lytton resigned rather than serve under the Liberals who had attacked him. His successor was the Liberal peer Lord Ripon, one of his critics. Ripon inherited a stalemated war: despite Roberts's and Stewart's victories, the British controlled only towns garrisoned and ground covered by their guns, although they were too strong for the Afghans to eject. The daily grind of convoy guards, skirmishes, and ambushes took a toll on Anglo-Indian morale.[41] Lytton had sought a political solution, and found it in his biblical phrase, 'a ram caught in a thicket'.[42] Abdur Rahman, Sher Ali's nephew and former pensionary of the Russians, was the best candidate for British purposes and played his cards well. To the Afghans he was 'a champion of the prophet', but to the British he would be a bulwark against the Russians. His aim, to ensure there would be no British envoy at Kabul, removed a possible source of conflict, judging by Cavagnari's fate. Abdur Rahman was greeted by local Amirs in friendship and by tribesmen with joyful fusillades of rifle shots. Leaders of Afghan resistance accepted him, knowing the British would evacuate once he was in power. Stewart was

---

[36] Elsmie, *Sir Donald Stewart*, 344.   [37] Ibid., 321.
[38] Brian Robson (ed.), *Roberts in India: The Military Papers of Field Marshal Lord Roberts 1876–1893* (Stroud: Army Records Society, 1993), 157, 160–61; also, Roberts to Burne, 1 Feb 1880, Eur Mss D951/3, f. 161.
[39] David James, *Lord Roberts* (London: Clowes & Son, 1954), 146–47.
[40] Dolaucothi L13663, 4 June 1880; Hills to V. Pugh, 14 Aug 1880, L14205, National Library of Wales.
[41] Robson, *Afghan Way of War*, 128–29.   [42] Genesis 22:13.

eager to withdraw the army to preserve the morale of Indian regiments, too long far from home, once a political solution was reached. Costs of the campaign soared as it became increasingly difficult to gather supplies. On 27 June, Abdur Rahman with some ambiguity accepted Ripon's terms. At a durbar at Kabul on 22 July, he was declared Amir.[43]

Abdur Rahman had a rival, however, in Ayub Khan, son of Sher Ali, Herati Sirdar, able leader and soldier, also a self-avowed champion of the Prophet. British intelligence reported Ayub had seventeen infantry regiments and impressive artillery. Ayub had to delay his planned advance from Herat until he had settled internal squabbles. The trigger for his march was the proclamation of Abdur Rahman as Amir. In hot weather, Ayub led his force 253 miles in just twenty-five days. From Primrose's Kandahar garrison a brigade was dispatched (not two brigades as some accounts state) to support the irregulars of the British-nominated Wali of Kandahar, Sher Ali, against Ayub. The Wali's men deserted to their supposed enemy.[44] On 27 July at Maiwand, Brigadier Burrows's 2,000 riflemen, 500 sabres, and twelve guns faced Ayub's 8,000 regular troops, thirty-two guns, 3,000 other mounted men, with irregular tribesmen and ghazis.[45] The Afghan guns were well served and Ayub made use of a shallow ravine running parallel to the British front to give cover against rifle and artillery fire. Nonetheless, the British held off Afghan attacks for four hours. However, the withdrawal of smoothbore cannons to replenish ammunition limbers caused inexperienced Indian soldiers to panic, believing their line was collapsing.[46] Defeat came swiftly. A host of Afghans rose from the ravine and folds in the ground to envelope and overwhelm Burrows's line of battle. One hundred men of a veteran British battalion, the 66th (Berkshire), made a heroic stand. Afghan casualties were said to be *beshumar* – 'countless'. An Afghan participant reported them as over 3,000. Burrows lost nearly 1,000 dead and only 168 wounded, an imbalance that showed the hazards of Afghan war 'when the women come out to cut up what remains'.[47]

---

[43] Betty Balfour, *The History of Lord Lytton's Indian Administration 1876 to 1880* (London: Longmans, 1899), 409.

[44] Robson, *Afghan Way of War*, 130–31.   [45] Some accounts give a total of 15,000.

[46] It is alleged that a young heroine, Malalai, saved the day for Ayub when his army wavered. She stood up waving her veil as a standard and calling out, in verse and then song, to rally her countrymen. A bullet then killed her. The story has many improbabilities. No British nor Indian participant saw her. Malalai is a figure helpful to Afghan nation-building.

[47] The best-known line of Rudyard Kipling's 'The Young British Soldier'. For the battle, L. Maxwell, *My God! Maiwand* (London: Leo Cooper, 1979); B. Robson, 'Maiwand, 27th July 1880', *JSAHR* LI (1973): 194–221; Robson, *Road to Kabul*; 'The Kandahar Letters of the Rev. Alfred Cane', *JSAHR* LXIX (1991): 146–60, 206–20; T. A. Heathcote, *Afghan Wars* (London: Osprey, 1980), 148–51.

The Kandahar garrison of 5,000 men and thirteen guns had to defend walls extending 6,000 yards. Primrose expelled the Afghan population to prevent treachery. On 8 August, Ayub's main force arrived and his artillery opened a continuous bombardment. On the 13th, they occupied two suburbs.[48] Ripon and his Commander-in-Chief, Haines, decided to launch two relief forces, one under Major-General Robert Phayre by the obvious route from Quetta, the other an elite force under Roberts from Kabul to retrace Stewarts's previous route in reverse.[49] By virtue of his local rank in Afghanistan, Roberts would supersede Primrose.[50]

From Quetta, Phayre experienced delays assembling transport animals to cross Baluchistan's scorching desert, and faced a tribal uprising fomented by the news of the British defeat at Maiwand. Expecting to start mid-August, he did not march until the 30th, and on 5 September was just drawing clear of the Khojak Pass.[51]

Roberts's 313-mile march in 23 days became legendary. After the publication of MacGregor's journal, the tendency was to belittle it, but this was unjust. It was essential to restore British prestige throughout the empire and Roberts's feat helped accomplish that goal. Indian bazaars were alive with rumours, seriously worrying to India's rulers. Russian sources were clear: 'According to intelligence from India, the Mahommedan population of that country is greatly excited by the advantages which Ayub Khan has so far obtained over the English. In order to suppress this excitement it is necessary, at all hazards, to demolish Ayub Khan's army'.[52] Political officer Lepel Griffin wrote, 'I see immense & national interests at stake in this Kandahar expedition. On its success or failure the most gigantic issues may depend'.[53] The Russian Soboleff wrote, 'General Roberts decided on an heroic exploit, and in spite of its incredible difficulty carried it out'.[54] Much credit for the march's success was due to Chapman, Stewart's Chief of Staff on his march, who was then doing the same job for Roberts. Chapman spelled out the column's debt to the Afghans: 'we owe it to Abdur Rahman's efforts, or to the withdrawal of Mushk-i-alam's fanatical opposition, that the people

[48] Heathcote, *Afghan Wars*, 151–53.
[49] Elsmie, *Sir Donald Stewart*, 375; *Kandahar Correspondence*, 56–57, 61, 68, 66b, 74–74a.
[50] On Primrose, see Caroline Jackson, 'General James Primrose: Reconstructing a life', *JSAHR* 97: 388, 389, 390 (Spring, Summer, Autumn 2019).
[51] Robson, *Road to Kabul*, 251–53.
[52] Merewether Papers, Translation of Russian Abstract, 28 August 1880, OL, Eur Mss D625/14, British Library.
[53] Rodney Atwood, *The Life of Field Marshal Lord Roberts* (London: Bloomsbury Academic, 2015), 104.
[54] Major-General A. N. Soboleff, *The Anglo-Afghan Struggle*, trans. and condensed by Major W. E. Cowan (Calcutta: Government Printer, 1885), 137, 143, 144.

remained to sell their grain and flour'.[55] Abdur Rahman and his allies were sure to help the British knock out his rival, Ayub. Roberts's old friend James Hills shrewdly commented, 'Abdur Rahman ... of course has done everything in his power to keep the tribes quiet who are in Roberts' patch for he wishes him to go along as fast as he can & do what he himself would have to try & do hereafter, namely knock [Ayub] out of turn'.[56] 'This is a grand thing for Bobs', wrote Stewart to his wife, 'If there is any fighting, he can't help being successful, and his success must bring him great credit'.[57]

The speed of the march left native carriers and doolie bearers struggling at the rear. Footsore soldiers with poor footwear fell out. Their commander also suffered, but not from his boots. Near the march's end, Roberts was stricken with what he told his wife and one biographer was a fever,[58] but according to a medical board was a duodenal ulcer. Since autumn 1879, he had suffered from 'a continuous pain in his chest, a feeling of weariness and occasional passing of blood'.[59] He was completely prostrate for four days, and forced to travel in a doolie, a conveyance for the sick. Would he be well enough to command in the coming battle?[60] On the morning of 31 August, however, close to Kandahar, Roberts rose from the doolie, mounted his famous grey, Vonolel, and led in. He requested several thousand pairs of new boots be sent. Nine soldiers and eleven followers were dead or missing.[61]

Roberts's famed 'luck' had given the opportunity to redeem himself after the hangings. Now it placed his enemy for a knock-out blow by the best regiments British India could muster. Ayub was a skilful general, and he held strongly defended villages, walls loop-holed, his formidable artillery ready.[62] The Afghans did not enjoy their usual numerical superiority, at 12,800 being only slightly more numerous than Roberts's men. Ayub's force included 5,000 ghazis, two thirds armed only with sword and spear. Even his guns were outmatched. The Afghans did not understand the fuses on captured British ammunition and consequently few shells burst.[63] British artillery wrought havoc with segment shell, layers of

---

[55] *Kandahar Correspondence*, vol. 1, 228a.
[56] Dolaucothi L14205, 21 August 1880, National Library of Wales; *Kandahar Correspondence*, vol. 1, 228a–230.
[57] Elsmie, *Sir Donald Stewart*, 376.
[58] James, *Lord Roberts*, 159; C. R. Low, *Major-General Sir Frederick Roberts: A Memoir* (London: W. H. Allen, 1883), 365.
[59] Roberts Papers 5504, Item no. 38, Results of a Medical Board of Officers, Kandahar, 8 September 1880, National Army Museum.
[60] Diary quoted, James, *Lord Roberts*, 159.
[61] IOL, L/MIL/5/684, no. 13117, British Library; *Kandahar Correspondence*, vol. 1, 183.
[62] MacGregor, *Second Afghan War*, vol. 6, 36.   [63] *Kandahar Correspondence*, vol. 2, 8.

cast iron balls around an explosive charge. The overwhelming British victory ended with the 92nd (Gordon Highlanders) Regiment and 2nd (Prince of Wales's Own) Gurkha Regiment racing for the enemy guns. All thirty-two were taken including two captured at Maiwand.[64] Roberts, in possibly his only mistake, had sent General Hugh Gough's cavalry too far to the left, and there was no serious pursuit. The victory, however, was decisive enough. Maiwand had been avenged, and the rumors in Indian bazaars subsided. The victors lost forty dead and 228 wounded. They buried 1,200 Afghans on the field and Roberts estimated the enemy wounded to be roughly the same equal number.

Anatomy of a Battle: Ahmed Khel

The Battle of Ahmed Khel has been virtually forgotten, unlike Maiwand and Kandahar, Roberts's subsequent victory. It clearly illustrates, however, British strengths and Afghan weaknesses throughout the campaign.

On 19 April 1880, Stewart's men spotted an Afghan force on a rocky spur and rapidly deployed. British guns opened fire. Scarcely had this been done when 'an enormous mass of men with standards formed on the hilltop [wrote Stewart], a considerable number of horsemen [were] riding along the ridge with the intention of sweeping to the rear of our line to attack the baggage'. Successive waves of swordsmen on foot seemed to envelope the British position. The Afghan horsemen on Stewart's left poured down two ravines and struck a squadron of the 19th Bengal Lancers before they could charge. Stewart thought the situation 'critical' at this juncture, made worse by a mass of 2,000 horsemen at the far end of the Afghan line who galloped down on the British gun batteries. The error of ordering the 59th (2nd Northamptonshire) Foot to take up a fresh position allowed a tidal wave of Afghan swordsmen to strike them while the men were forming up and had not fixed bayonets. The Afghans charged just when Colonel E. F. Chapman, Stewart's Chief of Staff, had ridden forward to tell Brigadier-General R. J. Hughes, commanding the infantry, to prepare for attack. Chapman wrote, 'in an incredibly short space of time two long lines of swordsmen seemed to spring up from the hill ... the whole hill seemed to be moving'. The Afghans' bravery was magnificent, but Captain R. Elias of the 59th Foot wrote, 'Anyone with the semblance of a heart under his khaki jacket could not help feeling

---

[64] Headlam papers, letter from H. L. Gardner, 1 Dec 1935, Royal Artillery Archives, formerly Woolwich; Major-General Sir J. Headlam, *History of the Royal Artillery from the Indian Mutiny to the Great War* (Woolwich, Royal Artillery Institute, 1940), vol. 3, 55–56; MacGregor, *Second Afghan War*, vol. 6, 35–41.

something like pity to see them advancing with their miserable weapons in the face of our guns and rifles'.[65]

The battle had been on a knife edge, the speed of the Afghan advance catching Stewart by surprise. He and his staff drew their swords to defend themselves. Superior weaponry, training, and fire discipline proved decisive. The Indian cavalry made flank attacks, while in the centre the British and Gurkha regiments kept their cohesion and shot down large numbers of the Afghans with volleys. Reserve artillery fired onto the Afghan horsemen heading towards the column's baggage. An hour's fierce fighting decided the battle. The Afghans were thrown back and streamed away. Some 2,000 Hazaras co-operating with Stewart were waiting a mile or two distant and pursued the defeated Ghilzais, killing those they could catch. The Afghans lost an estimated 3,000 killed and wounded, while British losses were seventeen killed and 124 wounded.[66] Over 800 bodies were counted, and later Afghans erected a monument to 1,100 'martyrs' on the battlefield.[67]

Aftermath

The price of war in Afghanistan for British India was heavy in gold but less in men. The conflict cost £19.5 million, of which Britain paid £5 million. The British and Indians lost 1,850 killed in battle, the Afghans, an estimated 5,000.[68]

For British and Indian soldiers, the fighting ended with their evacuation. A special medal was struck for those who marched from Kabul to Kandahar. Stewart would succeed Haines as Commander-in-Chief, India. Roberts would go to Madras (Chennai) to command the southern army before taking over from Stewart. Brigadier Charles Gough wrote that Roberts's victory 'has brought the war to a close in a complete and satisfactory manner and will also completely establish Abdul [sic] Rahman on the throne'.[69] This was only partly true. British statesmen

---

[65] Captain Elias in the *Royal United Services Institute Journal* XXIV, 669–70, as cited in Johnson, *Afghan Way of War*, 127.
[66] Stewart's Dispatch, 5 May 1880, IOL, L/MIL/5/683, no, 11,834, British Library; Chapman's words in, 'Two years under Field-Marshal Sir Donald Stewart', 261–62; Captain Elias's in the *Royal United Services Institute Journal* XXIV, 669–70; Robson, *Road to Kabul*, 192–95, and Johnson, *Afghan Way of War*, 126–27.
[67] Elsmie, *Sir Donald Stewart*, 331–33, 333–35; Chapman, 'Two years under Field-Marshal Sir Donald Stewart', 259–60.
[68] Robson, *Road to Kabul*, appendix 297. Hanna estimated 50,000 deaths altogether. More on each side perished of disease. Hanna, *Second Afghan War*, vol. 3, 564.
[69] Gough Papers 8304-32-204 and 249, 20 November 1879 & 5 September 1880, National Army Museum; cf. Elsmie, *Sir Donald Stewart*, 388.

continued watching Afghanistan, uncertain of the future. The British held Kandahar for the Wali, against the wishes of their new ally Abdur Rahman. The city lay astride the strategic route from Herat to the Bolan Pass. A hot debate was conducted in Parliament as to whether it should be given up. Gladstone's ministry did just that, ignoring the wishes of senior Indian Army soldiers. Meanwhile, Ayub faced a mutiny among his men at Herat. He made overtures to the British laying claim to Kandahar, but they made over the city to Abdur Rahman and, in April, his appointed governor arrived for the handover. Ayub, however, advanced as soon as the British left Kandahar, arriving in July 1881, greeted as Sher Ali's son and victor of Maiwand.

Haines shrewdly wrote that while Roberts had won a 'superb' victory, 'I have constantly to keep the fact prominently before my colleagues that it does not finally dispose of Sirdar Mahomed Ayub Khan as a possible source of future trouble. Many a defeated man has refitted his shattered forces in Herat'.[70] Ayub was a skilful general, but at Kandahar, he was routed and fled west, seeking asylum first in Persia and then, in 1887, in India. Abdur Rahman, 'the Iron Amir', consolidated his rule in a series of bloody internal wars. Intent on internal reform and peace abroad, Alexander II accepted that the Second Afghan War had reduced Afghanistan 'to a tributary of the British Empire'.[71] Britain had secured her aim of a friendly buffer state guarding India's North-West Frontier. This policy worked, although that of weakening the Pashtuns on British India's frontier and launching punitive military expeditions less so, as shown by the Great Frontier Rising of 1897. Abdur Rahman was bound to the British by treaty and fear of military retaliation; despite one or two wobbles, he stayed loyal.[72] The Russians considered the next forty years 'a dark page' in their diplomacy.[73] Not until 1919 would war between Afghans and British recur. By then, the Victorian world had been made anew.

Further Reading

Atwood, Rodney. *The Life of Field Marshal Lord Roberts*. London: Bloomsbury Academic, 2015.

Balfour, Lady Betty. *The History of Lord Lytton's Indian Administration 1876 to 1880*. London: Longmans, 1899.

---

[70] Haines Papers, to Dillon 5 October 1880, 8108/9-32, no. 12, National Army Museum.
[71] Fuller, *Strategy and Power in Russia*, 332–35.
[72] K. Surridge, 'The Ambiguous Amir: Britain, Afghanistan and the 1897 frontier uprising', *Journal of Imperial and Commonwealth History* 36, 3 (Sept 2008): 417–34. Gillard, *Struggle for Asia*, 141.
[73] Marshall, *Russian General Staff and Central Asia*, 139.

Barfield, T. *Afghanistan: A Cultural and Political History*. Princeton: Princeton University Press, 2010.
Chapman, E. F. 'The march from Kabul to Kandahar in August and the battle of the 1st September, 1880'. *Journal of the Royal United Services Institute*, XXV (1882): 282–315.
Elsmie, G. R. *Field Marshal Sir Donald Stewart: An Account of his Life, Mainly in his Own Words*. London: Constable, 1903.
Fuller, W. C. *Strategy and Power in Russia 1600–1914*. Toronto: Maxwell Macmillan, 1992.
Gillard, D. *The Struggle for Asia 1828–1914*. London: Methuen, 1977.
Hanna, H. B. *The Second Afghan War 1878-1879-1880: Its Conduct and its Consequences*. 3 vols. London: Constable & Co, 1899–1910.
— *Lord Roberts in War*. London: Simpkin, Marshall, Hamilton, Kent & Co., 1895.
Heathcote, T. A. *The Afghan Wars 1839–1919*. London: Osprey, 1980.
Hensman, Howard. *The Afghan War 1879–1880*. London: W.H. Allen, 1881.
Hopkirk, Peter. *The Great Game: On Secret Service in High Asia*. London: Murray, 1990.
Johnson, Rob. *The Afghan Way of War*. London: Hurst & Co, 2011.
Lieven, Dominic. *Empire: The Russian Empire and its Rivals from the Sixteenth Century to the Present*. London: Pimlico, 2003.
Maxwell, Leigh. *My God! Maiwand*. London: Leo Cooper, 1979.
Moreman, T. R. *The Army in India and the Development of Frontier Warfare, 1849–1947*. Basingstoke: Macmillan, 1998.
Roberts, Frederick S. *Forty-One Years in India: From Subaltern to Commander-in-Chief*. London: Richard Bentley & Son, 1897.
Robson, Brian. *The Road to Kabul: The Second Afghan War 1878–1881*. Staplehurst: Spellmount, 1996.
Streets, Heather. 'Military influence in late Victorian and Edwardian popular media: The Case of Frederick Roberts'. *Journal of Victorian Culture VIII*, part ii (2003): 231–56.
Trousdale, William. *War in Afghanistan 1879–1880: The Personal Diary of Major General Sir Charles Metcalfe MacGregor*. Detroit: Wayne State University Press, 1985.
Younghusband, G. J. *The Story of the Guides*. London: Macmillan, 1908.

8   The Anglo-Zulu War, 1879

Ian Knight

On 18 December 1877, a meeting took place on the troubled borders between the newly-annexed British colony of the Transvaal and the independent kingdom of Zululand. On a long, low, stony ridge later dignified with the name Conference Hill, Sir Theophilus Shepstone, the Administrator of the Transvaal, met with a party of 500 Zulus, headed by many of the country's leading representatives, including senior councillors of the Zulu King, Cetshwayo kaMpande. Shepstone, who had grown up on the frontiers of the British Cape Colony, and was fluent in several African languages, had moved to Natal not long after it had become a British colony in 1846. Shrewd and inscrutable, he had pursued his own vision of the expansion of British interests in southern Africa and had carefully fostered his own reputation among Africans; he was universally known among Africans as *Somtsewu*, 'Father of Whiteness.'[1]

Shepstone, who had a long history of diplomatic dealings with the Zulu kingdom and expected to be treated with courtesy and respect, found the Zulu mood to be hostile; the King's representatives addressed him sharply, and berated him for failings in his policies. The meeting broke up with angry exchanges, and Shepstone retired insulted and indignant.[2] Yet the outcome did not reflect Shepstone's shortcomings alone, but rather the fact that the relationship between the British and the Zulu kingdom was increasingly strained, and that the Zulus were becoming aware of shifts in British policy which seemed to them increasingly hostile. For many Zulus, indeed, the meeting at Conference Hill would come to be seen as the moment war between the two became inevitable.

---

[1] Jeff Guy, *Theophilus Shepstone and the Forging of Natal* (Pietermaritzburg: University of Natal Press, 2013), 57.
[2] Richard Cope, *Ploughshare of War: The Origins of the Anglo-Zulu War of 1879* (Pietermaritzburg: University of Natal Press, 1999), 162.

Background

The Zulu kingdom was situated north of Natal in the eastern coastal strip between the uKhahlamba (Drakensberg) mountains and the Indian Ocean. A series of economic and ecological pressures had resulted in conflict among the region's cattle-owning African societies and these were exploited, in the early-nineteenth century, by the ambitious King of the small Zulu clan, Shaka kaSenzangakhona. By the mid-1820s, Shaka had incorporated many of his neighbours and had formed a new centralized, economically and militarily strong kingdom.[3] Rumours of his rise had reached the Cape at a time when, in the wake of Napoleon's defeat at Waterloo in 1815, British interests were expanding around the world. In 1824, a group of Cape merchants established contact with Shaka who allowed them to set up a small trading enclave on the shores of a lagoon known as the Bay of Natal. It was a decision Shaka came to regret as it proved a portal through which British interests expanded into the region.

In 1836, many of the Dutch frontier farmers at the Cape resolved to place themselves beyond British authority and trekked into the interior. Concerned that they might use the bay as a means to allow rival European powers to establish themselves in the region, the British government in London decided to secure formal possession of the area. In 1842, British troops clashed with Boer Trekkers and, and after annexing the territory the following year, Natal was established as a colony in 1856.

In effect, the British acquisition of Natal effectively deprived the Zulus of an area over which they had exerted huge influence. White settlement of the colony grew slowly while its African population continued to be inextricably bound to the Zulu kingdom, often through a history of conflict; many of those groups within the colony had either resisted incorporation into the Zulu kingdom or had fled as political refugees. In his capacity as Secretary for Native Affairs, Theophilus Shepstone oversaw the division of land between white settlers and the black population and devised methods of administration that essentially subverted African traditional authority to his own. While managing diplomatic relations with the colony's African neighbours, Shepstone consistently sought to manipulate African society to comport to his own vision of British interests. Nevertheless, despite occasional tensions, successive Zulu Kings took pains to remain on good terms with the British and regarded them as allies within the broader rivalries within the region.

---

[3] John Laband, *Rope of Sand: The Rise and Fall of the Zulu Kingdom in the Nineteenth Century* (Johannesburg: Jonathan Ball, 1995), 19–30.

148   Ian Knight

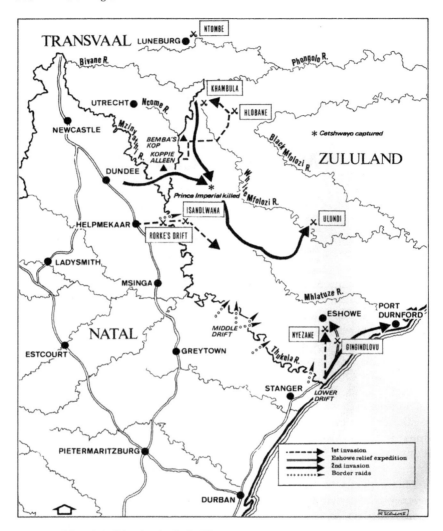

Map 8.1 The Anglo-Zulu War, 1879

For the Zulu, the most pressing diplomatic concern was the growing presence of the Boers on their western flank. Thwarted in Natal, the Boers had established a republic across the mountains in the interior of South Africa, the Zuid Afrikaansche Republiek (ZAR), known as the Transvaal. Throughout the 1860s, Boer frontier farmers began to encroach steadily on land the Zulus considered theirs. Aware of this tension, Shepstone largely supported the Zulu claims in an attempt to negate the spread of Boer influence. In 1873, he attended the ceremonies to install a new Zulu King, Cetshwayo kaMpande. Cetshwayo was glad to receive the show of British support, and worked to maintain the good, albeit sometimes volatile, relations which had existed between the Zulus and the British since 1824. At the same time, he was well aware of the paradigm of British expansion in southern Africa; 'First', he said, 'comes the trader. Then the missionary. Then the red soldier',[4]

Tensions between the British and Boers grew in southern Africa considerably as the economic value of the region rose after the discovery of diamonds in 1867 in the area around what later became known as Kimberley. For Imperial visionaries like Shepstone, the land offered untapped markets; the people, cheap labour. The solution proposed in the early 1870s by the Colonial Secretary, Lord Carnarvon, to safeguard British interests was Confederation, which would bring together the region's disparate groups under loose but effective British control, a scheme which he had enacted in Canada just a few years earlier. It was not, however, without obvious challenges since not only could many of the African and Boer groups be expected to resist but the largest British colony, the Cape, would need to be reassured that it would not have to bear the costs. London proposed a careful wielding of the stick and carrot, championing the advantages of the scheme whilst hinting at coercion for those who did not. In 1877, at Shepstone's prompting, Britain annexed the Transvaal, as a key element in the confederation, citing the republic's financial difficulties and conflicts with its African neighbours. The move caught the most Republican elements in the Transvaal by surprise, and Shepstone convinced himself that the lack of immediate opposition meant that the Boers acquiesced to the move.

At the same time, a new British High Commissioner was sent to the Cape with instructions to implement Confederation.[5] Sir Henry Bartle Frere was an experienced Imperial proconsul who had enjoyed a distinguished career in India, and whose ability to act on his own initiative in Britain's interests had afforded him considerable leeway. Frere brought with him a global perspective on British affairs locally, a wariness of rival European powers, and even a suspicion that Cape Town itself might be vulnerable to attack by Russian gun-boats.[6] For Frere, the resolution of

---

[4] Frank Emery, *The Red Soldier: Letters from the Zulu War 1879* (London: Hodder and Stoughton, 1977), title page.
[5] Cope, *Ploughshare of War*, 196–216.
[6] Damien P. O'Conner, *The Zulu and the Raj: The Life of Sir Bartle Frere* (Knebworth: Able Publishing, 2002), 98–101.

local conflicts was a matter of some urgency as a step towards ensuring unchallenged British influence across the region.

Frere quickly came to the conclusion that the suppression of remaining indigenous African independence would greatly aid the cause, not least by offering a promise of British military protection to settlers across the colonies and republics, but also by making African groups themselves compliant. In the Ninth Cape Frontier War, 1877–78, for example, Frere attempted to crush the Xhosa once and for all. With the annexation of the Transvaal, however, Britain had inherited the ZAR's long-standing boundary dispute with the Zulus and it was the Zulus who enjoyed the most formidable military reputation in the region. Influenced by Shepstone, Frere came to believe that the Zulus posed the most obvious threat to the safe implementation of Confederation.

* * * * *

In its immediate aftermath, the literature of the war was largely confined to the official *Narrative of Operations Connected with the Zulu War of 1879* and the reminiscences of British officers who took part. Although rich in insight into their personal experiences, it was inevitably limited in perspective, with little attention devoted to the politics of the war, the view of the ordinary British soldier or of the Zulus. The controversies surrounding Lord Chelmsford's actions resulted in a selective editing of his papers by the Hon. Gerald French, published in 1939 as *Lord Chelmsford and the Zulu War*, but it was not until 1948 that a professional historian, Sir Reginald Coupland, published the first study of the iSandlwana (Isandlwana) campaign, *Zulu Battle Piece*. Despite interviewing at least one Zulu veteran of the campaign, however, Coupland limited himself entirely to British sources, thus embodying the limitations of studies of the war to that point. In 1964, however, the feature film *Zulu* – based on the battle of Rorke's Drift – reignited popular interest in the war and it was followed two years later by Donald R. Morris's monumental and gripping popular history, *The Washing of the Spears.* Morris's view of both events at iSandlwana and of Zulu society was largely based on colonial interpretations, however, and a vigorous analysis of iSandlwana by F. W. D. Jackson, published initially in the *Journal of the Society for Army Historical Research* (1965) and later revised and expanded as *The Hill of the Sphinx*, effectively challenged much of Morris's interpretation. The advent of the centenary led to fresh studies within South Africa which, in the case of Jeff Guy, considered the war within a broader context of economic and social conflict, while John Laband re-interpreted the war from the hitherto largely ignored Zulu sources. Indeed, Laband's *Rope of Sand* (1993) offered a ground-breaking history of the nineteenth-century Zulu kingdom with the Zulus at the forefront of their own story. Laband's work with Paul Thompson in mapping the sites rescued the battlefields from becoming a largely mythologized landscape. By the 1990s, academic scholarship was increasingly influencing popular history to present a more even-handed and complex approach to the war in books such as Ian Knight's *Brave Men's Blood* and *Zulu Rising*.

Outbreak of War

Cetshwayo regarded the British in Natal as a friendly power and yet, as an independent ruler and a traditionalist who set great store by Zulu history and custom, he was not prepared to see his country subverted by his neighbours. He had hoped that British intercession in the Transvaal might bring an end to the festering border dispute but once it was clear that in fact the British would support the Boers, he attempted to ward off an open breach by diplomacy whilst at the same time preparing his people for the possibility that they might have to fight in defence of their country.

Frere's opinion that the British should wage war against the Zulu was reinforced by their seemingly aggressive attitude displayed at Conference Hill. He hoped that the disputed boundary with the Transvaal might provide a *casus belli* but in fact a Boundary Commission appointed to look into the dispute in March 1878 largely vindicated the Zulu position. Frere refused initially to release the report and, in July 1878, a growing frustration among the Zulu border communities led to an incident which played into his hands. Two wives of Sihayo kaXongo, a Zulu border Chieftain, deserted their husband and took refuge on the Natal bank, provoking Sihayo's sons to cross the border, arrest them, return them to Zulu soil, and execute them according to tradition.[7] In fact, such 'hot pursuit' actions were relatively common on both sides and tolerated; now, however, Frere interpreted the move as proof of Cetshwayo's defiance and aggressive intent. After consulting with his military adviser, Lieutenant-General Lord Chelmsford, Frere called Zulu representatives to a meeting on 11 December 1878. He told them that the Boundary Commission had found largely in their favour, but the award was conditional upon Cetshwayo disbanding the Zulu military system and accepting a British resident at his court. He was given thirty days to comply – if he did not, he would find himself at war. Frere was acting

---

[7] Ian Knight, *Zulu Rising, The Epic Story of iSandlwana and Rorke's Drift* (London: Macmillan, 2010), 7–11.

considerably beyond his authority. Already involved in the Second Afghan War (see Chapter 7), the Disraeli government was reluctant to sanction adventures elsewhere; Frere, however, gambled that by the time the government could respond, he would already be at war and he did not expect the campaign to be a long or difficult one.

British and Zulu Forces

Although the Zulu military system was the cornerstone of national defence it was not a full-time professional body. It was essentially a part-time citizen militia in which all young men were conscripted into regiments, called *amabutho*, and required to provide both civil and military service to the king when required.[8] The system was designed to give the king direct control over the country's most important resource, its manpower, and bonding within each *ibutho* was strengthened by regimental names, the common age of the members, and by distinctive ceremonial uniforms of feathers and furs. In fact, however, although large royal homesteads existed to serve as barracks when the army was assembled, logistical practicalities meant that the regiments were only mustered for short periods, and the men spent most of their time living with their families. Although membership of the *amabutho* was a life-time obligation, the burden fell mostly on younger regiments. Marriage was an important rite of passage within Zulu society marking the onset of full adult responsibilities, and the system tacitly acknowledged that it brought about different priorities. Married men were exempt from the brunt of service, and were only expected to muster for great national ceremonies or in times of serious crisis; for that reason, the Zulu kings had assumed the prerogative to grant permission to marry, something which they did en masse, when the men within a particular ibutho were in their late 30s and were reaching the end of their most energetic period of service.

Each ibutho was divided into wings and companies and the senior officers were appointed by the King. Traditionally, the Zulus fought at close-quarters with a large, cow-hide shield and a short spear designed for stabbing, and their tactics had been developed to allow as many men to reach close combat as possible. Known as *izimpondo zankomo*, the 'horns of the beast', their favourite attack formation was an encircling one in which the most mature, experienced regiments launched a frontal assault in a body known as the 'chest' while younger, faster regiments

---

[8] Ian Knight, *The Anatomy of the Zulu Army: From Shaka to Cetshwayo* (London: Greenhill Books, 1995), 61–95.

swept round in 'horns' on either side. Although the warrior ethic pervaded Zulu life, by 1879 few of the younger regiments had any practical experience, while only a small number of older men had taken part in the last war against whites, a clash with the Boer Voortrekkers in 1838. The King and his military advisers were well aware of the growing impact firearms had and attempts had been made to import firearms in large numbers. The vast majority were obsolete patterns, however, often in poor condition, and supplied with limited powder and shot. The limitations of their guns became apparent in the early stages of the forthcoming conflict and reinforced their natural conservatism and reliance on traditional weapons.

Chelmsford, the senior British military officer in southern Africa, was an experienced commander who had fought in the Crimean War and the Indian Rebellion (see Chapter 1), and had served on the staff of the expedition to Abyssinia (see Chapter 4). He was an establishment figure, conservative in his views toward the military, and enjoyed royal support. As a commander, he lacked dash but he was thorough and practical, and cautious of the lives of his men.[9] Most recently, he had commanded during the later stages of the Ninth Frontier War where he had formed distinct impressions of local African fighting techniques. In his view, the enemy could seldom be drawn into an open fight but, when it was, it could be defeated by superior firepower. Despite the fact that he commissioned an intelligence report which meticulously noted the strength, organization, and tactics of the Zulu army, Chelmsford could not quite free himself from that early impression of local warfare.

Like most Victorian commanders in colonial theatres, Chelmsford was short of resources. He had at his disposal just eight battalions of regular infantry, two artillery batteries, some companies of Engineers, and no regular cavalry. In addition, he was able to draw upon the Royal Naval to supply a Naval Brigade. To make up for his wanting numbers, he had to turn to Natal. The colony maintained a number of small, part-time mounted volunteer units for local defence and, after some resistance, the Natal government agreed to make these available. A much larger resource was Natal's African population, most of which was historically antagonistic towards the Zulu kingdom; the Natal government, however, was reluctant to arm them for fear of possible insurrection, and it was only at the very end of 1878 that they gave way. Several regiments of both mounted and infantry auxiliaries – the Natal Native Contingent – were raised but while the small, mounted units were efficiently organized and equipped, the foot

---

[9] John Laband (ed.), *Lord Chelmsford's Zulu Campaign 1878–1879* (Stroud: Alan Sutton, 1994), xix–xxviii.

contingents were only issued one firearm for every ten men, and for the rest carried the same weapons as their Zulu counterparts.

On the eve of war, Chelmsford's forces totalled just over 5,000 infantry, 1,500 mounted troops and 10,000 auxiliaries.[10] British reports numbered Cetshwayo's army at 40,000 men – in fact no more than 25,000 would be fielded on any single occasion.[11]

Strategy and War Aims

Chelmsford was painfully aware that he was fighting the Zulu on their terrain. In order to contain an enemy much more mobile than his own force, Chelmsford initially planned to invade from five different points along the Natal and Transvaal borders, converging on Cetshwayo's royal homestead oNdini (Ulundi). Yet Zululand possessed no roads, only a series of traders' wagon tracks, and Chelmsford's troops would be required to carry all their supplies and equipment – food, ammunition, tents – with them. A frantic scurry towards the end of 1878 saw his transport requirement bolstered by civilian wagons bought or hired from the settler population at extortionate rates, but even so it was still impossible to equip five offensive columns. Two were reduced to supporting defensive roles and, instead, Chelmsford planned to invade with three columns – one advancing up the most direct route from Natal along Zululand's coastal tracks, another through the central border via Rorke's Drift, and the third from the disputed Transvaal border in the north. Chelmsford's greatest fear was that he would not be able to bring the Zulus to battle, and that by advancing from separate points upon oNdini he would give the Zulus no option but to fight. Once he did, he was entirely convinced that superior British firepower would win the day. Neither he, Frere, nor Shepstone expected the campaign would last long; the prevailing view in Natal was that Cetshwayo was an unpopular tyrant, and that the kingdom could collapse at the first sharp shove.[12]

Cetshwayo was determined to act only on the defensive and within his own borders, hoping that the role of the injured party would serve him well in future peace negotiations. In fact, the Zulu army had only limited logistical support and it was important, therefore, that it strike quickly. Lacking the resources to attack all the British columns at once, the King and his councillors intended to strike at them piecemeal, and hope that

---

[10] Intelligence Branch, War Office, *Narrative of the Field Operations Connected with the Zulu War of 1879* (London: HMSO, 1881), 145–46.
[11] Laband, *Rope of Sand*, 219.
[12] Laband (ed.), *Lord Chelmsford's Zululand Campaign*, xxxiv.

any victory would force the British to negotiate. Despite the odds of a pre-industrial society taking on the greatest world power of the age, morale within the Zulu army was high, fuelled by widespread indignation at British presumption.[13]

The Course of the War

As Frere had intended, Cetshwayo could not comply with the British demands. The Zulu army, including the married amabutho, was mustered and ritually prepared for war. Yet Cetshwayo still hoped a direct confrontation might be avoided and resolved to hold his troops at oNdini until the British intentions became apparent. That happened quickly enough.

Even before the ultimatum expired on 11 January 1879, the British left (No. 4) column, commanded by Colonel H. Evelyn Wood crossed into territory claimed by the Zulu. On the British right, the coastal column (No. 1), under Colonel Charles Pearson, was forced to delay its advance until the 12th due to the sudden onset of heavy rains which raised the level of the Thukela (Tugela) river.

Chelmsford himself had decided to accompany his Centre Column (No. 3), which he regarded as his main thrust. Punctilious to form, he crossed the Mzinyathi River, the boundary, at Rorke's Drift early on the morning of 11 January. The crossing was unopposed, and, on the opposite bank, Chelmsford established his first camp on Zulu soil. A few miles directly ahead of him, the track passed close to the homestead of Sihayo kaXongo. Chelmsford was keen to underline the punitive façade of the British invasion, and in any case could not afford to leave a potentially hostile Zulu force unchallenged. The next morning, he took most of his troops to attack Sihayo. Neither Sihayo nor his senior sons were at home, however; they were attending the muster at oNdini, and his homestead was defended by only 200 warriors. After a sharp skirmish among the boulders of a line of cliffs – an incident reminiscent of the fighting on the Cape frontier – the Zulus were dispersed, and Sihayo's homestead was looted and burned.[14] Chelmsford noted that the Zulus had fought well but had been dispersed easily enough; the first hint that an air of complacency was settling over him and his men.

Once news reached oNdini of the incident, the King considered his options. Of the invading columns the Centre Column appeared the most aggressive. Cetshwayo, his Commander-in-Chief, Mnyamana Buthelezi,

---

[13] Knight, *Zulu Rising*, 248. [14] Ibid., 206–17.

and his generals decided on a strategy of containment against the flanking columns while directing their main response against the British centre. Zulu loyalists in the north and coastal districts were directed to harass the invaders in their areas, and while a detachment of royal amabutho from oNdini, about 5,000 men under Godide kaNdlela, was despatched to support resistance at the coast, the rest were directed against Chelmsford. On 17 January, the Zulu army set out, some 25,000 men, under the command of two of the king's most trusted generals, Ntshingwayo kaMahole and Mavumengwana kaNdlela marching towards Rorke's Drift.

In the coastal district, slowed by the recent rains, Pearson's column advanced through the undulating countryside towards a deserted mission station called Eshowe, situated thirty miles from the border. Chelmsford ordered him to construct a supply depot and be prepared to co-ordinate future movements with the progress of the remaining columns. Early on the morning of 22 January, while his wagons were crossing the narrow Nyezane River, Pearson's scouts spotted Zulu parties on a hill directly ahead. He ordered his auxiliaries to drive them off but the ensuing skirmish brought forth a much larger force: 6,000 Zulus, a mix of local elements and the amabutho despatched from oNdini, had been shadowing Pearson for the past twenty-four hours.[15] Godide hoped to attack the British on the road but the river encounter had provoked the attack prematurely. As Pearson hurried his men up the track and formed a firing line, Godide hurriedly tried to manoeuvre his amabutho. Only the uMxhapho regiment of the left horn was able to deploy properly, sweeping round towards the British rear but it was eventually checked by heavy fire.[16] As the Zulu attack stalled, Pearson counter-attacked forcing the Zulus to withdraw. Pearson lost just fifteen men; the Zulus, as many as 400. The battle demonstrated Zulu courage but the outcome was largely shaped by the poor co-ordination of the Zulu attacks, their lack of sufficient numbers, and the discipline of British troops. The following day, the British occupied Eshowe.

Meanwhile, Lord Chelmsford remained at Rorke's Drift, his advance delayed by the poor state of the roads. On 20 January, he ordered his forces forward and reached the foot of a rocky outcrop known as iSandlwana, an isolated sandstone peak rising some 400 feet from the

[15] Ian Castle and Ian Knight, *Fearful Hard Times: The Siege and Relief of Eshowe* (London: Greenhill Books, 1994), 49–73.
[16] In Pearson's force was a single Gatling gun, landed by men of HMS *Active*, and although it jammed after a short burst, this was the first time a machine gun was used in a hostile action by a British force.

surrounding plain and looking eerily like – as the men noted – the sphinx badge of the 24th Regiment. He established camp laid out in regimental blocks across the forward slopes at the foot of the hill. Although the view ahead was clear for about twelve miles, it was shut in by a high ridge a mile away to the south and a lower escarpment just a few hundred yards to the north. The camp, intended to be temporary, was not subject to Chelmsford's standing orders for permanent camps, and therefore there was no attempt to fortify it.

Indeed, Chelmsford's intelligence sources suggested that the main Zulu army was advancing to confront him. Scouting ahead with his staff, he identified the hills to the south as a vulnerable spot, and, the following day, he directed most of his auxiliary and mounted troops, commanded by Major John Dartnell, to scour through them. Spending an exhausting day marching through miles of rugged country, Dartnell found most of the Zulu homesteads deserted as the men had gone to join the King's army and the non-combatants had fled into hiding. Late that evening, however, at the furthest point of their reconnaissance, Dartnell's men encountered several hundred Zulus crossing their front. Chelmsford's orders had been to return to iSandlwana that night, but concerned that his men would be vulnerable in the dark and that the intelligence value of his discovery would be lost, Dartnell opted to remain and sent a report back to Chelmsford.[17]

The report reached Chelmsford at about 2.30 a.m. on the 22nd and presented a dilemma. The Zulus seemed to be acting as he had anticipated, avoiding an open fight and instead exploiting the difficult terrain on his right front. If he waited until morning the Zulu might either overrun Dartnell or simply melt into the hills. Chelmsford decided to act promptly. Unable to move out immediately with his entire column, he decided instead to split his force, took half his men and left the rest to guard the tents and baggage. As he was leaving, a member of his staff reminded him that a supporting column, some 350 auxiliary troops under Brevet-Colonel Anthony Durnford, had been ordered to Rorke's Drift. A hasty note was scribbled ordering Durnford forward to iSandlwana.

While Chelmsford searched for the enemy, the force left behind suffered a terrible defeat (see 'Anatomy of a Battle: iSlandlwana' section). But the Battle of iSandlwana was not the only battle of the war fought on 22 January. Cetshwayo had determined only to fight in defence of his country but about 4,000 men, held in reserve at

[17] Knight, *Zulu Rising*, 269–76.

iSandlwana and commanded by the King's younger brother, Prince Dabulamanzi kaMpande, had been held back during most of the fight and were eager to engage the British. Reaching the Natal border a few miles below the crossing at Rorke's Drift, Dabulamanzi realized that the frontier farms on the opposite bank were exposed and took his men across the river to raid. Some Zulus peeled off to sweep downstream while the rest, perhaps 3,500 – the uThulwana, iNdlondlo, uDloko and iNdluyengwe amabutho – moved leisurely upstream. Ahead of them lay a small border supply depot which Chelmsford had established at the mission station at Rorke's Drift. It consisted of a hospital and a commissariat detachment guarded by one infantry company, B Company, 2nd Battalion 24th (2nd Warwickshire) Regiment of Foot, and a company of auxiliaries.

The first the garrison at Rorke's Drift heard of iSandlwana was when survivors streamed past the post. Unable to evacuate the sick, the senior officers, Lieutenant John Chard, Royal Engineers, and Lieutenant Gonville Bromhead, 24th Regiment, decided to make a stand. There were over thirty wagonloads of supplies stockpiled at the post, heavy sacks of mealies (corn) and Army biscuit, and with these Chard marked out a defensive perimeter. When the auxiliaries broke and fled, Chard was left with scarcely 150 men to defend the post. At about 4.30 p.m., the amabutho began its attack.

The defence of Rorke's Drift lasted throughout the night. Early in the evening, the Zulus pushed their way into the hospital, forcing the defenders to drag the patients from room to room. Chard could not defend the entire perimeter and withdrew to a small area in front of the remaining building. Yet the compact nature of the defensive position made it difficult for the Zulus to concentrate against it in sufficient numbers and the barricades were enough to negate their skills at close-quarter combat. In the early hours of the morning, the Zulus withdrew. Although Chard's men were exhausted, his losses were remarkably light – just seventeen killed. In contrast some 350 Zulu bodies were scattered around the post, and dozens more lay out in the surrounding country; their total losses were perhaps as high as 600 men.[18]

Chelmsford, meanwhile, had spent much of the previous day searching for the Zulu army in vain. Finally, he returned to iSandlwana, only to find his camp destroyed and littered with the dead of his garrison. His men spent a terrible night on the battlefield, lying among the bodies, and returned to Rorke's Drift the following morning. At one point they

---

[18] Ian Knight, *Nothing Remains but to Fight: The Defence of Rorke's Drift* (London: Greenhill Books, 1993), 72–116.

passed some of Dabulamanzi's warriors in retreat but both sides were too exhausted to embark on a new round of fighting. Chelmsford was relieved to find Rorke's Drift had held but in a grim postscript to the battle his men, made vengeful by the sight of iSandlwana, passed over the field, killing the Zulu wounded.

The defence of Rorke's Drift was undeniably gallant – eleven of its defenders were awarded the Victoria Cross – but it was brutally clear to most onlookers that Chelmsford's invasion had failed less than a fortnight after it had begun. Leaving his men at Rorke's Drift, he hurried to the colonial capital to prepare Natal for a Zulu counterattack. That attack, however, never came. Cetshwayo remained on the defensive, his army exhausted. He allowed his regiments to return home, undergo the necessary purification rituals, and rest.

For Frere, iSandlwana was a political calamity, throwing the spotlight onto an adventure which London had never fully authorized. Nevertheless, although the fallout would eventually lead to Frere's recall and the abandonment of confederation, the Conservative government felt that restoring British military prestige was essential. Reinforcements far exceeding those demanded by Chelmsford at the start of the war were hurried to southern Africa.[19]

The Zulu victory had, furthermore, left Chelmsford's flanking columns unsupported. In the coastal sector, Pearson opted to reduce the strength of his garrison, sending his auxiliaries back to the border, and dig in, surrounding the Eshowe mission with the most complex system of entrenchments built during the war. Learning the lesson of Rorke's Drift Cetshwayo forbade his men from making a direct assault on Eshowe but instead directed them to harass the British whenever they emerged from their fort. For three months, Pearson and his 17,00 men were effectively besieged.

In the north, Wood's column remained active, conducting a low-key war of raids and counter-raids against local Zulu groups. These included a section known as the abaQulusi, who had been established in the area a generation before to guard the interests of the Zulu Royal House, and the followers of a renegade Swazi Prince, Mbilini waMswati, who had given his allegiance to Cetshwayo, and who was to emerge as the most dynamic guerrilla leader on the Zulu side throughout the war. On 12 March, Mbilini scored his greatest success, launching a surprise attack on a convoy of the 80th Regiment (Staffordshire Volunteers) of Foot which was stranded on the banks of the swollen Ntombe River, killing over

---

[19] O'Conner, *The Zulu and the Raj*, 166–78.

60 men and capturing wagonloads of ammunition. He would continue to harass the Transvaal border communities until he was killed in a skirmish a few weeks later.

By the middle of March, both sides were ready to launch fresh offensives. With Pearson cooped up at Eshowe, the Zulu high command considered Wood's column to be the most active threat, and in mid-March the amabutho who had triumphed at iSandlwana were reassembled to drive him out. At the same time, Chelmsford tried to recover the initiative. His priority was to extricate Pearson but, in order to confuse the Zulu, he directed Wood to make a diversionary attack in the north.

Hlobane, a flat-topped mountain, had long served as an abaQulusi stronghold. The summit was surrounded by a line of cliffs. Perhaps lured by the prospect of capturing Zulu cattle guarded on Hlobane, Wood resolved to attack. On the night of 27 March, two detachments of mounted troops set out from his base at Khambula to attack either end of the mountain at first light.[20] The approach was difficult and the attack went awry from the start when one detachment, deciding the route up was impractical, withdrew from the field. The other, under Wood's right-hand man, Lieutenant-Colonel Redvers Buller, succeeded in reaching the summit but once up the abaQulusi cut the lines of retreat.

As Buller's men swept across the hill driving cattle before them, to the south, they saw long columns of warriors streaming in their direction. It was the King's main army, and its arrival was purely coincidental. Although most of it continued towards Khambula, three amabutho were detached to assist the defence of Hlobane. Their approach threw the British on the summit into confusion, the units scattering in their hurry to withdraw. One unit ran straight into the Zulus and was overrun, and the rest were forced to descend by a steep rocky pass while under attack. The action at Hlobane was a debacle, producing for the British the worst butcher's bill of the war after iSandlwana – around 200 British and auxiliary troops killed.[21]

The Battle of Hlobane alerted Wood to the Zulu intentions. His position at Khambula consisted of two wagon-laagers and a small earthwork redoubt on the top of a commanding rise, and, despite the mauling at Hlobane, he had two battalions of infantry, a battery of guns and the remnants of his irregulars to defend it. Early on the morning of 29 March, the Zulu army could be seen deploying from its overnight

[20] Huw Jones, *The Boiling Cauldron: The Utrecht District and the Anglo-Zulu War 1879* (Bisley: The Shermershill Press, 2006), 259–82.
[21] Intelligence Branch, *Narrative of Field Operations*, 160.

bivouac several miles away, the extending horns sweeping across miles of open countryside. After Rorke's Drift, Cetshwayo had warned his generals not to attack well-defended positions, but the younger men in his army saw it as their duty to attack the invaders wherever they found them. By about 9.30 a.m., Wood noticed that, while the Zulu right had taken up a position close to the camp, the rest of the army was still manoeuvring. This gave him the opportunity to lure the Zulu right into an unsupported attack, and he directed his mounted men – survivors of Hlobane – to ride out and volley fire from close range.[22] The young amabutho on the Zulu right immediately rushed forward to attack but, once the mounted men were safely back within the laager, the British met them with such an intense fire that the attack was driven back. The Zulu left came into action but the attacks remained uncoordinated, allowing Wood to meet each one in turn. By early afternoon, the amabutho began to withdraw and Wood sent his mounted men to attack without mercy, killing many exhausted warriors. The pursuit continued late into the afternoon, and the Zulu army disintegrated. Some estimates put the Zulu losses at 2,000 dead, and many more wounded.[23] Wood's own losses were just twenty-eight men killed.[24]

The defeat at Khambula was the first serious check to Zulu ambitions in the war, and it was followed within days by another at the opposite end of the country. Chelmsford had crossed the Lower Thukela with the intention of relieving Eshowe. On the night of 1 April, his men camped in a square laager on a rise near a Zulu homestead called kwaGingindlovu. His scouts reported that the Zulu had assembled between him and Eshowe, and at first light they could be seen deploying to attack.[25] These were the men Cetshwayo had retained in the district, some 10,000 men commanded by Somopho kaZikhale and Dabulamanzi. Chelmsford met them with infantry four deep on all sides, and supported with two Gatling guns, artillery, and rockets. Although the Zulu attacks were determined, they collapsed in the face of an impenetrable curtain of fire. The following day, Chelmsford relieved Pearson's garrison.

The battles of late March and early April allowed Chelmsford to complete his plans for a fresh invasion of Zululand. He believed that after iSandlwana, Britain needed a decisive end to the war to restore its prestige. He was also aware that the Government, unsatisfied with his performance, had sent Major-General Sir Garnet Wolseley to replace him. He pulled Pearson back from Eshowe and merged his command

---

[22] Laband, *Rope of Sand*, 263–77.   [23] Ibid., 276–77.
[24] Intelligence Branch, *Narrative of Field Operations*, 161.
[25] Castle and Knight, *Fearful Hard Times*, 198–214.

with the relief column to form a new body, the 1st Division, which he instructed to advance up the coast. A second column, the 2nd Division, composed of reinforcements, was assembled on the Ncome River, north of Rorke's Drift. Wood retained his independent command, known now as the Flying Column, but Chelmsford directed it to move south and advance in tandem with the 2nd Division.[26]

For Cetshwayo, the options to face a new British offensive were limited. His amabutho still had the will to fight but it was clear that they were unlikely to resolve the war through military means. As the British pressed their advance, the King turned to diplomatic means but his attempts failed.

At the end of June, the combined 2nd Division and Flying Column descended into the valley of the White Mfolozi River, the last geographical obstacle before oNdini. After several days of preparations, on 3 July, Chelmsford sent Buller and his mounted men across the river to scout out a position from which to launch an attack. The Zulus had anticipated such a move and ambushed Buller's men, chasing them back across the river, but Buller had secured the intelligence Chelmsford needed. The next morning, Chelmsford crossed the river with nearly 5,000 troops, two Gatling guns, and twelve field guns.

Chelmsford formed his men into a large square, four ranks deep on all sides, with his guns, cavalry, auxiliaries, and ammunition carts in the centre.[27] The square slowly marched to a rise in a grassy plain amidst the cluster of royal homesteads, the spot selected by Buller. The amabutho emerged and encircled the square on all sides. Chelmsford held his infantry in hand until the Zulus were 400 yards away and then opened fire. The battle lasted less than an hour. Only once did a Zulu attack get close to the British lines.[28] Chelmsford unleashed his cavalry – the 17th (Duke of Cambridge's Own) Lancers with a troop of the 1st (King's) Dragoon Guards and his Irregulars – who rode into the Zulus with such force that an orderly retreat turned into a rout. The auxiliaries were sent out to kill any wounded Zulus that remained. The defeat was total. Over 1,000 Zulus were killed, while only 13 British troops were lost. The great

---

[26] On 1 June, while accompanying the 2nd Division, Prince Louis Napoleon Bonaparte, the young, exiled heir to the Imperial throne of France, who was attached to Chelmsford's staff, was killed by a Zulu scouting party while on patrol. See, Ian Knight, *With His Face to the Foe: The Life and Death of Louis Napoleon, The Prince Imperial, Zululand 1879* (Staplehurst: The Spellmount Press, 2001), 194–221.
[27] John Laband, *The Battle of Ulundi* (Pietermaritzburg: Shuter and Shooter, 1988), 28–42.
[28] An attack on the right rear of the British square reached to within nine paces before being driven back. Melton Prior, *Campaigns of a War Correspondent* (London: Edward Arnold, 1912), 119.

royal homesteads, including oNdini itself, were set on fire, and, by early afternoon, the British had retired across the river.

Anatomy of a Battle: iSandlwana

The camp at iSandlwana was commanded by Lieutenant-Colonel Henry Pulleine. The garrison consisted of six companies of the 24th Regiment, two light field guns, and detachments of Natal Mounted Volunteers and auxiliaries left as picquets. At about 9.30 a.m., several hours after Chelmsford had left, a force of about 2,000 Zulus appeared on a ridge just north of the camp. Pulleine stood his men to but the Zulus did not attack, and after about an hour withdrew beyond the skyline. Shortly afterwards Durnford arrived with his men. British forces at iSandlwana now numbered some 1,700 men. Durnford directed some of his mounted auxiliaries to follow the Zulu withdrawal and determine their intention. At about noon, one of the detachments pursued Zulu foragers over a rise and located the main Zulu army.

The Zulu army had moved into the territory of *inkosi* Sihayo, acquiring key intelligence. Local warriors who had remained to guard their homes joined the main army. It was one such party which Dartnell encountered the previous night. The army rested in the sheltered Ngwebeni valley, hoping to let the day pass as the coming night was a night of the new moon, an inauspicious omen for launching an attack. The Zulu regimental commanders were actually in discussion when Durnford's men appeared on the rise above them and suddenly the collective tension in the Zulu ranks, stoked by pre-battle rituals, snapped. The nearest regiment to the British incursion rose up to attack, dragging those amabutho alongside with it.

From his position in the camp, below the escarpment, Pulleine could see nothing of the Zulu attack but, alerted to its presence, deployed his infantry on a low rocky rise which commanded a chain of erosion gulleys draining off the escarpment. Two companies sent onto the heights were soon driven back, while far on Pulleine's right Durnford's own detachment blundered into the Zulu left and was forced to retire. For a while, as the Zulus crested the hill and descended towards the camp, the 24th Regiment's fire kept them at bay while Durnford had his men dismount and defend a stream bed. Yet the British position was far too extended, and Durnford was in danger of being cut off by Zulus pressing between him and Pulleine's command. He had little option but to withdraw, leaving Pulleine's right exposed. Realising the danger, the companies of the 24th Regiment stopped firing and retired towards the tents just as the Zulus made a fresh attack along the length of their line. In a matter of minutes, the British position collapsed as the Zulus drove between the British detachments in order to prevent them from reforming. Fighting raged hand to hand as the 24th Regiment was pushed through the camp, only to find that the Zulu right horn had already cut behind them. The Zulu horns never managed to meet, allowing room for small numbers, mostly auxiliaries, to escape, but the bulk of the British infantry were destroyed on the slopes below iSandlwana or in the valley beyond.[29] The dead included Durnford, Pulleine, and 1,300 of their men. By about 3.30 p.m., the fighting was over and the Zulus set about looting the camp before, exhausted, retiring with their wounded. The victory had been a dramatic one, but costly; at least a thousand Zulus had been killed outright, and hundreds more were so badly wounded that they would die on the long walk home.[30]

Technology and the Royal Navy

Chelmsford possessed a number of advantages throughout the war. The Royal Navy could bring reinforcements to the Cape and directly to Durban (Port Natal) without interference in a matter of weeks. Communications had been aided by the undersea telegraph cable which had been laid as far as Madeira, and a message could reach London from South Africa within three weeks. Within southern Africa, however, communication was more problematic, since the telegraph was limited to major centres while a planned railway out of Durban had yet to be completed. Although the British Army relied on heliographs elsewhere, there were none in Natal at the start of the war, and most messages were carried by rider.

Chelmsford had a number of 7-pounder, muzzle-loading field-guns, designed as mountain guns but mounted on heavier carriages for the local terrain. These fired a variety of projectiles from shrapnel-filled airburst shells to cannister for use at close range but they were widely held to be too light for the task required of them. Later in the campaign, he was reinforced by a battery of 9-pounders. The British Army was beginning to experiment with various carriage-mounted hand-cranked machine guns and a Gatling gun, as mentioned earlier, was first used in action in Zululand; later, a section of two Royal Artillery Gatlings took part in the closing stages of the war. The British were also equipped with a number of 9-pounder Hale's rockets, fired from troughs, and

---

[29] Knight, *Zulu Rising*, 350–423.
[30] W. C. F. Molyneux, *Campaigning in South Africa and Egypt* (London: Macmillan, 1896), 196–98.

24-pounders fired from tubes. The rockets were unstable and notoriously unreliable but were valued for their incendiary qualities and the psychological effect it was hoped they would have on the enemy.[31]

It was in his infantry, however, that Chelmsford placed his greatest trust. They were armed with the Mark II Martini-Henry rifle, the first British purpose-built single-shot breach-loading rifle. It was robust and easy to use, sighted to a maximum range of 1,700 yards but at its most effective on the battlefield at ranges of less than 400 yards. Each infantryman carried 70 rounds of ammunition on the march and battalion reserves were kept at forward camps; although the question of ammunition supply has become part of the mythology of the Anglo-Zulu War, there is no evidence that a failure of supply influenced the outcome of iSandlwana or any of the subsequent battles.[32]

Aftermath

It was immediately clear to both sides that the war was over with the British victory at oNdini. Cetshwayo had not stayed to see the defeat, and in the days after the battle retired to the safety of loyal chiefs in the north. Chelmsford began to withdraw his command and tendered his resignation. Upon his arrival, Wolseley, the newly appointed High Commissioner, Governor of Natal and the Transvaal, and Commander-in-Chief in South Africa, had little to do but supervise mopping up operations and dispose the area's political future. He re-occupied oNdini, and, from a camp near the burned-out ruins, accepted the surrender of individual Zulu chiefs. On 28 August, the King himself was captured by British Dragoons in the Ngome forest. Wolseley sent him into exile at the Cape.[33] The last shots of the war took place a few days later in the Ntombe valley, where a few Zulu die-hards, who had refused to surrender, were blown up by British Engineers in the caves in which they had taken refuge.

For the British, events had already moved on. The Spring election of 1880 led to Disraeli's defeat and the creation of a Liberal government led by William Gladstone. Gladstone rejected further direct involvement in Zululand. Wolseley, after dividing Zululand into thirteen parts, with rule given to many British collaborators, withdrew, paving the way for a

---

[31] For the weapons and uniforms of British forces, see Ian Knight, *British Forces in Zululand 1879* (London: Osprey Publishing, 1991), 9–63.
[32] Knight, *Zulu Rising*, 377–81.
[33] With British backing, Cetshwayo returned to Zululand in 1883. He died the following year in the midst of civil war.

decade of civil war which proved more costly than the British invasion. There was no political will to pursue confederation and Frere was recalled to justify his actions. The war had cost the lives of seventy-six British officers and over 1,700 men, including auxiliaries in action, and a further 347 of disease. Thousands of transport animals were either killed or worked to death. For the Zulu, it had been worse – perhaps 10,000 men dead, thousands more wounded, the King deposed, the great royal homesteads and hundreds of family homes destroyed, and thousands of head of cattle taken.

Further Reading

Castle, Ian and Ian Knight. *Fearful Hard Time: The Siege and Relief of Eshowe*. London: Greenhill Books, 1994.

Cope, Richard. *Ploughshare of War: The Origins of the Anglo-Zulu War 1879*. Pietermaritzburg: University of Natal Press, 1999.

Emery, Frank. *The Red Soldier: Soldiers Letters from the Zulu War*. London: Hodder and Stoughton, 1977.

Guy, Jeff. *The Destruction of the Zulu Kingdom: The Civil War in Zululand 1879–1883*. London: Longmans, 1979.

Jackson, F. W. D. *Hill of the Sphinx: The Battle of Isandlwana*. London: Westerners Publications, 2002.

Intelligence Branch, War Office. *Narrative of the Field Operations Connected with the Zulu War of 1879*. London: HMSO, 1881.

Knight, Ian. *Brave Men's Blood: The Epic of the Zulu War*. London: Greenhill Books, 1990.

Nothing Remains but To Fight: The Defence of Rorke's Drift. London: Greenhill Books, 1993.

Zulu Rising: The Epic Story of the Battles of iSandlwana and Rorke's Drift. London: Macmillan, 2010.

Laband, John. *Kingdom in Crisis: The Zulu Response to the British Invasion of 1879*. Manchester: Manchester University Press, 1992.

Laband, John (ed.) *Lord Chelmsford's Zululand Campaign*. Stroud: Alan Sutton, 1994.

Rope of Sand: The Rise and Fall of the Zulu Kingdom in the Nineteenth Century. Johannesburg: Jonathon Ball, 1995.

Laband, John and Paul Thompson. *Field Guide to the War in Zululand and the Defence of Natal 1879*. Pietermaritzburg: University of Natal, 1983.

Morris, Donald. *The Washing of the Spears: The Rise and Fall of the Zulu Nation*. New York: Simon & Schuster, 1965.

9 The First Anglo-Boer War, 1880–1881

John Laband

Background

In his manual on the conduct of colonial small wars, Col. Charles E. Callwell made frequent reference to the First Anglo-Boer Boer War of 1880–1881 as a classic case of 'operations of regular armies against irregular, or comparatively speaking irregular forces'. Not that the former invariably held the advantage but as Callwell pointed out, the Transvaal campaign provided a devastating demonstration of the effects of modern fire and movement tactics as successfully practise by mounted Boer irregulars against far less militarily deft professional British soldiers.[1]

At the time, British loyalists in South Africa appropriately dubbed the war the Transvaal Rebellion because the Boers of the Transvaal Territory, which Great Britain had annexed on 12 April 1877, took up arms in December 1880 to regain their independence. For the same reason, Afrikaner nationalists long celebrated their successful rebellion against British imperialism as their First War of Independence.[2]

Lord Beaconsfield's Tory administration had annexed the Transvaal in the belief that India was central to British commercial interests and her status as an imperial power, and that its security depended on the Royal Navy's control of the African coaling stations and sea routes through the Suez Canal and around the Cape. To secure South Africa as a strategic link in this chain, it was considered essential to knot together a politically-stable British confederation of the subcontinent's British colonies and white settler states under the crown.[3] The Zuid-Afrikaansche Republiek (ZAR), or South African Republic – founded by Dutch-speaking farmers (or Boers) migrating in the 1830s out the British-ruled

---

[1] C. E. Callwell, *Small Wars: Their Principles and Practice*, 3rd ed. (London: HMSO, 1906), 4, 21–23.
[2] On what the war has been called, see John Laband, *The Transvaal Rebellion: The First Boer War 1880–1881* (Harlow: Longman Pearson, 2005), 4–7.
[3] C. F. Goodfellow, *Great Britain and South Africa Confederation (1879–1881)* (Cape Town: Oxford University Press, 1966), 49–59.

Cape Colony into the interior of South Africa – was included in this scheme, even though Britain had recognized its independence by the Sand River Convention of 17 January 1852.[4]

Before the Witwatersrand gold rush began in 1886, the Transvaal Territory was a poor colonial acquisition with few resources. Its society was dominated by between 36,000 and 45,000 Boers, most of whom were sparsely sprinkled across the countryside on their 6,000-acre farms, all of them fundamentalist Calvinists, and resolutely pre-industrial in outlook.[5] There was also a 5,000-strong 'English' community of non-Dutch white aliens, two-thirds of whom lived in the sparse scattering of little villages which usually consisted of no more than a small church, courthouse, market square and a few dozen houses. Even Pretoria, the largest town and the capital, had a civil population of around only 2,250. This small 'English' element, on whose support the British administration relied, disproportionally controlled almost all mercantile and commercial business and was deeply resented by the Boer majority.[6] The African population of the Transvaal was estimated at between 700,000 and 800,000 and outnumbered the whites who lorded it over them by 20 to 1. They would play little part in the war, but feared correctly that if the British were ousted, their situation would deteriorate under restored Boer rule.[7]

The first Administrator of the Transvaal Territory, Sir Theophilus Shepstone, found it no easy task to mollify his new Boer subjects, most of whom objected to annexation.[8] They sent two unsuccessful delegations to London in 1877 and 1878 to object to annexation, and when the second reported back on 10 January 1879 to a public meeting at Wonderfontein, the resolution was taken to continue to agitate, and to set up a shadow Boer administration.[9] Initial British disasters during the

---

[4] D. H. Heydenrych, 'The Boer Republics, 1852–1881', in Trewhella Cameron and S. B. Spies (eds.), *An Illustrated History of South Africa* (Johannesburg: Jonathan Ball, 1986), 150.
[5] For a detailed description of Boer society in the Transvaal, see Laband, *Transvaal Rebellion*, 26–40.
[6] John Laband, 'Burying the Union Jack: British loyalists in the Transvaal during the First Anglo-Boer War 1880–1881', *History of Intellectual Culture* 4, 1 (2004): Special Issue: British World Conference, 2003: 2–8.
[7] Laband, *Transvaal Rebellion*, 38–41, 186–87, 223–24.
[8] Deryck M. Schreuder, *The Scramble for Southern Africa, 1877–1895* (Cambridge: Cambridge University Press, 1980), 61–64; Bridget Theron, 'Theophilus Shepstone and the Transvaal Colony, 1877–1879', *Kleio* 34 (2002): 104–27.
[9] Louis Scott, 'Boereweerstand teen Gedwonge Britse Bestuur in Transvaal, 1877–1880', in F. A. van Jaarsveld, et al. (eds), *Die Eerste Vryheidsoorlog van Verset en Geweld tot Skikking deur Onderhandeling 1877–1884* (Pretoria and Cape Town: Haum, 1980), 15–27.

Anglo-Zulu War of 1879 led many to believe that if it came to open resistance they might well be able to defeat the British. So, when Sir Bartle Frere, the High Commissioner, met the Boer leaders in April 1879 and offered them self-government within a British confederation, they held out for complete independence.[10]

Colonel Owen Lanyon replaced Shepstone as Administrator of the Transvaal on 4 March 1879. A tough soldier, Lanyon's style of administration proved unbending and authoritarian and did nothing to reconcile the dissident Boers to British rule. His superior was the pushy General Sir Garnet Wolseley, who had been appointed on 28 May 1879 as High Commissioner in South- Eastern Africa and Governor of Natal and the Transvaal. When Wolseley arrived in Pretoria in September 1879 after having imposed a settlement on the defeated amaZulu, he grandiloquently informed the resentful Boers that 'as long as the sun shines daily the British flag shall fly over the Transvaal'.[11] He too failed to conciliate them. Ironically, his crushing of the Bapedi in the Second Anglo-Pedi War of November–December 1879, instead of impressing the Boers with the benefits of British rule, freed up the Boer leaders to focus on anti-British agitation now that the longstanding Pedi threat along the Transvaal's eastern frontier had been removed.[12] At the mass meeting of *burgers* (citizens) held at Wonderfontein from 10 to 15 December 1879, the Queen's sovereignty was publicly denounced. Paul Kruger, previously the Vice-President of the ZAR, emerged as the dominant figure and ramped up agitation against British rule.

On 24 April 1880, Major-General Sir George Pomeroy Colley succeeded Wolseley.[13] Academically brilliant and an experienced staff officer, Colley was one of Wolseley's protégés, a member of his 'Ashanti Ring', a coterie of reform-minded officers.[14] The framing and implementation of defence policy in South- Eastern Africa were

---

[10] G. H. Le May, *Afrikaners: An Historical Interpretation* (Oxford: Blackwell, 1995), 73–78; Basil Worsfold, *Sir Bartle Frere. A Footnote to the History of the British Empire* (London: Butterworth, 1923), 213–25.

[11] Entry of 11 September 1879, in Adrian Preston (ed.), *Sir Garnet Wolseley's South African Journal 1879–80* (Cape Town: A. A. Balkema, 1973), 112.

[12] For the Second Anglo-Pedi War, see John Laband, *Zulu Warriors: The Battle for the South African Frontier* (New Haven and London: Yale University Press), 265–77.

[13] For Colley's earlier career, see Ian F. W. Beckett, 'George Colley', in Steven J. Corvi and Ian F. W. Beckett (eds.), *Victoria's Generals* (Barnsley: Pen & Sword Military, 2009), 74–80.

[14] For 'Wolseley's Ring', see Ian F. W. Beckett, *A British Profession of Arms: The Politics of Command in the Late Victorian Army* (Norman: University of Oklahoma Press, 2018), 76–87.

Colley's preserve alone, and he acted independently of the lack-lustre General Officer Commanding Her Majesty's Forces in South Africa, Lieutenent- General the Hon. Leicester Smyth, with his Headquarters in Cape Town.

Such was the situation in the Transvaal when William Gladstone's second Liberal administration took office in April 1880. His government was preoccupied at home by the agrarian agitation of the protracted and intractable Irish Land War, and was divided over what policy to pursue regarding the Transvaal. The Transvaal Boers hoped that the Liberals would be more amenable than the Tories had been. Indeed, Gladstone himself sympathized with their demand for self-determination, and his government agreed that the Tory confederation agenda should be abandoned in due course. Nevertheless, the conservative Whig faction in his cabinet prevailed for the moment, and the government decided it must show firmness to uphold the imperial image in South Africa. Gladstone accordingly wrote to the Boer leaders on 8 June 1880 to confirm he would not let the Transvaal go, citing his government's obligation to the British settlers in the Transvaal and its duties to the Africans.[15] With that, Gladstone's administration took its eyes off the Transvaal and fixed its attention on the dangerous Irish question closer to home. Disillusioned by Gladstone's refusal to consider the retrocession of the Transvaal, Kruger and his close associates decided that further meetings and protests were pointless, and that they should start preparing for an armed uprising.[16]

* * * * *

Despite the First Anglo-Boer War's significance in undoing British plans to confederate southern Africa, works dealing with the campaign have been swamped by the voluminous literature on the Second Anglo-Boer War. That is understandable. The First Anglo-Boer War was a very small campaign by comparison, with only a few thousand men engaged on either side. Yet it is also possible that English-speaking historians have tended to shy away from it because (a rare enough occurrence for the Victorian era) it proved an unmitigated humiliation for British arms.

---

[15] Deryck M. Schreuder, *Gladstone and Kruger. Liberal Government and Colonial 'Home Rule' 1880–1885* (London: Routledge and K. Paul; Toronto: University of Toronto Press, 1969), 81–85.
[16] Paul Kruger, *The Memoirs of Paul Kruger, Four Times President of the South African Republic, Told by Himself* (London: T. Fisher Unwin, 1902), 165.

At the time, two war correspondents who witnessed events and interviewed participants, both brought out books in 1882: Charles Norris-Newman of the *Standard's: With the Boers in the Transvaal and Orange Free State*, and Thomas Fortescue Carter of the *Times of Natal's: A Narrative of the Boer War*. The latter, with its meticulous detail and even-handed approach has long been regarded as the standard history of the war. Col. William Bellairs, who was the Officer Commanding the Transvaal District throughout the war, published his meticulous, military account of events as *The Transvaal War* (1885) with his wife, Lady Bellairs, credited as editor because he was still a serving officer. The chapters devoted to the Transvaal campaign in Lieutenant-General Sir William Butler's biography, *The Life of Sir George Pomeroy-Colley* (1899), are essential for coming to grips with the British commander's erratic leadership.

Thereafter, for more than half a century, no book in English on the First Anglo-Boer War appeared until Oliver Ransford's popular account, *The Battle of Majuba Hill: The First Boer War* (1967). This was soon followed by Joseph Lehmann's *The First Boer War* (1972), a thorough, popular retelling. A new direction was taken by Ian Bennett, *A Rain of Lead* (2001), who concentrated in great detail on a single episode of the war, namely the siege of Potchefstroom, and there is room for more studies of this kind. Another different approach was taken by John Laband in *The Transvaal Rebellion* (2005) where he tackled the war from the perspective of the clash of the antagonists' military cultures, and took especial note of the British loyalists in the Transvaal who introduced an element of civil war into the conflict. In all accounts of the Transvaal campaign the critical battle of Majuba has received especial attention, and is the focus of two recent works, Ian Castle's *Majuba 1881* (1996), and John Laband's *The Battle of Majuba Hill* (2017).

For Afrikaners, or those who have approached it from the Boer standpoint, the war remains a matter for celebration, and the centenary of the conflict generated several excellent studies. A number of well-researched academic theses and dissertations were submitted at South African universities. Several scholarly studies have been published, most noteworthy being the collection of research essays in Afrikaans edited by F. A. van Jaarsveld, A. P. J. van Rensburg, and W. W. Stals, *Die Eerste Vyrheidsoorlog* (1980), covering all aspects of the war. Colonel George Duxbury's *David and Goliath* (1981) is a succinct, authoritative account of the campaign written when he was Director of the South African National War Museum.

172   *John Laband*

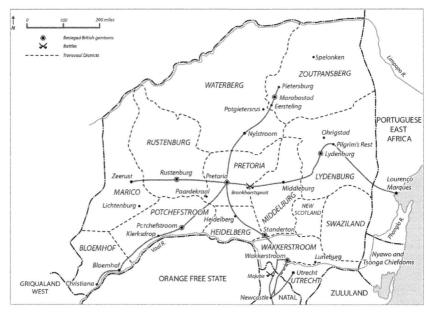

Map 9.1 The First Anglo-Boer War, 1880–1881.
John Laband, *The Battle of Majuba Hill: The Transvaal Campaign, 1880–1881* (Solihull: Helion & Company, 2017).

Outbreak of War

For the Transvaal Boers, having to pay taxes to the British administration symbolized their resented submission to alien rule, but Lanyon was nevertheless determined to bring tax evaders to book. When on 11 November 1880 the *landdros* (magistrate) in Potchefstroom put P. L. (Piet) Bezuidenhout's wagon up on auction in execution of costs relating to his non-payment of taxes, a hundred well-armed burgers under P. A. (Piet) Cronjé rode into the village to support Bezuidenhout. Lanyon had no alternative but to send in troops to arrest them. The Officer Commanding the Transvaal District was Col. William Bellairs and he had available only about 1,500 British troops, already overstretched in small garrisons in Pretoria, Rustenburg, Lydenburg, Marabastad, Standerton and Wakkerstroom.[17] When troops from the

---

[17] Lady Bellairs (ed.), *The Transvaal War 1880 –81* (Edinburgh and London: William Blackwood and Sons, 1885), 43. By 16 December, there were 1,759 troops in the garrison.

Pretoria garrison arrived in Potchefstroom on 18 November, Cronjé's men refused to be intimidated, and a stand-off ensued. Finally accepting the seriousness of the situation, on 25 November Lanyon called on Colley for reinforcements.[18]

Colley was reluctant to comply. The two rebellions that had broken out in October 1880 in the neighbouring Cape-administered territories of Basutoland and the Transkei seemed of greater concern to Natal's security than the situation in the Transvaal, and Colley was unwilling to significantly deplete the Natal garrison.[19] Meanwhile, grasping the political potential of events in Potchefstroom, the Boer leaders called a mass meeting at Paardekraal. On 13 December the gathering resolved to reconstitute the old republican *volksraad* (parliament) and elected a triumvirate to lead it consisting of Kruger, Piet Joubert, a former acting Vice-President, and Marthinus Wessel. Joubert was elected *Kommandant-Generaal* (Commandant-General) which gave him supreme military command. On 16 December – the anniversary of the symbolically charged victory of the Voortrekkers over the amaZulu at Blood River (Ncome) in 1838 – the provisional Boer government proclaimed the restoration of the the ZAR and placed it under martial law. Joubert sent out far and wide to mobilize the approximately 7,000 mounted burgers he believed available to him.[20]

British and Boer Forces

The Boer commando system, a militia in which every able-bodied burger between sixteen and sixty was required to serve without pay as part of his civic responsibility, had been formalized in 1715 on the Cape frontier by the Dutch East India Company and had been replicated in the Boer republics.[21] The burgher on commando was expected to provide himself with a rifle and fifty rounds of ammunition, his own horse and saddlery, and to carry eight days' rations. He was accompanied by black servants, or *agterryers*, who had always been an inseparable part of the commando system and who carried out all the behind-the-line services including digging trenches and helping with the wounded. No structured military

---

[18] Ian Bennett, *A Rain of Lead: The Siege and Surrender of the British at Potchefstroom* (London: Greenhill Books, 2001), 45–48.
[19] Colley to Lord Kimberley, 26 December 1880, (C. 2866), no. 3, British Parliamentary Papers (BPP).
[20] J. E. H Grobler, 'Paardekraal: Eensydige Herstel van die Onafhanklikheid', in Van Jaarsveld et al., *Eerste Vryheidsoorlog*, 104–106, 108.
[21] George Tylden, 'The development of the commando system in South Africa, 1715 to 1922', *Africana Notes and News* (13 March 1958–December 1959), 303–13.

training took place, no uniforms were issued, and the outspokenness and informality of the men, even towards their officers who were elected by popular vote, led the British to believe the Boer forces were necessarily inferior and undisciplined. But this was gravely to underestimate the Boers' military effectiveness.

Boer tactics were based on two interconnected, well-tried elements: horses that gave mounted men the advantages of mobility and surprise and permitted swift tactical withdrawals, and small arms that laid down a devastating fire. (The third classic element, the ox-wagon laager, had lost its usefulness except as a mobile base camp.) Operating as mounted infantry, the Boers employed coordinated infantry fire and movement tactics in which well-aimed covering fire by selected marksmen made it difficult for the defenders to show themselves to fire back at their assailants. With an enemy on the move, the Boers used their efficient forward scouting to locate the target and to approach under cover of dead ground to bring the commando unseen to within effective rifle range. And Boer musketry was excellent. As habitual hunters they knew how to make the best use of terrain, and their engrained skills resulted in accurate individual fire and in the initiative essential in scattered irregular warfare.[22]

The British forces in South Africa were of a different order. Once reinforcements had been injected during February 1881, all elements of the British forces were represented in the war: cavalry regiments, batteries of Royal Artillery, companies of Royal Engineers, battalions of infantry, squadrons of mounted infantry, and naval brigades. As a consequence of the sweeping army reforms undertaken by Edward Cardwell, Secretary of State for War in William Gladstone's first cabinet (1868–74) – reforms much deplored by H. R. H. Prince George, Duke of Cambridge, the Field Marshal Commanding-in-Chief, and his conservative coterie[23] – these troops were short-service soldiers.[24] Conditions were improving for the rank and file in the late Victorian army, but although the purchase of commissions had been abolished in 1871, an amateurish, gentlemanly ideal still prevailed where dash and flair were at a greater premium than technical military knowledge. Even

---

[22] Willian Kelleher Storey, *Guns, Race, and Power in Colonial South Africa* (Cambridge: Cambridge University Press, 2008), 133–43.
[23] Beckett, *British Profession of Arms*, 98–102.
[24] Edward Spiers, 'The Late Victorian Army 1868–1914', in D. G. Chandler and I. Beckett (eds.), *The Oxford History of the British Army* (Oxford: Oxford University Press, 2003), 187–200. The regimental numbers and county affiliations which characterised individual battalions were subsequently changed to territorial titles in new regiments with the implementation in 1881 of the recommendations of the Ellice Committee on the Formation of Territorial Regiments.

so, during the late-Victorian era efforts were being made to transform tactical practices. 'Bush-fighting', with its emphasis on marksmanship in extended order, had been encouraged through culminating experience in colonial campaigns and by the advent of breech-loading rifles that made it possible to load and fire more rapidly, and to do so while kneeling or lying down.[25] Nevertheless, marksmanship was not practised regularly enough, and the men relied upon their officer's orders to set their sights correctly.

Compared to the drably-dressed Boers, the British forces in their overseas field dress were colourfully attired. Their frocks and tunics for officers were scarlet for dragoons, Royal Engineers, and infantry, and blue for all other units except the Rifles, who wore dark green. Headgear was the white cork sun helmet stained light brown on campaign. Highland regiments retained their kilts, and those arriving from India, along with the hussars, wore khaki tunics. The naval brigades were dressed in blue and white.[26]

Colley did not raise African levies for logistical and combat support as was normal in colonial campaigns because the racial conventions of the time made it simply unthinkable to unleash them against white Boer settlers.

Strategy and War Aims

The Boers' strategy, once they had taken up arms, was straightforward. The scattered British garrisons had to be immediately neutralized through blockade and starved into submission. Any sorties were to be repelled to prevent the British forces in the Transvaal from concentrating and making a thrust towards Heidelberg (the rebels' provisional capital) or Potchefstroom. Most importantly, they had to be prevented from attacking the Boer forces blocking a British advance from neighbouring Natal in the rear. If they were successful in these objectives, the Boer leadership intended to negotiate the restoration of their independence from their position of strength.

British aims were equally uncomplicated. The blockaded garrisons had to hold fast while a relief column was assembled in Natal, marched to their rescue and secured Pretoria, the seat of the administration. The

---

[25] All the new tactical ideas were readily available in War Office, *Field Exercise and Evolution of Infantry*, Pocket edition (London: HMSO, 1877).
[26] Scarlet as a battledress would only be officially discredited by the Colour Committee of 1883, and the last time it was worn on campaign was in Zululand in 1888.

British knew that the forces at their disposal in Natal were hardly sufficient for a major offensive, but promised reinforcements would take up to two months to arrive, and the beleaguered garrisons might not be able to hold out that long. The decision was therefore taken not to wait but to advance as soon as possible and force the mountain passes held by the Boers. The British presumption was that they would defeat the 'amateur' Boer forces in the field, relieve the blockaded garrisons, and crush the rebellion. That achieved, British rule would be restored.

It was debated how the anticipated British reinforcements should be deployed. The suggestion was that a westerly column should advance from Cape Town, take the Boer forces in the Transvaal in the rear, and distract them from their operations in Natal, but fear that this manoeuvre would inflame pro-Boer agitation in the Cape led to its abandonment.[27] The reinforcements were consequently sent to Natal where the British had repeatedly failed to break though the Boer positions and had suffered three humiliating reverses, but before they had built up their full strength, the British government brought the campaign to a halt. In the course of negotiations, the Boers achieved their primary objective of regaining their independence from Britain.

The Course of the War

The first shots of the Boer rebellion were exchanged at Potchefstroom on 16 December,[28] and on the same day the Boers leaders sent an emissary to Lanyon requiring him to hand over the Transvaal to them.[29] The Administrator responded on 18 December by ordering Colonel Bellairs 'to put down insurrection wherever it may be found to exist'.[30] Bellairs urged Lanyon to concentrate the scattered British garrisons in Pretoria, but Lanyon was reluctant to abandon any post entirely. He made the strategic mistake of ordering elements of the Marabastad, Wakkerstroom, and Lydenburg garrisons to make hazardous marches to Pretoria through a hostile countryside, leaving the three outposts to be held by reduced garrisons.

When news reached Colley on 19 December of the rebellion, he began forming a column to advance into the Transvaal. The Boer Triumvirate

---

[27] Sir G. C. Strahan to Lord Kimberley, 3 January 1881, (C. 2754), enc. 2 in no. 45, BPP.
[28] Bennett, *Rain of Lead*, 71–75.
[29] S. J. P. Kruger, M. W. Pretorius, P. J. Joubert et al. to Sir O. Lanyon, 16 December 1880, (C. 2838), enc. no. 7, BPP.
[30] Proclamation by Lanyon, 18 December 1880, War Office [WO] 32/7812, enc. 2 in no. 079/3975, The National Archives (TNA), Kew.

had anticipated this. In order to prevent Bellairs from concentrating a field force strong enough to take the main Boer forces disputing Colley's advance from Natal in the rear,[31] the Boer forces investing the British posts were ordered to blockade the garrisons, repel any sorties, and starve them into submission. It was essential to intercept the British forces ordered to concentrate on Pretoria, but the Boers succeeded with only one of them.

On the afternoon of 20 December, a mile to the east of Bronkhorstspruit, Commandant Frans Joubert, leading a commando of 300 men, ambushed Lieutenant Colonel Philip R. Anstruther's column of 252 officers and men and a straggling train of baggage wagons as it proceeded from Lydenburg. Within fifteen minutes the British had suffered 156 casualties to the Boers' five and the mortally wounded Anstruther surrendered.[32] News of the British defeat at Bronkhorstspruit flared through the Afrikaner populations of southern Africa, stimulating their nationalist aspirations and support for their gallant blood brothers in the Transvaal.[33] The British, trying to explain away their defeat, blamed it on Boer 'treachery' and this perception did irreversible damage to their image in the eyes of the British public.[34]

In Pretoria, Potchefstroom, Standerton, and Wakkerstroom many of the loyalist civilians who had not fled the Transvaal took refuge from the besieging Boers with the British garrisons in their forts, or behind hastily erected defences where they suffered considerable privations. The men organized themselves into volunteer units to support the regular troops and saw incessant military action against the Boers blockading the forts. Elsewhere, in Rustenburg, Lydenburg, and Marabastad, where the forts were rudimentary and the garrisons small, the civilians prudently decided to remain neutral. In other villages without a British garrison – Middelburg, Zeerust, Utrecht – civilians made no attempt to resist the Boers and 'loyalists' suffered heavy exactions.[35]

---

[31] J. E. H. Grobler, 'Die Beleëring van die Britse Garnisoene', in Van Jaarsveld et al., *Eerste Vryheidsoorlog*, 130.

[32] For a recent account of the battle, see Laband, *Transvaal Rebellion*, 93–100.

[33] Charles Norris-Newman, *With the Boers in the Transvaal and Orange Free State in 1880–1*, 2nd ed. (London: Abbott, Jones, 1882), 131–33, 142–45. The term 'Afrikaners' for Dutch-speaking settlers was already widely current by the 1870s, and the language was becoming distinct from Dutch. Afrikaner national consciousness was stimulated by the mounting challenge of British imperialism, and was expressed in cultural as well as political terms.

[34] For the popular denigration of the Boers in the British press, see Joseph Lehmann, *The First Boer War* (London: Jonathan Cape, 1972), 122–24.

[35] Laband, *Transvaal Rebellion*, 52–3, 89–90, 109–23, 134, 137–38, 179–82, 186–87, 219–21, 235–36.

Meanwhile, Colley was cobbling together what troops he had available for a relief column, the Natal Field Force (NFF).[36] He was very short of mounted men and artillery, but no reinforcements were forthcoming from the Cape where the anxious Lieutenant-General Smyth kept them back on account of the Transkei rebellion and the Gun War in Basutoland. Colley consequently requested the War Office for reinforcements. The long sea passages involved meant they would not arrive before February 1881, and before they did so the Bronkhorstspruit disaster and parlous state of the British garrison in the Transvaal forced Colley's hand. On 30 December the NFF finally concentrated at its forward base in the village of Newcastle between Pietermaritzburg and the Transvaal border. It numbered only 1,462 officers and men, but short-handed as he was, Colley nevertheless firmly believed that the discipline, organization, and trained skill of his troops gave them the advantage over amateur Boers.[37]

Commandant-General Joubert anticipated that the NFF must advance into the Transvaal over Laing's Nek where the road traversed a semicircle of hills, six miles in length, just south of the border. By 18 January a Boer commando of 600 or more men had occupied Laing's Nek which was overlooked by the neighbouring heights and commanded to the west by the flat-topped Majuba Mountain.

On 26 January, the advancing NFF constructed an entrenched camp below Mount Prospect about five miles from Laing's Nek. On the morning of 28 January, Colley led out 1,211 officers and men to break through at Laing's Nek.[38] Advancing with Regimental and Queen's colours flying (the last time that British infantry would carry them into battle), they found themselves under devastating flanking fire from the Boers behind their rocks and breastworks. Unable to carry the Boers positions despite a desperate bayonet charge, the British withdrew after suffering 200 casualties, including most of Colley's staff. In contrast, Boer casualties numbered only forty-three, mainly from artillery fire. Despite his defeat, Colley could not fall back for fear of the adverse political repercussions both in South Africa and Britain, and the disheartening effect it would have on the beleaguered garrisons in the Transvaal, and dug in at Mount Prospect.[39]

---

[36] Operations of the NFF are detailed in the Journal of the Natal Force, 19 December 1880 to 12 March 1881 in *War and Peace in South Africa 1879–1881*, ed. Paul H. Butterfield (Melville: Scripta Africana Series, 1987), 170–220.
[37] Norris-Newman, *With the Boers*, 129–30.
[38] For an account of the battle, see Laband, *Transvaal Rebellion*, 146–60.
[39] Lt. Gen. Sir William F. Butler, *The Life of Sir George Pomeroy-Colley* (London: John Murray, 1899), 293–94.

Meanwhile, in London, the cabinet was trying to find a way out of this unwelcome little war without too much damage to British prestige, and without further aggravating anti-British nationalist sentiment in its other South African colonies. To make matters worse, Colley's defeat came inopportunely at precisely the moment when Gladstone was distracted by his government's efforts to ram the Coercion Act, aimed at curbing the activities of Irish Land League, through a reluctant, filibustering parliament.[40] Consequently, on 29 January the government eagerly grasped the offer of mediation by President Johannes Brand of the Orange Free State who was eager to broker a settlement before his own neutral Boer republic was drawn into the war. For their part, the Boer leaders in the Transvaal were keen to negotiate while they still held the military advantage.[41]

Unaware of these political developments, Colley decided he must remove the Boer threat to his long and fragile line of communications by making a demonstration in force along the road back to Newcastle. On the morning of 8 February, he led out a force of 273 all ranks. When it reached a triangular-shaped plateau, known as Schuinshoogte, about a mile and a half south of the Ingogo River, it was encircled by a Boer commando of 250 men under Field Commandant-General Nicolaas Smit. Pinned down and unable to break off the engagement, Colley waited for nightfall to make a hazardous retreat across rivers flooded by the afternoon's thunderstorms. British casualties numbered 142, or half of Colley's force. By contrast, Boer casualties came to only seventeen men.

With almost a quarter of the NFF dead or wounded, Colley and his men were deeply demoralized. Standing strictly on the defensive, they were cheered when reinforcements finally began marching upcountry under the command of the experienced and energetic Brigadier-General Sir Evelyn Wood.[42] But the government had no stomach for a renewed offensive. On 16 February the Colonial Secretary, the Earl of Kimberley, authorized Colley to suspend all hostilities pending negotiations,[43] and on 19 February ordered him to fix a 'reasonable time'" within which the Boers must respond to Kimberley's peace proposal.[44]

---

[40] R. C. K. Ensor, *England 1870–1914* (Oxford: Clarendon Press, 1968), 72–73.
[41] Schreuder, *Gladstone and Kruger*, 100–17.
[42] Stephen Manning, 'Evelyn Wood', in Steven J. Corvi and Ian F. W. Beckett (eds.), *Victoria's Generals* (Barnsley: Pen & Sword Military, 2009), 30–37.
[43] Kimberley to Colley, Telegram, 16 February 188, (C. 2837), no. 34, BPP. Kimberley also telegraphed Wood and Brand to ensure that his message got through to the Boers and was not smothered by Colley.
[44] Kimberley to Colley, telegram, 19 February 1881, (C. 2837), no. 50, BPP.

At this point Colley balked. Believing he would soon be strong enough to break through at Laing's Nek, on 21 February he wrote, as ordered, to Kruger opening peace negotiations but, disregarding Kimberley instructions, insisted on an unmeetable deadline of 48 hours.[45]

As Colley seems to have intended, his letter took several days to reach Kruger,[46] and once 48 hours had passed without a response, he could convince himself that 'by the rules of war and of honour he was free to move'.[47] Keeping his own government in the dark, Colley prepared to seize the summit of Majuba Mountain in a night attack. Majuba commanded the right of the Boer position, and Colley calculated that the outflanked Boers would be forced to withdraw from Laing's Nek, thus opening the road to the Transvaal. He also appears to have calculated that he would gain all the credit since Wood was away, bringing up more reinforcements.[48] What is without doubt (as he admitted to his wife in a last letter) was that, like a desperate gambler, he was preparing to stake the campaign and his reputation on the turn of a single card.[49]

Colley began his doomed attack on the night of 26 February. His troops seized the summit, but instead of retiring, the next morning the Boers successfully stormed Majuba and routed the British, driving them back to their camp. Colley was killed on Majuba, and Wood was sworn in as Acting Governor of Natal and Administrator of the Transvaal, entrusted with the command of the gravely demoralized troops of the NFF.[50] Wood knew that with the steady build-up of reinforcements he would soon have 15,000 troops in the field: more than enough to guarantee the success of a renewed offensive.[51] But the government was not interested, and insisted on his reaching a settlement with the Boers. To his chagrin, Wood was consequently saddled with the odium of pursing negotiations he privately deplored, and his 'abject surrender' (as many saw it) stalled his career for a number of years.[52] Indeed, Majuba long remained a stain on the British army's honour that it strove to remove.

[45] Colley to Kruger, 21 February 1881, quoted in Butler, *Pomeroy-Colley*, 344.
[46] Schreuder, *Gladstone and Kruger*, 132.   [47] Butler, *Pomeroy-Colley*, 360.
[48] Butler, *Pomeroy-Colley*, 352, 361–62, 364; Oliver N. Ransford, *The Battle of Majuba Hill: The First Boer War* (London: Thomas Y. Crowell, 1967), 66, 71–72.
[49] Colley to Lady Colley, 26 February 1881, Butler, *Pomeroy-Colley*, 367–68.
[50] Manning, 'Evelyn Wood', 38. On 4 March 1881, Kimberley appointed Sir Frederick Roberts, who had become a popular hero on account of his recent success in the Second Afghan War, to succeed Colley. But when Roberts arrived in Cape Town on 28 March the war was already over. Somehow convinced that Wood had made peace to foil him because he was a member of the 'Ashanti Ring' that rivalled his own 'ring'. Roberts immediately returned to England. See Laband, *Transvaal Rebellion*, 215.
[51] For a list of the troops due in South Africa by April 1881, see *The Times*, 10 March 1881.
[52] Sir Evelyn Wood, *From Midshipman to Field Marshal*, vol. 2 (London: Methuen, 1906), 115; Manning, 'Evelyn Wood', 39, 42.

Through the determined meditation of President Brand, Wood (now holding the local rank of major general) met Joubert on Sunday, 6 March at O'Neill's cottage, half-way between the British camp and the Boer positions on Laing's Nek. The two commanders agreed to an armistice up to midnight on 14 March.[53] With Kruger's arrival at O'Neill's cottage on 16 March negotiations reconvened. After tough bargaining, the terms of an armistice were eventually ratified on 23 March. The British acknowledged the complete independence of the Transvaal people subject to British suzerain rights. In return, the Boers agreed to disperse in order to await the final settlement of a Royal Commission. The ensuing Pretoria Convention was signed on 3 August 1881, and the last British troops evacuated the Transvaal on 18 November.[54] British settlers across South Africa were convinced that Gladstone and his ministers had thrown the Transvaal loyalists to the Boers to secure a shameful peace, and petitioned and protested with outrage.[55]

Anatomy of a Battle: Majuba

At 11.00 p.m. on the moonless night of 26 February, Colley led out a mixed force of twenty-seven officers and 568 men (two companies of the 58th Regiment, two companies of the 3/60th Rifles, three companies of the 92nd Highlanders and a company-strength Naval Brigade drawn from the *Boadicea* and *Dido*), as well as three newspaper correspondents and an unrecorded number of African guides and servants who carried three days' rations for the troops.[56] The daytime Boer picquet regularly posted on Majuba had been withdrawn in order to be present at the Sunday divine service to be held early the next morning at the Boer laagers on the Transvaal side of Laing's Nek.[57] When the first British troops breasted the summit at 3.40 a.m. on Sunday, 27 January (the rear

---

[53] Heads of Conditions of an Armistice Proposed to be Agreed between the British and Boer Forces, 6 March 1881, P. J. Joubert Collection (JC) 26, no. 2529: 1881, National Archives Repository, Pretoria (NARP).

[54] Subsequently, the London Convention of 27 February 1884 removed the nebulous concept of the Queen's 'suzerainty'.

[55] For the range and scope of the protests, see Laband, 'British Loyalists', 9–14.

[56] For two of the most recent accounts in English of the battle, see Ian Castle, *Majuba 1881: The Hill of Destiny* (London: Osprey Military, 1996), 60–85; and John Laband, *The Battle of Majuba Hill: The Transvaal Campaign, 1880–1881* (Solihull: Helion & Company, 2017), 103–22. For an account in Afrikaans, see C. M. Bakkes, 'Die Slag van Majuba, 27 Februarie 1881', in Van Jaarsveld et al., *Eerste Vryheidsoorlog*, 179–97.

[57] Brig. W. Otto, 'Die Slag van Majuba 27 Februarie 1881', *Scientia Militaria: South African Journal of Military Studies* 1, 11 (1981): 2.

of the labouring column was not finally up until dawn began to break), they discovered it deserted.

The troops found themselves on the summit of Majuba, roughly triangular in shape. It has a rocky perimeter of about three quarters of a mile that slopes inwards to form a basin, in some places nearly forty feet below the outer line of boulders. It is bisected from east to west by a low rocky ridge. Colley was satisfied with the apparent strength of the position, but his confidence was misplaced. With the detachment of two companies of the 3/60th Rifles and one of the 92nd Highlanders to secure his lines of communication, he had only nineteen officers and 383 men left to hold the position. The men were placed in extended skirmishing order with 15-pace intervals between files and with reserves in support. A further mixed reserve, drawn from all the units, was formed up in the hollow behind the rocky ridge close by Colley's headquarters beside the hospital and commissariat. Colley failed to order perimeter entrenchments, essential in an era of accurate, long-range rifles fire.[58] Knowing this, several of Colley's junior officers and the Naval Brigade took the initiative and improvised stone breastworks.

The Boers did not expect to have to fight on the Sabbath, and were scandalized as well as astounded at the unexpected and unwelcome sight of the British on the mountain above them.[59] But they overcame their initial panic when they realized that there was to be no supporting British attack on Laing's Nek itself, and that they could concentrate undistracted on retaking Majuba. Nicolaas Smit coordinated Boer strategy. He led one mounted force to the lower northern slopes of Majuba and directed a second group of about 150 horsemen to ride around the western side of the mountain to prevent any British reinforcements reaching Colley and to cut off a British withdrawal.

The Boers at the base of Majuba dismounted and Smit formed them into two assault groups under Commandant Joachim Ferreira and Assistant Field Cornet Stephanus Roos, soon joined by a third to Roos's left under Field Cornet Stephanus Trichard. During the morning, further volunteers swelled their numbers to about 450 men. Smit deployed a cordon of the older and less physically active Boers at the foot of the mountain to mount covering fire for the skirmishers working expertly up the slopes in two supporting lines, taking every advantage of the natural cover of thick bush and of the dead ground.

---

[58] War Office, *Field Exercise*, 382–402.
[59] Joubert to Kruger, 27 February 1881, Argief Boeren Voormannen (BV)13, p. 454, NARP; Kaptein G.E Visser, 'Die Eerste Vryheidsoorlog: Enkele Aspekte met die Britse Siening van die Boere en die Verskille tussen Boer en Brit', *Scientia Militaria: South African Journal of Military Studies* 1, 11 (1981): 74.

When at about 8.00 a.m. the British on the summit realized they were under attack, they felt no alarm. But by 10.30 a.m., Colley was becoming concerned by the weight of incessant Boer covering fire that deterred his men from exposing themselves along the skyline to fire down at the Boer assault groups. With British fire suppressed, the Boers extended their line and closed in on the British in a classic pincer movement. Somewhere between 12.30 p.m. and 12.45 p.m., they stormed the British defences in several places and opened enfilading fire on the remaining troops holding the perimeter. In the ranks the over-confidence of the morning was overtaken by perplexity and anxiety. At first the British fell back before the advancing Boers in reasonable order, but then gave up any further attempt at a stand. They simply threw themselves over the edge of the southern side of the mountain in a desperate *sauve qui peut*, bounding and tumbling down the steep, boulder-strewn slopes, many dropping their rifles as they went. Colley was fatally shot through the head, although the circumstances surrounding his last moment are unclear.[60]

At about 1.45 p.m., the troops Colley had posted along his line of communication came under attack from the mounted Boers who Smit had despatched around the western flank of Majuba, and from a fresh group on foot under Commandant J. Uys who hurried up from Laing's Nek to the north-east. Almost surrounded, the troops withdrew with great difficulty at about 3.00 p.m. to Mount Prospect Camp. The garrison advanced their 9-pounders and Gatling guns to deter the Boers from advancing any further and cutting off the British retreating from Majuba, and mounted men were sent out to carry exhausted fugitives away on their horses. In the camp, frenzied preparations were made to repel a Boer assault but, judging the defences too strong, the Boer did not press on and firing ceased by 3.30 p.m.[61]

The British suffered 242 casualties with eighty-one men taken prisoner. With close to half their force lost, this was a crushing defeat, made even starker when compared to the mere seven Boer casualties. The Boers, astonished by the extent of their victory over professional soldiers, chose to regard it as nothing less than God's support in their fight for freedom.[62]

The Role of Technology and the Royal Navy

Commodore F. W. Richards, commanding H. M.'s vessels at the Cape of Good Hope and along the West Coast of Africa, who had his naval

---

[60] See Butler, *Pomeroy-Colley*, 404–06; and Lehman, *Majuba*, 247–48.
[61] Joubert to Kruger, 1 March 1881, BV 13, p. 473, NARP.
[62] Kruger to Joubert, 5 March, JC 26, no. 2457:1881, NARP.

base at Simon's Town, provided Colley with a Naval Brigade and artillery from two corvettes, HMS *Boadicea* and HMS *Dido*.[63] The Royal Navy also played a support role, transporting reinforcements from England, India, Halifax, and Gibraltar to Durban, where they disembarked. In 1880, the narrow-gauge railway inland went only as far as Pietermaritzburg. The troops had to march from there to the front while their supplies were brought up by ox-wagon over rudimentary tracks.

The British government kept in close telegraphic contact with Colley through the submarine cable that since December 1879 had linked London to Durban via Aden.[64] Field telegraph lines linked Durban to Colley's headquarters and to the British garrisons in the Transvaal, but these were regularly severed by the Boers. Colley had then to resort to a chain of heliograph stations or to dispatch rider.[65]

Both sides were armed with the latest single-shot breech-loading rifles and carbines. The British were issued with the Mark II Martini-Henry rifle fitted with a triangular socket bayonet.[66] The most popular rifle with the Boers was the British-made 1866 pattern Westley Richards, but some still preferred the old muzzle-loading hunting musket. The Boers had no artillery to speak of, but the British army deployed 9-pounder Rifled Muzzle Loaders and 7-pounder RML Mark IV steel mountain guns. In addition, the Naval Brigade was equipped with 24-pounder Hale's rockets and Gatling guns.[67]

Aftermath

The Transvaal campaign brought the British army's leadership, marksmanship, discipline, and grasp of modern fighting techniques into question. The subsequent 1881 Report on Musketry Instruction recommended radical improvements in musketry, but these amounted simply to better training in methods already set down in the army's

---

[63] Commodore F. W. Richards to the Secretary of the Admiralty, 10 January 1881, (C. 2866), no. 37 and encs, BPP.

[64] John Laband, *Historical Dictionary of the Zulu Wars* (Lanham, Toronto and Oxford: The Scarecrow Press, 2009), 227, 283.

[65] The British employed the Mance pattern heliograph, devised in 1869. Its flashes could be seen up to fifty miles away through a telescope, but visibility depended on the amount of sunlight.

[66] Although the Martini-Henry Mark III was accepted into service in August 1879, it was designed for the British Volunteers, Militia, and the troops of dominion governments rather than for British regulars.

[67] Kaptein R. von Moltke, 'Wapentuig van die Eerste Vryheidsoorlog', *Scientia Militaria: South African Journal of Military Studies* 11, 1 (1881): 8–29.

regulations.[68] Ultimately, the army's weak showing in the war lay with its poor execution of existing military doctrine, rather than with the doctrine itself.

With the retrocession of the Transvaal, Gladstone's government abandoned the previous Tory administration's confederation policy. In doing so, it placated Afrikaner sentiment and defused the real possibility of a united Afrikaner front challenging continuing British preponderance in South Africa. It would require the new circumstances of the 1890s and of resuscitated imperial interest in South African confederation to revive the call for Afrikaner nationalism and to lay the path to the Second Anglo-Boer War.[69]

Paradoxically, the very extent of Boer success in the war of 1880–81 would lie at the root of their military failure in the conventional stage of their Second War of Independence. Their leaders banked on initial military successes encouraging Afrikaners across the sub-continent to flock to their cause, and on the British once again losing heart and negotiating a settlement.[70] It was a fatal miscalculation.

Further Reading

Beckett, Ian F. W. 'George Colley'. In Steven J. Corvi and Ian F. W. Beckett (eds). *Victoria's Generals*. Barnsley: Pen & Sword Military, 2009.

Bellairs, Lady (ed.) *The Transvaal War 1880–81*. Edinburgh and London: William Blackwood and Sons, 1885.

Bennett, Ian. *A Rain of Lead: The Siege and Surrender of the British at Potchefstroom*. London: Greenhill Books, 2001.

Butler, Lt. Gen. Sir William F. *The Life of Sir George Pomeroy-Colley, KCSI, CB, CMG Including Services in Kaffraria – in China – in Ashanti and in Natal*. London: John Murray, 1899.

Carter, Thomas Fortescue. *A Narrative of the Boer War: Its Causes and Results*, New edition. Cape Town: J. C. Juta; London: John Macqueen, 1896.

Castle, Ian. *Majuba 1881: The Hill of Destiny*. London: Osprey Military, 1996.

Davey, A. M. 'The Siege of Pretoria 1880–1881'. *Archives Year Book for South African History*. Nineteenth Year, vol. 1. Parow, South Africa: The Government Printer, 1956.

Duxbury, George R. *David and Goliath: The First War of Independence, 1880–1881*. Saxonwold: South African National Museum of Military History, 1981.

Laband, John. *The Battle of Majuba Hill: The Transvaal Campaign, 1880–1881*. Solihull, UK: Helion & Company, 2017.

---

[68] Report of the Committee on Musketry Instruction in the Army, 1881, WO 33/37, TNA.
[69] F. A. van Jaarsveld, trans. F.R. Metrowich, *The Awakening of Afrikaner Nationalism 1868–1881* (Cape Town: Human and Rousseau, 1961), 220–1.
[70] Denis Judd and Keith Surridge, *The Boer War* (London: John Murray, 2002), 106.

'Burying the Union Jack: British loyalists in the Transvaal during the First Anglo-Boer War 1880–1881'. *History of Intellectual Culture* 4, 1 (2004): Special Issue: British World Conference, 2003, 19 pp. (on-line journal).

The Transvaal Rebellion: The First Boer War 1880–1881. Harlow: Longman Pearson, 2005.

Lehmann, Joseph. *The First Boer War*. London: Jonathan Cape, 1972.

Norris-Newman, Charles. *With the Boers in the Transvaal and Orange Free State in 1880–1*, 2nd ed. London: Abbott, Jones, 1882.

Ransford, Oliver N. *The Battle of Majuba Hill: The First Boer War*. London: Thomas Y. Crowell, 1967.

Spiers, Edward. *The Late Victorian Army, 1868–1902*. Manchester: Manchester University Press, 1992.

Van Jaarsveld, F. A., A. P. J. van Rensburg, and W. A. Stals (eds.) *Die Eerste Vryheidsoorlog van Verset en Geweld tot Skikking deur Onderhandeling 1877–1884*. Pretoria and Cape Town: Haum, 1980.

10 Egypt and the Sudan, 1881–1885

Rob Johnson

Background

The Egyptian Campaign of 1881–82 was an efficient combined operation that generated dynamic geo-strategic consequences. The irony was that the British Liberal government sought to avoid a full-scale intervention in 1881 but was compelled to act when the Egyptian Army launched a nationalistic coup against Britain's client government. Similarly, the British government was even more reticent about involving itself in the deliverance of the Sudan in 1884–85 from an insurrection under the leadership of Muhammad Ahmad bin Abdullah, who styled himself the 'Mahdi'. The region seemed to have little national interest, but once again, the British were drawn in.

The chapter analyzes the forces involved and Lord Wolseley's calculations during both interventions. It traces the manoeuvres of the belligerents, and the significance of the Battle of Tel el-Kebir, the disaster of Hicks's mission, and the fall of Khartoum. The relative importance of British, Egyptian, and Sudanese technology, tactics, cohesion, and leadership are assessed through operations such as the battles of Suakin, Abu Klea, and Tofrek. Despite the historiographical apotheosis of Charles Gordon, the garrison commander at Khartoum, and, latterly, the proto-nationalist Mahdi, the focus here is the operational one, especially the severe challenges of colonial campaigning.

The success of Wolseley's lightning land operations actually furthered the deterioration of security in Egypt's colonial possessions in the Sudan. It also deepened Anglo-French rivalry which set in motion a 'scramble' for African territory. The chapter concludes with an evaluation of the consequences, including the anachronistic attempts to visualize Arabi and Muhammad Ahmad as liberation leaders.

★ ★ ★ ★ ★

The Anglophone historiography was dominated by the character and the manner of the death of Gordon, with a handful of contemporary accounts of the relief expedition. In it, the Mahdi was largely condemned as a savage and forgotten. Sudanese writers have tried to recover his reputation and emphasized his place as the leader of a national revolution.[1] Some of the hagiography reached the absurd, however, such as Ismail Abd-el Gadir's biography that claimed the Mahdi's face was lit 'like a morning star' and he was a dispenser of justice, adored by the masses, and ever victorious in battle. More useful to military scholars are the accumulated records of Sudanese and European officers, which recalled events they had been involved in, some of which remain in Khartoum's national archives.[2] Despite the polarized historiography, we can now evaluate the campaign in terms which address the undoubted courage of the belligerents, the varied performance of modern technologies, and the narrow margin of success and failure on both sides.

Introduction: The Occupation of Egypt

While ostensibly part of the Ottoman Empire, a new, assertive Egyptian nationalist identity emerged under the leadership of Mehmet Ali in the 1820s. His rule was ruthless but modernising, and, with French assistance, he created a fleet and an army that conquered the Sudan and defeated the Ottomans. Great Britain would not permit the dismemberment of the Ottoman Empire, however, as the Sultan's domains provided a strategic buffer zone that contained the threat of Russian expansionism. Britain and France prioritized the Ottomans, not Egypt. That changed, however, when successive Egyptian rulers increased their expenditure and attracted significant foreign investment. The most extravagant project was the construction of the Suez Canal which resulted in crushing domestic taxation. Ismail Pasha, who titled himself *Khedive*, continued to borrow vast sums from European banks until he approached bankruptcy.[3]

When the Khedive was compelled to sell shares in the Suez Canal in 1875, the British Prime Minister, Benjamin Disraeli, ensured his country acquired the dominant interest, which, when combined with the fact that four-fifths of commercial shipping was in British hands, increased British influence in regional and global commerce. The crippling debts of Egypt,

---

[1] Fergus Nichol, *The Mahdi of the Sudan and the Death of General Gordon* (London: Sutton, 2004), xxii, xxiv.
[2] Stephen Manning, *Soldiers of the Queen* (Stroud: Spellmount, 2009), 162–68.
[3] Nichol, *The Mahdi of the Sudan*, xxii, xxiv.

Egypt and the Sudan, 1881–1885

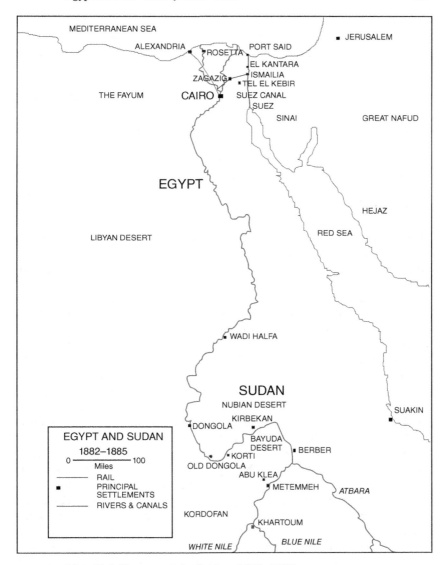

Map 10.1 Egypt and the Sudan, 1882–1885

which had reached £81 million in 1876, forced Ismail to default on repayments, with the result that he had to accept the imposition of an International Commission of Debt to reform the entire system. France and Britain each provided a Controller-General of Finance, giving rise to a system of 'Dual Control'.[4] By 1878, they had also established a supervisory position within Egyptian politics. Both powers, despite the extensive level of influence they now exercised, were nevertheless reluctant to turn Egypt into a colony, for that would demand enormous expenditure and responsibility.

Angered by the severe curtailment of his spending, Ismail tried to plot against the Dual Control, invoking religious and nationalist sentiments to mobilize his countrymen. Few listened: they were exhausted by their ruler's misgovernment.[5] In 1879, Britain and France agreed to have Ismail removed in favour of his more reasonable son, Tewfik. However, amongst educated and wealthy Egyptians there was deep resentment that foreigners effectively governed the country, and they begrudged the new taxation regime which favoured the peasantry.

The Egyptian Army officer corps, which had enjoyed privileges over their countrymen under Ismail, were dismayed by the cuts and changes imposed. The officers were divided between indigenous Egyptians from the peasantry on one side and those of Ottoman-Turkish and Circassian descent on the other. Many of the cuts in personnel had fallen on the Egyptian *fellahin* officers, generating resentment. Colonel Ahmet Arabi ('Urabi) was one of these men and he had suffered a significant fall from grace under Ismail after a previously meteoric career. In 1880, Arabi led objections but he was arrested as the elites attempted to silence him. Anticipating the action, Arabi had already arranged that three loyal regiments would march to rescue him. Faced with mutiny, the Khedive gave way. Arabi and his comrades then pledged their grateful allegiance to Tewfik and the affair seemed closed. However, within weeks, the elites made another attempt to remove Arabi, and, once again, the army declared its loyalty to its Egyptian officer corps.

The French, having secretly first supported the officers, now grew concerned by the nationalist rhetoric it had evoked. When nationalists contemplated a constitutional system, the French demanded the British government issue, with them, a joint note guaranteeing the Khedive's powers. The effect was instantaneous within Egypt, uniting all in resentment of foreign hubris, for it exposed how little control the Egyptians really had over their own affairs. Arabi and his comrades began to assert themselves in the government of the country, awarding higher pay and

---

[4] Ronald Robinson and John Gallagher, *Africa and the Victorians* (London: Macmillan, 1961), 76 and following; Thomas Pakenham, *The Scramble for Africa* (London: Weidenfeld and Nicolson, 1991), 124.

[5] Juan Cole, *Colonialism and Revolution in the Middle East: Social and Cultural Origins of Egypt's Urabi Movement* (Princeton: Princeton University Press, 1993), 234–72.

investment to the army. Attacks on Europeans rose significantly, and a joint Franco-British naval flotilla moved to Alexandria to deter any threat to the Khedive and the 90,000 Europeans in Egypt. The Egyptian Army, determined to throw out foreign control, began to construct earthworks and batteries facing the British and French ships.

On 11 June, a riot in Alexandria against Christians left fifty Europeans dead. Rather than intervene, the British and French governments still favoured Ottoman mediation. This was not sufficient to prevent a flood of departures by anxious European civilians. Businesses and services closed down, and the resulting economic downturn fuelled the anger of Egyptians and increased the high-handedness of their army. The British Prime Minister, William Gladstone, still opposed to any form of intervention or violence, fearing escalation, but to placate his colleagues he permitted contingency plans to be devised, and these fell to General Sir Garnet Wolseley as Adjutant General.[6] The concept of operations Wolseley formulated was for two infantry divisions and a cavalry brigade to first secure the Suez Canal and then advance on Cairo, a more extensive design than the simple restoration of order in Alexandria.

The Outbreak of War

Around the port, Egyptian batteries continued to build up, with over 180 guns arranged in a four-mile arc. Admiral Sir Beauchamp Seymour, commanding the Royal Navy's force at Alexandria, issued warnings that this constituted an intolerable threat, but when these were ignored, he issued an ultimatum on 10 July 1882, stating that, unless the forts and their guns were surrendered to him, he would fire on them.[7] The French government, disapproving of the statement, withdrew its ships, but, with the Egyptians openly defiant, Seymour delivered his bombardment. Eight battleships and eleven gun-boats fired all day into the Egyptian defences. The Egyptian gunners stood as long as they could, scoring hits on some ships, but, by 4.30 p.m., their guns had all been silenced. The Egyptian troops abandoned the city to looters, while angry citizens sought out European civilians for vengeance. For three days there was widespread destruction and disorder in which a further 100 Europeans

---

[6] Alexander Schölch, 'The "Men on the Spot" and the English occupation of Egypt in 1882', *The Historical Journal* 19, 3 (1976): 773; A. G. Hopkins, 'The Victorians and Africa: A reconsideration of the occupation of Egypt, 1882', *The Journal of African History* 27, 2 (1986): 363–91; M. E. Chamberlain, 'Sir Charles Dilke and the British intervention in Egypt, 1882: Decision making in a nineteenth-century cabinet', *British Journal of International Studies* 2, 3 (1976): 231–45.
[7] M. J. Barthorp, *War on the Nile* (Poole: Blandford, 1982), 33.

were killed, until, reluctantly, Seymour landed bluejackets and marines on the harbour to take control.

Meanwhile, Major-General Sir Archibald Alison, commanding at Cyprus, had embarked his men ready to seize the Suez Canal, but, realizing the imperative to secure Alexandria, he diverted his force there, landing two battalions to relieve the naval contingent.[8] The Khedive was brought to the palace at Alexandria for his protection, and, with news of hostile Egyptian troops constructing a fortified base just fourteen miles from the port, at Kafr el-Dauar, Alison began to throw up a defensive cordon of his own. The Royal Navy assisted with the construction of an armoured train, complete with naval guns, which could rush marines and troops to the perimeter.

It was clear that order had broken down in Egypt, and, to protect national interests, secure the European residents, and to restore the country's governance and prosperity, a larger military intervention was required. The British Cabinet was divided. Some insisted on a limited action that took possession of the Canal alone. Others urged a more comprehensive campaign that took back Cairo. There was further disquiet when France refused to participate because of anxieties about German military opportunism against their borders. Gladstone compromised by insisting on a short-term expedition to restore the Khedive and the rule of law. Wolseley was therefore commissioned to execute the mission on the understanding it would be concluded rapidly.

British and Egyptian Forces

Arabi, promoted Commander-in-Chief by a group of notables in light of Tewfik's alignment to the British, now faced the prospect of invasion. His objective was to protect Cairo, which meant covering several routes from the coast, including the railways which radiated out across the Nile Delta. There was no question of holding the shores against the powerful guns of the Royal Navy, so the plan was to conduct a defence in depth using the interior lines of communication. Once the axis of the British attack became clear, forces could be concentrated against it. The line from Alexandria had been blocked already by the fortifications erected at Kafr el-Dauar, but it was likely the British would advance either from Alexandria or perhaps Damietta or Rosetta. Arabi did not think it possible that the British would land along the Suez Canal, such as Ismailia, because of the distances and difficulties of moving across country from

---

[8] The 1st Battalion South Staffordshire Regiment and 3rd Battalion King's Royal Rifle Corps.

there. Internal waterways, such as the Sweetwater Canal, and the various channels of the Nile, served as useful obstacles to the British and could provide defensive lines for the Egyptians. Fortunately, Ferdinand de Lesseps, the French engineer, controlled all the Suez Canal traffic and his hostility to the British could be relied upon to hinder their movements. Arabi appears to have accepted de Lesseps's insistence that the Canal would in any case be neutral in the conflict. He also believed that Gladstone's government would not want to conduct a military operation and would seek to come to terms.

The Egyptian Army had expanded from its peacetime establishment of 9,000 men to a theoretical 60,000, with some 6,000 tribesmen in support.[9] Actual figures for the army were difficult to ascertain. In the early 1870s, the Khedive had claimed to have 100,000 men but the official figure in 1881 was around 18,000 in the Delta and 40,000 in the Sudan. A significant portion of the army of the upper Nile was made up of conscripted and enslaved Sudanese soldiers led by Egyptian officers, while most of the garrisons were ill-trained *bashbuzuq* (militia). In the subsequent campaign, Egyptian infantry battalions consisted of both ethnic Egyptian and Sudanese men who were treated with the same disdain by their own officers.[10] In 1881, with men recalled to the army, the Delta forces were distributed as 30,000 men along the north coast, from Kafr el-Dauar to Damietta: 11,000 held in reserve at Cairo, and 12,000 positioned to cover any advance from the north-east. The posture of the Egyptian Army was defensive, but there was confidence in their prospects. Having driven off a British force that approached Kafr el-Dauar (which was, in fact, a demonstration), morale amongst the Egyptian officers was high. Arabi established his headquarters in an elaborate tent at this site of 'victory' and sought to bolster his reputation as an honourable officer by insisting on the protection of Europeans in Cairo and elsewhere.[11]

The army appeared to be a modern one as it was organized along European lines. Regular infantry battalions consisted of four companies, each of 200 men. The soldiers were equipped with the American-made 11 mm (.433) Remington rolling-block rifle and sword bayonet. Cavalry,

---

[9] Barthorp, *War on the Nile*, 53, 63; Philip Haythornthwaite, *The Colonial Wars Sourcebook* (London: Arms and Armour/Cassell, 1995), 170.

[10] Alice Moore-Harell, 'The Turco-Egyptian Army in Sudan on the eve of the Mahdiyya, 1877–80', *International Journal of Middle East Studies* 31 (Feb 1999): 19–37; Ronald M. Lamothe, *Slaves of Fortune: Sudanese Soldiers and the River War, 1896–1898* (London: Boydell and Brewer, 2011), 11–43.

[11] Peter Mansfield, *The British in Egypt* (Newton Abbott: Victorian and Modern History Book Club, 1973), 48.

formed in regular squadrons, carried the carbine variant of the Remington, while irregulars carried obsolete rifles and bladed weapons. In artillery, the German-made guns were of the latest variety, consisting of 500 (80 mm and 90 mm) breech-loading field pieces, and several 90 mm muzzle-loading rifled howitzers.

If the weapons and defensive posture were the Egyptians' strengths, then their weakness lay primarily in their personnel. Few of the officers had any practical experience of war, and those that had were the survivors of the defeat in Abyssinia (see Chapter 4). The gunners and engineers were considered the best of the army, but the reluctant rank and file were conscripted from the *fellahin* peasantry of the Nile Valley, and, despite the appearance of modernity, the soldiers were treated with contempt by their leaders. Families feared their men being taken to the army, and some took to self-mutilation to avoid the service.[12] Recruits were rounded up and sometimes chained when taken to their barracks, and thereafter pay and food were offered episodically; their accommodation was bad, and discipline excessively harsh. The *kourbash*, a leather whip, was administered liberally by NCOs. It was not known how they would fight behind prepared positions, but British intelligence considered the motivation of the Egyptian fighting forces to be low.

The total British force brought to bear against Egypt consisted of 16,400 men from Britain, 7,600 from the Mediterranean garrisons, and 7,000 from India, with forty-eight guns and a siege train. They deployed swiftly compared with the Crimean campaign just twenty-five years before, thanks to improvements in shipping and organization. It took just four weeks, from the point of mobilization to the arrival of units in the field, to be prepared for action.[13]

The British Army faced a number of challenges in the late-nineteenth century, making its capabilities all the more remarkable. There was a significant increase in demands for its deployment after 1879, and yet its manpower, being voluntary, remained fairly static in number and, despite having to compete with wages in the private sector, budgets were constrained.[14] In addition, the last quarter of the century was a period of rapid technological change. The increasingly lethality of weapons had forced the army to adopt loose skirmishing formations and to reconsider the role of cavalry in 'shock action'. In India, on the North-West Frontier, khaki drab had already been introduced for camouflage, and

---

[12] Cole, *Colonialism and Revolution in the Middle East*, 84–109.
[13] Edward M. Spiers, *The Victorian Soldier in Africa* (Manchester: Manchester University Press, 2004), 79.
[14] There were, in 1879, eighty-two battalions overseas and just fifty-nine at home.

while the army that sailed to Egypt wore its traditional scarlet and green uniforms of the past, the environment, enemy's weapons, and the numerical odds would demand much of the army's personnel and leadership.

The British Army had no General Staff and was rather dependent on the experience of its officers in pragmatic improvisation, borne of colonial garrison duty and expeditionary warfare. The difficulty was knowing precisely what techniques and requirements there would be in any one campaign. There were often criticisms about supplies and hospital arrangements, particularly when lines of communications were extended or medical support was found to be inadequate after significant engagements.[15] While officers were aware of the potential for new weapons, as they had witnessed in South Africa between 1879 and 1881 (see Chapter 9), there was a concurrent awareness that close order tactics, forming squares, and cavalry charges could still have a vital role to play against very large numbers of highly-motivated, cohesive, but less well armed adversaries. The army therefore continued to emphasize the importance of tight discipline and control, in part to ensure a careful expenditure of ammunition when operating over very large distances from logistical bases.

The standard infantry weapon in Egypt was the Mark II Martini-Henry rifle, which was a lever operated breach-loader using all-metal cartridges, with a range up to 1,800 yards. During the campaign in Egypt, soldiers' accounts make no mention of any detrimental effects by sand or fouling, but refer to the significant 'kick' of the rifle in the shoulder, caused by the eighty-five grains (5.5 g) of black powder propellant. In the fighting along the Sweetwater Canal, infantrymen recorded opening fire at 900 yards and firing for several hours.[16] At the Battle of Tel el-Kebir, each infantryman carried a fighting order of 100 rounds of ammunition, along with bayonet, rations, and a water canteen. The cavalry was issued with a carbine variant but tended to make use of the *arme blanche* in engagements. Both of these forces were supported by the Royal Navy's Gatling guns, the crank-handled, rotary firing, spring-loaded weapon which could fire a steady continuous 400 rounds per minute, out to one mile, to suppress an area target. The turning motion of the barrel allowed the mechanism to cool, which greatly reduced the risk of jamming, but the hot and sandy conditions in Egypt created their own challenges. For longer range fire, the Royal

---

[15] See, for example Sergeant C. Spraggs, Diary, 17 September 1882, Acc. Nbr. 7706/14, National Army Museum, London.
[16] Spiers, *The Victorian Soldier in Africa*, 84.

Artillery's weapons consisted of the 9-pounder horse artillery gun and the 12-pounder for the field artillery, that could reach out to 3,500 yards but crews could also improvise: In one incident, an abandoned enemy Krupp gun was mounted on a disused railway car and opened up at very long range on retreating Egyptian forces.[17]

Strategy and War Aims

Reinforcements were initially sent to General Alison at Alexandria, but this was part of Wolseley's deception plan. He had always intended to fix Arabi at Kafr el-Dauar and advance from Suez against Cairo. He estimated that Arabi would have to fight in the vicinity of Tel el-Kebir to save his capital. Not only had Wolseley devised the plan himself, but he had also been instrumental in its administration and organization, creating the later popular epithet for efficiency as 'All Sir Garnet'. Tents, fuel, transport animals, and hospitals were arranged in Cyprus and Malta. Royal Engineers were allocated to railway management, military police were deployed, there was a postal unit, a staff for managing war correspondents, and a logistics staff to allocate, transport, and then distribute ammunition, rations, and stores.

Wolseley had joined the army in 1852, served in Burma and in the Crimea, where he was wounded in both campaigns, and then served in the Indian Mutiny (see Chapter 2). Such was his courage and skill that he was promoted to Lieutenant Colonel at the age of twenty-five. He worked as a staff officer in China (see Chapter 3) and then Canada, organizing the Red River Campaign in 1871, before being promoted as Assistant Adjutant General in the War Office during critical army reforms. He then took command of the successful expedition against the Ashanti (Asante) (see Chapter 6), a campaign marked by exceptional efficiency and attention to detail. He went on to appointments in India, Cyprus, and South Africa, taking part in the closing stages of the Zulu War of 1879 (see Chapter 8). He returned to Britain as a modernising Quarter Master General and then Adjutant General, before taking command of the Egyptian Campaign force. As the senior officer, he instilled much confidence in his men.

Wolseley calculated that the revolt had to be defeated at its heart, in the city of Cairo, and to secure the Suez Canal (to prevent it being blocked to shipping), it made sense to make the main thrust from that direction towards the capital. The force at Alexandria would fix the attention of the

[17] Ibid.

Egyptian Army while Wolseley's force got into position. The line of communication from Ismailia, on the Canal, would be shorter too, only seventy-five miles compared with 120 miles from Alexandria. Wolseley ruled out trying to advance across the Nile Delta because of the dense cultivation, numerous irrigation channels, and the risk of igniting a popular revolt that would hamper his supply column.

Alison was ordered to make a demonstration of force at Kafr el-Dauar, which had the effect that Wolseley intended. The sensationalism of the press unwittingly added to the deception. In Alexandria, the vernacular media amplified the stories, which seemed to convince all of their veracity. For five weeks, Arabi languished at his fortifications, unaware that Wolseley was out manoeuvring him to the east. Wolseley knew that, as soon as Arabi realized, he would try to resist around Tel el-Kebir, and it was here that the British Army intended to inflict a decisive defeat on the Egyptian Army.

The Royal Navy moved swiftly to seize Ismailia and simultaneously blocked traffic from entering the Suez Canal from the southern end. Port Said was taken by Royal Marines and sailors in a night operation, which captured the Egyptian troops in their beds. Within an hour, the entire port had been secured. Meanwhile, Wolseley had quietly re-embarked the Guards Brigade, and its cavalry and artillery support, at Alexandria, and they joined the forces concentrating off Port Said. To create confusion, a message was telegraphed to the War Ministry in Cairo stating that Ismailia had fallen to 5,000 British troops and therefore a relief attempt was pointless. The message was accepted as entirely valid, even though, at the time, the British forces had not even secured that vital railhead on the Canal.[18] As the British maritime convoy made its way along the waterway, the Royal Navy seized Ismailia, with reinforcements of the 1st Royal West Kent's rushing in on gun-boats.

Once Ismailia was secure, Wolseley intended to reduce the force at Alexandria, now under Lieutenant-General Sir Edward Hamley, and bring more men to join his advance from Suez, but, until he had landed sufficient numbers, he required the Alexandria force to continue to distract and pin the Egyptians.

The Course of the War

Unloading Wolseley's force took time, as a vast number of stores, men, and horses had to be moved off a narrow landing area. The Egyptians lost

[18] Ibid., 81.

another opportunity at this moment, when their advanced guard in the area withdrew to concentrate at Tel el-Kebir. On the other hand, the Egyptian engineers were busy building a dam across the Sweetwater Canal at Magfar to deny British forces sufficient supply. Wolseley regarded this as a critical factor that necessitated immediate action. He therefore moved with those troops that had disembarked on 23 August, the 1st Division, with the Household cavalry, and part of N/A Battery, Royal Horse Artillery (RHA) and used them to drive off the nearest Egyptian forces.

To exploit this unexpected early success, Wolseley ordered his men forward to Kassassin, a lock further up the Sweetwater Canal. In two days, he had achieved more than he had anticipated, so the priority was to adjust his system of supply to support his advanced units. This was crucial because the numbers that Wolseley could bring up was limited entirely by what could be supplied. Some wheeled transport was improvised to ease the constraints. At this anxious time, Wolseley also had to contend with the ambitions of Hamley at Alexandria, who requested permission to assault Kar el-Dauar. Wolseley curtly refused and ordered that the Highland Brigade be embarked to join him at Kassassin.[19]

The Egyptians realized that the Kassassin force was relatively small (of brigade strength) and preparations were made for a counter-attack that would drive off the British. An attempt to envelop the British force at night was checked by a chance encounter with the Household Cavalry which was itself conducting a wide flank march. The moonlight charge, at close quarters, broke through the Egyptian infantry before their firepower could have much effect. In the brief action, British losses were nine killed and seventeen wounded, but the Egyptian force had simply ceased to exist, such was the speed and weight of the attack.

For the next twelve days, Wolseley established his rail and canal communications, brought up his entire force, and accumulated his stores. Detailed reconnaissance was made of the main Egyptian position at Tel el-Kebir. On 12 September, Arabi had dashed eastwards to meet the new threat, and his Arab guides, perhaps eager not to offend him, reported that the British were weak at Kassassin and cut off from their supplies at Ismailia. Arabi decided to seize the opportunity and advanced. What he encountered was not a weak force, but 8,000 British troops, supported by another brigade, the Guards, just ten miles off. The British were ready and waiting when the Egyptians appeared on two axes. While guns engaged on both sides, the Guards Brigade were

---

[19] The Military Journal of the Hon. G. H. Gough, entry for 5 October 1882, GB 133 Eng MS 1375, John Rylands Library, University of Manchester.

ordered up with the objective of hitting one of the Egyptian formations in the flank. The Egyptians seemed to hesitate, so a general advance was ordered, and Arabi's force, deterred by the scale and firepower they had encountered, began to withdraw. By mid-morning, the British had pursued them as far as the main defences at Tel el-Kebir and some thought was given to making a sudden attack while the Egyptians were pulling back. Such a move might not only have incurred unnecessary casualties, but could have run into a much larger enemy reserve, and so it was decided not to press on.

The Anatomy of Battle: Tel el-Kebir

At Tel el-Kebir, ditches and earthworks some four miles long had been constructed, with ten artillery bastions at intervals, the whole position resting on the banks of the Sweetwater Canal.[20] Behind the first line there were more entrenchments and guns, while, 1,000 yards out to the front, there was a redoubt. The ground was flat, open, and exposed. The ramparts of the Egyptian positions were protected by two parallel ditches between six and nine feet deep, designed to catch an assaulting force in a killing zone at close quarters. The ramparts themselves stood six feet high and ten feet deep. Within these defences were some 20,000–30,000 regular Egyptian troops and seventy-five guns, distributed as fourteen battalions in the first line, three in reserve, and three more to the south of the canal.

To reduce the effectiveness of the defences and to maximize the impact of a mounted pursuit in daylight, Wolseley opted for a night attack. This had the added advantage of making the final assault at dawn and taking advantage of the cooler conditions for his marching men. To maximize the element of surprise, there was to be no preliminary bombardment, and every man was to remain silent for the seven-mile approach. Divisions would proceed with one brigade forward and the other 1,000 yards behind, and each division, covering a 1,000-yard frontage, was to maintain a gap of 1,200 yards from the next.[21] The Cavalry Division and RHA was posted to the open, northern flank, ready to ride in behind the position once the infantry had broken through. The artillery would be held with the reserve brigades, ready to come into action at the moment of contact. The Indian Infantry Brigade, consisting

---

[20] Egyptian Defences at Tel El Kebir, 13 Sept 1882, WO 33/40, no. 211, The National Archives.
[21] British Formation for Attack at the Battle of Tel-el-Kebir, Derived from General Wolseley's Report, 10 Sept 1882, WO 33/40, no. 209, TNA.

of a British battalion and four Indian ones, was to remain south of the canal, ready to move on to Zagazig, an important railway junction some fifteen miles behind the front. It was to be supported by a naval brigade, Gatling machine guns, and 40-pounder naval gun.

Darkness and the need for secrecy briefly threw the British off their axis, but discipline ensured that, despite the error, all was corrected, dressing restored, and the axis re-established without a sound. As the night wore on, the alignment of stars shifted and so, with it, went the entire British force. The result was that the troops would arrive in slightly different points than they had intended. Fortunately, this meant that the Highland Brigade did not collide with the advanced Egyptian redoubt, which would have blown the element of surprise.

When Egyptian sentries, only 200 yards in front of the ramparts, raised the alarm, the Highlanders fixed bayonets, and stepped up their pace, while frantic Egyptian soldiers jumped to their fire steps. Their first shots engaged the Highlanders at 100 yards, but the Scotsmen were now unstoppable. Released from their imposed silence, they yelled loudly, and started to scramble over the double ditches with the Egyptians pouring fire into their ranks as they slid and clawed their way over. The weight of fire meant, for a moment, it looked as if the assault might stall in the 'kill zone'. General Hamley, who had been spoiling for a fight at Alexandria, was having none of it, and demanded that the attackers press on.[22] His encouragement and presence in the front lines meant the Egyptian position was cleared and he pushed the reserve companies forward. They crossed a second fire-swept glacis and dived into the Egyptian entrenchments, wrestling their way along them with bayonets. On the right of the Highland Brigade, the Black Watch were struggling to capture a five-gun redoubt and the close quarter battle lasted a full twenty-five minutes. When the Rifles came up, the action finally tilted in the British favour.

The Highland Light Infantry had a similar problem with a four-gun bastion. The ditches were deeper and wider, and the Sudanese troops holding it refused to give way. The Highlanders just couldn't get in and had to fall back to regroup until the Duke of Cornwall's Light Infantry came up in support. A renewed attack here finally carried the position, but it took forty-five minutes to secure it.

---

[22] Alexander Innes Shand, *The Life of General Sir Edward Bruce Hamley* (Edinburgh: W. Blackwood, 1896), vol. 2, 107, 152; See also, G. Tylden, 'Tel-el-Kebir, 13th September, 1882', *Journal of the Society for Army Historical Research* 31, 126 (Summer 1953): 52–57; Hugh Chisholm (ed.), 'Sir Edward Bruce Hamley', *Encyclopædia Britannica*, 12 (Cambridge University Press, 1911), 896.

Meanwhile, the 1st Division had swarmed over the first line of ramparts only to find that the Egyptians had pulled back a short distance to fire a volley into the British lines as they came over. The losses could not stop the attack though, which had taken on its own momentum. Egyptian gunners fired enfilade from their redoubt that was under attack by the Black Watch, until they were silenced, and the intrepid N/2 battery, Royal Artillery, threw their guns and limbers over the Egyptian ramparts to engage at close quarters. One gun's wheel broke in the manoeuvre, earning accolades for this daring unit. With artillery support, the 1st Royal Irish Fusiliers, who had advanced in textbook short rushes, also managed to get into hand-to-hand fighting with the Egyptians. Elsewhere, individual companies were now reforming and wheeling to deliver fire into the Egyptian flanks, and more British guns were coming into action.

The Cavalry Division was also engaged, taking on the northern most redoubt of the defences. To the Egyptians, it seemed as if the British were coming through at every point, and, initially wavering, their entire line finally gave way. The Cavalry Division now started to sweep the retreating troops southwards towards the bridge of Tel el-Kebir, while the Guards, Highlanders, and 1st Division continued to drive the Egyptians backwards. By 6.00 a.m., the entire position was taken.

To the south of the canal, the Indian Brigade had swung southwards and come in on the Egyptian right flank, supported by the fire of the Gatling guns. The accompanying cavalry caught the retreating Egyptians as they pulled out, breaking up their formation entirely. All that remained of the Egyptian Army was a mass of fugitives, trying desperately to reach the safety of the town. Arabi abandoned his men, leaving his positions strewn with 2,000 Egyptian dead and a multitude wounded. Wolseley had lost fifty-seven men and 412 wounded. The victory was therefore comprehensive. As Wolseley had predicted, resistance was broken, and the Indian Brigade took Zagazig without difficulty. At one point, the Indian troops found themselves marching parallel to the demoralized *fellahin* soldiers but not a shot was fired.[23]

The Cavalry Division pressed on towards Cairo, which it reached the next day. The inhabitants were eager to avoid destruction, and the Egyptian leaders wished to come to terms with the British too. They warned that if the cavalry tried to enter the city there would be rioting. Undeterred, Colonel Herbert Stewart, leading a party of Indian cavalrymen, ordered that the Citadel surrender and the garrison lay down their

---

[23] Barthorp, *War on the Nile*, 73.

arms. Moreover, Arabi was to be handed over. Two squadrons took possession of the 10,000-strong garrison and their arms under cover of darkness and Arabi was brought in.

Aftermath

To retain order, a force of 10,000 British troops was established in Egypt, but the balance returned home. There was praise for Wolseley for the rapid and decisive victory. He was made a viscount and granted financial reward. There was considerable admiration for the Royal Navy too, which had made the success of the campaign possible. Indeed, it is important to note that the Royal Marines and Sailors had been in the vanguard of almost every action, including the assault on Tel el-Kebir.

The plan was for Arabi to be handed over to the Khedive, but the Egyptian leader was cautioned that execution, for him or his comrades, would be unacceptable. In the event, they were court martialled on charge of rebellion, but death sentences were commuted to exile. Arabi was sent to Ceylon, and, when he returned in 1901, he had been forgotten. His reputation was restored by nationalists in the 1950s, eager to claim that his revolt had been the first national uprising against colonial rule. In fact, the British government was deeply opposed to permanent occupation. Gladstone was eager to restore the status quo ante bellum, and regain French confidence, but with Egypt's army defeated, its government on an uncertain footing, and its finances in disarray, he knew he could not simply abandon the country. He believed that the moral imperative was to ensure that Egypt was reorganized to enjoy representative government, sound financial management, and security for its people. British advisors and administrators were to be sent to realize this ambition, but this merely prolonged the administration from London, inviting the very accusations of foreign control that Gladstone had sought to avoid.

For security, a gendarmerie was created under Colonel Valentine Baker, while the Egyptian Army was reconfigured under Major-General Sir Evelyn Wood. The problem was that Egypt needed to find a solution for its Sudanese colony, which, in light of the defeat in 1882, was being mobilized by a millenarian military leader known to his followers as the Mahdi.

Outbreak of War: The Mahdist Revolt

The Egyptians had conquered the various disunited clans of the upper Nile from 1819 onwards, so that, by the 1870s, the Khedive's dominion extended to the equatorial belt of Africa, some 800 miles south of Khartoum. Nevertheless, Egyptian authority was resented. The corrupt and idle administration, backed by some 40,000 reluctant and conscripted peasant soldiers and irregulars, allowed slavery of the black population to flourish.[24] Although officially outlawed, local Arabs were adept at bribing officials. The most enterprising of these was the ruthless Zobeir Rahama, who had carved out control of Darfur province and 'awarded' it to the Khedive in return for the status of Pasha. Despite the size of Egypt's Sudanese empire, the financial crises of the regime led to the further deterioration of its governance and abuses of power.

The Khedive sought to deflect European criticism by appointing General Charles Gordon, a successful administrator and military officer who had crushed the Tai'ping on behalf of the Chinese Imperial government in the 1860s, as the Governor of Sudan's Equatorial Province. Gordon pursued the slave-traders with great energy and resolution, his Christian convictions giving him a fearless disregard for his own security. His admonition of corrupt officials endeared him to many southern Sudanese. In 1877, he defeated the rising of the tribe of Zobeir Rahama, the Bahr el-Ghazal. Zobeir's own son was killed and the slave system smashed. Gordon was eventually to step down in 1879, but his replacement, Muhammad Ra'uf Pasha, was ineffectual. The Egyptian administrators returned to their corrupt practices, which only served to highlight the benevolence of Gordon, and, crucially, inspired the possibility of a better authority than that of Cairo.

In 1881, Mohammed Ahmed, a boat-building apprentice, emerged as a teacher of a radical form of Islamism, seeking, like so many of that type, to renew, regenerate, and purge the Muslim faith of all forms of external influence.[25] An attempt to arrest the preacher for his incitement to violent resistance ended in utter failure when the two Egyptian companies sent to capture him were beaten, routed, and annihilated by an angry mob. Mohammed Ahmed believed the incident was evidence of his divine mission and he declared himself Mahdi. He claimed to have visions and the gift of prophesy. He told his followers that he had been sent by God to not only deliver Sudan and Egypt from all non-believers and apostates, but the whole world. Despite the confidence of his predictions, he nevertheless fled the Nile and took refuge in the remoteness of Kordofan province. Raids and assassinations were organized and in

---

[24] A. I. M. Ali, *The Slave Trade and Slavery in the Sudan, 1820–1881* (Khartoum: Khartoum University Press, 1972).
[25] Peter Holt, *The Mahdist State in the Sudan, 1881–1898*, 2nd ed. (Oxford: Clarendon, 1970), 26.

December 1881, the Mahdists ambushed 1,400 Egyptian troops and followers near Fashoda and killed them all.[26] It was not all unrelenting success, however. The Egyptian Army managed one or two small victories. Their problem was that, with insufficient resources, badly-led and scarcely motivated to hazard their lives, the Egyptian troops were too often beaten.

Sudan's garrisons were besieged and overwhelmed. Critically, an entire brigade of 4,000 was attacked and wiped out in southern Kordofan.[27] The Mahdists successes, the defeat of the Egyptians, and the absence of the expected retribution not only emboldened Mohammed Ahmed, they ignited the population of the Sudan in revolt. By the end of 1882, the Mahdists had established control of much of the region, with the exception of the major urban centres and the Nile valley. Faced with certain destruction, Egyptian soldiers held out in these locations. At El Obeid, the garrison refused to capitulate until starvation and defection forced them to surrender. The Mahdists had soon acquired modern rifles, artillery, and ammunition.

Following the British intervention in 1882, the Egyptian Army in the Nile had been reduced in size to just 6,000 men and was undergoing retraining, so very few troops were available to make a counter offensive against the Mahdi. The British government wanted to reduce British influence to a small, affordable garrison at Alexandria and refused to consider any British force being sent to Sudan. The result was that the Egyptian authorities recalled 10,000 men of Arabi's old army, with a handful of British officers in an advisory role. Colonel William Hicks, who had been retired from the Indian Army, was invited to lead an expedition with the majority of these men with the Egyptian rank of Major-General. Short of money, Hicks accepted, but it was clear to him and his fellow officers that the rank and file were undisciplined, unmotivated, and largely untrained. Hicks himself had no experience of desert warfare but he won some early successes around Khartoum and it was logical to next recover El Obeid in Kordofan.[28] He was denied any further manpower or funds, so he was compelled to set out with what he had: 7,000 infantry, some mounted Sudanese irregulars, fourteen guns, six machine guns, and a large baggage column.

The Mahdi lured Hicks's men into a trap at Kashgil.[29] There were few survivors, and the 40,000 Mahdists were now armed with a total of nineteen Krupp guns, some 21,000 modern rifles, and an array of other,

---

[26] Charles Royle, *The Egyptian Campaigns, 1882 to 1885* (London: Hurst and Blackett, LTD, 1900), 216.
[27] Barthorp, *War on the Nile*, 79. [28] Royle, *The Egyptian Campaigns*, 236.
[29] It is alleged that, in addition to a vast charge from several directions, some Mahdists had hidden in pits with camouflaged roofs, attacking the Egyptians from behind. Corroboration of such claims is impossible. Report of Bimbashi Mahmud Effendi

older weapons.[30] Soon after Hicks's defeat, Darfur Province fell to the Mahdi, while the southern garrisons of the Equatorial Province were effectively cut off from Khartoum. On the Red Sea coast, the Arab-Hadendoah slave owner, Osman Digna (Uthman Abu Bakr Diqna), inspired by the news of the Mahdi's success, joined the spreading revolt and laid siege to the port of Suakin.

The effect of Hicks's defeat went further. Gladstone was again consulted about the Sudan, but he reiterated his objections to intervention. The British advised the Egyptian government to abandon Sudan altogether, but it was unclear how the remaining garrisons were to be evacuated without massacre. Some Egyptians considered the notorious slaver Zobeir Pasha as a man who could strike a bargain with the Mahdi, but his reputation made him unpalatable to the British. Instead, it was decided that Gordon should be sent.[31] London regarded Gordon as someone who could produce reliable observations on the extent of the Mahdist revolt, but Cairo saw Gordon as a man who could evacuate Khartoum and the other remaining garrisons. Sir Evelyn Baring, the British Consul-General, had some misgivings about Gordon as a candidate, fearing that a devout Christian heading into a region engulfed by an Islamic revolt might further enflame the situation.

At Suakin, the situation continued to deteriorate. General Valentine Baker, an officer with recent military experience in Turkish service, commanded a force of old soldiers that had advanced to relieve the besieged garrison at nearby Tokar. When, at El Teb, Osman Digna's large force appeared suddenly, the Egyptian cavalry tried to retire but ran into their own infantry and threw them into disorder. As they tried to reform, the charging Hadendoah crashed into them and in the resulting hand-to-hand struggle, some two-thirds of Baker's men were killed and wounded. He rallied the routed survivors and struggled back to the port.

To hold Suakin, the Royal Navy landed a detachment of Royal Marines, until General Graham, en route to India with three British infantry battalions and a cavalry regiment, relieved them soon after. Graham demanded that Osman Digna withdraw, but when no reply came, Graham advanced on 29 February 1884 to defeat the Hadendoah who had entrenched themselves at El Teb, along with the guns they had captured from Baker.

Abdallah, Statements on the Destruction of Hicks Expedition, CAIRINT 3/9/197, National records office, Khartoum; Nichol, *The Mahdi of the Sudan*, 186.

[30] It is alleged that a third of the Egyptian survivors surrendered and 500 escaped. Royle, *The Egyptian Campaigns*, 249.

[31] C. Brad Faught, *Gordon: Victorian Hero* (Dulles: Potomac, 2008), 79–80.

Conscious that the Hadendoah could make surprise attacks at close quarters, Graham organized his brigade in a large square, with machine guns and field artillery at the corners.[32] In this formation, the men marched, advancing onto the left of the Hadendoah fortifications. The Sudanese response was to fire all they had at the British forces, and when this failed to stop the advance towards them, they launched a series of desperate rushes. Each of these was cut down by the disciplined fire of the British regulars. Gradually, the Hadendoah positions were cleared and the Sudanese started to pull back. The British cavalry of the 10th and 19th Hussars set off in pursuit, only to be ambushed by a concealed force just off their axis. The rear squadrons halted, turned about, and then charged their would-be attackers, resulting in a chaotic melee in the thorn scrub. The Hadendoah threw themselves down and tried to cut the horses legs, inflicting casualties, so many troopers dismounted to open up with their carbines, which turned the tide. The Sudanese forces then collapsed and retreated.

Graham had not yet brought Osman Digna to terms and so he continued his advance to Tamai on 13 March 1884, marching in two large square formations. Once again, the action was initiated by a sudden ambush, this time with thousands of Hadendoah surging up from ravines closest to the British troops. The York and Lancaster Regiment, which was nearest the onslaught, fired a volley, which inflicted severe losses, but the momentum of the Sudanese charge brought them into a close quarter fight. The corner machine gun had jammed, the crew were cut down, and a gap had opened in the formation. The result was another chaotic hand to hand fight with bayonets and spears. Meanwhile the second British square had been able to cut down a second charge, and the mass of tribesmen, stung by this intense fire, had veered off to the right and piled into the seething mass of the melee that was underway. The second square therefore advanced rapidly to fire into the side of the assailants, while the British cavalry peeled off to produce the same effect on the Hadendoah's other flank. The combined fire turned the tide and the Sudanese now fell back, leaving over 2,000 dead behind them.[33]

---

[32] Graham's command consisted of 3,342 infantry, gunners, and sappers, 864 cavalry, and 28 guns, while Osman Digna's army at that point was estimated at 15,000. The British force consisted of the 10th Hussars, the 19th Hussars, and the Mounted Infantry; the infantry were formed of 1st Battalion Black Watch, 3rd Battalion King's Royal Rifle Corps, 1st Battalion Gordon Highlanders, 1st Battalion Royal Irish Fusiliers, 1st Battalion York and Lancaster Regiment, and Royal Marine Light Infantry, supported by the Royal Artillery, the Royal Engineers, and the ubiquitous Royal Navy.

[33] Some estimates were as high as 4,000 but even the lower figure of 2,000 represented a fifth of Osman Digna's entire force.

As the square regrouped and advanced again, small parties continued to rush forward, only to be cut down by volleys of rifle and machine gun fire. Tamai was a British victory, but it had cost 119 killed and 112 wounded, mostly from the melee. Graham knew, however, that he had inflicted grievous losses on Osman Digna and he requested permission to press on to the Nile at Berber. The British government at home refused and ordered his forces back to Suakin, losing a significant opportunity in the process.

Gordon, meanwhile, had reached Khartoum, and, while warning that the termination of Graham's advance would lead to the severance of communications down the Nile, he set about assessing the situation. His arrival had been greeted with enthusiasm in the city, not least because locals believed Gordon would put to an end the abuses of the Egyptians and deter the Mahdists from attacking them. Gordon did not disappoint. He wiped out local debts, freed prisoners, abolished torture, cut taxation, and, most popular of all, ignored local slavery on which local merchants depended. He also announced his intention to evacuate the Egyptians and therefore his willingness to see a Sudanese administration established. His choice was Zobeir Pasha, but London, about to lose their telegraph link with Khartoum, would not hear of it. Gordon was cut off, surrounded, and outnumbered, and the Mahdi's army was closing in from all directions.

British and Mahdist Forces

The Mahdi styled his men originally as *dervish* (poor) before repudiating the title later in favour of *ansar* (seekers), but, despite subsequent claims that this was a national revolt, his followers were from a great variety of groups, invariably divided, but held together by certain grievances and religious faith.[34] While the peoples were generally identified as black or of Arab descent, there were fifty-six major tribes in the Sudan, with 600 sub-clans. Some occupied positions of prestige and power, while others were treated as slave stock and fought for their survival.

The British Army had initially encountered the eastern Sudanese, the Beja, who were sub-divided into the Hadendoah (from: Hada-, chief; -endowa, people), Bisharin, Ababda, Beni-Amer, Amarar, Shukaria, Hallengra, and Hamran. British soldiers were struck by the distinctive hair styles of the Hadendoah, which was clumped into three bunches with fat, and they nick-named them the 'fuzzy-wuzzy'. Despite the

---

[34] Nicoll, *Mahdi of Sudan*, 36.

disarming epithet, immortalized by Rudyard Kipling, there was some respect for the dauntlessness of the Beja as fighters. Armed with a small hide shield and leaf-bladed spear or knives, these fighters ran full tilt at the British lines, regardless of the casualties they suffered, at least initially. They soon learned to make better use of the terrain to conceal themselves and avoid the full force of Western firepower.

The Baggara (Baqara) inhabited the northern Kordofan and were nomadic cattle herders by tradition, but they became a loyal core of the Mahdi's forces during the revolt. The Kabbabish (literally 'the sheep and goat herders') were also regarded as an 'Arab' population and they occupied the area between Darfur and Dongola on the Nile. To the south and east, along the Blue Nile and Atbara, were the Arabic-speaking Hassania, Shukria, and Ja'alin. The latter group claimed descent from the Prophet's family and were amongst the most zealous to join the Mahdi. The arc of groups to the south were blacks, including, from the west of the Nile, the Shilluk; east of the Nile, the Dinka; and south of Fashoda, the Nuer. Some of these men were conscripted into the Mahdist forces, and some continued to resist the self-proclaimed prophet, preferring to take their chances on Anglo-Egyptian service.

The Mahdist army was organized in three loose divisions, each commanded by a Khalifa and identified by a giant, coloured standard. The black flag division, led by Khalifa Abdullah, was drawn from the Western Sudan; the green standard, under the direction of Ali wad Hilu, was made up of men from the central Sudan; and the red flag division, from northern Sudan, was commanded by Mohammed esh Sherif.[35] Within these broad divisions, groups of men led by minor emirs would attach themselves. In theory, the flag divisions were made up of rubs ('quarters', or regiments of approximately a 1,000 men) which consisted of riflemen, spearmen, swordsmen, mounted men, and administrative personnel. Traditionally, such groupings only emerged in time of crisis, but in the revolt, attempts were made to put these detachments on a permanent 'standing' footing, based in settlements. The model of standing forces was the slave-owners' *jihadiyya* standards (rifle companies) led by a *ra's mi'a* (leader of a hundred). These companies were subdivided into platoons, each with their own commander.

The technology with which the Ansar were armed varied a great deal. Captured arms were the most modern, but there were older weapons, including a large, tripod-mounted muzzle-loading musket that fired a

---

[35] Ibid., 4, 103.

large-calibre round. A number of men carried the leaf-bladed spear, throwing javelins, and double-edged swords known as kaskaras. There may have been great potential in the captured modern weapons, but shortages of ammunition, lack of training, and an absence of skilled operators limited their effectiveness. It was the relative weakness in fire power that led to the dependence on the tactics of, first, a large fusillade of fire, followed second, by a charge of men with bladed weapons. To advance over longer distances at speed, the men would jog at a steady pace, usually in silence. The final rush was delivered with chanting, often prayers, which increased in volume until they could get close to their enemies. The combination encouraged their comrades, but induced fear in undisciplined adversaries.

The most significant challenge for the Egyptian forces in their efforts to crush the Mahdist rising had been the availability of manpower, although the scattered arrangement of their garrisons made concentration even more difficult. The lack of funding, resources, and willing personnel added to the problems, and the standard of Egyptian officers was, frankly, low. The strength of the Egyptian Army was in its weapons technology, which was far better than that of the Mahdists, but, once these weapons were captured, it enhanced the Sudanese resistance significantly. Egyptian defeats caused a surge of support for the Mahdi and further demoralized the Khedive's isolated troops. Several garrisons capitulated when besieged and some were betrayed and captured. Others, fearing massacres, held out, including Khartoum.

The Egyptian Army was attempting to reform when actually fighting a conflict. Eight battalions had been formed in the north after 1882, with the 1st Brigade under British officers, and the 2nd Brigade under Egyptian and Turkish commanders. The disciplinary system was altered to the British model, abolishing the brutal practises of the past. However, the army in the Sudan had not been exposed to these modernizing influences.

The disarray in the Egyptian army meant that British forces had to stem the advancing tide of Mahdism. Unlike the campaign of 1882, the British Army had switched to khaki (or grey) tropical uniforms, more suitable to the climate. The heat, distances, and the labours of campaigning up the Nile nevertheless meant the conflict was considered 'more against nature' than an enemy.

The Camel Corps had been designed for just this purpose. It consisted of hand-picked men from the units serving on the Nile and divided into specific detachments, supported by some light artillery and machine guns. It was, in all, one of the most unusual contingents ever formed by the British Army and designed specifically for the Nile campaign.

A total of 9,000 men, and 40,000 tons of stores had to be moved up the Nile. Initially this involved rail transportation, and then movement up the river by whalers, with eight to ten regular soldiers to a boat. The troops described dust storms and heat that were 'fearful' but the river transit was hazardous and often exhausting.[36] All ranks described the conditions as 'trying', with added discomforts from flies, thirst, sunburn, and infections that, periodically, claimed lives.

Despite long marches and the difficulties of keeping camels concentrated alongside the marching troops, the British Army's emphasis on discipline, control, and cohesion was valuable. In the face of Sudanese attacks, often in large numbers, the British soldier was expected to maintain a regular rate of fire and steadiness in receiving a charge. Less cohesive forces would have been unable to endure, as the fate of Hicks's army had proven, but the combination of their superior firepower and the strength of their cohesiveness produced confidence.[37] The concern was over the proportions of casualties suffered, with losses caused primarily by hand to hand fighting and sniping into night bivouacs.[38] Medical arrangements, especially for those travelling back down the Nile, were considered inadequate. Perhaps the greatest blow to morale came, though, with news of Khartoum's fall and the loss of Gordon.[39]

Strategy and War Aims

After considerable public pressure to save Gordon, and an appeal from Queen Victoria, the British government finally agreed to send a relief column up the Nile. Wolseley was selected to lead the relief force on the strength of his reputation for successful and short expeditionary campaigns in West Africa and Canada. He was also a personal friend of Gordon. Wolseley ordered the brigade of 6,000 men to march up alongside the river to make certain of its water supply. To traverse the cataracts, whalers were required, operated by Canadian boatmen, and a vast store of supplies accumulated. The alternative route, from Suakin, was considered, but rejected, because it was thought that the line of communication would be more vulnerable and it could only be made secure by the time-consuming construction of a railway. So much time had been lost in political procrastination that there was now pressure to move

---

[36] Spiers, *The Victorian Soldier in Africa*, 114.   [37] Ibid., 118.
[38] Lieutenant Henry W. D. Denne to his father, 26 January 1885, PB 64/8, Gordon Highlanders Museum, Aberdeen.
[39] Captain J. E. Blackburn, 'With the Nile Column from January 17 to March 7 1885', *Royal Engineers Journal* 15 (1885): 154–55.

swiftly. On 17 November 1884, a note from Gordon, stating he had just forty days supplies left (which had taken thirteen days to reach Wolseley) added to the urgency.[40]

At Korti, Wolseley had to decide whether to continue with his whole force along the great bend in the Nile out to the east or to cut across the desert, the shortest route to Khartoum. He calculated that the arrival of a relatively small force of British troops would be enough to deter the Mahdists and probably lift the siege, but it meant breaking an established military maxim of never dividing one's force in proximity of the enemy. Any force sent across the desert, mounted on camels, also had to be self-contained in terms of logistics and strong enough to defeat a large Mahdist army sent against it.[41]

The Course of the War: The Relief Expedition

There were multiple challenges for Wolseley to overcome in operating up the Nile. Since there was no permanent logistics system for the army, the bulk of the riverine traffic was entrusted to the private contractor Thomas Cook and Sons. While practised in moving and supplying small numbers of tourists, the company had no experience of transporting a brigade and all its impedimenta. When the steamers ran out of coal during the build-up of troops and supplies at Wadi Halfa, thirteen more precious days were lost. The railway that reached the forward depot was also in poor repair, adding more frustrating friction. Camels, supplied to the army, were not in the peak of condition. One private soldier described them as 'diseased and swarming with maggots'.[42] Learning to ride these sickly mounts took more time. The boats that Wolseley had brought out from Britain had to be rowed upstream, against the Nile current, and, with the waters falling in this season, there were more cataracts to negotiate. The staff work was not systematized either, and depended on individuals, some of whom were rivals, which only added to misunderstandings and delays. The unifying element was Wolseley himself, and he commanded great loyalty, but that tended to constrain commanders, who preferred to wait for his instructions rather than act on their own initiative.

It took three months, from the moment of authorization, to get the first unit away on the river on 6 November 1884. Each battalion would follow

---

[40] Royle, *The Egyptian Campaigns*, 360–61; Anthony Nutting, *Gordon* (London: Constable, 1966), 264; Barthorp, *War on the Nile*, 100.

[41] Royle, *The Egyptian Campaigns*, 313; Nicoll, *Mahdi of Sudan*, 251; Barthorp, *War on the Nile*, 99–100; For a critical assessment, see Thomas Pakenham, *The Scramble for Africa* (London: George Weidenfeld and Sons, 1991), 232.

[42] Barthorp, *War on the Nile*, 96.

in turn to manage the supply chain, which meant that the last unit to embark would leave Wadi Halfa on 19 December. Wolseley urged his men to make greater haste, offering a bounty to the battalion that made best speed to Dongola: the fastest was the 1st Royal Irish which made the passage in thirty-eight days.[43] Wolseley was informed, in the note from Gordon, that five steamers had been sent out from Khartoum to Metemmeh, about 100 miles north of the city, there to await the relief forces. This news, and knowledge of Gordon's dwindling supplies, meant that Wolseley moved the point of riverine concentration to Korti, the shortest distance from Metemmeh as the crow flies. The Camel Corps, which had marched patiently alongside the river for 360 miles, arrived at this new concentration point on 14 December. This was, in effect, the date which Gordon had estimated to be the limit of his logistics.

The estimates from Wolseley's staff were that, since the first battalion had arrived at Korti on 17 December, it would not be until 22 December that the entire river column could be brought in.[44] Time had, in effect, run out, and Wolseley decided to gamble and send the Camel Corps to Metemmeh, across the desert, and then press on up the Nile to Khartoum. This meant a march of 176 miles, with every expectation of resistance by a larger number of Sudanese fighters at any point. To augment this advance, and possibly deceive the Mahdi, Wolseley also sent four battalions under Major-General W. Earle upriver as an advanced guard, with the intention of capturing Berber before pushing on to Metemmeh. Here there was to be a new base for supplies.

Unfortunately, the shortage of baggage camels meant that the Camel Corps, or Desert Column, would have to first establish a forward base at Jakdul Wells in the desert, and then return the ninety miles to collect the balance of supplies, so as to make the final leg across to Metemmeh. Under Major-General Sir Herbert Stewart, the first camel-borne force set off on 28 December and returned on 5 January to collect the balance. As he did so, Wolseley informed him that another note and verbal report had been received from Gordon: Khartoum was besieged and under attack, but it was a shortage of rations that most threatened the garrison. Gordon had added that Wolseley should proceed in strength as a large Mahdist force had gathered at Khartoum, and he cautioned that Berber should not be left in Mahdist hands in his rear. Wolseley therefore decided to modify his plans. The Camel Corps was to continue to

---

[43] Evelyn Wood, *From Midshipman to Field Marshal* (London: Methuen, 1096), vol. 2, 173–74; Royle, *The Egyptian Campaigns*, 321; Barthorp, *War on the Nile*, 99.
[44] Barthorp, *War on the Nile*, 100; Pakenham, *The Scramble for Africa*, 233.

Korti but avoid a dash on to Khartoum. Instead, it was to join the river steamer force that Gordon had left and fortify itself. In the meantime, Earle was to capture and hold Berber, leaving a battalion entrenched there, while the balance joined the Desert Column at Metemmeh. Only when he had united all his forces, would Wolseley continue to Khartoum. The interval would be used to ascertain in more detail, from the steamer force, the exact conditions Gordon faced. Wolseley retained the contingency, if the city was imminently in danger of falling, of sending the Camel Corps on, but all this depended on better intelligence.

Anatomy of Battle: Abu Klea

The 1,400-strong Camel Corps made its way across the desert as planned, leaving detachments at the critical wells to facilitate the passage. On the second day, small detachments of Mahdists were observed, and, as the Desert Column approached a line of low hills above the next set of wells, it was evident that a larger force had assembled. With little daylight left, Stewart decided to halt the column in a square formation, with a zariba of rocks, piled two feet high, and thorn bushes, around the perimeter. Higher ground was picqueted for early warning of any attack, but during the night, sniping and drumming denied much rest. At dawn on 17 January, the weight of fire increased, resulting in casualties, but Stewart had already resolved to push on and clear his enemy from the hills ahead.[45] The 1st Royal Sussex Regiment was detailed to hold the zariba with the baggage, while the main body moved off in a large square, with the Hussars, Scots Guards, and Mounted Infantry forming a screen. Harassing fire continued, but it was the broken nature of the ground that necessitated a halt, as the 'walls' of the square became stretched.

At that moment, 5,000 Ansar fighters sprang out of the scrub some 500 yards away and charged towards the square. Recovering the skirmishers meant that firing could commence only at 200 yards, but at this range it proved devastating. A 7-pounder gun fired shrapnel and the Mounted Infantry beside them fired volleys, which brought down dozens. The charge veered away to the right, where the ground afforded some cover. The attack, though, had been the signal for other groups of Ansar to charge, and the left rear corner of the square, which was trying to regroup from its extended lines in the march, was their target. Here, a small gap had opened up between the units. As men were wheeled to fill it, the Navy detachment ran their Gardner gun twenty yards off to a flank

---

[45] Nicoll, *Mahdi of Sudan*, 256.

and opened fire, and the 4th and 5th Dragoon Guards were detailed to support them. Just as the Ansar men came within the last few lethal yards of the Gardner, it jammed, and the crew were cut down. The Dragoon Guards were still trying to adjust their front but the Ansar were now upon them, dashing into the gap at the rear of the square.

The rest of the rear of the square was soon a mass of stabbing and thrusting blades and bayonets. Seeing the danger, the rear ranks at the front of the square, who stood on slightly higher ground, turned and fired into the mass in the gap, and the casualties this inflicted caused the Ansar to waver and then fall back as rapidly as they had come. To cover their withdrawal, mounted Ansar horsemen made a charge, but the men at the rear face of the square now had a chance to use the full effect of their weapons, so the large body of horsemen was defeated. Pockets of Ansar men still fighting were now finished off. The action had lasted ten minutes, and, in that time, 1,100 Ansar had been killed and many more wounded.[46] The estimated size of the Ansar force had been between 8,000 and 14,000, but it had been dispersed with significant loss. By contrast, the British had suffered seventy-three killed and ninety-four wounded.

Having cleared their way to the wells, the Desert Column was able to make a night march over the remaining twenty-three miles to Metemmeh. Nevertheless, just after dawn on 19 January, Stewart could see another large force of Ansar advancing from the Nile. He ordered the construction of another defensive zariba to protect the stores and animals, but this work came under a steady and increasing volume of fire from skirmishers. Stewart was mortally wounded and command devolved to Sir Charles Wilson, who, following Stewart's plan, assembled another square to cover the last four miles to the river. The zariba was held by the Heavies, 19th Hussars, gunners, and a Royal Navy detachment, and from this position they could direct artillery fire against the enemy groups forming on either side of the square.

Wilson's force marched steadily, occasionally halting to fire into the groups that tried to remain hidden in the scrub. As they approached a final ridge, the Ansar rose in a vast mass and hurled themselves down the slopes. Relieved that the enemy had shown himself and presented such a clear target, the British soldiers cheered and delivered volley fire which inflicted crops of casualties. The momentum of the attack carried the Ansar over the bodies, but between 400 and 100 yards, the fire became more effective still. Count Gleichen, who was present, noted that not a

---

[46] The Mahdist account of the action at Jabal Abu Tulayh testified that a great many 'companions' were martyred. Nicoll, *Mahdi of Sudan*, 252.

single man got within eighty yards, and described the Mahdists being 'mown down like grass'.[47] The Ansar reserve, observing the fate of the attacking groups at Abu Kru, simply turned and made off. Once again, Mahdist casualties were heavy, and the losses on the British side small – twenty-three had been killed.

The Desert Column reached the Nile, but it was clear that Metemmeh was not held by Gordon's steamer force, which was nowhere to be seen. Fortunately, on 21 January, four steamers appeared from Khartoum with 400 men on board, all utterly relieved to see the Camel Corps. They brought news that a large Mahdist force was on its way and they handed over Gordon's journal and a note which suggested Khartoum could be held. The steamer force was anxious that Wilson's men make best speed to the city, but Wilson was eager to conduct a reconnaissance to prevent another surprise attack. Throughout the next day, Wilson collected fuel for the steamers and made his reconnoitres, without much success. While ready late the next day, Wilson decided to wait until the following morning before pressing on, convinced that no imminent threat now existed.[48]

Two steamers set out on 24 January, carrying 240 Sudanese soldiers and the 1st Royal Sussex, and while making good progress on the first day, one of the vessels ran aground on the 25th and was not freed from the mud for many hours. The same thing happened on the 26th, with precious time lost again. Finally, at 11.00 a.m. on 28 January, the steamers sighted Khartoum. Over the next hour, they came under increasing fire from the banks, and Wilson scanned the city skyline for some indication of the garrison.

Aftermath

Khartoum was an uninspiring settlement with a population of around 50,000, two-thirds of whom were black slaves. A further fifth were not Sudanese, but Egyptians, Syrians, Greeks, and Turks, all eager for protection from the Mahdi's retribution. The confluence of the Blue and White Nile rivers provided security on three sides, while the open south and east was now marked by an 8-foot ditch and a rampart, four miles in length. To augment this obstacle, the ditch and glacis were strewn with broken glass, spikes, and electrically-operated mines. On the far side of the rivers lay two redoubts, the Omdurman and the

---

[47] Lt. Col. Count Gleichen (ed.), *The Anglo-Egyptian Sudan* (London: HMS0, 1905), vol. 1, 248–49 and vol. 2, 180–81; See also Manning, *Soldiers of the Queen*, 165–67.
[48] Nicoll, *Mahdi of Sudan*, 253.

North Fort. To garrison the defences, Gordon could call on 6,000 Egyptian troops and irregulars, 2,400 Sudanese regulars, and 3,000 volunteers and citizens. There were seven river steamers, armed with artillery and machine guns for mobile fire support and sorties, and the whole city had commenced the siege with six months supplies and a great volume of munitions.

Despite his orders to evacuate the city, Gordon vacillated about his mission.[49] He oscillated between obedience to his government's instructions and defiance of the Liberal administration, in part because he was troubled by the idea of abandoning the people of the Sudan to a Jihadist revolt. If Khartoum was held, he reasoned, the revolt could be broken and a more enlightened Sudanese government brought in, perhaps with British protection and benign guidance. The result was that, by March 1884, Gordon had only evacuated 2,000 Egyptian civilians and sick military personnel. Nevertheless, when Khartoum was cut off by the Mahdists, Gordon had little choice but to resist and therefore try and save the city's population from massacre. He expected relief to come, even when Berber, and several provinces, fell into the hands of the Mahdi.

The greatest threat to Gordon's garrison was starvation and the sicknesses associated with it. In late November, Gordon learned of the forward British detachment established at Korti, and he used the information to encourage his hungry and weary garrison. A band played on the roof of the residency to encourage the troops, despite daily shelling and sniping. The steamers were used to give fire support against the repeated raids on the river forts, especially the Omdurman fortifications. But it was food that was dwindling fastest, and on 14 December Gordon estimated he had just two weeks' left. He wrote in his last journal entry that he thought the city might hold for ten days and, if it fell, he recorded 'I have done my best for the honour of our country'.[50] His strong Christian convictions, this sense of duty, and a moral conscience to protect all those who came under British control appealed deeply to the Victorian public at home, and it was his iconic position – the solitary hero facing a desperate situation in a distant and hostile country – that seemed to contrast so strongly with a comfortable and complacent government.

Gordon's situation grew critical through the first days of January, although the discovery of additional stores produced some relief. Nonetheless, the city and its garrison were hunting dogs and rats to

---

[49] Nutting, *Gordon*, 234, 239, 246–47; Pakenham, *The Scramble for Africa*, 221.
[50] Gordon's last entry for his diary, 14 December, as cited in Royle, *The Egyptian Campaigns*, 360; Nutting, *Gordon*, 264.

eat, and gnawed on goatskin water bags. When the food at Omdurman fort ran out altogether, the soldiers, who were too weak to escape, were authorized to capitulate on 12 January 1885. It was an indication to the Mahdists that the end was coming.

Nevertheless, the news of the defeat of the Ansar at Abu Klea, brought in by one of Gordon's spies, indicated that the relief force might still arrive in the nick of time. Further reports came in that the British had secured Metemmeh, just ninety-six miles away, and hope rose for a few days. Many of the Mahdists were just as concerned about the approach of the British forces and some urged an immediate assault and others a withdrawal into the desert. Such was the gravity of the situation in the garrison that a delegation of the city urged Gordon to make terms with the Mahdi. Gordon refused, just as the Mahdi would not give up at this final moment. Convinced of his own rhetoric, and eager to take Khartoum before the British could reinforce it, the Mahdi resolved that the Ansar would make the final assault on 26 January. Gordon, aware that the assaulting forces were assembling, issued orders that every man, from eight to eighty, was to come to the defences for 24 hours, promising that the British Army would soon arrive.

It was not enough. In the early morning, the defences were breached at the south-west and eastern corners, and, despite desperate fighting by the outnumbered Egyptian regulars, within an hour, the Mahdists had overwhelmed the city defenders. Khartoum was utterly sacked, with thousands of civilians killed amidst the looting.[51] During the carnage, Gordon was killed and decapitated, his head being presented to the Mahdi himself.

Wilson's flotilla arrived two days after the city had fallen. The bitterness of being 'too late' was to haunt the entire disconsolate expedition for the rest of the campaign and Gladstone for the rest of his career. Wolseley was informed in the middle of April that the government had decided to terminate the Sudan operations. It was a decision that concluded a campaign which was in danger of drift: there were no strategic interests for Britain to protect in the Sudan. The reason for the campaign had gone when Gordon was killed at Khartoum, so, beyond the punitive desire to chastise the Mahdi, it was hard to see what a conquest of the region would achieve. The Sudanese had little desire to see the Egyptians reinstalled and the British government would not pay for the significant costs of making Sudan a colony, not least when the operations had already cost £7 million. The objective would have been to establish a

---

[51] Nicoll, *Mahdi of Sudan*, 259.

Sudanese government, but, not only would this condone a slave-economy, it was likely it would fall to the Mahdi and his legions, and probably perpetuate the massacres that had engulfed Khartoum. The British Army therefore pulled back to Egypt.

The withdrawal did Gladstone little good. His government was defeated in June 1885, and the public who had once regarded him as the GOM, the Grand Old Man, now styled him the MOG, Murderer of Gordon. The vacillation shown by his administration had contributed directly to the fall of Khartoum, but Liberal leaders resented Gordon's, and the army's, demands for military intervention which they believed served no interest and wasted tax-payers' money. Yet the Liberals reputation for appeasing violent enemies of Britain, such as the Jihadists of the Sudan, the Afrikaners of Transvaal, or Irish terrorists, was punished in the elections. Conversely, Gladstone's most vehement critic, Wolseley, never truly recovered from the ordeal of the campaign either. His health declined, and while he became Commander-in-Chief of the British Army in 1895, he lost much of his reformist energy.

Despite the tendency of some Sudanese and recent historians to eulogize the achievement of the Mahdi, his absurd vision of greatness was exposed within weeks of his victory at Khartoum. Bitter disagreements broke out between the various tribes and factions of the Sudan. The idea that the *Mahdia* represented some national foundation is equally false.[52] There was resentment at the systems of taxation, the demands to observe moral strictures imposed by the new Jihadist authorities, and the profiteering of the leaders. The Mahdi had issued his threats to conquer Egypt, demanding that all bow to his authority, but he was struck down in June 1885 with typhus. For all his grandiose claims to be the equivalent of the Prophet, he ended his days in the corner of a stable block, vomiting and weak. His successor, the Khalifa Abdullah, set about consolidating his power and purging his rivals, but the Sudan, wracked by famine, misgovernment, and crop failures, was left in an acute hiatus for fourteen years (see Chapter 13).

Further Reading

Abu-Salim, Muhammad Ibrahim (ed.) *Al-athar al-kamila lil-imam al Mahdi*, 7 vols. Khartoum: Khartoum University Press, 1990–94.
Barthorp, M. J. *War on the Nile*. Poole: Blandford, 1982.
Blunt, Wilfred Scawan. *A Secret History of the English Occupation of Egypt*. London: T. Fisher Unwin, 1907.

---

[52] Ibid., 268–69.

Brackenbury, Major-General Henry. *The River Column: A Narrative of the Advance of the River Column of the Nile Expeditionary Force*. Edinburgh and London: W. Blackwood and Sons, 1885.
Burleigh, B. *Desert Warfare, Being the Chronicle of the Eastern Soudan Campaign*. London: Chapman and Hall, 1884.
Colville, Colonel H.E. *History of the Soudan Campaign*. London: Harrison and Sons, 1889.
de Cosson, Major E. A. *Days and Nights of Service with Sir Gerald Graham's Field Force at Suakin*. London: J. Murray, 1886.
Elton, Lord (ed.) *General Gordon's Khartoum Journal*. London: W. Kimber, 1961.
al-Gaddal, Muhammad Sa'id. *Lawhali-tha'ir Sudani: al-imam al-Mahdi Muhammad Ahmed bin Abdallah (Portrait of a Sudanese Revolutionary: The Imam Muhammad Ahmed bin Abdallah)*. Khartoum: Khartoum University Press, 1985.
Gleichen, Count. *With the Camel Corps up the Nile*. London: Chapman and Hall, 1888.
Holt, Peter. *The Mahdist State in the Sudan, 1881–1898*, 2nd ed. Oxford: Clarendon, 1970.
Knight, Ian. *Queen Victoria's Enemies (2): Northern Africa*. London: Osprey, 1989.
Kochanski, Halik. *Sir Garnet Wolseley: Victorian Hero*. London: The Hambledon Press, 1999.
Lehmann, John. *All Sir Garnet*. London: Jonathan Cape, 1964.
Mansfield, Peter. *The British in Egypt*. London: Victorian and Modern History Book Club, 1973.
Maurice, Col. J. F. *A Military History of the Campaign in Egypt, 1882*. London: HMSO, 1887.
Nichol, Fergus. *The Mahdi of the Sudan and the Death of General Gordon*. London: Sutton, 2004.
Robinson, Ronald and Gallagher, John. *Africa and the Victorians: The Official Mind of Imperialism*. London: Macmillan, 1961.
Robson, Brian. *Fuzzy-Wuzzy: The Campaign in the Eastern Sudan*. Tunbridge Wells: Spellmount, 1983.
al-Sayid-Marsot, A. 'The Occupation of Egypt', in Andrew Porter (ed.) *The Oxford History of the British Empire: The Nineteenth Century: Volume III*. Oxford: Oxford University Press, 1999.
Symons, J. *England's Pride: The Story of the Gordon Relief Expedition*. London: Hamish Hamilton, 1965.
Tylden, Major G. 'Tel el Kebir'. *Journal of the Society for Army Historical Research*, XXXI (1953): 52–57.
Warner, P. *Dervish: The Rise and Fall of an African Empire*. London: TBS, 1973.
Williams, M. J. 'The Egyptian Campaign, 1882'. In Brian Bond (ed.) *Victorian Military Campaigns*. London: Hutchinson, 1967.
Wolseley, Sir Garnet. *In Relief of Gordon*, ed. Adrian Preston. London: Hutchinson, 1967.

11 The Third Anglo-Burmese War and the Pacification of Burma, 1885–1895

Ian F. W. Beckett

The British conquest of Upper Burma, an area of 140,000 sqaure miles with a population of four million, took only three weeks in November 1885. The occupying force under Major-General Sir Harry Prendergast concentrated at Rangoon between 5 and 11 November 1885. It crossed into Burmese territory on 11 November, seized Minhla in the only serious engagement on 17 November, received a message of surrender from King Thibaw on 27 November, and took Mandalay on the following day. Thibaw and Queen Supayalat were sent into exile on 29 November. Prendergast had easily accomplished his mission to occupy Mandalay, dethroned Thibaw, and avoided 'unnecessary conflict with the people'. He lost four killed, four drowned, and twenty-six wounded, and inflicted an estimated 250 casualties on the Burmese.[1]

Burma was formerly annexed, becoming a province of India on 26 February 1886. The Burmese government had been paralyzed by the speed of the British advance and effectively decapitated. The structures of national and local political power and of social organization were all dismantled by February 1886 and replaced by an entirely new colonial administration supplanting some 300 years of traditional authority. However, there was disorder and arson in Mandalay amid the collapse of central authority with too few troops available to prevent it. Disbanded Burmese soldiers merged with existing bandits known as *dacoits* while more distant ethnic minorities from the capital such as the Chins, Karens, Kachins, Mons, and Shans were no more willing to accept British rule than that of the Burmese in the past. It added to the complexity of what became the longest campaign fought by the Victorian army. What one political officer characterized as a war of 'little affairs' and Rudyard Kipling dubbed the 'campaign of the lost footsteps' took

---

[1] Intelligence Branch, Army Headquarters, *Frontier and Overseas Expeditions from India, Volume 5: Burma* (Simla: Government Monotype Press, 1907), 144, 146.

ten years.[2] Pacification thus embraced not only the initial occupation of the Third Anglo-Burmese War (1885–86) and the ongoing suppression of the dacoits from 1885 to 1891, but also major expeditions against the hill tribes between 1889 and 1895.

Background

The ruling dynasty at the court of Ava was established in the mid-eighteenth century as an absolute (and unstable) monarchy with frequent bloody conflicts waged between rival heirs. So far as the British were concerned, the instability of Burma posed a strategic threat to the north-eastern frontier of India. Great Britain also had significant economic interests in the region. Burmese incursions into the small independent border-states of Assam, Cachar, and Manipur resulted in the First Anglo-Burmese War (1824–26). In February 1826, Burma ceded the Arakan and Tenasserim to the British, agreeing to a commercial treaty, and paying an indemnity. The commercial treaty yielded little of value since the Burmese declined to trade in either rice, a staple food for its people, or in silver. Teak became the basis of trade. General corruption led to increasing attempts at extortion on the part of Burmese officials towards British merchants seeking to penetrate further into the interior as teak forests in Lower Burma became exhausted. Following various incidents, a British blockade of Rangoon resulted in the Second Anglo-Burmese War (1852–53). The Burmese ceded Lower Burma and hundreds of square miles of valuable teak forest in June 1853.

Modernization was attempted by King Mindon (reigned 1853–78) but under the pliable and indolent Thibaw, who succeeded to the throne in 1878, declining revenues, increasing economic difficulties, and poor rice harvests exacerbated the breakdown of royal administration. The British perception was that the real power behind the throne was Thibaw's capricious wife and half-sister, Supayalat, who was held responsible for the slaughter of thirty-one of Thibaw's male siblings. Unrest in the Shan States precipitated the collapse of central control and security in other areas, accelerating the loss of revenues at the same time that the royal court's extravagance increased.

* * * * *

---

[2] Harold Fielding Hall, *The Soul of a People* (London: Macmillan, 1906), 66; Rudyard Kipling, *From Sea to Sea and Other Sketches: Letters of Travel*, Single volume ed. (London: Macmillan, 1900), 218.

Despite its longevity and controversies, the campaign has been little studied. The Government of India did produce an official history of the initial and ongoing operations in six volumes between 1887 and 1893. A section was also devoted to the operations in the fifth volume of the Indian Army Intelligence Branch's *Frontier and Overseas Expeditions from India* in 1907. While the latter has been reproduced in a modern edition, the six-volume official history is only available in the former records of the India Office, now held in the British Library's Asia, Pacific and Africa Collection. Sir Charles Crosthwaite, the British Chief Commissioner from 1887 to 1890 published *The Pacification of Burma* in 1912. There are a few memoirs and contemporary accounts by journalists, but only two monographs dealing solely with the Third Anglo-Burmese War and/or subsequent pacification have appeared in print since 1945, namely A. T. Q. Stewart's, *The Pagoda War: Lord Dufferin and the Fall of the Kingdom of Ava, 1885–86* in 1972 and, from the Burmese perspective, Ni Mi Myint's *Burma's Struggle against British Imperialism, 1885–95* in 1983.[3] More recent analysis is confined to academic journals and unpublished doctoral theses.[4]

Outbreak of War

A trading dispute gave the British the excuse to act. In reality, they were alarmed by the Franco-Burmese treaty signed in January 1885. Under its terms, there were agreements for the French to build a railway between Hanoi and Mandalay, to establish a new bank jointly owned by the French and Burmese, and for the French to control of Burmese ruby

---

[3] Ni Mi Myint, *Burma's Struggle against British Imperialism, 1885–95* (Rangoon: Universities Press, 1983); A. T. Q. Stewart, *The Pagoda War: Lord Dufferin and the Fall of the Kingdom of Ava, 1885–86* (London: Faber & Faber, 1972). For an overview, see Kaushik Roy, *The Army in British India: From Colonial Warfare to Total War, 1857–1947* (London: Bloomsbury, 2013).

[4] Ian F. W. Beckett, 'The Campaign of the Lost Footsteps: The pacification of Burma, 1885–95', *Small Wars and Insurgencies* 30 (2019), 994–1019. See also M. S. Ali, 'The Beginnings of British Rule in Upper Burma: The Study of British Policy and Burmese Resistance, 1885–90', Unpub. Ph.D., London, 1976; Michael Aung-Thwin, 'The British "pacification" of Burma: Order without meaning', *Journal of Southeast Asian Studies* 16 (1985): 245–62; Michael Charney, 'Armed rural folk elements of pre-colonial warfare in the artistic representations and written accounts of the pacification campaign (1886–1889) in Burma', in Michael Charney and Kathryn Wellen (eds.), *Warring Societies of Pre-colonial Southeast Asia: Local Cultures of Conflict within a Regional Context* (Copenhagen: NIAS Press, 2018), 155–81; Takahiro Iwaki, 'The village system and Burmese Society: Problems involved in the enforcement process of the Upper Burma Village Regulation of 1887', *Journal of Burma Studies* 19 (2015): 113–43; Jordan Wingfield, 'Buddhism and insurrection in Burma, 1886–90', *Journal of the Royal Asiatic Society* 20 (2010): 345–67.

The Third Anglo-Burmese War and the Pacification of Burma   223

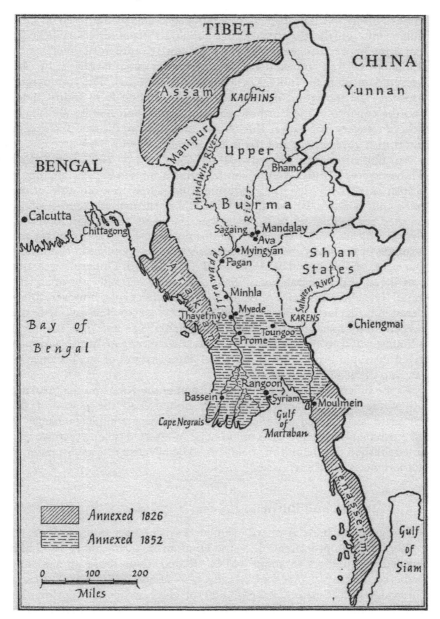

Map 11.1 Burma, 1885–1895.
R. T. Q. Stewart, *The Pagoda War* (London: Faber & Faber, 1972)

mines. From the new capital of Mandalay, Thibaw imposed a £2.3 million fine on the Bombay-Burma Trading Corporation for allegedly exporting more teak than they had bought. Commercial interests in Rangoon wanted annexation and the policy was favoured by the Secretary of State for India, Lord Randolph Churchill. The commercial pressure, the spectre of French influence extending from Indo-China, and the collapse of the Burmese government as indicated by the steady flow of refugees into Lower Burma all contributed to the exasperation of the British government and the Indian authorities with Thibaw.

An ultimatum was despatched on 22 October 1885 demanding Thibaw accept British control over Burma's foreign policy; appoint a British envoy with direct access to the King; agree on arbitration of the fine; and facilitate British trade with China through Burma. Thibaw rejected the ultimatum on 5 November 1885 and occupation followed. British officials with experience of Burma opposed annexation on the grounds of the likely military and financial costs, predicting significant Burmese opposition. The Viceroy of India, Lord Dufferin, was not convinced of the desirability of intervention and certainly not of annexation. The alternative of a protectorate and indirect rule, however, foundered on the lack of any acceptable successor to Thibaw, and the perceived incapacity of the Hluttaw (Council of State) or any local administration to function effectively as a guarantor of British interests given the rapid breakdown of any local authority and of any pretence of law and order following occupation.

As the official history put it, the expulsion of the King and the breaking up of the Burmese army 'completely undermined the power of the Hlutdaw [sic]; so that what actually occurred was a complete collapse of all central authority, and this could not be re-asserted till an executive was re-established throughout the country'.[5] The effective re-establishment of authority was to take ten years.

British and Burmese Forces

The regular Burmese army was estimated at 15,650 men but volunteers responding to a proclamation by the Hluttaw on 7 November 1885 had swelled its numbers to about 24,000–28,000. Only those immediately gathered for the defence of Mandalay – about 4,000–5,000 men – surrendered but barely 2,000–3,000 of their weapons were seized. Former soldiers, most of whom had not faced the British, merged with

---

[5] H. E. Stanton, *The Third Burmese War, 1885, 1886 and 1887: History of the War prior to the Annexation of the Country* (Calcutta: Superintendent of Government Printing, 1887), 52.

dacoits to wage guerrilla struggle. At the time of the British invasion, much of the Burmese army was engaged in fighting the Shans, dacoits, and assorted dissidents with real royal authority not extending much beyond Mandalay. Far from welcoming the British as expected, the Burmese generally resented the removal of a King who if weak politically was still semi-divine in their eyes. Many Burmese soldiers immediately resolved to fight on. Opposition was also fuelled by unwittingly symbolic evidence of disrespectful British attitudes to traditional authority such as the use of parts of the royal palace as an Anglican chapel, a British club and the Chief Commissioner's office, and rumours of wanton destruction of property, ill-treatment of monks and women, and summary executions.[6]

The increasing spread of resistance has been characterized as deriving from a combination of Burmese patriotism, millenarianism, and continuing banditry.[7] A number of royal or claimed royal princes evaded capture and deportation after the fall of Mandalay. Some such as the Myinzaing Prince, who died of fever in August 1886, proved a magnet for initial resistance. So did monks (*pongyi*) such as U Ottama, who was only captured in July 1889. Monks lost status and influence through the removal of the monarchy and the Hluttaw's proclamation in November 1885 invoked the supposed threat to the Buddhist faith, portraying the British as heretics. Many of the nobility and gentry did not contest British rule. They were supplanted by Burmese with local influence such as Boh Swe, hereditary *thugyi* (headman) of Mindat. Boh Swe was eventually killed in October 1887. There were then also the dacoits such as Bo Hla U, an active bandit on the Lower Chindwin since 1883, who simply turned into a resistance leader: he was killed in an internecine quarrel in April 1887.[8] Revolt spread to Lower Burma in 1886, the first Chief Commissioner, Sir Charles Bernard, recognizing in March that 'these outbreaks are not dacoity but incipient rebellion of a part of the population evoked by affairs in Upper Burma'.[9]

In some ways, resistance was not so much to the British – and thereby indicative of national or proto-national loyalties – as to any centralizing authority. Accordingly, alongside royal princes, monks, and bandit leaders, village communities themselves could take up arms with internal conflict between villages where some backed the British. In this respect, there was a separate civil war running alongside the overall pacification campaign.[10]

---

[6] Thant Myint-U, *The Making of Modern Burma* (Cambridge: Cambridge University Press, 1983), 199–200.
[7] Ibid., 202–07.   [8] Myint, *Burma's Struggle*, 65–66.   [9] Ibid., 78.
[10] Charney, 'Armed Rural Folk', 155–81.

It was convenient for the British authorities to refer to all opponents as dacoits since this suggested that they were the enemy of the British and the Burmese population alike. The Commander-in-Chief in India, Lieutenant-General Sir Frederick Roberts, believed that dacoity was 'not the work of "patriots" but of restless spirits who have lived by the trade all their life'.[11] Whatever the source of leadership or motivation, dacoit bands led by those characterized as *bohs* could range from a handful to as many as 4,000 men. Invariably the British distinguished between bohs and their followers, suggesting the significance of local leadership. It is impossible to gauge the numerical strength of opposition to the British or the losses inflicted on the Burmese.

Intimidation was applied by the dacoits to the local population in order to ensure their assistance although, in many cases, banditry was so long established that coercion was not required.[12] Troops disarmed villagers, which left them more at the mercy of dacoits.[13] Grattan Geary of the *Bombay Gazette* recorded of the plight of villagers: 'They will be shot as dacoits if they have arms; if they have none, they will be robbed and possibly murdered by the dacoits'. The choice, he claimed, was 'dacoiting or being dacoited'.[14] It was exceptionally difficult to gain any information and equally hard to distinguish between dacoits and peaceful villagers.[15] Given the intimidation and the lack of intelligence, it was concluded as Crosthwaite later put it that the only course was to make villagers 'fear us more than the bandits'.[16]

Steadily progress was made and the last major expedition in Burma proper was the Wuntho expedition in 1891 on the edge of the Shan States. When the campaign turned to the hill tribes, however, the Shans, Kachins, and Chins were far more organized with villages invariably fortified with earth breastworks, stockades, and spiked approaches. The Chins soon adapted to guerrilla tactics and were the most durable of all the opponents of the British, the last significant leader surrendering only in May 1894. A police as opposed to an army operation to dislodge a force of Chinese Shans from the Bhamo district occurred as late as March 1898.

---

[11] Roberts to Churchill, 28 Feb 1886, Roberts Mss, 7101-23-100-1, National Army Museum (NAM).

[12] Hall, *Soul of People*, 61–64; Sir Charles Crosthwaite, *The Pacification of Burma* (London: Edward Arnold, 1912), 103–04.

[13] 'Mandalay in 1885–88: The letters of James Alfred Colbeck', *SOAS Bulletin of Burma Research*, vol. 2 (2004), 47–76, 50.

[14] Grattan Geary, *Burma, after the Conquest* (London: Sampson Low, Marston, Searle & Rivington, 1886), 45–46, 74.

[15] Edmund Browne, *The Coming of the Great Queen: A Narrative of the Acquisition of Burma* (London: Harrison & Son, 1888), 270–75.

[16] Crosthwaite, *Pacification*, 103–04.

From the British perspective, the force initially provided to Prendergast totalled 11,844 men from the Bengal and Madras Armies, of whom 3,029 were British regulars.[17] No land transport was provided beyond some 2,000 Punjabi coolies, many of whom proved too old to carry the burdens required of them as well as succumbing to disease.[18] Transport was supplemented therefore in December 1885 by 100 royal elephants and 300 ponies from the Manipur Cavalry but half the elephants were without mahouts and untrained, and half the ponies were unserviceable.[19] Brigadier-General George White complained that the force had been equipped 'as a fish to fight a dog'.[20] British control extended no further than the range of the expeditionary force's rifles with insufficient troops to occupy the country as a whole.[21]

Flying columns – usually no more than 200 men – were organized but often arrived too late to prevent dacoits raiding villages or to catch them. White, commanding in Mandalay, concluded that the most effective response would be 'close occupation of the disturbed districts by military posts'.[22] Initially, ten posts were established along the Irrawaddy. This was soon extended to twenty-five as it was recognized that these were necessary to maintain military ascendancy, provide centres for the more well affected Burmese, protect lines of communication, and support the civil power. Posts were extended to cover the routes from Toungoo to Mandalay and from Toungoo to Thayetmyo. Posts usually consisted of a bamboo stockade and parapet, fronted by a ditch filled with thorns or prickly pear, and a liberal use of bamboo spikes beyond. Paths were cleared between posts to facilitate movement and communication. By the summer of 1886 there were forty-three posts in Upper Burma and forty-seven in Lower Burma concentrated on the Sittang and the Irrawaddy. By March 1887, there were 141 posts in Upper Burma.[23]

While the Burmese and hill tribes were poorly armed with mostly flintlock muskets, bows, and spears, British troops were armed with breechloading Martini-Henry rifles and Indian troops with the earlier Snider-Enfield breechloader. Despite the technological advantage in weaponry, the British had to overcome significant challenges of climate and terrain. Field Marshal Viscount Slim was later to write of Burma, 'It could fairly be described as some of the world's worst country, breeding the

---

[17] Stanton, *Third Burmese War* (1887), 32. [18] Browne, *Coming of Great Queen*, 192.
[19] *Frontier and Overseas Expeditions*, 168.
[20] Sir Mortimer Durand, *The Life of Field Marshal Sir George White VC*, 2 vols. (Edinburgh: William Blackwood & Sons, 1915), vol. 1, 326.
[21] *Frontier and Overseas Expeditions*, 164–65, 178. [22] Crosthwaite, *Pacification*, 15.
[23] John Nisbet, *Burma Under British Rule – And Before*, 2 vols. (London: Archibald Constable, 1901), vol. 1, 112–14, 126.

world's worst diseases, and having for half the year at least the world's worst climate'.[24] Only in the cooler season of November to January were conditions conducive to campaigning. North of Mandalay, it was pretty much impenetrable jungle with the Arakan Yomas and the Chin and Lushai hills all running north to south and, in the case of the Chin-Lushai hills, rising to 10,000–12,000 feet. In the case of the Chin-Lushai Hills, one British officer recorded, 'Approached through malarial valleys and *terai* which decimates the troops with sickness before they reach the inhabited heights, mountains and over paths so bad that sometimes it is only with infinite difficulty that five miles a day are accomplished'.[25] George White wrote on 3 January 1886 that the country was 'the most difficult I ever saw or thought of to plan operations in – everywhere water & jungle, both of which defy calculation as to time of march. The natives know nothing of distance, & the country is unsurveyed'.[26] The country was also cut north to south by the great rivers of the Sittang, Chindwin, Salween, and the main north-south artery of the Irrawaddy.

Troops relied on tracks and paths that had been well-trodden over the years but this could make them vulnerable to ambush. Dacoits likened British columns to buffalo moving through reeds which closed behind them. It was rare for the frequently fruitless marches to be less than seven hours.[27] In consistently high temperatures and humidity, disease flourished. Malaria, dysentery, and cholera posed the greatest dangers. Cholera broke out even before the fall of Mandalay.[28] Between November 1885 and October 1886, for example, there were ninety-one British and Indian fatalities from action but 930 deaths from disease with a further 2,032 men invalided to India. At any one time around twenty per cent of the field force were incapacitated by disease in 1885–86.[29]

The Strategy and Nature of Pacification

The pacification campaign proved controversial from the start. George White informed Roberts in June 1886 that it would be best to keep events out of the press for the 'operations we are constantly undertaking which

---

[24] Field Marshal Viscount Slim, *Defeat into Victory* (London: Cassell, 1956), 169.
[25] A. G. E. Newland, *The Image of War or Service in the Chin Hills* (Calcutta: Thacker-Spink, 1894), 6–7.
[26] Sir Mortimer Durand, *Life of White*, vol. 1, 326.
[27] Stanton, *Third Burmese War*, 72–74.   [28] Stewart, *Pagoda War*, 90.
[29] L. W. Bodé, *The Third Burmese War, 1885, 1886 and 1887: History of the War from the Annexation of the Country to the Commencement of the Winter Campaign of 1886-87* (Calcutta: Superintendent of Government Printing, 1888), 37; *Frontiers and Overseas Expeditions*, 228.

are so necessary would not long attract the tide of public sympathy towards us involving as they do heavy loss nearly always inflicted on the enemy with, I am happy to say, very slight loss on ourselves'.[30]

There had been unwelcome publicity given to the campaign by the correspondent of *The Times*, Edward Moylan. Moylan was deported from Mandalay in December 1885 for evading censorship regulations and reporting on the initial disorder. Moylan then used his considerable political contacts to be restored to his position, writing increasingly critical reports on the slowness of the pacification campaign and what he regarded as Prendergast's incompetence. Moylan happened on a story in January 1886 that, during a series of twenty-two exemplary executions of dacoits at Mandalay, the Provost Marshal, Colonel W. W. Hooper, had not only questioned men about to be executed by firing squad to try and extract intelligence but also, as an amateur photographer, delayed the order to fire so as to capture the death at the exact moment he exposed his negative. Hooper had not photographed the executions while actually on duty nor had he delayed the order to fire to set up the camera, yet, inevitably questions were raised in Parliament.[31] Dufferin, immediately forbade further executions for fear that they 'will strengthen the hands of those who may be disposed to criticise our conquest of the country'.[32] With the British government wary of adverse public opinion, Prendergast was relieved of the command in March 1886. Hooper was reprimanded and sent back to India with no chance of further promotion. Bernard was also removed in January 1887 following more criticism by Moylan.

Dufferin defended Burma policies in October 1886, arguing that a now critical British public had expected too much: 'They thought that the bloodless campaign of last November, and the capture of Theebaw and of his capital, had finished off the business; and they were delighted with the idea of having acquired a new Province in so inexpensive a manner. The Government of India, on the contrary, never indulged in these sanguine anticipations'.[33] Sir Charles Brownlow, the Assistant Military Secretary for India at the War Office, noted, 'The senseless British public went into the same hysterical rapture about the occupation of Mandalay as it did about Tel-el-Kebir. Its want of judgement and foresight, as proved by subsequent events in both instances is not very creditable to it and hence its impatience and disappointment'.[34] Equally, the Secretary of State for War, W. H. Smith, suggested the public was

---

[30] White to Roberts, 19 June 1886, White Mss, Eur Mss F108/3, APAC.
[31] Stewart, *Pagoda War*, 118–31, 140–41, 164–70.   [32] Ibid., 127–28.   [33] Ibid., 173.
[34] Brownlow to Roberts, 22 Aug 1886, Roberts Mss, 7101-23-12, NAM.

'very impatient knowing as little of the difficulties in the way of operations in Burmah as they would of operations on the moon'.[35]

Seen as a safe pair of hands, Lieutenant-General Sir Herbert Macpherson, Commander-in-Chief of the Madras Army, succeeded Prendergast in September 1886. When Macpherson died of fever within days of arrival in October, Roberts took personal command of operations. Roberts issued detailed guidance to column commanders. Columns must be provisioned for ten days with grain for horses and ponies to be obtained on the march. Supply depots had to be established and particular care taken of horses, ponies, and pack animals. Columns must be carefully co-ordinated and local guides obtained. Roberts stressed that 'the chief object of traversing the country with columns is to cultivate friendly relations with the inhabitants, and at the same time to put before them evidences of our power, thus gaining their good-will and their confidence'. The 'broadest possible margin' had to be drawn between dacoits, and villagers coerced into assisting them. The inhabitants, therefore, had to be treated properly. Military operations, however, had to inflict 'the heaviest loss possible' and column commanders were permitted to inflict punishments if civil officers were not present. They were also to disarm the villages although a certain number could be returned on licence to 'responsible villagers'. Roberts also suggested means of combatting ambushes with designated flanking parties told off to sweep into the jungle when a column was fired upon.[36] Since Roberts believed troops 'should make their presence felt everywhere', he set an ideal column at 50–100 British infantry, 100–200 Indian infantry, thirty mounted infantry, and two mountain guns.

The instructions displayed considerably more recognition of 'hearts and minds' than Roberts's conduct of operations in the Second Afghan War (1878–80), suggesting perhaps that he had learned lessons from the widespread criticism his methods had then attracted.[37] In February 1887 Roberts handed over command to George White.

Given the perceived unreliability of the Burmese, the new civil and military police intended to augment troop strength was raised mainly in India. The first police levy in February 1886 was for 1,122 men from Indian regiments to be supplemented by an additional 2,240 men recruited from northern India. Two more levies were authorized in

---

[35] Smith to Roberts, 5 Nov 1886, Smith Mss, WO 110/5, TNA.
[36] Brian Robson (ed.), *Roberts in India: The Military Papers of Field Marshal Lord Roberts, 1876–93* (Stroud: Alan Sutton for the Army Records Society, 1993), 357–62.
[37] Robert Johnson, 'General Roberts, the occupation of Kabul, and the problems of transition, 1879–80', *War in History* 20 (2013): 300–22.

March 1886 for the protection of the railway to be constructed between Toungoo and Mandalay, and for the Mogaung area. They were again drawn from northern India but also from Gurkhas. Further police were raised in March 1887.[38] Pay was not as attractive as for the Indian Army and there was a tendency to rely on lower caste recruitment. Wastage was also high, not least from disease. Generally, however, the notion of 'martial races' pervaded the process: Sikhs and Gurkhas were preferred. The hill tribes, notably the Karens, were seen as sufficiently 'martial' and more resistant to disease, with increased recruitment from 1892. Subsequently, Chins, Kachins, and Karens were also preferred for the Burma Rifles.[39]

By March 1887, there were 9,000 police in Lower Burma and over 17,000 military and civil police in Upper Burma under the command of Colonel Edward Stedman as Inspector-General. In fact, Burma was far more heavily policed in terms of the ratio of police to population than any other part of British India.[40] By the end of 1888, military police numbers in Upper Burma were 19,177, manning separate 192 posts.[41] In 1888, the minimum number of police in any post was raised from twenty-five to forty with the minimum strength of any patrol fixed at ten men. That year, military police casualties were forty-six dead and seventy-six wounded compared to an estimated 312 dacoits killed and 721 captured.[42] Civil and military police throughout Burma reached the strength of around 32,000 in 1888, a total not fully reduced until the 1920s.[43]

Troops were steadily reduced, priority being given to those units that had been engaged in the initial occupation.[44] At the beginning of 1887, the police manned fifty-six posts compared to 142 military posts. By 1889, only forty-one were held by troops but 192 by police.[45]

By 1888, steady progress was being made in Upper Burma, with few remaining larger dacoit bands or prominent leaders, more willingness on the part of the population to assist in the maintenance of law and order,

[38] H. E. Stanton, *History of the Third Burmese War, 1885, 1886 and 1887: The Winter Campaign of 1886–87, and Subsequent Operations up to March 31st 1888* (Calcutta: Superintendent of Government Printing, 1889), 136–37.
[39] Robert H. Taylor, 'Colonial forces in British Burma: A national army postponed,' in Tobias Rettig and Karl Hack (eds.), *Colonial Armies in Southeast Asia* (London: Routledge, 2009), 195–209.
[40] Myint, *Burma's Struggle*, 82–85.
[41] N. Newnham Davis, *History of the Third Burmese War, 1888–89: The Winter Campaign of 1888–89 and Subsequent Operations up to December 3rd 1889* (Simla: Government Central Printing Office, 1892), 77–78.
[42] Crosthwaite, *Pacification*, 97–98.
[43] Lalita Hingkanonta, 'The Police in Colonial Burma', Unpub. PhD, London, 2013, 181.
[44] Viceroy to India Office, 14 Jan 1887, IOR/L/MIL/7/9180, APAC.
[45] Nisbet, *Burma Under British Rule*, vol. 1, 141.

and an apparent recognition that the interests of the people were best served by doing so.[46] Resistance in Lower Burma was never as organized, mostly consisting of small and isolated bands. From an estimated 2,183 dacoits operating in Lower Burma in 1888, the number had declined to an estimated 181 by 1890.[47] Attention, therefore, turned to the Shan States and the Kachin and Chin Hills.

The Anatomy of Battle: Guerrilla War

The nature of guerrilla warfare meant that there were no significant battles but, instead, desultory engagements. There were over 100 engagements between April and July 1886 alone with twenty-nine in August and twenty-seven in September.[48] A typical action was that on 4 July 1886 when Jemadar Imam Khan of the 26th Madras Infantry with thirty men, escorting a convoy, was attacked by 200 dacoits. They were driven off without loss after an hour, the dacoits losing an estimated sixteen dead. That same day Lieutenant Gough of the 1st Royal Welsh Fusiliers was sent out from Ye-u with fifteen of his own men mounted on ponies, twelve lancers from the 2nd Madras Lancers, fifty men of the 21st Madras Infantry, and thirty police to disperse dacoits in the Teze area. He located and attacked the dacoit band at Lekse. They promptly fled: twelve dead dacoits were counted with Gough sustaining no casualties.[49] By 31 December 1886, the force had been increased to 31,571 men in Upper Burma and 4,176 in Lower Burma.[50] The field force was now reckoned to yield a ratio of one man for every 3 1/2 square miles of country compared to the original one man for every seven square miles.[51]

The pattern of campaigning hardly varied. One official account of the cold weather operations of 1887–88 recorded:

The story of the year is a record of endless marches by day and night, through dense jungle where the path could hardly be traced, along paths so thick in mud that the soles of men's boots were torn off as they marched, over sandy tracts devoid of water, over hills where there were no paths at all. Rarely was there the chance of an engagement to cheer the troops; stockades were found empty, villages deserted, camps evacuated, and yet everywhere there was the probability of a sudden ambush from every clump of trees or line of rocks, or at any turn of the road.[52]

[46] Note on State of Upper Burma, 14 July 1888, Thirkell White Mss, Eur Mss E254/10 (b), APAC.
[47] White, *Civil Servant*, 221–22. [48] *Frontier and Overseas Expeditions*, 197.
[49] Bodé, *Third Burmese War*, 16.
[50] Report on Operations for the Suppression of Brigandage, IOR/L/MIL/7/9181, APAC.
[51] *Frontier and Overseas Expeditions*, 241. [52] Ibid., 289.

In 1888, there were five engagements in March, four in April, three each in May and June, two each in July and August, one in September, two in October, and three in November, resulting in five British and Indian dead. Winter season operations saw fifty-one engagements between December 1888 and February 1889, with thirty-two British and Indian deaths.[53]

In the Shan States, an area of about 40,000 square miles and a population of 1.2 million, troops found it difficult to move during the rainy season, with the Shans able to return to 'old haunts' as soon as troops departed. Flying columns were more effective in the cold weather season when Gurkhas proved able to outmanoeuvre the Shans even in dense jungle-clad hills although this rarely resulted in much contact.[54] Generally, the British approach to all the hill tribes was to defeat resistance, impose an indemnity, insist on a continuation of the annual tributes previously paid to the Burmese King, and to establish a garrison with a resident political officer to represent British power.[55]

In the Kachin Hills, opposition resulted in four separate operations being mounted in 1888–89. The British resorted to the destruction of villages, crops, and livestock. Between January and May 1889, for example, the Mogaung Column commanded by Captain H. O'Donnell, the Staff Officer for the Burma District, destroyed twenty-four villages with a total of 355 houses, all household goods, 419,000 pounds of grain, fifty-nine buffaloes, and also fowls and pigs 'without number'.[56] The four expeditions together destroyed forty-six villages with 639 houses. The force suffered one dead and twenty-three wounded. It captured thity *dahs* (Burmese knives), seven guns, a number of spears, and a symbolic golden umbrella, but no enemy bodies were found although it was assumed from blood stains that the Kachins had sustained losses. The Kachins were largely pacified by December 1895 although, as recounted earlier, a police expedition was mounted in March 1898 to expel Chinese-Shans from the Bhamo district.

Like the Kachins, the Chins favoured fighting from stockades but soon adapted to guerrilla tactics. The British initially attempted negotiation but dacoits driven out of Upper Burma encouraged Chin raids down from the hills. The Chin Field Force was organized in response in December 1888. White, who accompanied the expedition, reported the Siyin Chins as the 'most difficult enemy to see or hit I ever fought'.[57] In

---

[53] Newnham Davis, *Burmese War*, Appendix I, iii–xvii.
[54] Diary of Expedition to the Shan States, Scott Mss, Eur Mss F278/51, APAC.
[55] Aung-Thwin, 'British sacification of Burma', 252.
[56] Report on Mogaung Field Force, 19 Apr 1889, IOR/L/MIL/7/9182, APAC.
[57] Crosthwaite, *Pacification*, 303–04.

November 1889, the Chin-Lushai Expedition was mounted to prevent further Chin raids into Burma and to open up a good road between Chittagong and Burma. Two columns totalling 3,608 fighting men and directed by William Penn Symons were deployed with an additional one advancing from Chittagong in India.[58] Great difficulties were encountered traversing the Chin Hills and malaria accounted for 207 deaths among troops and followers of the two Burma columns with a further 2,122 invalided: only nine troops or followers were killed.[59]

British columns could rarely carry more than ten days' food supplies with them carried by coolies, making it impossible to do much damage to the Chins or their crops. Ambushes were best met by rushes since it was found that the Chins would not stand to fight. They were especially skilful at night and it became practice to ring posts with tins on wires as a warning.[60] In 1892, larger columns broke up Chin combinations then dispersed into garrisons to harass further the Chins, destroy food supplies and impose disarmament. By 1900 the British military garrison in Burma was down to just 10,324 men.[61]

The Role of Technology

The pacification of Burma was not a campaign noted for the use of technology although British East India Company and Irrawaddy Flotilla Company steamers initially carried the occupying force to Mandalay. Those of the Irrawaddy Flotilla Company then routinely carried military guards or police to prevent dacoits crossing the rivers, as well as controlling piracy.

Paradoxically for a jungle campaign, cavalry and mounted infantry made a particular contribution. A small force of ninety-eight mounted infantry riding Burmese ponies was put together by Edward Browne drawn from the Rangoon Volunteer Rifles, Lower Burma police, and his own regiment – the Royal Scots Fusiliers – to give the British more mobility during the invasion.[62] When commanding Upper Burma, White requested three cavalry regiments for the intended 1886–87 winter operations. Mounted men offered greater mobility and some ability to outflank opponents even in jungle. Moreover, the Burmese were not used to horses as opposed to ponies and were apparently terrified of them. At peak, four Indian cavalry regiments were used but it was difficult to keep horses alive, 666 out of 2,092 being lost between October 1886 and

---

[58] *Frontier and Overseas Expeditions*, 330–32.   [59] Ibid., 335.   [60] Ibid., 320.
[61] Nisbet, *Burma Under British Rule*, vol. 1, 149.
[62] Browne, *Coming of Great Queen*, 132–33.

October 1887 to diseases such as relapsing fever (*surra*), lumbar paralysis (*kumri*), and anthrax.[63]

In addition, the mounted infantry was built up to a force of 825 men divided into companies of sevety-five, each attached to district headquarters and armed with carbines and artillery sword bayonets. Few of those drafted in had any experience of mounted infantry work. Indian soldiers had little knowledge of horse-mastership and took far longer to train to ride. There were few copies of the British regulations available in India so Penn Symons, whose services White had specifically requested, wrote his own instructions.[64]

Such was the perceived value of mounted infantry that it was decided to retain it as an element within the regular garrison in 1894. In April 1887, 1,600 men had been employed as mounted infantry, but it would now be established at 215 British and 300 Indian soldiers with increased pay to persuade infantrymen to volunteer for detached service.[65] Artillery was less successful as mules could not readily keep up with infantry and there were rarely defined targets. Gardner machine guns were used but they were often inaccurate due to the jolting of tripods and frequently broke down. Nonetheless, they had a good morale effect when employed.[66]

In many respects, measures introduced alongside purely military operations were more effective in bringing about pacification. These measures included rewards offered for information; pardons for surrenders; and the relocation of the rural population to more easily defended locations, which disrupted crop cultivation but cut the dacoits off from their base of support. Many villages were burned. Large scale disarmament was instituted by Bernard's successor as Chief Commissioner, Crosthwaite, in 1887. General pardons were often made conditional upon the surrender of guns. Disarmament became especially effective when coupled with the Upper Burma Village Regulation. The latter was drafted by Crosthwaite in February 1887 and implemented from October 1887 onwards. He regarded it as 'the most effective weapon in our battery for the restoration of peace and order'.[67] Traditional thugyi were replaced by appointed headmen who were made responsible for law and order, combing the function of thugyi and policeman. Thus,

---

[63] Stanton, *Third Burmese War* (1889), 211–17; 'Notes on Cavalry employed in Upper Burma from October 1886 to October 1887', *SOAS Bulletin of Burma Research* 2 (2004), 29–38.
[64] Durand, *Life of White*, vol. 1, 347.
[65] India Council to India Office, 29 May 1894, IOR/L/MIL/7/9199, APAC.
[66] Stanton, *Third Burmese War* (1889), 218–29.
[67] Crosthwaite, *Pacification*, 81–82, 106.

villagers had to respond to the headman's gong and perform any service required on pain of 24 hours in the stocks.[68] The Lower Burma Village Act was implemented in 1889 implementing the same conditions there.

Essentially, the Regulation and its various additional amendments imposed a uniform system on Burma although this was not always carried out consistently at local level.[69] It has also been argued that the British sense of pacification meant sufficient order to collect revenue: a wider psychological pacification was never realized.[70] The significance of the Village Regulation was that district commissioners were able to order the fencing of villages, the mobilization of villagers, collective fines, and the removal of those suspected of supporting or sympathizing with dacoits.[71] The latter led to large-scale removals while collective fines proved especially effective, as in the case of breaking up the support base for U Ottama around Minbu in November 1889. One notorious dacoit, Bo Ya Nyun, surrendered in May 1890 after rewards and pardons for defectors had robbed him of support.[72] Strict licensing of guns was introduced in May 1888, with requirements for license holders to act as special constables, and loss of guns resulting in confiscation of all within a village.

Railway construction between Toungoo and Mandalay assisted movement of troops but also served to provide wage income for up to 24,000 men, offering further reason for supporting the British administration, albeit that it was actually forced labour[73] Indeed, it was suggested that the railway was 'one of the most pacifying influences in the eastern districts'.[74] In the case of the Kanhow tribe among the Chins, it was suggested that those chiefs taken captive in the 1890–91 winter campaign and sent to Rangoon 'were much impressed by the wonders of civilization and the evidence they saw of the power of the white man'. Supposedly they vowed 'never again to withstand British arms'.[75]

Under the Shan States Act of November 1888, the hereditary *sawbwa* were retained with reduced powers since they appeared more recognizably as the kind of local chiefs with whom the British could work com-

---

[68] Michael Charney, *A History of Modern Burma* (Cambridge: Cambridge University Press, 2009), 7.
[69] Iwaki, 'Village system and Burmese society', 113–43.
[70] Aung-Thwin, 'British pacification of Burma', 245–62.
[71] Crosthwaite, *Pacification*, 105.   [72] Myint, *Burma's Struggle*, 62, 101.
[73] Ibid., 101–02; Roberts to Sladen, 3 Dec 1887, Sladen Mss, Eur Mss E290/52, APAC; W. R. Winston, *Four Years in Upper Burma* (London: C. H. Kelly, 1892), 69.
[74] White, *Civil Servant in Burma*, 168.
[75] J. H. Parsons and E. W. Dunn, *History of the Third Burmese War, 1890–91: The Winter Campaign of 1890–91* (Simla: Government Central Printing Office, 1893), 19.

pared to thugyi.[76] Over 7,000 weapons were taken from the Chins between 1893 and 1896.[77] The implementation of the Chin Hills Regulations in 1896, taking the Chin Hills into Burma as a scheduled district, however, led to further disorder until 1900.

Aftermath

As Kipling suggested, the 'Burmese business was a subaltern's war'.[78] Among those who served in Burma noted for later distinction were Henry Rawlinson, Henry Wilson, Richard Haking, and Ralph Clements, whose career was cut short by fatal appendicitis in 1909. Among brigade commanders, in addition to White, good reputations were made by William Lockhart, William Penn Symons, Cecil East, Robert Low, Edward Stedman, and William Gatacre. As White wrote on one occasion, Burma 'somehow finds out weak points very rapidly'.[79]

Yet, while reputations were made in the eyes of the India military authorities, the pacification of Burma was not viewed in the same way at the War Office in London. Seven separate bars were awarded for the India General Service Medal relating to operations in Burma between 1885 and 1893.[80] Pleas for a separate medal, however, were rejected. Both Roberts and White felt therefore that there had been too little reward for Burma, while some of those serving in 'police work' in Burma believed that issuing only a clasp was an economy measure.[81] The Military Secretary at the War Office, Sir George Harman, suggested there had been too little action and the Prince of Wales, too, was led to believe there had been few casualties.[82] Roberts was obliged to reduce the list of those being put forward for honours.[83] He felt keenly the difference in the number of awards for recent frontier actions against the Mahdists in Egypt, writing 'so long as Egyptian heroes can get decorations for a picnic lasting as many weeks you must not be surprised

---

[76] Myint-U, *Making of Modern Burma*, 216–17.
[77] *Frontier and Overseas Expeditions*, 355.
[78] Rudyard Kipling, 'A conference of the powers', *Many Inventions* (New York: Appleton, 1899), 33. First published in *The Pioneer*, 23/24 May 1890.
[79] White to Roberts, 3 Dec 1888, Roberts Mss, 7101-23-90, NAM.
[80] Burma 1885–87, Burma 1887–89, Chin-Lushae 1889–90, Burma 1889–92, Lushae 1889–92, Chin Hills 1892–93, Kachin Hills, 1892–93.
[81] Roberts to Cowell, 5 Aug 1887, Cowell Mss, 2009-02-110-417, NAM; White to Roberts, 28 May 1887, White Mss, Eur Mss F108/3, APAC; Major General Sir Francis Howard, *Reminiscences, 1848–90* (London: John Murray, 1924), 299. See also Lyttelton to Godley, 18 July 1887, Lyttelton Letter Book, Eur Mss F102/43, APAC.
[82] Pole-Carew to Roberts, 15 and 28 July 1887, Roberts Mss, 7101-23-59, NAM; Roberts to Pole-Carew, 5 Aug 1887, 7101-23-100-1.
[83] Roberts to Dufferin, 30 July 1886, Roberts Mss, 7101-23-98, NAM.

at my pressing the claims of those who have done what seems to me, more valuable work'.[84] Eventually, three VCs were won during the pacification, all by medical officers.[85] Subsequently, as operations in Burma became a long and exacting pacification campaign, few brigade commanders or staff officers were willing to undertake a full five-year term when regiments were being rotated after three years.[86]

Burma never proved to be of real commercial value to the British Empire beyond the Burmah Oil Company that began operations in 1886. In the end, too, Burma remained under British control for only sixty-two years after 1885, and that was disrupted by the serious Tharawaddy Revolt between 1930 and 1932, and by Japanese occupation between 1942 and 1945. At the time, desultory guerrilla warfare between 1885 and 1895 did not have the resonance with the British public of the campaigns in the Sudan or on the North-West Frontier of India. The pacification of Burma, however, has contemporary resonance, which makes its neglect the more surprising. Intended regime change was not accompanied by any consideration of the likely implications. The initial force deployed was not sufficient to ensure proper security in the aftermath of occupation. Prolonged insurgency necessitated deploying a force far larger than originally intended or anticipated. Evolving military and civil measures eventually brought order but proved destructive of Burmese society. British preference for the recruitment of hill tribes into police and armed forces equally sowed seeds for future divisions. The pacification of Burma was not just a campaign of lost footsteps but is one of forgotten footsteps.

Further Reading

Ali, M. S. 'The Beginnings of British Rule in Upper Burma: The Study of British Policy and Burmese Resistance, 1885–90'. Unpub. PhD, London, 1976.

Aung-Thwin, Michael. 'The British "pacification" of Burma: Order without meaning'. *Journal of Southeast Asian Studies* 16 (1985): 245–62.

Beckett, Ian F. W. 'The campaign of the lost footsteps: The pacification of Burma, 1885-95.' *Small Wars and Insurgencies* 30 (2019): 994–1019.

Browne, Major Edmond. *The Coming of the Great Queen: A Narrative of the Acquisition of Burma*. London: Harrison & Son, 1888.

Charney, Michael. *A History of Modern Burma*. Cambridge: Cambridge University Press, 2009.

---

[84] Roberts to Brownlow, 16 Jan 1887, Roberts Mss, 7101-23-103, NAM.
[85] Those awarded VCs were John Crimmin, 1 Jan 1889; Ferdinand Le Quesne, 4 May 1889; and Owen Lloyd, 6 Jan 1893.
[86] Arbuthnot to Roberts, 26 July 1890, Roberts Mss, 7101-23-2, NAM.

'Armed rural folk elements of pre-colonial warfare in the artistic representations and written accounts of the pacification campaign (1886–1889) in Burma'. In Michael Charney and Kathryn Wellen (eds.) *Warring Societies of Pre-colonial Southeast Asia: Local Cultures of Conflict within a Regional Context*. Copenhagen: NIAS Press, 2018: 155–81.

Crosthwaite, Sir Charles. *The Pacification of Burma*. London: Edward Arnold, 1912.

Geary, Grattan. *Burma, After the Conquest*. London: Sampson Low, Marston, Searle & Rivington, 1886.

Hall, Harold Fielding. *The Soul of a People*. London: Macmillan, 1906.

Intelligence Branch, Army Headquarters. *Frontier and Overseas Expeditions from India, Volume 5: Burma*. Simla: Government Monotype Press, 1907.

Iwaki, Takahirp. 'The village system and Burmese society: Problems involved in the enforcement process of the Upper Burma village regulation of 1887'. *Journal of Burma Studies* 19 (2015): 113–43.

Myint, Ni Mi. *Burma's Struggle against British Imperialism, 1885–95*. Rangoon: Universities Press, 1983.

Myint-U, Thant. *The Making of Modern Burma*. Cambridge: Cambridge University Press, 2001.

Newland, A. G. E. *The Image of War or Service in the Chin Hills*. Calcutta: Thacker-Spink, 1894.

Nisbet, John. *Burma Under British Rule – And Before*. 2 vols. Westminster: Archibald Constable, 1901.

Roy, Kaushik. *The Army in British India: From Colonial Warfare to Total War, 1857–1947*. London: Bloomsbury, 2013.

Stewart, A. T. Q. *The Pagoda War: Lord Dufferin and the Fall of the Kingdom of Ava, 1885–86*. London: Faber & Faber, 1972.

Taylor, Robert H. 'Colonial forces in British Burma: A national army postponed.' In Tobias Rettig and Karl Hack (eds). *Colonial Armies in Southeast Asia* London: Routledge, 2009.

Thirkell White, Sir Herbert. *A Civil Servant in Burma*. London: Edward Arnold, 1913.

Wingfield, Jordan. 'Buddhism and insurrection in Burma, 1886–90.' *Journal of the Royal Asiatic Society* 20 (2010): 345–67.

Winston, W. R. *Four Years in Upper Burma*. London: C. H. Kelly, 1892.

12 The Tirah Campaign, 1897–1898

Sameetah Agha

Background

In the summer of 1897, the British confronted a formidable armed revolt on the North-West Frontier of India. Along the length of the Frontier, from Waziristan to Swat, military outposts were attacked and captured, and military garrisons besieged by the Pukhtun tribes. While the British had faced consistent resistance from the tribes that inhabited the frontier region since they took over the trans-Indus districts after their conquest of Punjab in 1849, what was different in this case was the attempt of the tribes to unite and deliver simultaneous attacks, something the British had counted against happening.

In fact, a cornerstone and justification of the more aggressive British policy of expansion and occupation in the 1890s, 'The Forward Policy', was based on bringing the tribes into alliance and friendly relations to aid the British against a possible Russian invasion of the Indian empire. In 1886, Frederick Roberts, Commander-in-Chief, India, declared in a memorandum that the attitude of the tribes was the essence of any scheme for the defence of the North-West Frontier: 'If they are with us, we have no anxiety, if they are against us, we shall be in serious straits'.[1]

The British had faced ongoing and consistent opposition from the Afridis and Orakzais since 1849. While both tribes were to be reckoned with, because of the 'fighting men' they could muster (Afridis 25,000–30,000; Orakzais 20,000–25,000), the Afridis were regarded as the more powerful and among some of the fiercest fighters on the Frontier.[2] Prior to 1897, Afridi resistance led the British to conduct punitive military

---

[1] Frederick Roberts, Extract from a Memorandum, 17 August 1886, Proceedings of the Government of India, Foreign Department, Secret, National Archives of India, New Delhi.

[2] *Frontier and Overseas Expeditions from India*, vol. 2 (Simla: Govt. Monotype Press, 1910), 20.

expeditions against different Afridi clans in 1850, 1853, 1855, 1878, and 1879.[3]

According to contemporary colonial military historiography, the numerous punitive expeditions were necessary because the Afridis loved violence. 'With a Pathan, and especially an Afridi, fighting is his occupation, his pastime, and his only joy ... he must always be fighting somebody'.[4] While specifically referring to Afridis here, within the master narrative of frontier warfare generally, reprisals were forced upon the British due to tribal depredations, such as raiding, across the administered boundary against British subjects. However, an ongoing grievance represented by the Afridis, one that they would communicate again in 1897 prior to their attacks on the Khyber posts, has been glossed over both in contemporary and later literature – the British takeover of trans-Indus salt mines and the enhancement of the salt duty. Contrary to the view that Afridis liked to fight because of idleness, salt was one of the principal trades in which they engaged. Excavating, mining, and trading in salt derived from the salt range, both within India and into Afghanistan and further into Central Asia. In 1896, the Government of India increased the duty on Kohat salt from eight annas to two rupees, which amounted to a quadrupling of the price of salt for both consumers and traders.[5] However, due to the disruptions caused by colonial intrusion and their poverty, despite their opposition to imperial expansion, many Afridis enlisted in the Jezailchi corps, locally recruited levies, to guard the Khyber Pass in return for subsidies. Afridis also joined the British Army and fought in many of their campaigns. On the eve of the revolt in 1897, there were some 3,000–4,000 Afridis enlisted either directly in the British Army or under native chiefs. British military accounts frequently stated that Afridis made excellent and loyal soldiers who did not shy away from fighting their own kith and kin for the colonial government.[6]

The Orakzais, a tribe connected to, and neighbouring the Afridis, had also fought the British in several engagements. In retaliation, several punitive military expeditions were conducted against them in 1885,

---

[3] For an official outline of these expeditions, as well as the ones conducted against the Orakzais, see *Frontier and Overseas Expeditions*, vol. 2.

[4] A. K. Slessor, *The 2nd Battalion, Derbyshire Regiment in Tirah* (London: Swan Sonnenschein, 1900), 4–5).

[5] For British policy regarding the Trans-Indus salt mines and the role of salt in Afridi resistance, see Sameetah Agha, 'Trans-Indus salt: Objects, resistance, and violence in the North-West Frontier of British India', in Lipokmar Dzuvichu and Manjeet Baruah (eds.), *Objects and Frontiers in Modern India: Between the Mekong and the Indus* (New Delhi, New York: Routledge, 2019), 21–42.

[6] Leonard Julius Shadwell, *Lockhart's Advance through Tirah* (London: W. Thacker, 1898), 10.

1868, 1869, and 1891. In the years preceding 1897, the Orakzais had directly contested British occupation of Samana and it was only through punitive military operations (two Miranzais Expeditions in 1891) that they were coerced into acquiescence. L. White King, Deputy Commissioner, Kohat, in his official monograph on the Orakzais, acknowledged that the rising of the Orakzais in 1891, joined by the Afridis, lay in the occupation and building of forts in Samana which had 'practically destroyed their independence'.[7] In 1897, the Orakzais would reiterate the occupation of Samana and the incessant fines placed on them, as grievances for their revolt.

* * * * *

The history of the Tirah campaign is still dominated by contemporary accounts of the Tirah Expeditionary Force (TEF) written mostly by British officers or correspondents attached to the TEF.[8] Such accounts follow the engagements and difficulties encountered by the TEF. Given their semi-official nature, while such works contain criticism of tactics and logistics, they also served as justifications of military failures and losses incurred during the campaign and the lessons to be learned for the conduct of future campaigns.[9]

Subsequently while the Tirah campaign appears within general histories of colonial North-West Frontier, no book-length, comprehensive accounts have been published. In recent decades, there has been some attention to aspects of the war such as Keith Surridge's examination of the role of the Amir of Afghanistan in the tribal revolt, or the role of the TEF in contemporary media, the 'yellow press' in England.[10] Tim Moreman provides an incisive analysis of the tactical military lessons drawn from Tirah, and their impact upon the developing doctrine of

---

[7] L. White King, *Monograph on the Orakzais Country and Clans* (Lahore: Punjab Government Press, 1900), 84.

[8] Please see 'Further Reading' section.

[9] See for example Col. H. D. Hutchinson, *The Campaign in the Tirah 1897–1898: An Account of the Expedition Against the Orakzais & Afridis under Gen. Sir. William Lockhart* (London: Macmillan, 1898). However, amongst these works, Slessor's account is particularly illuminating. On several occasions, Slessor disputes the veracity and accuracy of information given out about the campaign including in the military despatches sent from Lockhart to the Government in India and to England. Slessor, *The 2nd Battalion*, 104–05.

[10] Keith Surridge, 'The Ambiguous Amir: Britain, Afghanistan and the 1897 North-West Frontier Uprising', *Journal of Imperial and Commonwealth History* 36, 3(2008): 417–34; Gelnn R. Wilkinson, 'Purple prose and the yellow press: Imagined spaces and the military expedition to Tirah, 1897', in Finkelstein, David and Douglas M. Peers (eds.), *Negotiating India in the Nineteenth-Century Media* (London: Macmillan Press, 2000), 254–76.

frontier colonial warfare.[11] Rob Johnson has devoted a chapter in *The Afghan Way of War* to reconstructing the Pashtun perspective of the war. Acknowledging the one-sided, British perspective of prevailing accounts as well as the paucity of sources, Johnson attempts to reconstruct the Pashtun perspective through their actions and comments recorded by British officers at the conclusion of the campaign.[12]

However, critical comprehensive histories that would address the many gaps that remain, such as the role of field hospitals, animal labor, British civil-military relations, military decision-making, gender relations and the role of women have yet to be undertaken. And in order to obtain a more complete picture of the Tirah campaign, or frontier wars in general, that incorporates the Pukhtun perspective, an examination of Pukhtun oral tradition is necessary.[13]

Outbreak of War

On August 23, 1897, an estimated *lashkar* (militia) of about 10,000 Afridis commenced attacks on British military posts in the Khyber. They captured and burnt the British forts at Ali Masjid and Fort Maude. On August 25, Landi Kotal, the most advanced post in the Khyber, was captured, and a large quantity of ammunition stored there

---

[11] T. R. Moreman, *The Army in India and the Development of Frontier Warfare, 1849–1947* (London: Macmillan Press LTD, 1998).

[12] Rob Johnson, *The Afghan Way of War: How and Why They Fight* (Oxford: Oxford University Press, 2012).

[13] In 1994–45, I undertook two visits to FATA (Federally Administered Tribal Areas, now Khyber Pukhtunkhwa) to gather oral narratives of the 1897 tribal revolt. In addition to Pukhtun poetry, through which memory and history is preserved and passed on, I was able to gather several Afridi accounts of the war. While it is beyond the scope of this essay to discuss them at length, one is particularly resonant here. Mir Hasan Gul, Aka Khel was the oldest surviving witness/participant of the war, that I interviewed. In some instances, his testimony corroborated British accounts and in others, he provided new counter-evidence of the war. According to Hasan Gul, Mullah Syed Akbar was the leader of the Afridis and Kamnarai was the leader of the Orakzais. Syed Akbar opposed British occupation consistently and the British tried to bribe him, both by giving him 'bags of money' as well as offering to send his blind son for treatment to England. According to Hasan Gul, while there were many who took money from the British in the form of 'Maliki' and even attained the status of Nawab, Syed Akbar refused. In addition to the occupation of the Khyber, the price of salt as a motive for the Afridi attacks was emphasized. As far as Afridi tactics, Hasan Gul provided many details such as, 'The Afridis attacked in groups of 10-20 ... they carried bread and *gur* (jaggery)'. A most extraordinary point that was described was that as the British retreated from Tirah, the Afridis released water through a system of irrigation that was used in Tirah, which led the ground to become muddy and the retreating British army along with their animals got stuck. (Mir Hasan Gul, Interview with Agha, Jamrud, Khyber, May 1995).

244 Sameetah Agha

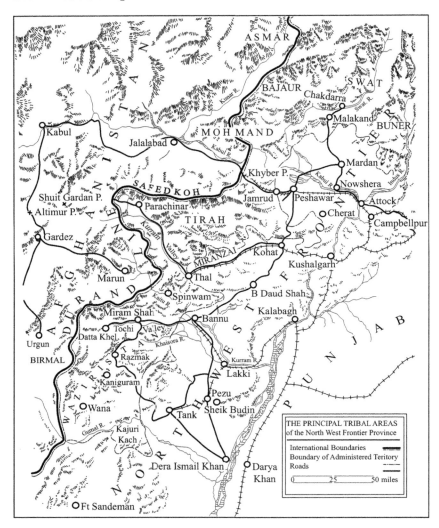

Map 12.1 The North-West Frontier of British India, c. 1900.
Redrawn from C. Repington, *Policy and Arms* (London: Hutchinson, 1924)

fell into Afridi hands. The official public response, communicated and echoed by the British press, was one of shock, humiliation and a loss of imperial 'prestige'. It was in order to recover imperial prestige that the Tirah expedition was sanctioned, to invade the summer home of the Afridis and Orakzais, a place that they held sacred and that had never been entered by a European before.

The combined Afridi-Orakzais attacks on the Samana forts occurred some days later in September. On September 12, the small post of Saragarhi, held by a small garrison of twenty-one men of the 36th Sikhs, was captured and the entire garrison killed. The attack was visible to the garrisons of Forts Lockhart and Gulistan 'but the enemy were in such force that it was quite impossible to do anything to save the situation'.[14]

Previous attacks that summer in other parts of the Frontier were described officially as 'sudden', 'fanatical' outbreaks. However, officials in the Khyber knew for several weeks of an impending Afridi attack on the Khyber. Captain F. J. H. Barton, the commandant of the Khyber Rifles, strengthened the posts by increasing the number of men within the garrison and the rations, supply of water, and rounds of ammunition. However, in an astonishing turn of events, Barton received peremptory orders to leave his garrison behind and withdraw from Landi Lotal. The garrison was left to fend for itself.

Initially, British authorities tried to make out that the Afridi levies had deserted to the lashkar and made no attempt to defend the post, an account that was repeated by contemporary writers such as by C. E. Callwell who wrote of the 'half-hearted resistance' of the Khyber Rifles.[15] However, Barton and Aslam Khan, his assistant, provided detailed reports of the fighting that took place that demonstrated that the Rifles fought hard against their fellow tribesmen, despite being deprived of their commanding officer, and with a large British force encamped within five miles of them that was not moved to help them.[16]

Detailed examination of the decision-making surrounding the loss of the Khyber reveals that the decision not to defend the Khyber was ultimately made by the Commander-in-Chief, India, George White.[17] Following the fall of the Khyber, White made a forceful case in the Governor-General's Council for not just the invasion of, but for the permanent annexation of Tirah. He was overruled by Viceroy Elgin and other members. However, the invasion of Tirah was sanctioned to punish the tribes and to recover imperial prestige, damaged as result of the loss of the Khyber – a loss that in all likelihood could have been averted.

---

[14] Captain H. L. Nevill, *Campaigns on the North-West Frontier* (London: J. Murray, 1912), 269.
[15] C. E. Callwell, *Tirah 1897* (London: Constable, 1911), 6.
[16] Telegram from Aslam Khan to Udny, 10 September 1897, Proceedings of the Government of India, Secret Frontier, February 1898, Directorate of Archives, Peshawar, Pakistan.
[17] For a detailed examination of the politics of the chain of command and sub-imperial decision-making surrounding the loss of the Khyber, see Sameetah Agha, 'Sub-imperialism and the loss of the Khyber: The politics of imperial defence on British India's North-West Frontier', *Indian Historical Review* 40, 2(2013): 307–30.

British and Afridi and Orakzai Forces

The TEF was the largest concentration of troops deployed on the North-West Frontier to date. On 3 September, the Government of India announced punitive operations against the Afridis and Orakzais; the goal being to reach Tirah. Lieutenant-General Sir William Lockhart was vested with supreme control of the campaign. He was on leave in England at the time and had to leave at a day's notice to make his way back to India. Two divisions forming the main column were to be mobilized consisting of infantry, cavalry, and mountain artillery. In addition, two columns were formed to operate in Peshawar and in the Kurram valley while one was held in reserve in Rawalpindi. The total number of the force totalled 54,440.[18] Over 70,000 transport animals were also mobilized for the TEF.

The concentration of forces that took place at Kohat, thirty-two miles by road from the railhead at Khusalgarh, was marked by delay. This was due to waiting for the arrival of troops including those already deployed with the Mohmand and Malakand Field Forces. Gathering transport and supplies for such a large force also contributed to the delay, especially challenging due to the number of expeditions being conducted simultaneously.

Contemporary writers emphasized the disorganization and chaos that was evident during the mobilization and commented that the resources of North India were simply not up to the demand of the field force. All provisions from biscuits, bully beef, and rum to warm clothing, tents, bedding, and of course ammunition and military equipment such as mountain artillery needed to be collected. Field hospitals and the telegraph department needed to be organized to accompany the expedition. Sappers and miners were needed to carve out paths, where none existed, for thousands to pass through. Provisions and transport would constantly come up short during the campaign. Callwell remarked that in a region of intense cold nights as Tirah would be in November and December troops have 'no business to be on the war-path without some warm clothing carried on their persons' and 'without some form of emergency ration at their disposal'.[19]

The Afridis and Orakzais were estimated to have 40,000–50,000 'fighting men'. However, due to the guerilla nature of the fighting that ensued after the attacks in the Khyber and Samana, it is difficult to know

---

[18] British officers 1,010; British troops 10,882; Indian troops 22,614; and noncombatants 19,934. Nevill, *Campaigns on the North-West Frontier*, 281.

[19] Callwell, *Tirah 1897*, 98.

how many actually engaged in operations against the TEF. While both Afridis and Orakzais had previously opposed the British through carrying out armed attacks, this was the first time that a large-scale combination of the two tribes took place. Mullah Syed Akbar, an Aka Khel Afridi considered by the British to be the most powerful of the Tirah Mullahs, played a key role in mobilizing the tribes to fight, as it was through his influence that the Orakzais were able to heal their differences and join the Afridis in a coalition to oppose the government. According to L. White King, Syed Akbar had an inner council of three who acted as his advisors and he was in communication with the most important Mullahs on the North-West Frontier.[20] It also appears that Syed Akbar played a key role in planning the strategy behind the attacks. While Afridis and Orakzais used large *lashkars* to launch attacks such as on the Khyber forts in August, thereafter during the campaign they resorted to smaller and dispersed groupings to snipe into camps or attack the rearguard of columns. Elected members of Afridi councils arranged all plans for action and decided on the number of men to be furnished from each clan or village. On taking the field, each combatant carried the minimum of provisions (bread and ammunition) on which they could live off for days. Not requiring a long line of communications and their familiarity with the terrain gave them astonishing mobility.

The Afridis and Orakzais had, for some years prior to the revolt, already been training to fight the British if and when necessary. In 1880, Mir Bashar declared himself *Badshah* (King) of Tirah, settled feuds among different clans, and raised 3,000 men who were paid regularly. He had officers in regiments who drilled the men daily and even had Pukhtun bagpipers who played on parade, while discharged Afridi sepoys instructed the men. Bashar's plan was to raise 20,000 men who would be trained and ready to attack the British or any other power who might invade them.[21]

By 1897, the Afridis were armed with long-range rifles such as the Martini-Henry and made themselves the masters of the few Lee-Metfords they captured during the campaign. They were frequently acknowledged 'as skilled a marksman as could be found in the world' by their British opponents.[22] Similarly, the Orakzais were well-armed

---

[20] King, *Monograph on the Orakzais*, 54.
[21] From W. M. Young, Secretary to Government, Punjab to the Secretary, to The Government of India, Foreign Department, 18 June 1880, Proceedings of the Government of Punjab, Directorate of Archives, Peshawar, Pakistan.
[22] Shadwell, *Lockhart's Advance*, 104.

and were manufacturing rifles, pistol, gunpowder, and caps for muzzle-loading rifles as well as breech-blocks and spring.

Strategy and War Aims

The British scheme for military operations was issued from the office of the Quartermaster-General towards the end of September, a month after the initial Afridi attacks. Its object was to punish the Afridis and Orakzais by an invasion of Tirah, which had never before been entered by a British force, and to 'exact reparations'. However, beyond the goal of reaching Tirah, no plan was outlined, nor was one communicated to the officers and troops of the TEF. The goal to strike a swift and decisive blow had failed at the outset due to the long delay in concentrating the forces. The troops would not move towards Tirah until the middle of October – a delay of another month. Many officers and correspondents with the expedition speculated while waiting to receive orders at every stage of the campaign and were uncertain whether the end goal was permanent annexation of Tirah.[23] Given the lack of clarity, beyond reaching Tirah, there was also an assumption that the tribes would crave terms soon after seeing such a large force. That assumption would prove to be a miscalculation.[24] The voluminous official and confidential telegrams between Lockhart and the Government of India and any action being subject to approval from England, demonstrated that Lockhart in actuality did not have the autonomy with which he appeared to have been vested. 'Sir William Lockhart, it is true, was vested with supreme political as well as military control of the expedition, but in these days, when Generals in the field are tied by the telegraph to their Governments, such independence is little more than nominal'.[25]

Afridis and Orakzais, both on the eve of the attack and in subsequent communications, repeatedly laid out their aims: (1) the evacuation of British troops from the Khyber and the Samana (2) lowering of the salt duty (3) return of Afridi women who had taken refuge in British territory across the administered boundary. Their strategy was to drive the British from the Khyber and Samana by delivering simultaneous attacks. However, the Orakzais would not commence their attacks until the Afridis had committed themselves. Therefore, the time lag between the two attacks may have lessened their overall impact, but in the short-term, the strategy was successful, especially for the Afridis with their capture of

---

[23] Hutchinson, *The Campaign in the Tirah*, 112. [24] Shadwell, *Lockhart's Advance*, 50.
[25] Slessor, *The 2nd Battalion*, 109.

the Khyber. However, once the expeditionary force began moving towards Tirah, Afridi tactics revolved around delaying and hampering the movement of the TEF by sniping into camps and attacking rearguards of the moving columns and foraging parties. Such tactics were largely successful as they resulted in inflicting heavy casualties upon the British forces without direct engagements.

The Course of the War

Assembling Forces: Preparation and Delay

From the perspective of the operations of the TEF, the campaign can be divided into four phases. The first phase involved extensive preparations. Everything from selecting the base of operations to the assembling and concentration of forces (human and animals), and especially arranging for supplies and transport, was marked by difficulty. While the merits of different sites for base of operations were debated at length, Kohat was selected for the main column under Lockhart's direct command and two other columns were formed at Peshawar and in the Kurram valley, all to meet and advance from Shinawari towards Tirah. The principal means of transport from Khusalgarh to Kohat and from there to the advanced base of Shinawari was by bullock-cart, which was slow and tedious. Even the breakdown of one cart caused a jam and blocked the movement of a hundred behind. The long trains of bullock-carts were subject to constant attacks and had to be guarded which required huge manpower including a cavalry escort.[26] The whole way to Shinawari was full of blocks and a thick cloud of dust enveloped the moving column.

On 11 October, the four days' march began from Kohat to the advanced base in Shinawari with the 2nd division leading. The 12 October was set as the date for the commencement of operations. Since Lockhart did not arrive in Kohat until 4 October, preparations were made by Major-General H. Yeatman-Biggs, and plans were constantly subject to modification. There was little organization around the concentration and movement of the thousands of men and animals pouring in and of the provisions that they needed. As Shadwell commented: 'From the 10th to the 20th October, one continuous stream of troops and animals moved along the road, sometimes as many as 2,000 carts alone leaving one post for the next; and if viewed from

[26] Ibid., 59.

an eminence, there did not appear to be a space of more than fifty yards, anywhere, that was not occupied by troops, transport animals, or bullock-carts'.[27]

March to Tirah

The next phase of the TEF was the march, or rather trek, towards Tirah. There was practically nil topographical information on Tirah and the routes leading to it. The British embarked on the march having to rely on native informants and treating the same information with suspicion. While 12 October had been set as the date for commencing the campaign, it was not until 17 October that Lockhart issued orders for the line of advance along the Khanki river into Khanki valley. It would take two weeks for the TEF to reach Tirah. The march was slow, arduous, and involved moving along difficult and steep mountain tracks, setting up camp, and then moving onto the next campsite. Once again, just the movement of transport and providing provisions for troops and animals was challenging if not near disastrous. In the absence of roads what were essentially goat tracks had to be continuously worked on to make them passable for the thousands of men and animals that comprised the TEF. Many times, the arrival of baggage to camp was delayed, due to the difficulties of moving the long column of pack animals, and troops were left without food and warm clothing. Supply of drinking water was challenging and troops had to resort to drinking muddy water. Opposition to the line of advance by the tribes involved remarkably accurate sniping into camps and attacks upon foraging parties.

The 25 October is particularly illustrative of the nature of such attacks. The first division sent out a strong foraging party, which was continually fired upon, resulting in thirteen casualties.[28] While sniping usually did not begin until night, on that day 'bullets were flying thick and fast' from 4.00–10.00 p.m., continuing at intervals all through the night.[29] Captain F. F. Badcock, an intelligence officer from the army headquarters was hit through his arm while sitting at lunch with other officers causing his arm to be amputated. Over fifty casualties occurred that night among the occupants of Karappa camp.[30] In the morning, six British and native soldiers were found cut up outside the camp.

The tribes were careful not to group together so firing back with artillery or rifles was useless, as it was difficult to know where to aim:

---

[27] Ibid., 66. [28] Ibid., 153. [29] Ibid., 154. [30] Moreman, *The Army in India*, 59.

Occasionally at night the constant firing led it to be imagined that they might be in considerable numbers and close by, a battery would be ordered to fire a star shell to light up the surrounding darkness, and enable the infantry to pour in a volley; but it seldom happened that the assailants could be seen. Even if two or three of them were for a moment visible, a volley fired when it was impossible to see along the sights of a rifle was not very apt to go near the mark, much less to hit it.[31]

After the losses of 25 October, a system of picketing the surrounding hills was set up. The officers and men also resorted to digging a sleeping place in the ground or piling stones around their resting place. This was impossible to do for the animals and every night animals continued to be hit.

The only direct engagement of the TEF that can be termed a 'battle' occurred during the two engagements to capture the Dargai Heights, a steep and precipitous ridge with a village of the same name, situated on top of the heights. The track leading up was barely a path with an exposed gap of about fifty yards along the line of approach. On 18 October, the British attacked the Dargai Heights. The goal of the action was to dislodge the Afridis from the top of the heights from where they had been firing upon the parties who were working on improving the tracks to allow for the passage of the column. The 1st Battalion 3rd Gurkhas supported by the 2nd Battalion King's Own Scottish Borderers were led by Lieutenant-General A. Power Palmer who charged and captured the heights by midday with a loss of three killed and nineteen wounded. Brigadier-General Westmacott's brigade conducted a reconnaissance of the heights and waited two hours for Brigadier-General Kempster's brigade to arrive. However, to their surprise, they were ordered, from the headquarters to evacuate the heights. This was a conspicuously strange decision since they would be re-ordered to take the heights and the identical action would be repeated on 20 October with far heavier losses. (For second battle of Dargai see following section.)

After the two engagements to clear Dargai heights, the march continued from the 21st to the 28th concentrating the two divisions. On 28 October, the Tirah Field Force moved toward Sampagha Pass. The four-mile-long road over the pass consisted of three ridges. While the ridges had been strengthened by the tribes with *sanghars* (stone defences), in contrast to Dargai, the tribes made no attempt to defend the more easily defensible passes, and instead 'waged guerilla warfare against the vulnerable columns of British and Indian troops melting away before determined assaults, pressing their attacks during withdrawals while all the time relentlessly harassing perimeter camps and convoys'.[32]

---

[31] Shadwell, *Lockhart's Advance*, 155.   [32] Moreman, *The Army in India*, 60.

Stay in Tirah

Maidan valley, the summer home of Afridis was a fertile valley, 6,000 feet high and about twelve miles long and six miles wide. The valley consisted of a series of terraced fields with *nullahs* (waterways) and lots of streams running thorough it. On 31 October, the TEF entered Maidan valley. The main goal of the expedition, to lift the veil from Tirah, had been accomplished. Lockhart had planted two divisions in the middle of Tirah. However, the goal of what is described here as the third phase of the campaign, was unclear. The inhabitants of Maidan had fled. There was no one around to 'exact reparations' from. Lockhart had thought that the fulfillment of terms would take ten days and he would be back on passage to England in November. However, as Slessor commented: 'It was one thing to advance into the heart of the country, but quite another, when there, to enforce terms, or even to make them known. Conditions of peace cannot very well be announced when none of the adversaries will come to listen to them, and the political officers found that for a long time they were powerless to persuade the jirgahs to come in, charm they never so wisely'.[33]

The lack of clarity also stemmed from the fact that the higher officials within the Government of India were not clear about future policy in the Khyber, Tirah or towards the Afridis and Orakzais. For the next three weeks during which the TEF occupied Maidan, Afridis consistently resisted the occupation making use of the rugged and broken up terrain and nullahs. Attacks were made upon reconnaissance and foraging parties, and long-range sniping into camps was constant, inflicting heavy casualties at times. Officers were shot while sitting down to eat or moving around camp. As Shadwell pointed out: 'Not a day passed but that some men or followers were killed or wounded by these wonderfully skilled marksmen, who are extremely difficult to see at all times, so expert are they in taking cover; and when, as was so frequently the case, they fired from long ranges with Lee-Metford rifles and smokeless powder, there was no smoke discernable to indicate even their approximate position'.[34]

During the engagement at Saran Sar in particular, heavy casualties were inflicted on the British troops. On 9 November, a reconnaissance was conducted by Westmacott to Saran Sar, a peak at the eastern end of Maidan about four miles away. However, the distance was broken up with precipitous ridges, watercourses, and wooded slopes. Westmacott arrived at the heights by noon but was told to wait there as Lockhart wanted to see the peak himself. The delay meant that the troops had to

---

[33] Slessor, *The 2nd Battalion*, 108.   [34] Shadwell, *Lockhart's Advance*, 188.

retreat over difficult ground in darkness and the casualties amounted to seventy killed. The brunt was borne by the 1st Battalion Northampton Regiment who lost nineteen killed and thirty wounded. While not pointing to Lockhart's role in the blunder directly, Callwell remarked that the 'mistake' in retreating at dusk was not the battalion's fault who were unpracticed in hill warfare, and were given no instructions on tactical methods suitable for such operations.[35]

After three weeks stay in Maidan, on 18 November Lockhart decided to move the camp about 3.5 miles away to Bagh. Nearly all the forage and grain in Maidan and its vicinity was exhausted and the large number of animals being buried there, had made the place unsanitary. Further, the Afridis regarded Bagh as sacred and it had a mosque known as the meeting place for the Afridis from where their attacks had been planned. The move to Bagh took a few days and during the evacuation, a scorched earth policy was employed where every dwelling was burnt and destroyed.[36] In Bagh, Mullah Sayid Akbar's house was destroyed, and the trees around the mosque burnt.

The cold weather had set in, troops suffered from frostbite frequently, and it had become evident that the field force would not be able to withstand being in Tirah during the harsh winter. During the campaign, there were 1,000 admissions to the field hospitals due to injuries and 11,000 from disease and exposure.[37] While most Orakzai clans had come in for negotiations and agreed to comply with British terms, only four out of eight sections of Afridis had come in to hear terms. On 23 November, Lockhart issued a proclamation to be circulated to the Afridis through messengers, that he was leaving Tirah because snow was coming, and he did not want his troops to be exposed to the cold of winter. As it was evident to many, the exit from Tirah, could not be regarded by the Afridis in any other way than 'the retirement of an unsuccessful force and a practical admission of failure'.[38]

Retreat from Tirah

According to Captain Nevill, the record of the withdrawal from Tirah, especially the march of the 2nd division, 'is unparalleled in Indian warfare since the disastrous retreat from Kabul in 1842'.[39] The withdrawal from Tirah began on 7 December with the plan that the two divisions of the main column would move to Peshawar marching down the Bara and Mastura valleys respectively. The freezing cold had set in. It

---

[35] Callwell, *Tirah 1897*, 88.   [36] Shadwell, *Lockhart's Advance*, 224.
[37] Slessor, *The 2nd Battalion*, 134.   [38] Ibid., 135.
[39] Nevill, *Campaigns on the North-West Frontier*, 297.

took several days to take down the camp and pack up. Telegraph lines and field hospitals had to be dismantled and packed up. Carrying the wounded back was an ordeal and required a *dhooly* (stretcher), which could weigh up to 100 pounds, and required eight to ten bearers. The transport officers went through the animals and shot those considered unfit for duty. As the soldiers, camp followers, dhooly bearers, and animal handlers marched back, they had to deal with heavy rain, frozen rivers and icy streams that had to be crossed while being subjected to constant sniping. Once again, the rearguards were attacked and suffered heavy casualties. On the 10th, it began to rain and the paths became so slippery that it was impossible for the laden animals to move on them. 'Added to this the men, and more especially the followers, were wet and chilled to the bone; the bedding and hospital tents were heavy with rain; the whole camp was deep in mud.'[40] Animals got bogged down or slipped in waterways and could not get out. The baggage fell off the animals and was entangled in ditches and streams. In the meantime, the Afridis were firing from all sides and men were in disarray trying to avoid bullets while dhooly bearers were struggling carrying the wounded on stretchers.

As the army trickled into Barkai, Richard Thomsett, the Principal Medical Officer attached to the Peshawar Column, stood and watched for several hours the return of the 'invaders and conquerers of Tirah', a sight that 'almost beggared description'. 'Highlanders, with their bare legs red from exposure, and some bleeding, and in many cases with no stockings on, their feet bring thrust into broken boots, passed by. They looked gaunt and rugged, with their faces and hands almost black, and many of them were devouring hunches of bread which had just been handed to them.'[41]

Anatomy of a Battle: The Second Battle of Dargai

On 18 October, the British attacked and captured the Dargai Heights. The order to evacuate came from the headquarters and was later justified for two reasons, both of which were based on miscalculations.[42] The second attack to capture Dargai occurred on 20 October. Yeatman-Biggs

---

[40] Shadwell, *Lockhart's Advance*, 265.
[41] Richard Gillham Thomsett, *With the Peshawar Column, Tirah Expeditionary Force* (London: Digby, Long & Co., 1899), 146.
[42] The decision appears to have been based on the assumption that the Afridis would not attempt to reoccupy the position; and secondly, that the water supply was three miles away so troops could not be left there. Hutchinson, *The Campaign in the Tirah*, 64–65. However, there were two sources of water close-by, a small *Talao* (tank) 100 yards below Dargai village and larger tank 500 yards to the East. Slessor, *The 2nd Battalion*, 60–61. On occupying the heights, Westmacott wanted to stay but the order to evacuate came from the headquarters. The goal had been to drive the tribes permanently from the

arrived at the Kotal and ordered a direct frontal attack to be led by the 2nd Battalion 2nd Gurkhas, supported by the 1st Battalion Dorset Regiment with the 1st Battalion Gordon Highlanders in reserve while the 2nd Battalion Derbyshire Regiment was to fire long range volleys from the village of Mamu Khan. This original order was modified several times leading in the end to the Gurkhas leading the attack supported by the Dorsets, the Derbys in 3rd place and the Gordons shooting long range. The orders were passed between the commanding officers but did not penetrate far back the long, drawn-out columns: 'The companies in rear simply followed on, playing blindly a game of "follow my leader", and having no notion as to the why or wherefore'.[43]

The slopes were so steep that soldiers had to keep halting to recover their breath. Two companies of the Gurkhas charged first under Colonel Eaton Travers losing sixty-seven men in ten minutes. The second rush of the Gurkhas was led by Major C. B. Judge, who was shot dead, and the Gurkhas fell back. Each company that attempted to charge forward was forced to fall back. Soon the troops were out of ammunition and the ammunition mules that were sent up lost their footing and rolled down the hill. After four hours of repeated attempts, the assault was at a standstill and the troops had not been able to move forward. The Gordons, whose long-range fire had not been very effective thus far, and the 3rd Sikhs were moved up. Yeatman-Biggs ordered them to charge with the Derbys, Gurkhas, and Dorsets in support. Lieutenant-Colonel H. H. Mathias addressed the troops: 'Highlanders, the General says the position must be taken at all costs. The Gordons will take it'.[44]

To their advantage, the Gordons were familiar with the ground, having been present at the scene two days before. Accompanied with rapid artillery fire, the men passed through the gap and dashed across the open space in extended order. With a large number wounded and three killed, including one officer, the companies got through. The leading troops were still about 200 yards below when the Afridis rapidly began to disperse. It was debated later whether they fled because they were running out of ammunition after several hours of firing rather than the action they confronted. When the heights were finally occupied there was no sign of the tribes and it appeared that their losses could not have been heavy. The British lost 199, including three officers killed and ten wounded and thirty-three men killed. The fighting was over for the day.

---

heights, but with the aid of reinforcements, they occupied the heights in even greater strength the following day.
[43] Slessor, *The 2nd Battalion*, 66.   [44] Ibid., 74.

The Role of Technology

Technology was a rather mixed affair during the Tirah campaign. On the one hand, the latest technologies of weaponry were deployed such as machine guns, mountain artillery, and rocket batteries. The Dum Dum (expanding) bullet was used for the first time in warfare and the Röntgen rays, which located bullets and splinters of lead in the body, for the first time in India. However, the crucial piece, on which almost every operation of the TEF depended, was transportation of people and baggage. Without railways and roads, the difficult mountainous terrain could only be traversed by animals.

There was no system in place for the urgent deployment of transport animals to the theatre of war. Transport animals were distributed in regiments all over India, and their number was not equal to the demand. Therefore, animals were taken by 'impressment', another word for force. A total of 103,597 camels, mules, donkeys, ponies, and bullocks were impressed for the 1897–98 operations of which over 70,000 were deployed in the Tirah operations. Every type of animal was gathered, 'the halt, the maimed, and the blind were collected with many undersized, half-starved and galled'.[45] All these animals had to be taken to 'passing stations' where transport officers would decide which ones were fit for service and then on to the base in Kohat. Both locations were at considerable distances from where the animals were found. No provision was made to feed the animals or their owners. Animals were packed in boxcars for days without food and water.

Correspondents and officers pointed out repeatedly how the transport animals were unfit for the expedition. Shadwell commented that the ponies were hardly able to carry any more than the heavy ordnance saddles with which they were equipped. 'Not only was much of the delay at the beginning of the campaign due (to use a very mild term) to the inferior transport, but a great many of the animals bought for the expedition, instead of being sent to Kohat ready equipped, were dispatched without pack-saddles, bridles, or any equipment at all.'[46]

The principal vehicle for transporting stores to the base was the bullock-cart. There were three types of carts each with their own set of problems. The bullock-cart drivers who were forced into service, and rarely saw any compensation, would tamper with their carts to make them break down. The *maundagi* carts were overloaded and again prone

---

[45] James L. Hevia, *Animal Labor and Colonial Warfare* (Chicago, London: The University of Chicago Press, 2018), 137.
[46] Shadwell, *Lockhart's Advance*, 74.

to frequent breakdowns.[47] Such mishaps, which occurred frequently, blocked the roads for the remainder of the transport and entailed difficulties in protecting the broken-down carts.

Throughout the campaign the delays, the breakdowns, and the numerous mishaps that occurred due to the problems with transport had a major impact on TEF operations. The difficulty of getting huge trains of pack animals across mountain tracks which were neither fit for the job, nor equipped properly, was not taken into account, nor planned for. For example, during the descent from Dargai to Kharappa many 'obligatory mules' that were carrying ammunition, water, and greatcoats were without saddles, so any jolt would send the load flying over a mule's head and drag it off a rock. With the delay and loss of baggage, troops would have to do without blankets, warm clothing, food, and water and the ammunition fell into the hands of the tribes.

In contrast to the Second Afghan War (see Chapter 7), when 'camel wastage' came under attention and criticism in England, following the Tirah campaign, it was impressment.[48] It is unknown how many impressed animals died, disappeared, or made it back after the campaign. Contemporary accounts are rife with descriptions of animals that died due to cold and starvation. 'These wretched beasts were constantly to be seen wandering about the outskirts of the camp, half dead with cold and hunger.'[49] Whether the animals procured for the TEF were unfit or ill-equipped to begin with, it is clear that transport mismanagement led to their deterioration and suffering, and had a tremendous impact on the operations.

Aftermath

The Tirah campaign cost £2.4 million and resulted in 1,150 British casualties, not including the people who died of sickness or succumbed to their wounds later. The number of casualties among the camp followers and other non-combatants such as animal drivers were not recorded. It is difficult to know the number of dead and wounded among the tribes, as they were never left behind. Most of the figures given in British sources regarding Afridi-Orakzais losses are estimates. However, their homes, crops, and villages that were burned and destroyed, would have likely taken years to rebuild.

---

[47] The term 'maundagi carts' referred to the system whereby a native contractor was paid per maund (about eithy-two pounds) delivered to destination. In order to be paid more, the native contractors tried to carry the 'maximum' load, so these carts were constantly overloaded and constantly broke down.
[48] Hevia, *Animal Labor*, 133–34.   [49] Slessor, *The 2nd Battalion*, 120.

From the military standpoint, and especially from the experience of the soldier who was part of the TEF, there were many lessons to be learnt.[50] The military effectiveness of the Afridis against an overwhelming army was striking, and their use of long-range weapons such as the Martini-Henry had transformed frontier warfare. What was especially notable was their skilled use of few arms of precision, acquired through capture, such as the Lee-Metford. In a note to the Viceroy, Lockhart stated, 'It is the accuracy of the fire, not the number of rifles that caused my recent losses'.[51]

While the failures of the TEF and the performance of the British troops came under scrutiny and were criticized by the press in India and in England, more broadly, the campaign demonstrated that the resources and organization to undertake such a large-scale military operation on the Frontier at a moment's notice were not in place. In England, the opposition criticized government policy, including during a heated debate in parliament surrounding the loss of the Khyber. Despite moments of political outcry and criticism by the press, it is difficult to assess if public attention sustained beyond the short-term over the events of the war.

Despite the immense destruction inflicted on the tribes, it was also questionable whether the campaign had succeeded in pacifying them or in recovering British prestige. The story of whether the long, drawn-out, and peacemeal 'compliance' of tribes with British demands for money and rifles indicated 'submission' was debatable. Sections of tribes continued their opposition, such as the Zakka Khel Afridis, and did not submit when the TEF withdrew from Tirah. In 1899, Captain George Roos-Keppel conducted a punitive expedition agaist the Chamkannis, a section of the Orakzais, to complete the unfinished business of the campaign.

The direct political result of the 1897 revolt was the end of the dual system of imperial control (Government of India and the local Punjab government) that had been in place since 1849 and the creation of the North-West Frontier Province in 1901 by Lord Curzon, the new Viceroy of India. In an attempt to avoid future costly expeditions on the Frontier, Curzon also began withdrawing Indian troops from military posts and replacing them with local militia. The Khyber was reopened and the Khyber Rifles were reinstated as guardians of the Pass. From the perspective of the Afridis and Orakzais, it is debatable if the aftermath of the war had dramatically changed imperial rule on the Frontier. However, the 1897 revolt remained the last instance of a major Afridi-Orakzais combination launched to resist British occupation of their lands.

---

[50] Moreman, *The Army in India*, 68–98.   [51] Ibid., 69.

Further Reading

Agha, Sameetah. 'Sub-imperialism and the loss of the Khyber: The politics of imperial defence on British India's North-West Frontier'. *Indian Historical Review* 40, 2(2013): 307–30.

Callwell, C. E. *Tirah 1897*. London: Constable, 1911.

Frontier and Overseas Expeditions from India, vol. 2. Simla: Govt. Monotype Press, 1910.

Hernon, Ian. *The Savage Empire: Forgotten Wars of the 19th Century*. Stroud: Sutton Publishing Limited, 2000.

Hutchinson, Col. H.D. *The Campaign in the Tirah 1897–1898: An Account of the Expedition Against the Orakzais and Afridis under Gen. Sir. William Lockhart*. London: Macmillan, 1898.

James, Colonel Lionel. *The Indian Frontier War: Being an Account of the Mohmund and Tirah Expeditions 1897*. London: Heinemann, 1898.

Johnson, Rob. *The Afghan Way of War: How and Why They Fight*. Oxford: Oxford University Press, 2012.

Mills, H. Woosnam. *The Tirah Campaign, Being the Sequel to the Pathan Revolt in North-West India*. Lahore, India: Civil and Military Gazette, 1898.

Moreman, T. R. *The Army in India and the Development of Frontier Warfare, 1849–1947*. London: Macmillan Press LTD, 1998.

Nevill, Captain H. L. *Campaigns on the North-West Frontier*. London: J. Murray, 1912.

Shadwell, Leonard Julius. *Lockhart's Advance through Tirah*. London: W. Thacker, 1898.

Slessor, A. K. *The 2nd Battalion, Derbyshire Regiment in Tirah*. London: Swan Sonnenschein, 1900.

Stewart, J. *The Khyber Rifles: From the British Raj to Al Gaeda*. Stroud: Gloucestershire, 2005.

Surridge, Keith. 'The Ambiguous Amir: Britain, Afghanistan and the 1897 North-West Frontier Uprising'. *Journal of Imperial and Commonwealth History* 36, 3(2008): 417–34.

Thomsett, Richard Gillham. *With the Peshawar Column, Tirah Expeditionary Force*. London: Digby, Long & Co., 1899.

Warburton, Robert. *Eighteen Years in the Khyber, 1879–1898*. London: J. Murray, 1900.

Wilkinson, Glenn R., 'Purple prose and the yellow press: Imagined spaces and the military expedition to Tirah, 1897'. In David Finkelstein and Douglas M. Peers (eds.) *Negotiating India in the Nineteenth-Century Media*. London: Macmillan Press, 2000.

Yate, Arthur Campbell. *Lieutenant-Colonel John Haughton, Commandant of the 36th Sikhs, A Hero of Tirah: A Memoir*. London: J. Murray, 1900.

13 Reconquest of the Sudan, 1896–1898

Edward M. Spiers

Background

Popular anguish erupted in Great Britain after the humiliating failure of the Gordon relief expedition. The killing of Major-General Charles 'Chinese' Gordon and the fall of Khartoum (25–26 January 1885) spawned an unprecedented Gordon cult, and demands of vengeance for the Christian martyr.[1] Despite this political turmoil, and the subsequent withdrawal of British forces to more defensible positions at Suakin on the Red Sea and Wadi Halfa on the Nile River, the Liberal government of William E. Gladstone survived. The intense passions aroused by the death of Gordon waned, as debates over Irish Home Rule arose, splitting the Liberal party.[2]

The Mahdist state also survived the death of Muhammad Ahma bin Abdullah, the Mahdi (or Expected Guide) in June 1885, as Khalifa 'Abdallāhi consolidated his regime in the aftermath. Sudanic scholars such as A. B. Theobald and P. M. Holt emphasized the achievements of establishing a civil and military administration over a disparate array of peoples, across an area of nearly one million square miles, and over a period of thirteen years.[3] Norman Daniel even asserted that 'British contemporaries at first saw the [Mahdist] movement much as we see it to-day, as the religious expression of national feeling'.[4] A contrary impression of the Mahdist state as one born in religious fanaticism, and steeped in oppression and bloodshed, owed much to the writings of Major F. Reginald Wingate, when director of intelligence for the

---

[1] Douglas H. Johnson, 'The death of Gordon: A Victorian myth', *The Journal of Imperial and Commonwealth History* 10, 3 (1982): 285–310.

[2] Richard Hill, 'The Gordon literature', *The Durham University Journal* 47, 3 (1955): 97–103.

[3] A. B. Theobald, *The Mahdiya: A History of the Anglo-Egyptian Sudan, 1881-1899* (London: Longmans Green, 1951), 35; P. M. Holt, *The Mahdist State in the Sudan 1881–1898* (Oxford: Oxford University Press, 1977), 264–66.

[4] Norman Daniel, *Islam, Europe and Empire* (Edinburgh: Edinburgh University Press, 1966), 416.

Egyptian Army. Although his *Mahdiism and the Egyptian Sudan* sold poorly, he assisted in the writing of two popular works by escapees from Omdurman, namely *Ten Years' Captivity in the Mahdi's Camp* by Father Joseph Ohrwalder and *Fire and Sword in the Sudan* by Rudolf Slatin, a former Governor-General of Darfur province and advisor to the Khalifa.

These themes reappeared in the early historiography of the war, notably the magisterial, two-volume work of Winston Churchill, *The River War*, which dominated coverage of the campaign. More recent accounts include Philip Ziegler, *Omdurman*,'Ismat Hasan Zulfo, *Karari: The Sudanese Account of the Battle of Omdurman*, and Henry Keown-Boyd, *A Good Dusting: The Sudan Campaigns 1883–1899*. Important source-based biographies include Archie Hunter, *Kitchener's Sword-Arm: The Life and Campaigns of General Sir Archibald Hunter*, M. W. Daly, *The Sirdar: Sir Reginald Wingate and the British Empire in the Middle East*, and John Pollock, *Kitchener: The Road to Omdurman*. Scholarly accounts of the British and international aspects of the campaign appear in Edward Spiers's edited volume, *Sudan: The Reconquest Reappraised*, and the role of Sudanese soldiers in Ronald Lamothe, *Slaves of Fortune*.

Of critical importance, though, were the early writings of Wingate and his accomplices. By chronicling and exaggerating the despotism, debauchery, and depravations of the Khalifa's rule, they found a receptive audience in Britain, reviving interest in the Sudan and in the cause of avenging Gordon's death. They insisted, too, that the time was ripe for action, and that the Mahdist state was tottering after a succession of internal revolts and widespread famines.[5] Sudan still threatened Egypt and Suakin as evidenced by several frontier skirmishes since 1885, but the reformed Egyptian Army (EA) had generally triumphed, notably in engagements at Toski (1889) and Tokar (1891). By 1896, those Gladstonian radicals who had championed religious nationalism in the Sudan, found themselves marginalized as a Conservative government reviewed the news from Africa.

Outbreak of War

Of prime concern to Lord Salisbury, the Conservative Prime Minister and Foreign Secretary, was neither the lurid accounts of life in the Sudan nor the movement of a French expedition through the province of Bahr El Ghazal towards the White Nile but the devastating defeat of an Italian

---

[5] Edward M. Spiers 'Introduction', in Edward M. Spiers (ed.), *Sudan: The Reconquest Reappraised* (London: Frank Cass, 1998), 1–10.

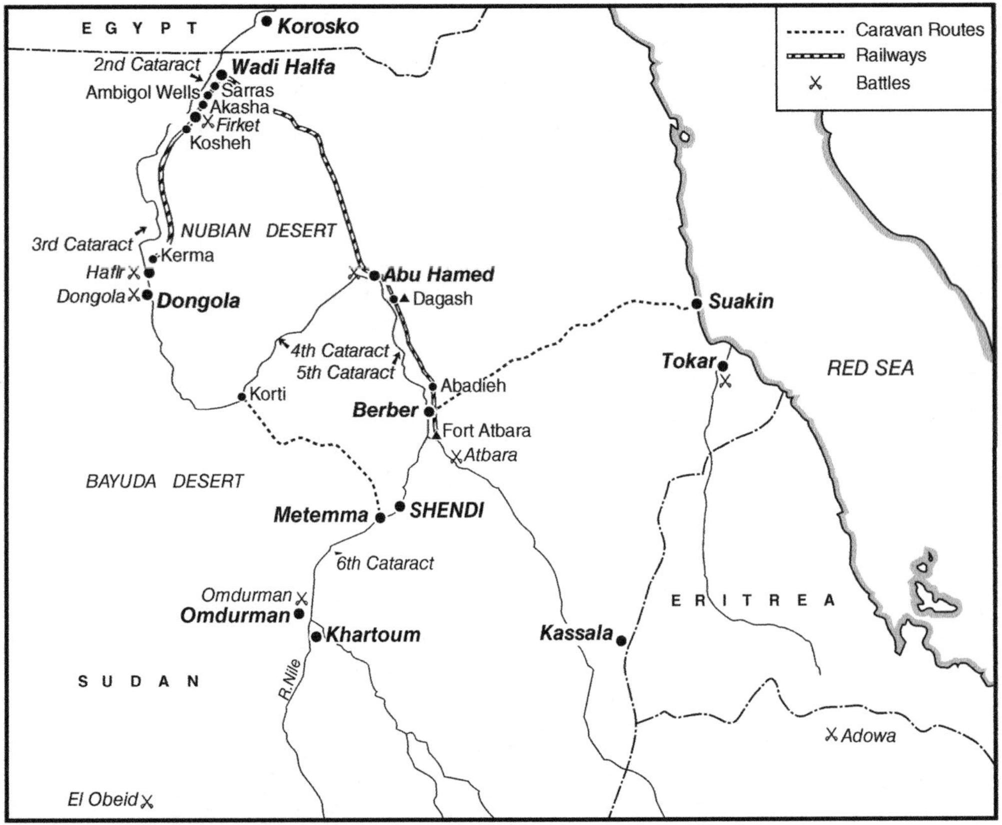

Map 13.1 Reconquest of the Sudan, 1896–1898

army by the Abyssinians at the Battle of Adowa (Adwa) on 1 March 1896. As the Italian government pleaded for a diversion to relieve pressure on its garrison at Kassala, European priorities took precedence over African considerations.[6] Seeking to improve Britain's relations with the Triple Alliance, Lord Salisbury reversed the policy of non-involvement in the Sudan, confirmed only four months previously.[7] In communicating the cabinet's decision of 12 March to Lord Cromer, Britain's Agent and Consul-General in Egypt, he insisted that the initial move should only encompass the northern province of Dongola, and that planting 'the foot of Egypt rather farther up the Nile' should not involve the expense of sending additional British troops to Egypt.[8] So contrary to post-colonial assertions (without evidence) that the campaign was launched to forestall French imperial ambitions, it began with distinctly limited objectives.[9]

British and Mahdist Forces

The core of what eventually became an Anglo-Egyptian Army was the Egyptian Army (EA), reformed and trained by British officers and NCOs. By 1896, it had become a compact and well-organized force of sixteen battalions of infantry (ten Egyptian and six Sudanese), three batteries of artillery, one Maxim battery, eight squadrons of cavalry, a Camel Corps of eight companies, and support units.[10] Colonel (later Major-General Sir) Horatio Herbert Kitchener, as the Sirdar (Commander-in-Chief) of the EA, commanded the Anglo-Egyptian forces. For the Dongola campaign, these numbered over 9,000 Egyptians and Sudanese apart from 520 North Staffordshires and some Maxim gunners.[11] By 1898, with the addition of the first British Brigade (four infantry battalions of Lincolnshires, Warwickshires, Cameron and Seaforth Highlanders), Kitchener commanded 14,000 men and, in the final advance on Omdurman, 8,200 British, including a Second Brigade (Grenadier Guards, Northumberland Fusiliers, Rifle Brigade and Lancashire Fusiliers), artillery, and the 21st Lancers, and 17,600 EA

---

[6] David Steele, 'Lord Salisbury, the "False Religion" of Islam, and the reconquest of the Sudan', in Spiers (ed.), *Sudan*, 11–33.
[7] Earl of Cromer, *Modern Egypt*, 2 vols. (London: Macmillan, 1908), vol. 2, 82.
[8] Lord Salisbury to Lord Cromer, 13 March and 1 April 1896, Salisbury Mss., vol. A113, nos. 8 and 12, Hatfield House Muniments (HHM).
[9] Ronald M. Lamothe, *Slaves of Fortune: Sudanese Soldiers and the River War 1896–1898* (Cambridge: James Currey, 2011), 18.
[10] Viscount Wolseley to Lord Lansdowne, 8 May 1896, CAB 37/41, The National Archives (TNA).
[11] Henry S. L. Alford and W. Dennistoun Sword, *The Egyptian Soudan: Its Loss and Recovery* (London: Naval & Military Press, 1898), 133.

soldiers, with forty-four guns and twenty Maxims on the land, thirty-six guns and twenty-four Maxims on the river.[12]

Defending Dongola was the Mahdist army of the north, approximately 10,000 men under Muḥammad wad Bushāra, with an advanced force of 3,000 men at Firket (Firka). Further south Emir Mahmud deployed 12,000 infantry, 4,000 cavalry, and ten guns at the battle of Atbara (8 April 1898), and at Omdurman (2 September 1898), the Khalifa had 52,000 men, including 14,000 Baggara horsemen and sixty-three 'assorted and inferior' guns.[13]

Strategy and War Aims

By relying upon the Egyptian Army, British planners minimized the costs of the campaign and reduced the exposure of British troops to the Sudanese climate. Cromer, ever mindful of Egyptian finances, described Kitchener as a 'first-rate military administrator', a 'rigid economist',[14] and a man who was 'cool and sensible knows his subject thoroughly – and is not at all inclined to be rash'.[15] The remarkably successful Dongola phase, completed in six months, at a minimal cost £E715,000, and with only a few battlefield casualties (forty-seven killed and 122 wounded), permitted a nineteenth-century form of 'mission creep'.

Kitchener now promoted to Major-General and knighted, visited London where he persuaded the Chancellor of the Exchequer to fund a railway across the Nubian Desert. Lord Salisbury acknowledged that Kitchener's 'campaign against the Chancellor of the Exchequer was not the least brilliant and certainly the most unexpected of all his triumphs'.[16] The Chancellor, Sir Michael Hicks Beach informed the House of Commons that Britain had now accepted that Egypt could never be secure so long as a hostile power occupied the Upper Nile valley.[17] As opportunities arose, British goals widened: Berber was seized (6 September 1897) after it was found evacuated by Mahdist forces, and Kitchener called for British reinforcements after intelligence reported that the Khalifa had planted his standards outside Omdurman (December 1897), a possible preliminary to an advance northwards.[18]

---

[12] Edward M. Spiers, 'Campaigning under Kitchener', in Spiers (ed.), *Sudan*, 59, 65.
[13] Theobald, *Mahdiya*, 198, 200, 221–222, 228.
[14] Cromer, *Modern Egypt*, vol. 2, 87–88.
[15] Cromer to Salisbury, 15 March 1896, Salisbury Mss. vol. A109, No. 24, HHM.
[16] Salisbury to Cromer, 27 November 1896, Salisbury Mss. vol. A113, No. 34, HHM.
[17] *Parliamentary Debates*, Fourth Series, XLV (5 February 1897), 1439–49.
[18] Edward M. Spiers, 'Intelligence and command in Britain's small colonial wars of the 1890s', *Intelligence and National Security* 22, 5 (2007): 661–81.

After victory at Omdurman Kitchener, accompanied by two Sudanese battalions and a contingent of Cameron Highlanders, moved up the Nile to confront Commandant Jean-Baptiste Marchand at Fashoda (19 September 1898). In seeking to establish French influence in the Upper Nile valley, Marchand had the support of a few permanent officials in Paris but after the confrontation, France announced its withdrawal from the Sudan (7 November 1898).[19]

The Khalifa's aims were less complex: he wanted to preserve the Mahdist state, having recently lost the province of Tokar to the British (1891), Kassala, the largest town in eastern Sudan, to the Italians (1894), and seen the French and Belgians gain footholds in the southernmost provinces of Bar al Ghazal and Equatoria. Alerted by spies about Kitchener's incursion, he demanded a forward defence of Dongola but, after the defeat at Firket (7 June 1896) and the evacuation of Dongola town (23 September 1896), faced the prospect of a full-scale invasion. The Khalifa sent Mahmud's army north, convinced that the invasion would follow the route of the relief expedition and cut across the Bayuda Desert to Metemma. Meanwhile he exhorted his far-flung forces to concentrate outside Omdurman other than those guarding his eastern and southern provinces or repressing rebellious tribes in Darfur.[20]

Frustrated by the ill discipline of Mahmud's army, the Khalifa tried to micromanage its movements but never surmounted the problems of transport and supply. Despite his warnings, Mahmud failed to reinforce Berber and his army struggled subsequently to reach the village of Nakheila, before scattering after defeat at the battle of Atbara. Even further south at the Sabluka (Sabaluqa) gorge on the Sixth Cataract, where a garrison was building defences, the Khalifa could not provide supplies and provisions. Confounded by logistical problems, he abandoned the Sabluka forts and brought all his forces back to Omdurman.[21] Ultimately having never left his capital, and lacking any operational plan to achieve his aims, the Khalifa was unable to counter the advance of Kitchener's forces.

The Course of the War

The Dongola campaign constituted the first phase of the reconquest. Kitchener, despite personal fears of supersession by a more senior

---

[19] J. F. V. Keiger, 'Omdurman, Fashoda and Franco-British Relations', Spiers (ed.), *Sudan*, 166; Darrell Bates, *The Fashoda Incident of 1898: Encounter on the Nile* (Oxford: Oxford University Press, 1984).

[20] 'Ismat Hasan Zulfo', trans. by Peter Clark, *Karari: The Sudanese Account of the Battle of Omdurman* (London: Frederick Warne, 1980), 55, 57, 71.

[21] Holt, *Mahdist State*, 213–15, 218–19, 221.

general, had several advantages. His chain of command stretched from the Foreign Office through Cairo, where Cromer remained a staunch supporter, informing Lord Salisbury that he was 'very much pleased with Kitchener' and hopeful that 'the War Office won't interfere with him too much'.[22] Kitchener also secured an Indian brigade to garrison Suakin, enabling him to concentrate the EA, with the 1st Battalion, North Staffordshires in reserve, for the advance up the Nile. Having served on the relief expedition, he knew the roadless and rocky terrain, and appreciated that a successful advance would depend upon mastering the requirements of transport and supply.

In these matters Kitchener, despite his autocratic and secretive manner,[23] received capable assistance from Brevet-Colonel (later General Sir) H. M. Leslie Rundle as his chief of staff, Major (later General Sir) F. Reginald Wingate, the director of intelligence,[24] and Brevet-Colonel (later General Sir) Archibald Hunter, commander of the frontier field force and later commander of the Egyptian Division.[25] Commanding three battalions, Hunter moved ahead and, by 20 March, established an advance base at the village of Akasha, seventy miles south of Wadi Halfa. As Akasha was within striking distance of Firket, where the Mahdists had assembled their forward troops, Hunter concentrated on fortifying his position while Kitchener sent supplies forward by camel convoys and repaired the railway from Wadi Halfa.

Restoring and extending the railway enabled the advancing force to bypass the Second Cataract and to sustain a presence deep inside Dongola province. The immense task of ordering all the sleepers, fastenings, stores and provisions, engaging engineers and artisans in Egypt, raising a railway battalion of 800 men, and instructing them as the work progressed, devolved upon Lieutenant E. Percy C. Girouard, a young French Canadian, who joined the expedition at the end of March. He impressed Lieutenant Harry L. Pritchard, RE, as knowing 'exactly what was wanted, and had the head, the energy and the pluck to do it. He was here, there, and everywhere, instructing, shoving things along, gradually getting organization and system to take the place of chaos, and under his guidance every one became slowly, but noticeably more proficient at the work'.[26]

---

[22] Cromer to Salisbury, 15 March 1896 and 13 June 1896, Salisbury Mss., vol. A109, Nos. 24 and 61, HHM.
[23] Ian F. W. Beckett, 'Kitchener and the politics of command', in Spiers, *Sudan*, 47–48.
[24] M. W. Daly, *The Sirdar: Sir Reginald Wingate and the British Empire in the Middle East* (Philadelphia: American Philosophical Society, 1997).
[25] Archie Hunter, *Kitchener's Sword-Arm: The Life and Campaigns of General Sir Archibald Hunter* (Staplehurst: Spellmount, 1996).
[26] An Officer (Henry L. Pritchard), *Sudan Campaign 1896–1899* (London: Chapman & Hall, 1899), 18–19.

By 21 May, the railway reached Ambigol Wells, twenty-two miles from Akasha, and allowed Kitchener to bring the EA forward for an assault on the Mahdists at Firket. Armed with precise intelligence from Wingate about the dispositions of the 3,000 Mahdists, Kitchener divided his command into two: a river column of three infantry brigades and two batteries of field artillery, about 7,000 men under Hunter's command, and a desert column under Major John F. Burn-Murdoch, some 2,000 strong, including seven squadrons of cavalry, eight Camel Corps companies, a Horse Artillery battery, and the Maxim machine guns of the only British troops involved. While the river column moved south on the afternoon of 6 June, the desert column swung east and then south to approach Firket from the rear. In a 4.30 a.m. assault on 7 June, the two columns caught the enemy by surprise and routed them. Half of the Mahdists became casualties, including 800 dead, and 600 surrendered. The Egyptian Army suffered twenty killed and eighty-three wounded. The victory boosted the morale of the EA and its officers: 'a complete success', wrote Burn-Murdoch, 'Most of the Emirs were killed'.[27] Kitchener applauded the controlled advance and fire discipline, while Cromer exulted in a victory on the date forecast by the Sirdar, and in the performance of the Egyptian troops not least in the 'hazardous' night march and surprise achieved.[28]

Thereafter progress slowed, as Kitchener needed the Nile to rise before moving men and supplies forward, while he extended the railway to Kosheh. In the meantime cholera and other diseases swept down from Egypt via the railway and camel convoys, killing far more men than would ever be lost in action.[29] Fortunately, the cholera passed as mysteriously as it had come: by 13 August, Burn-Murdoch recorded in his diary that the Egyptian cavalry had not had any cholera 'for nearly two whole weeks, so may be said to be clear of it'.[30] Another delay occurred on 28 August when freak winds and rain washed away twelve miles of railway between Wadi Halfa and Akasha, whereupon Kitchener assigned three and a half thousand labourers, working day and night, to the repair. Personally assisting in the work, Kitchener saw the line repaired in a

---

[27] Burn-Murdoch, TS diary, 14 June 1896, Add. Mss. 1986-05-26-17, National Army Museum (NAM).
[28] Kitchener to Cromer, 8 June 1896, and Cromer to Salisbury, 13 June 1896, Salisbury Mss., vol. A109, no. 67 and no. 61, HHM.
[29] Compared with the forty-seven killed in action and 122 wounded, some 260 Egyptian soldiers, 640 camp followers and nineteen British soldiers died from disease. Lt.-Col. E. W. C. Sandes, *The Royal Engineers in Egypt and the Sudan* (Chatham: Institution of Royal Engineers, 1937), 166.
[30] Burn-Murdoch, TS diary, 13 August 1896, Acc. 1986-05-26-17, NAM.

week.[31] Once four gun-boats and three steamers were hauled over the Second Cataract, Kitchener could launch his expeditionary force in its final advance. Gunners on the river and land silenced their Mahdist counterparts at Hafir (19 September), and on entering Dongola (23 September 1896), the expeditionary force found that Bishara and his army had fled. Apparently Bishara had wanted to launch a suicidal attack but his emirs seized and bound him before retreating across the Bayuda Desert.[32] Kitchener's forces moved on to seize Korti and Merowe.

On 1 January 1897, Kitchener began construction of his next railway. Having already jettisoned the options of crossing the Bayuda Desert or of advancing by rail from Suakin – the failures of the mid-1880s – he gambled upon crossing the unchartered and seemingly waterless expanses of the Nubian Desert. He also employed a broad gauge of 3 feet 6 inches, so matching the gauge of the Cape-Cairo railroad as favoured by Cecil Rhodes. Accordingly, when Girouard returned to England to purchase fifteen new engines and 200 trucks, Rhodes lent him several 70-ton and 80-ton locomotives previously destined for the Cape and Natal railways.

Construction of the Sudan Military Railway began slowly as workshops had to be built in Wadi Halfa, 1,500 platelayers trained, and rolling stock brought from England. By the end of April, only thirty-seven miles of the 230-mile track had been laid. Completion of the Dongola line to Kerma took priority so that supplies could be concentrated at Merowe before advancing to the projected railway terminus of Abu Hamed. Once the Dongola line had reached Kerma (4 May), resources were switched to the other track and progress accelerated. By 5 June, Kitchener reported that '63 miles had been laid. My railway battalion laid the other day 1,900 yards in 4 hours & 10 minutes so you see they are pretty smart & can do 2 miles a day if we could only get the materials up'.[33] In an extremely vulnerable process rail-laying gangs toiled across a desolate and barren terrain under a ferocious tropical sun. Hindered by dust storms, derailments, inexperienced staff, and other problems, the railway struggled forwards, always keeping a reserve of 10,000 gallons of water at the railhead.[34]

---

[31] Henry Keown-Boyd, *A Good Dusting: A Centenary Review of the Sudan Campaigns 1883–1899* (London: Leo Cooper, 1986), 152.
[32] Zulfo, *Karari*, 66.
[33] Kitchener to Sir Evelyn Wood, 5 June 1897, Acc. Mss. 1968-07-234, Kitchener-Wood Mss., NAM.
[34] Sandes, *Royal Engineers*, 231.

Kitchener's 'luck' persisted: his railway gangs found hitherto unknown sources of water deep underground at seventy-seven miles from Wadi Halfa, and later at 126 miles from Wadi Halfa.[35] Meanwhile the Khalifa, despite knowing about the railway's construction, neither understood its importance nor exploited its vulnerability. Having expected an invasion across the Bayuda Desert, he sent Mahmud's army to Metemma, which the Jaalin refused to evacuate, and so the army stormed the town (1 July), and spent months repressing the Jaalin people. On 3 July Kitchener wrote, 'The Dervishes are divided amongst themselves & the Khalifa is having trouble'.[36]

Kitchener now ordered Hunter to seize Abu Hamed with a flying column of 3,600 troops, predominantly Egyptian and Sudanese infantry, with six guns, four machine guns, thirty cavalry, a medical detachment, and 1,300 camels carrying eitghteen days' supply of food and ammunition. On 29 July, they left Merowe on the 118-mile march over broken and rocky terrain, with Lieutenant M. G. E. Manifold, RE, unwinding a telegraph line to keep in touch with Merowe. Marching mostly at night in the hottest time of the year, the mission was completed in seven and a half days – a testimony to 'the excellent marching power of the "Black" and the Egyptian'.[37] Armed with accurate intelligence, Hunter launched a preparatory bombardment at 6.00 a.m. on 7 August. The assault led by officers on horseback followed in an arc formation into the teeth of a volley at 100 yards. Hunter lost eighteen killed, including Major H. M. Sidney and Lieutenant Edward Fitzclarence, and sixty-one wounded, but destroyed the 700-man garrison (only one hundred more than Wingate had forecast). By 7.30 a.m., the Mahdists had lost 450 killed and twenty wounded, with another 180 taken prisoner, including the Mahdist commander, Emir Mohamed el Zayn: fifty fled.[38] Kitchener now sent three gun-boats on reconnaissances of Mahmud's camp and forts outside Metemma and shelled them heavily (16–17 October and 3 November). He also completed his railway to Abu Hamed (31 October), and ordered Hunter to seize the evacuated town of Berber (6 September), another 130 miles upriver.

Kitchener's line of communications was now over-extended and highly vulnerable. Desperate to extend the railway, a distraught Kitchener even tendered his resignation over financial difficulties in

---

[35] Ibid., 231–35.
[36] Kitchener to Wood, 3 July 1897, Acc. Mss. 1968-07-234, Kitchener-Wood Mss., NAM.
[37] An Officer, *Sudan Campaign*, 105.
[38] Kitchener to Hunter, 27 July 1897, Hunter Mss., 1/3, Sudan Archive, University of Durham (SAD).

October 1897 before rescinding the letter.[39] As the end of the year approached, he had his army scattered along the Nile with a brigade in Berber, relying upon a daily delivery of fifty tons of supplies from the Nile; a nearby dockyard of Abadieh (where the three gun-boats could be serviced rather than bring them back over the newly found Fifth Cataract); and an advanced camp at the Atbara.[40] This army may have confounded its critics by victories at Firket and Abu Hamed but both battles had been fought with excellent intelligence, the benefit of surprise, and overwhelming numerical advantages. However laudable this performance, the EA could not face the main army of the Khalifa alone,[41] and when Wingate's intelligence indicated that this army might move north (which it never did), Kitchener took the 'momentous & important step' of requesting British reinforcements.[42]

While Kitchener brought his British battalions forward, reaching Abu Hamed, over 1,000 miles from Cairo by steamer and railway in a mere eleven days, and began rigorous training and acclimatization under their commanding officer, Major-General William F. Gatacre ('Old Backacher' as the ranks described him), the Khalifa reviewed his options.[43] Having failed to exploit interior lines of communication, he had relied upon a passive defence of the north without ever reinforcing Mahmud's army.[44] Mahmud had failed to control the rapacious behaviour of the western tribesmen after the sack of Metemma, eventually sending all the local women to Omdurman (hence numerous Jaalin would join the 'friendlies' that later accompanied Kitchener's army on its final march).[45]

Even worse, Mahmud had allowed the evacuation of Berber, the second richest town in the Sudan, so allowing the valuable trade route to Suakin to fall into the hands of the enemy. Osman Digna, leading an army of 4,000 Mahdists, had now left eastern Sudan and joined forces with Mahmud's army. The veteran commander urged the 30-year-old Mahmud to leave the Nile (and the harassment of Kitchener's gun-boats) to move eastwards and 'fall upon Berber unawares'.[46] Mahmud complained to the Khalifa but he supported Osman Digna and, in mid-February 1898, Mahmud's army began to cross the Nile to Shendi. It

---

[39] Kitchener to Cromer, 18 October 1897, and Cromer, telegram, 24 October 1897, Salisbury Mss., Vol. A110, No. 64, and no. 67, HHM.
[40] Cromer, telegram, 2 January 1898, FO 78/5049, TNA.
[41] Col. A. Hunter to F. B. Maurice, 12 July 1896, Maurice Mss., 2/1/2, King's College London, Liddell Hart Centre for Military Archives (LHCMA).
[42] Maj. F.R. Wingate diary, 31 December 1897, Wingate Mss., 102/1/69, SAD.
[43] 2nd Lt. H. P. Creagh-Osborne Diary, 9–20 January 1898, Longe Mss., 643/1/4-7, SAD.
[44] 'Mahmoud in Captivity', *Lincoln Gazette*, 30 April 1898, 7.
[45] Zulfo, *Karari*, 72–3 and 79.   [46] 'Mahmoud in Captivity', 7.

moved up the eastern bank and made an exhausting desert crossing. Lacking supplies and transport, Mahmud defied the entreaties of Osman to move further east and, on 20 March, encamped his forces at Nakheila on the northern bank of the Atbara River.

As spies and refugees apprised Wingate of the divisions within Mahmud's command, and the army's north-easterly movement, Kitchener concentrated his forces.[47] Under a scorching sun the Lincolns, Warwicks, and Camerons marched across the desert, covering 120 miles in five days, with one day's rest: by midway through the march Lieutenant Ronald F. Meiklejohn (Warwicks) recalled, 'some had no soles on their boots: many had the skin off their feet: others were worn out. We left about 150 men & two officers (Caldecott & Christie): the Lincolns left 180: the Camerons 200: and these waited for two gunboats to arrive & bring them on. We had had no food now for 26 hours & no sleep for even longer'.[48] Eventually the exhausted British soldiers reached Berber as did the Seaforths, who only left Cairo on 2 March, and spent a week at Assouan camp, before catching up with the other battalions by train, boat, and by riding camels through the night, wearing their kilts.[49] Yet these units received splendid receptions on arrival from their Sudanese counterparts and reciprocated in kind when the Sudanese marched through the British camp en route to the Atbara.[50]

By 21 March, the Sirdar brought his combined forces about seven miles up the Atbara and sent cavalry to reconnoitre the enemy's position, twenty miles distant. Having tried to goad the enemy into an attack by dispatching gun-boats to destroy its almost undefended reserve at Shendi, Kitchener found Gatacre and Hunter in disagreement about an offensive. Remarkably, he referred the matter to Cromer but by the time Cromer replied, the senior command had agreed to launch an assault.[51] On 4 April, Kitchener began moving his army forward in short marches and, on the following day, another reconnaissance patrol had to escape being cut off, with an incoming officer, Captain Douglas Haig impressed by the discipline and fighting resolve of the 'Gyppie Cavalry'.[52] On the evening of 7 April, Kitchener prepared his men for their final night

---

[47] Intelligence Report, Egypt, No. 59, 13 February to 23 May 1898, 4, SAD.
[48] Lt. R. F. Meiklejohn, 'Nile Campaign', 27 February 1898, Acc. No. 1974-04-36, NAM.
[49] 'Letter from a Nairn Man at Atbara', *Nairnshire Telegraph*, 25 May 1898, 3.
[50] Meiklejohn, 'Nile Campaign', 3 and 10 March 1898, Acc. No. 1974-04-36, NAM; Capt. Samuel Fitzgibbon Cox, Diary, 3 and 15 March 1898, LR 770, Museum of Lincolnshire Life (MLL).
[51] Cromer, *Modern Egypt*, 2, 98–102.
[52] Captain Douglas Haig to Henrietta, 11 April 1898, Acc. 3155, No. 6, Haig Mss., National Library of Scotland (NLS).

march to attack Mahmud's camp at dawn. His final exhortation: 'remember Gordon. The men before you are his murderers' resonated through the ranks.[53]

Kitchener's plan to attack across open ground from the north (and not enfilade the enemy from the trees and scrub to the west) was bound to prove costly but it kept his units coordinated and facilitated the use of disciplined firepower. He deployed three brigades in a firing line that stretched over 1,500 yards. The EA brigades of Lieutenant-Colonels John G. Maxwell and Hector A. Macdonald were on the right and centre, that is, three Sudanese battalions in each firing line, with an Egyptian battalion in each reserve (and the 3rd EA brigade under Lieutenant-Colonel D. F. Lewis held in reserve). The British Brigade was on the left, with only the Cameron Highlanders in the firing line and the Lincolns, Seaforths, and Warwicks in columns behind. Unlike the Sudanese battalions which were deployed in lines to maximize their firepower, and advance in a series of rushes, the Camerons under Gatacre's orders were to walk towards the zariba, firing volleys, and then tear holes in the zariba to let the other units through.

At 6.15 a.m. on Good Friday, 8 April, Kitchener's artillery, supported by a rocket battery under the command of Lieutenant David Beatty, RN, opened their bombardment at about 600 yards; it lasted until 7.40 a.m. Thereafter the general advance began with bands, flags, and the pipes playing 'The march of the Cameron Men'. The Camerons walked forward, stopping periodically to fire volleys and only at 300 yards when the enemy opened fire, did they begin firing independently on the move.[54] While the Sudanese soldiers, firing as they moved, entered the encampment first, the British firing ceased temporarily on reaching the zariba. As gaps were torn, and officers moved to the front, the bulk of the British casualties occurred but all units pressed through, 'firing and bayoneting' the enemy in its stockade and trenches.[55] By 8.35 a.m. the most ferocious hand-to-hand battle of the campaign was over, as Mahdists fled across the river, leaving 3,000 dead, including forty emirs, and Mahmud captured by the Xth Sudanese (and possibly saved by the intervention of Captain George M. Franks).[56]

---

[53] 'Soldier's letter from the Soudan', (Dundee) *Evening Telegraph*, 13 May 1898, 4; 'The Battle of Atbara', *Nottinghamshire Guardian*, 21 May 1898, 5; 'The Battle of Atbara', *Sunderland Daily Echo*, 18 May 1898, 4.

[54] Capt. D. Cameron to Sir W. Cameron, 5 June 1898, Acc. No. 1983-05-55, Cameron Mss., NAM.

[55] 'A Notts. soldier on the battle of Atbara', *Nottinghamshire Guardian*, 18 June 1898, 5.

[56] Capt. G. M. Franks to T. J. Franks, 9 April 1898, Franks Mss., 403/2/6, SAD.

The victory had had a heavy cost (568 killed and wounded, with the majority of the casualties among the Sudanese and a disproportionate number of Cameron Highlanders).[57] It testified to the limitations of a frontal attack, even aided by modern firepower, against an entrenched enemy. Gatacre's attack formation was, as Hunter claimed, 'as bad as bad could be', resulting in a slow advance, limited fire effect, and a jumble of units once they reached the zariba.[58] Firepower prevailed, nonetheless; the artillery caused extensive damage and set much of the camp on fire, the Maxims deterred and scattered the Mahdist cavalry (with Osman Digna), and 'Gatacre's bullet' proved its worth (the British had prepared Dum Dum ammunition by filing the tips off their bullets). As Captain Henry Rawlinson noted, 'Few seemed to have moved after they had first fallen'.[59] Maximizing the effect of the firepower was the morale, discipline, and determination of the attacking soldiers, with Private H. Matthews (Lincolns) commending the Sudanese, who had 'advanced in grand style and there is no doubt about it they are good fighters'.[60]

Following the rout of Mahmud's army, the Anglo-Egyptian Army withdrew to its 'summer quarters', spending four months in various encampments until the Nile rose sufficiently to permit a flotilla of gunboats to cross the Sixth Cataract. Disease and boredom proved the principal threats, and despite sanitation instructions, the drinking of unfiltered water from the Atbara brought both diarrhoea and enteric fever. By early August, the cemetery outside the Highlanders' camp at Darmali had fifty graves, prompting Captain John Spencer Ewart (Cameron Highlanders) to record: 'Our stay at Darmali had cost us more lives than the battle of the Atbara: it is ever so in war; the climate is the soldier's most deadly foe'.[61] Meanwhile the Egyptians transformed the advance base into Fort Atbara, while the railway reached Atbara on 3 July, enabling two trains to deliver about 350–400 tons of supplies on a daily basis thereafter. It also brought three new twin-screw, heavily armed, and armour-plated gun-boats, *Melik*, *Sultan*, and *Sheikh* in prefabricated sections for assembly at Abadieh. As Winston Churchill aptly remarked, 'On the day that the first troop train steamed into the fortified

---

[57] 'Montrose soldiers at Atbara', *Evening Telegraph*, 14 May 1898, 5.
[58] Hunter to Sir W. Cameron, 25 April 1898, Acc. No. 1983-05-55, Cameron Mss., NAM.
[59] H. Rawlinson, Journal, 8 April 1898, Acc. No. 1952-01-33-4, NAM.
[60] 'A Horncastrian at the battle of the Atbara', *Horncastle News and South Lindsey Advertiser*, 28 May 1898, 5.
[61] Monro of Williamwood Mss., Capt. J. Spencer Ewart, Diary, 9 August 1898, Monro of Williamwood Mss., RH4/84, National Records of Scotland (NRS), Edinburgh.

camp at the confluence of the Nile and Atbara Rivers, the doom of the dervishes was sealed.'[62]

In addition to the Second British Brigade under the command of Brigadier-General the Hon. Neville Lyttelton (Brigadier-General Andrew Wauchope assumed command of the 1st Brigade and Gatacre, divisional command), Kitchener brought forward a fourth Egyptian Brigade, another two companies for the Camel Corps, a ninth squadron for the Egyptian Cavalry, the 32nd and 37th field batteries RA (with six 9-pounder guns and six 5-inch howitzers), four mule-drawn Maxim machine guns, a detachment of 16th company RGA (with two 40-pounder guns), and the 21st Lancers under Colonel R. H. Martin. In addition, 2,500 'friendlies' were raised under Major the Hon. E. J. Montagu Stuart-Wortley. Once the Nile was in full flood, limiting recourse to riverine transport, supplies and stores had to be pre-positioned and guarded as far as, and just south of, the Sixth Cataract (again without any interference from the Khalifa).

Units moved in sequence southwards, passing the abandoned town of Metemma, 'a most extraordinary sight', as Fitzgibbon-Cox remarked, the place being 'strewn with the skeletons of human beings and animals'.[63] On 23 August 1898, at Wad Hamed, Kitchener reviewed his army (all save the Lancers, Rifle Brigade and machine-gun detachments), and nearly 23,000 men stretched across two miles of bush-covered terrain. The army resumed its advance, camping again on the 28th, before completing another exhausting march to reach the village of el Egeiga on 1 September.

Anatomy of a Battle: Omdurman

As the army encamped, Stuart-Wortley's irregulars and six gun-boats cleared the forts and villages on the eastern bank, enabling Major F. B. Elmslie's 37th battery to begin shelling Omdurman, including the large white dome of the Mahdi's tomb with 50-pound lyddite shells. On the following morning, they moved further south, clearing the forts on the western bank and at Khartoum, and breached the walls of the citadel in three places to provide pathways for advancing troops. In effect the gunners had protected Kitchener's flank, silenced the enemy's guns, and struck at the heart of Mahdism.[64] The effects were visible to both

[62] Winston S. Churchill, *The River War* (London: Sceptic, 1987), 183.
[63] Fitzgibbon Cox, Diary, 17 August 1898, LR-770, MLL.
[64] Maj. F. B. Elmslie, 'Some experiences in Egypt', *Minutes of the Proceedings of the Royal Artillery Institution* XXVI (1899): 55–67.

armies: Yusuf Mikha'il, a Coptic clerk with the Khalifa's army, wrote that 'There was a natural and embarrassed silence in the ranks of the army'.[65]

By 'shaping' the battlefield, Kitchener was also trying to goad the Khalifa into an attack (and avoid costly street-fighting within Omdurman). Holding an excellent defensive position with a clear field of fire, Kitchener had defences constructed in an arc facing west (shelter trenches for the EA, a zariba for the British) over one mile and used searchlights from the gun-boats to sweep the ground beyond his perimeter throughout the night. Within the Khalifa's council only the wily Osman Digna, who had fought the British for fifteen years, argued for a night attack but the 25-year-old Shaykh al Din, the Khalifa's eldest son, insisted 'Let us not be like mice or foxes slinking into their holes by day and peeping out at night'.[66] Whether influenced by this rhetoric, or the difficulties of shooting at night and controlling his forces, the Khalifa preferred to annihilate the infidel in the morning.

Far from simply launching a fanatical assault, the Khalifa planned a two-pronged offensive. In the first wave regular forces under Osman Azraq and Ibrahim al Khalil, with artillery and rifle fire, would fall upon the front and left flank of the enemy. If this failed, Osman Azaq was supposed to withdraw and lure the Anglo-Egyptian forces out of their defences, and beyond the covering fire of the gun-boats, whereupon they would be ambushed from forces held in reserve behind rocky outcrops (the Black Standard, commanded by the Khalifa's brother, Ya'qub, to the south and the Green Standard and *mulazimin* under Shaykh al-Din from the Kereri Hills to the north). With Osman Digna guarding the route to Omdurman, this was a flexible plan relying upon surprise, shock action, and coordinated assaults from different directions but it overlooked the enemy's immense superiority in firepower, relied upon inexperienced commanders such as Shakyh al-Din, and lacked any means of rapid communications across several miles of terrain.

The result was an utter disaster. When the first wave of Mahdists, with their spears, banners, and drums, appeared on the crest line, stretching over two miles, it was a sight, as Captain J. K. Watson (EA) described, 'never to be forgotten'.[67] At 6.45 a.m. 32nd Field Battery opened fire at 2,500 yards, followed by long-range fire from the maxims (1,700 yards) and British infantry (1,500 yards) but the really murderous fire occurred at 800 yards. Despite their bravery, none of the Mahdists reached the Anglo-Egyptian line, including a magnificent charge by Baggara

---

[65] Zulfo, *Karari*, 148.   [66] Ibid., 151.
[67] Capt. J. K. Watson to his Father, 7 September 1898, Acc. No. 1983-04-112, Watson Mss., NAM.

horsemen. By 8.00 a.m. the first phase of the battle was over. Firepower had prevailed, not least the 'splendid volleys' of Wauchope's brigade: as Major F. Ivor Maxse (EA) observed, 'I cannot speak too highly of the excellent fire discipline of this Brigade'.[68]

The cavalry were less fortunate. On the right flank the nine squadrons of Egyptian cavalry, six companies of the Camel Corps, and Horse Artillery engaged the *mulazimin* in the Kereri Hills before retreating under the covering fire of the gun-boats. On the other flank, Colonel Martin led 320 troopers of the 21st Lancers to harass retreating Mahdists and head them off from Omdurman. Fired upon by a small band of riflemen from a *khor* (dried watercourse), the lancers charged without any reconnaissance only to find that Osman Digna had concealed another 2,000 spearmen in the khor. In a brief but ferocious encounter, for which the regiment earned three Victoria Crosses, the lancers charged through the mass of spearmen, rallied, reformed, and dispersed the enemy with carbine fire. Although the gallantry of the regiment earned many plaudits, and the charge became the iconic image of the battle, the costliness and futility of the event received widespread censure. In losing one officer and twenty men killed, forty-six men wounded, and 119 horses killed or wounded, the regiment was now out of action and unable to pursue the retreating enemy. 'The Colonel', wrote Captain Douglas Haig, 'sh[oul]d be strongly reprimanded for what he did: there was no object in his charging, while the casualties were enormous'.[69]

At 9.00 a.m., Kitchener launched his advance towards Omdurman, with his units deploying in echelon order, the two British brigades soon moving ahead on the left. Criticized at the time, the formation unravelled as the two central brigades struggled to keep up with the British, opening a gap of about a mile and exposing the vulnerable right flank of three battalions of long-service Sudanese soldiers, three batteries of artillery, and eight Maxims under Macdonald.[70] This flank duly encountered the Black Standard on its left but not in a surprise, coordinated assault, as Ya'qub waited twenty minutes for news of Shaykh al-Din. Drawn up in line formation with the eighteen guns and eight Maxims in front, the Sudanese annihilated Ya'qub's suicidal charge, then turned round ninety degrees in textbook fashion, when the Green Standard charged from the north. The Ninth Sudanese pivoted in an arrowhead – half facing north,

---

[68] Maj. F. I. Maxse to his Father, 13 September 1898, 219, Maxse Mss., West Sussex Record Office.
[69] Haig to Henrietta, 6 September 1898, Acc. 3155, No. 6, Haig Mss., NLS.
[70] Col. N. S. Sparkes to Mrs. Turnure, 13 September 1898, Acc. No. 1966-04-44, Sparkes Mss., NAM.

half south – and as Sudanese firepower destroyed the Green Standard,[71] the Lincolns came up to extend the line, firing 'a good many volleys'.[72] By 11.30 a.m., firing ceased, as Kitchener's army continued its advance on Omdurman, having crushed the Khalifa's army, killing some 10,800 and wounding another 16,000 while suffering only forty-eight fatalities and 382 wounded.

The Role of Technology and the Royal Navy

The railway, aptly described as 'the deadliest weapon that Britain ever used against Mahdism', was the foundation of victory.[73] Strategically, it changed the entire calculus of the campaign. By shortening the time of the journey from Wadi Halfa to Abu Hamed from eighteen days by camel and steamer to 24 hours (depending upon the serviceability of the engines), the railway enabled Kitchener to move his forces into the heart of the Sudan, independent of season or of the height of the Nile. Operationally, it transformed the way the campaign unfolded, providing Kitchener with an unprecedented degree of mobility in a remarkably economical campaign. The railway allowed the Sirdar to concentrate his forces at places and times of his choosing, and sustained the morale of his men in the advance upon Omdurman by delivering food, mail, ammunition, and medical supplies.[74] As Colonel Hunter admitted during the Dongola expedition:

> More than two-thirds of the work is calculating the quantity of supplies required and where to have them and by what time. In fact, war is not fighting and patrolling and bullets and knocks, it is one constant worry about transport and food and forage and ammunition and seeing that no-one is short of stuff and that collisions don't take place on a single line of railway.[75]

Equally impressive was the rapidly constructed communications network. During the Dongola campaign, the field telegraph covered 630 miles with nineteen telegraph offices along the main and auxiliary railway lines, and transmitted 277 messages per day.[76] Advanced units,

---

[71] Lamothe, *Slaves*, 169–71.
[72] Spiers, 'Campaigning under Kitchener', in Spiers (ed.), *Sudan*, 71.
[73] George W. Steevens, *With Kitchener to Khartum* (Edinburgh: Blackwood, 1898), 22.
[74] On the building and significance of the Sudan Military Railway, see Edward M. Spiers, *Engines for Empire: The Victorian Army and its Use of Railways* (Manchester: Manchester University Press, 2015), 96–114.
[75] Hunter to Capt. J. R. Beech, 23 July 1896, 964/2/28, Hunter Mss., SAD.
[76] Lieutenant M. G. E. Manifold, 'The field telegraph, Dongola expedition, 1896', *Royal Engineers Journal* 27 (1897): 3–5.

as in Berber, received telegraphic communications within a month as ground wire was laid over 236 miles, while poling parties followed often 150 miles or more behind the wire-laying party.[77]

Just as important was transport, supply, and communications along the Nile, where a flotilla of ten gun-boats, accompanied by other vessels, dominated the river. The Royal Navy provided seven of their commanders, three of whom – the Hon. Horace L. A. Hood, David R. Beatty, and Colin R. Keppel – would enjoy prestigious naval careers, despite in the cases of Beatty and Keppel narrowly surviving when their gun-boats, *El Teb* and *Zafir*, were wrecked or sank. In dominating the river, gun-boats provided reconnaissance, mobile firepower suppressing shore-based defences, mechanized transport by towing other vessels, artillery support at Omdurman, and exploitation of the triumph by moving past Khartoum and up the Blue and White Niles.

Aftermath

The aftermath of Omdurman included a brief controversy about the treatment of Mahdist dead and wounded, a long-term diplomatic triumph, and another battlefield victory. When the war correspondent, E. N. Bennett criticized Kitchener for neglect of the enemy wounded, he provoked staunch support for the Sirdar,[78] as water had been taken out to those left on the battlefield even if the expedition's medical staff could not treat so many wounded.[79] Kitchener compounded this controversy by destroying the Mahdi's tomb (lest it became a place of pilgrimage) and by speculating upon what he should do with the Mahdi's skull (after dispersing rest of the skeleton in the Nile).[80]

These controversies, though, barely dented a reputation already boosted by the widely-reported Gordon memorial service, held in the ruins of his palace in Khartoum (4 September), a proposal to build a Gordon Memorial College on the banks of the Nile, and then the triumph at Fashoda (19–21 September 1898). Unaware of Marchand's strength (only twelve officers and 120 *tirailleurs*), Kitchener took a company of Cameron Highlanders, two Sudanese battalions, a battery of

---

[77] Sandes, *Royal Engineers*, 243.
[78] Hugh Cecil, 'British correspondents and the Sudan campaign of 1896–98' in Spiers (ed.), *Sudan*, 119–23.
[79] Spiers, 'Campaigning under Kitchener' in Spiers (ed.), *Sudan*, 74.
[80] John Pollock, *Kitchener: The Road to Omdurman* (London: Constable, 1998), 149–51.

artillery and four Maxims on three gun-boats and two stern-wheelers towing barges. After a journey of 500 miles, Kitchener negotiated in French, and in claiming to represent Khedive Abbas Hilmi, had the Egyptian flag raised. The French subsequently abandoned their claim to the Upper Nile.[81] Kitchener had earned his peerage.

The Khalifa, nonetheless, remained the focus of a potential revolt, especially as an army of Ahmad Fadil tried to join his residual forces. As Ahmad Fadil survived various actions, and managed to join the Khalifa in Kordofan, Kitchener's brother, Walter, led a two-week expedition to find the Khalifa in January 1899 but this proved abortive. In the succeeding months, desertions nearly halved the Khalifa's forces, and on 24 November 1899, Wingate led a well-armed body of 3,600 men to defeat the Khalifa, killing him and his faithful emirs at Um Dibaykarat.[82]

Further Reading

Alford, H. S L. and Sword, W.D. *The Egyptian Sudan: Its Loss and Recovery*. London: Macmillan, 1898.
Bates, D. *The Fashoda Incident of 1898: Encounter on the Nile*. Oxford: Oxford University Press, 1984.
Churchill, W. S. *The River War*, 2 vols. London: Longmans, 1899.
Cromer, The Earl of. *Modern Egypt*, 2 vols. London: Macmillan, 1908.
Daly, M. *The Sirdar: Sir Reginald Wingate and the British Empire in the Middle East*. Philadelphia: American Philosophical Society, 1997.
Holt, P. M. *The Mahdist State in the Sudan 1881–1898*. Oxford: Clarendon Press, 1959.
Hunter, A. *Kitchener's Sword Arm: The Life and Campaigns of General Sir Archibald Hunter*. Staplehurst: Spellmount, 1996.
Keown-Boyd, H. *A Good Dusting: A Centenary Review of the Sudan Campaign 1883–1899*. London: Leo Cooper, 1988.
Lamothe, R. M. *Slaves of Fortune: Sudanese Soldiers and the River War 1896–1898*. Oxford: James Currey, 2011.
Pollock, J. *Kitchener: The Road to Omdurman*. London: Constable, 1998.
Sandes, Lieutenant-Colonel E.W.C. *The Royal Engineers in Egypt and the Sudan*. Chatham: The Institution of Royal Engineers, 1937.
Spiers, E. M. (ed.) *Sudan: The Reconquest Reappraised*. London: Frank Cass, 1998.
Spiers, E. M. 'Intelligence and command in Britain's small colonial wars of the 1890s'. *Intelligence and National Security* 22, 5 (2007): 661–81.

---

[81] Ibid., 144–48.
[82] 'The end of Mahdism: An interesting letter', *Yorkshire Herald and York Herald*, 13 December 1899, 6.

Spiers, *Engines for Empire: The Victorian Army and its Use of Railways*. Manchester: Manchester University Press, 2013.

Theobald, A. B. *The Mahdiya: A History of the Anglo-Egyptian Sudan, 1881–1899*. London: Longmans Green, 1951.

Ziegler, P. *Omdurman*. London: Collins, 1973.

Zulfo, I. H. trans. Clark, P. *Karari: The Sudanese Account of the Battle of Omdurman*. London: Frederick Warne, 1980.

14 The South African War, 1899–1902

Stephen M. Miller

Background

Although hostilities may have ended between Boers and Britons with the Pretoria Convention of 1881 (see Chapter 9), tensions did not dissipate. In the aftermath of the First Anglo-Boer War, relations between Great Britain and the two Boer Republics, the Transvaal (South African Republic) and the Orange Free State, continued to be hampered by British strategic and economic interests, on the one hand, and, by Boer desires to assert republican sovereignty, on the other. The Transvaal witnessed a gold rush in the 1880s. Its population grew rapidly as investors and migrant workers, both from Southern Africa and from around the world, made their way to the republic which only a few years earlier had been teetering on the edge of economic bankruptcy. In Great Britain, the economic growth of the Transvaal was perceived as a threat to the viability of its South African colonies, Natal, and Cape Colony, potentially reducing them to a status of dependency. Further complicating matters, Kaiser Wilhelm II's policy of *Weltpolitik* led to an increased commitment to the German penetration of neighbouring South West Africa (Namibia). British administrators envisioned a not-too-distant future when the gold trade could be redirected through German territory and, in the event of a second war, the Boers could turn to the Germans for assistance. The War Office carefully considered this possibility in its war planning.

In December 1895, the diamond and gold magnate and Prime Minister of the Cape Colony, Cecil Rhodes, attempted to both assist and shape British colonial policy as well as to promote his own ambitions by destabilizing the Transvaal through an armed insurrection of the Uitlanders, the mostly white, English-speaking, migrant population of Johannesburg. The result was the failed Jameson Raid. Although no hard evidence at the time was revealed, it seemed to the Boers, Germans, and British Liberals, that Joseph Chamberlain, the British Colonial Secretary, was involved in the scheme. Had Lord Salisbury's Conservative government wanted a war in the aftermath of the Jameson Raid, however, the timing could not have been worse. By the summer of 1896, the Sirdar of Egypt, then Colonel Sir Horatio Herbert Kitchener, was readying a force for the invasion of the Sudan (see Chapter 13) and the largest uprising on the North-West Frontier of India was about to erupt around Tirah in 1897 (see Chapter 12). As Ronald Robinson and John Gallagher have argued in their seminal work, *Africa and the Victorians*, it was not until 1899 that the British government could focus its attention on squarely on South Africa.[1]

Sir Alfred Milner was appointed the British High Commissioner in South Africa and Governor of the Cape Colony in 1897. Like Rhodes, he feared the implications of a strong independent Transvaal, and also like Rhodes, he saw the need to remove Paul Kruger as its President. Unlike Rhodes, however, Milner pursued victory through democratic election. By 1899, the Uitlander population had grown larger than the Burgher population in the Transvaal. With Chamberlain's support, Milner championed the cause of the Uitlanders, demanding the extension of suffrage in the Transvaal by easing eligibility, specifically targeting the residency requirement. If the Uitlanders could vote, he believed, those who were willing to work with the British could be installed in positions of power, Kruger would be removed, and the Transvaal could be transitioned into a British-dominated federation of South African colonies, something Benjamin Disraeli's Conservative government had attempted in the 1870s. At the Bloemfontein Conference, 31 May–5 June 1899, Milner pushed Kruger on the franchise issue, believing a 'big concession of the franchise question would be such a score that we could afford to let other concessions drop quietly into the background or settle them by compromise.'[2] Milner's attempt failed, albeit his policy won a lot of support at home, particularly among those who became recently enfranchised by the Third Reform Act of 1884 and were sympathetic to the plight of the Uitlanders. Kruger knew, however, what he would be giving up by reducing the residency requirement and the Bloemfontein Conference closed without any agreement. Limited Boer concessions in August were rejected by Milner when they included challenges to Britain's suzerainty over the region. The concessions were hollow; Kruger knew Milner could not accept any assertion of Boer autonomy.[3]

---

[1] Ronald Robinson and John Gallagher with Alice Denny, *Africa and the Victorians*, 2nd ed. (London: Macmillan, 1981), 410–61.

[2] Secret Papers Related to Affairs in South Africa, Colonial Office (CO) 879/56/572, A. Milner to J. Chamberlain, 4 June 1899, telegram no. 97, The National Archives (TNA), Kew.

[3] Bill Nasson, *The South African War 1899–1902* (London: Arnold, 1999), 34.

Although war was not inevitable, the Boers began to prepare for it nevertheless. The Orange Free State, which had clung to its neutrality throughout the First Anglo-Boer War, had no intentions of standing on the sidelines yet again. M. T. Steyn, the President of the Orange Free State, had tried to prevent war at the Bloemfontein Conference but now worked with his neighbour towards coordinating a united resistance to any British military threat. An offensive strategy, promoted by Jan Smuts, the Transvaal's state attorney, was generally accepted by commando leaders. It called for a rapid invasion of the Cape Colony, to promote rebellion among the Boer population, and of Natal, in order to seize Durban and the colony's main ports in order to hinder British operations and reinforcement.[4] Businesses which had produced tools for the goldmines were transformed into armaments producers to supplement the weapons which had been imported since the Jameson Raid. Food, clothing, and other essential supplies were organized through a Commissariat. Smuts, anticipating a protracted war, also encouraged planning to keep the mines and farms producing.[5]

Although Great Britain had more or less sorted out its immediate imperial military demands in North Africa and in India, it remained reluctant to jump into another conflict. Ironically, Chamberlain cautioned Milner and urged him to continue to work for a settlement. Lord Lansdowne, the Secretary of State for War, made some concessions to Lord Wolseley, the Commander-in-Chief of the British Army, who since the summer had been urging for, among other things, the mobilization of an army corps, but Lansdowne feared any decisive action might provoke the Boers. Wolseley was not immediately worried about that possibility. He knew, rightly so, that the Boers would have been extremely reluctant to begin a war in South Africa's winter months when its commandos made up of mounted burghers would be challenged by limited grazing opportunities. But as June and July rolled into August and September, Lansdowne still refused to raise an adequate number of men needed for the impending war, nor did he obtain the necessary supplies to support a force overseas or take measures to improve military intelligence.[6]

As early as April 1899, Salisbury's cabinet had met with some senior military officers to discuss strategy in the event of a war in South Africa.

---

[4] Peter Warwick, 'Introduction to Part II, in P. Warwick (ed.), *The South African War: The Anglo-Boer War 1899–1902* (Harlow: Longman, 1980), 59.
[5] Denis Judd and Keith Surridge, *The Boer War* (New York: Palgrave, 2002), 93.
[6] Report of His Majesty's Commissioners Appointed to Inquire into the Military Preparations and Other Matters Connected with the War in South Africa, cd 1790, 1904: XI, 8793.

One of the participants at that meeting was the fifty-nine-year-old veteran of many of Britain's small wars, longtime member of the Ashanti Ring, and former Adjutant-General, Sir Revers Buller. Buller was not aging well. He had gained a lot of weight, he was drinking more and more, and he had come to doubt his own leadership abilities. After his failures at the 1898 Aldershot general maneuvers, he was overheard second-guessing himself and muttering, 'I have been making a fool of myself all day'.[7] Nevertheless, Buller emerged as Lansdowne and Wolseley's compromise candidate to lead British forces in South Africa. Even after the Bloemfontein Conference failed to resolve the Anglo-Boer differences and war seemed more likely, neither Lansdowne nor Wolseley would provide Buller with the support he needed. But Buller is also to blame for the shortcomings in British war preparations. He did not assert himself and failed to demand the necessary action needed, preferring to merely complain to his brother in their correspondence. Buller's strategic plan was not endorsed by the Cabinet until 29 September.[8] War erupted only a week later, and the British were simply not ready.

* * * * *

British publishers were quick to produce books about the South African War even before the conflict came to its end. By 1910, readers had access to hundreds of volumes which told the story of the entire war or part of it, of a regiment, or of a general. Soldiers of all ranks, regular and volunteer, published their memoirs, journals, and letters from the front. The historical accuracy of these works varied dramatically. Sir Arthur Conan Doyle's pro-imperial *The Great Boer War* was perhaps the most popular history of the war and it was revised sixteen times between 1900 and 1902. The most useful of these early works were Leo Amery's edited seven-volume, *The Times History of the War in South Africa 1899–1902*; Frederick Maurice and M. H. Grant's four-volume, *(Official) History of the War in South Africa, 1899–1902*; and, the two-volume, *The War in South Africa, A German Official Account*, translated by W. H. Waters. As Ian F. W. Beckett has shown, these works are still essential resources for modern day researchers but they are each flawed in their own way.[9] The only Afrikaans work

---

[7] Wm. St. John Fremontle Brodrick Midleton, *Records & Reactions 1856–1939* (New York: E.P. Dutton, 1939), 132–33, as cited in Geoffrey Powell, *Buller: A Scapegoat? A Life of General Sir Redvers Buller 1839–1908* (London: Leo Cooper, 1994), 114.

[8] Report of His Majesty's Commissioners Appointed to Inquire into the Military Preparations and Other Matters Connected with the War in South Africa, cd 1790, 1904: XI, 14953.

[9] Ian F. W. Beckett, 'Early historians and the South African War', *Sandhurst Journal of Military Studies* 1 (1990): 15–32.

comparable to the above three was J. H. Breytenbach's six-volume *Die Geskiedenis van die Tweede Vryheidsoorlog in Suid-Afrika, 1899–1902* written over a thirty-year period in the mid-century and still unfinished at the time of his death.

In the late 1970s and the early 1980s, both the quality and the scope of the scholarship increased. The methods of social historians began, at last, to penetrate military history. Ten years later, the impact of cultural history began to leave its mark as well. In Peter Warwick's edited collection, *The South African War: The Anglo-Boer War*, a group of historians discussed aspects of the war ranging from black participation to Boer collaborators, and from the role of women in the war to British societal attitudes during the conflict. The 'Second Anglo-Boer War' was finally becoming the 'South African War'. One of the contributors to the volume, S. B. Spies, published his seminal work in 1977, *Methods of Barbarism? Roberts and Kitchener and Civilians in the Boer Republics, January 1900–May 1902*, which examined the Great Britain's scorched earth policy, and its use of concentration camps and their impact on the Transvaal and the Orange Free State. Finally, it is worth mentioning, Thomas Pakenham's exhaustively researched yet extremely readable, *The Boer War*, published in 1979. Although a traditional military account of *The Boer War*, Pakenham raised the bar for popular historians.[10]

Although some very important works came out earlier, like Bill Nasson's 1991, *Abraham Esau's War: A Black South African War in the Cape, 1899–1902*, it was the approach of the centennial which renewed academic historians' interest in the war. Works like Fransjohan Pretorius's 1999, *Life on Commando During the Anglo-Boer War, 1899–1902*, really changed the landscape of the war's historiography. Military biographies and books examining Imperial forces, the role of the Volunteers, and the British command structure were joined by works on concentration camps, commemoration, race and gender, and a plethora of local histories.[11]

Outbreak of War

Although the British government had been expecting war since April 1899, as noted above, it had taken few actions to prepare for it. It failed to make the necessary arrangements in Great Britain and take precautionary measures in its South African colonies. It also failed to heed its 'men on

---

[10] Unlike most of the earlier literature, Pakenham attempted to vindicate Buller.
[11] Please see the 'Further Reading' section at the end of this chapter for a selection of these works and others.

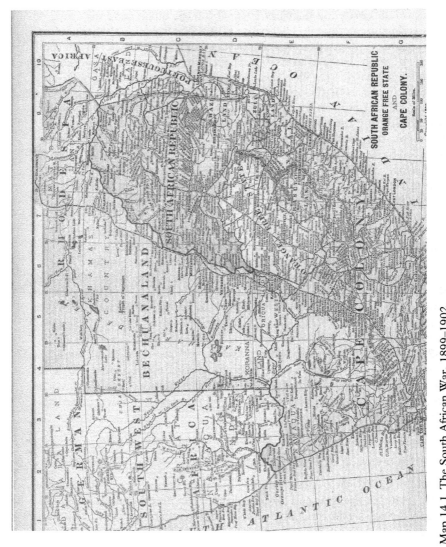

Map 14.1 The South African War, 1899–1902.
W. Harding, *War in South Africa* (Chicago: Dominion Company, 1899)

the spot', Lieutenant-General Sir William H. Goodenough, the General Officer in Command in South Africa, and his successor, Major-General Sir William Butler, who warned about the difficulties of holding advanced positions, especially in the Northern Natal.[12] Nevertheless, it proceeded to incite the Boers in early September by delivering to Kruger a series of demands which included revising the franchise and recognizing British suzerainty. It went short, however, of threatening an immediate armed response if Kruger's government failed to accept the terms, but it made the Cabinet's position clear. This was the so-called penultimatum. At the same time, the British government announced that it would be readying a military expedition and dispatching 10,000 troops to defend its South African colonies.[13] The Boers rejected the penultimatum on 17 September.

Although Steyn still held out for the chance of peace, Kruger had come to accept the inevitability of war. He also endorsed Smuts's plan to strike quickly and decisively, bringing the war to the British colonies. This strategy would be hampered or perhaps even thwarted by the arrival of 10,000 British reinforcements. Therefore, abrupt action was necessary. Commandos in the Transvaal were mobilized on 28 September and, a few days later, the Orange Free State followed suit.

The rejection of the penultimatum finally convinced Salisbury that war was his only path to protecting British political and economic interests in the region. As Boer burghers were mobilizing, the British Cabinet met to hammer out the language of an ultimatum and issue orders to the War Office to finally mobilize the troops for which Buller had asked. Kruger and Steyn, however, did not wait for the British ultimatum to be delivered. Instead, on 9 October, they delivered an ultimatum of their own, reasserting republican sovereignty and demanding that all British troops in transit turn back and all troops who had come to South Africa after 1 June leave at once. In the future, they stipulated, all differences between the two parties must be resolved by arbitration. They gave Salisbury's government 48 hours to accept their terms or face war.[14] The British responded that the terms could not be accepted, nor could they even be discussed, and, on 11 October, Boer commandos crossed into Natal. The South African War had begun.

---

[12] Butler was forced to step down in August 1899 for his perceived pro-Boer sentiment. William F. Butler, *An Autobiography* (London: Constable and Co., 1911), 417–20.
[13] Iain R. Smith, *The Origins of the South African War 1899–1902* (London: Longman, 1996), 368–70.
[14] Further Correspondences of the Affairs in the South African Republic, Ultimatum of 9 October, CO 879/59/600, TNA.

British and Boer Forces

The Commando system had evolved throughout the nineteenth century in both the Orange Free State and the Transvaal. Effectively, all white males between the ages of sixteen and sixty were expected to participate in military service when called upon. Although increasing urbanization worried some at the top, particularly in the Orange Free State, that some of the burghers did not possess the qualities and skills of earlier generations, most of the men mobilized in late September and early October 1899 owned their own firearms and knew how to use them. Similarly, the majority were experienced horsemen. Increasing centralization of command meant more decisions were being made at the top and more systematic planning was being conducted in the years leading up to the war. Commissariats in both Republics were responsible for supplying most food, clothing, ammunition, and other supplies. As the war went on, government stocks dried up and local *landdrosts* (magistrates) likewise could not provide commandos with many of the basics.

When war was declared, the two Boer Republics mobilized between 32,000 and 35,000 burghers; by the end of the year, that number had risen to 45,000.[15] A few thousand Europeans also volunteered to fight for the Boer cause and made their way from Germany, Holland, and elsewhere, although most proved ineffectual combatants.[16] Black South Africans played a far greater role in the war in terms of numbers and contribution to the Boer war effort. Although most were not armed and served as laborers, servants, and scouts, at times *agterryers* (after-riders) did fight alongside burghers. Perhaps as many as 10,000–15,000 volunteered or were coerced or forced to join the commandos at the start of the war.[17] Although women played several significant roles in the war, including providing food and clothing for the war effort, generally speaking they were not permitted on commando. Only a few cases of armed women fighting side by side with burghers have been revealed.[18]

British forces in South Africa were greatly outnumbered by the Boers at the start of the conflict. They numbered only 10,000 in January

---

[15] Fransjohan Pretorius, *Life on Commando During the Anglo-Boer War 1899–1902* (Cape Town: Human & Rousseau, 1999), 25.

[16] Emanoel Lee, *To the Bitter End: A Photographic History of the Boer War 1899–1902* (New York: Penguin, 1985), 50–56.

[17] Bill Nasson, *Abraham Esau's War: A Black South African War in the Cape, 1899–1902* (Cambridge: Cambridge University Press, 1991), 96, as cited in Fransjohan Pretorius, *The Anglo-Boer War 1899–1902* (Cape Town: Struik, 1998), 79.

[18] See, for example Sarah Raal, *Met die Boere in die veld: die ervarings van die skryfster* (Kaapstad: Nasionale Pers, 1937).

1899 and then grew slightly in August. In September, an additional 10,000 men were ordered to Cape Town, Port Elizabeth, and Durban to shore up defences. It was the delivery of those reinforcements which precipitated the Boer ultimatum and ultimately determined the timing of the war's onset. In the last week of September, the government seemed to finally accept the inevitability of the war and an army corps, 40,000 men, was mobilized on Salisbury Plain.

Despite the initial danger that British colonists faced in the short run, in the long run, the Boers could not hope to match the British manpower and materiel war effort. Great Britain had an enormous advantage over the republics in its ability to recruit, mobilize, and supply a large expeditionary force. It possessed the population, transportation and communication systems, and industrial base to overwhelm the opposition if the government deemed it appropriate and was willing to spend the money and the political capital. By January 1900, over 100,000 British soldiers were in South Africa. By war's end, nearly 450,000 troops had been raised to defeat the Boers.

In the aftermath of Black Week in December 1899 (see the 'Course of the War' section), the British government authorized, under varying terms, Militia, Imperial Yeomanry, and Volunteers (including the City of London Imperial Volunteers), to serve overseas. In addition, small numbers of men made their way to Natal and Cape Colony and joined locally raised units. Over 100,000 of these volunteers supplemented regular forces.[19] The training of these men differed by organizational force and by the year in which they were recruited. The first contingent of Imperial Yeomanry, for example, was organized and trained in Great Britain at the start of 1900; whereas, the second contingent was rushed to South Africa about a year later, with the expectation that the men would receive their training after they arrived in Cape Town. These units suffered from a lack of *esprit de corps* and many men who would have been rejected for service during training exercises at home were allowed to serve because it was too costly to send them back.[20] Although some units were easily integrated into existing battalions and benefited from serving alongside seasoned veterans, like Volunteer Service Corps recruits, others remained separate from Regular Army units and had more challenging experiences acclimating to the war.

---

[19] Frederick Maurice and M. H. Grant, *(Official) History of the War in South Africa, 1899–1902*, vol. 4 (London: Hurst and Blackwood, 1906–1910), appendix 13.
[20] Stephen M. Miller, *Volunteers on the Veld: Britain's Citizen-Soldiers and the South African War, 1899–1902* (Norman: University of Oklahoma Press, 2007), 152–53.

Great Britain also turned to its empire after Black Week. In addition to foodstuffs, horses, and other supplies, the War Office accepted the offer of approximately 30,000 imperial troops raised in Australia, Canada, New Zealand, and its South African colonies. The War Office was not happy with its own volunteer recruits. Too many, it believed, were urban, lacking in physique, and had little or no experience with guns and horses. To counter the Boer, these organizers dreamed of recruiting rugged Australians from the bush and Canadians from the western prairies. They did manage to get some of these, but especially in Canada, recruiters had more success in large urban areas and most of the recruits were drawn from the lower-middle and skilled working classes.[21] Like the British volunteers in general, these troops varied in quality and were often hampered by poor discipline.

The Indian Army played a vital role in the expansion and maintenance of the British empire in the nineteenth century. British officials, however, reached a decision early on that they would not employ Indian troops in South Africa.[22] Officially, they would not use African troops in the war either. Nevertheless, black Africans performed vital ancillary duties. They drove wagons, cared for horses, built fortifications, and loaded and unloaded supplies.[23] In the latter stages of the war, they confiscated Boer livestock and participated in farm burning. And, at times, they were armed and provided security, particularly in the more remote sectors of the countryside.

Strategy and War Aims

The standard interpretation of the war's causes argues that Great Britain was the aggressor. It claimed suzerainty over the Republics and therefore direction of their external affairs which the terms of the London Convention of 1884 did not justify. Just a few months before the war began, for example, the Transvaal and the Orange Free State were not invited to The Hague Conference for fear of offending Great Britain and no state was willing to insist that they be allowed to participate. Great Britain also wanted to safeguard the economic interests of its South

---

[21] Carman Miller, *Painting the Map Red: Canada and the South African War 1899–1902* (Montreal, Kingston: McGill-Queen's University Press, 1993), 59.

[22] David Omissi, 'India: Some perspectives of race and empire', in David Omissi and Andrew S. Thompson (eds.), *The Impact of the South African War* (New York: Palgrave, 2002), 216–17.

[23] Peter Warwick, *Black Participation and the South African War 1899–1902* (Johannesburg: Ravan, 1983), 21–25.

African colonies by preventing the Republics from gaining railway access to Portuguese East Africa (Mozambique) and German South West Africa and thus preserve traditional trading routes through Cape Town, Port Elizabeth, and Durban. Many alleged, at the time, and some continue to argue that British officials and the City of London wanted to further their own personal interests and those of friendly capitalists who felt restricted by Kruger's policies.[24] Regardless of the motives, most historians continue to see Salisbury's Conservative government's pursuit of a brazen imperial policy as the main cause of the war.

At the time, in Great Britain, those who showed sympathy towards the Boers and agreed with the above statement were labelled pro-Boers by their detractors. No doubt, pro-Boers were in the minority in the country. Yet, even as late as September 1899, most Britons had no reason to support an aggressive war in South Africa. The Boer ultimatum, however, gave the government the propaganda tool it needed. It could now argue that it did not want the war but it would not shy away from it and most newspapers and periodicals were quick to support the claims. The Boer invasion of Natal and Cape Colony, which immediately followed the outbreak of hostilities on 11 October, offered further 'proof' that the Boers were the aggressors.[25]

An offensive was deemed necessary by Boer war planners. British defences along the borders had to be removed, it was essential that transportation networks which would allow British reinforcements to flow into the interior be interrupted, and, if possible, Boers in the British colonies needed to be incited to rise up and join the invading forces. In the Cape Colony, General Piet Cronjé's commandos cut off the remote town of Mafeking on 13 October and, three weeks later, Kimberley, the centre of the diamond industry, was besieged as well. The major Boer thrust into Natal was led by Commandant-General Piet Joubert. By the end of October, the Boer offensive had pushed British forces out of Northern Natal. Colonists, fearing the invaders and also the possibility of Zulu action, made their way to the coast in droves. The Boers laid siege to Ladysmith on 2 November, cutting off the main British garrison in the colony and leaving Pietermaritzburg as well as the Natal port cities vulnerable to attack.

British war planning was hampered from the beginning by administrative inaction, local political intervention, and lack of drive and

---

[24] P. J. Cain and A. G. Hopkins, *British Imperialism: Innovation and Expansion 1688–1914* (London: Longman, 1993), 379–80.
[25] See, for example *Daily Telegraph* (London), 11 October 1899, 8; and, *Times* (London), 11 October 1899, 7.

inventiveness on the part of Buller. Whereas Boer strategy called for an offensive, British planning before the war, cognizant of manpower limitations, called for a defensive posture. Butler warned that attempting to hold advanced positions in the Cape Colony and Natal would be disastrous and that strategy was best served by pulling back from the frontier, destroying important bridges, guarding mountain passes, and utilizing local sources to obtain information on the enemy's movements. In Natal, this included giving up Ladysmith and retiring across the Tugela River. These measures were necessary to give Great Britain time to mobilize its forces for a future offensive.

Buller had other plans. His experiences with Wolseley in the Gold Coast (Ghana) in 1874 (see Chapter 6) and in Egypt in 1882 (see Chapter 10) led him to believe that the best strategy was to seek a decisive victory by gathering his forces together, marching through the Orange Free State, and then striking at Pretoria, the capital of the Transvaal. The Boer offensive, resulting in the Mafeking, Kimberley, and Ladysmith sieges, however, forced him to cast aside his plan. Salisbury's government was not willing to risk the political fallout if those towns fell to the Boers. In addition, local forces were also interfering with Buller's strategy. Lieutenant-General Sir George White, former Commander-in-Chief of the Indian Army, was sent to Natal in September. White was inclined to heed Butler's advice and to pull his forces out of northern Natal. After meeting with the Governor of Natal, Sir Walter Hely-Hutchinson, and General Officer Commanding of Natal, Major-General Sir William Penn Symons, however, White agreed to hold the advanced positions. Hely-Hutchinson convinced him that pulling back would endanger settlers and could lead to a Zulu insurrection and Penn Symons, who White had served with in India and trusted, insisted that the number of British forces was sufficient to hold Dundee and points north of Ladysmith.[26] White, later, would also make the political calculation, one supported in London, that abandoning Ladysmith could not be done regardless of the military benefits. Perhaps, Buller could have intervened and demanded a retreat but in the end, he allowed his officers in the field and the politicians at home and in South Africa to make the decisions for him. There would be no massed thrust into the Orange Free State. Instead, Buller would be reactive. His army corps, which finally began arriving in early November, would be divided and sent to prepare

---

[26] Mortimer Durand, *The Life of Field-Marshal Sir George White* (Edinburgh, London: William Blackwood and Sons, 1915), 33. Also see Stephen M. Miller, *George White and the Victorian Army in India and Africa: Serving the Empire* (London: Palgrave-Macmillan, 2020).

for responses in Natal and the Cape Colony. Buller, himself, would not go to Cape Town to direct the war, nor to Orange River Station to command the relief of Kimberley and then strike at Bloemfontein, but would head to Natal to personally take over the relief of Ladysmith. For both actions, Buller would be roundly criticized. Later, he justified these decisions in his official report to the War Office: 'I therefore decided upon every ground that the deliverance of South Natal must be my first object ... I should have preferred to have devoted every possible man of my forces to Natal ... But at the same time I felt it impossible to ignore Kimberley. That town represented to the Native the symbol of British power and property in South Africa; and I feared the effect of its fall'.[27]

The Course of the War

Generally speaking, the South African War can be examined in three phases. During the first phase, as mentioned earlier, the Boers enjoyed a distinct advantage in manpower and benefitted strategically from their rapid advance into Natal and the investment of Mafeking and Kimberley in the Cape Colony. Although by late 1899, Buller and his generals had sizable forces at their disposal, British offensives in Natal and in both the western and eastern Cape Colony failed. The second phase, in which set-piece battles were still the norm, began early in 1900. Field Marshal Lord Roberts replaced Buller as Commander-in-Chief, more reinforcements arrived giving the British a great advantage in manpower, and a major offensive was launched into the Orange Free State from the western Cape. After the Boers suffered a critical defeat at Paardeberg, British forces pressed on to Bloemfontein. The Orange Free State's capital fell in mid-March 1900, and after a brief delay, Roberts's forces continued their advance into the Transvaal. Johannesburg was captured on the last day of May and both colonies were annexed by the British government. In Natal, Ladysmith was relieved at the end of February, and in May, Buller, began his advance northwards, joining Roberts in the Transvaal the following month. Finally, the third phase, which began roughly in June 1900 and overlapped the second phase, is marked by Boer guerrilla activity and a British counter-insurgency. The British attempted to thwart Boer tactics, which included hit-and-run strikes against weak outposts and communication and transportation networks, by containing Boer commandos through their use of concerted drives in conjunction

---

[27] War Office (WO) 132/24 p. 17, TNA.

with a constricting network of blockhouses, a scorched earth policy, and the construction of a concentration camp system. This third phase ended with the Treaty of Vereeniging, signed on 31 May 1902.

The Boer invasion of Natal was expected. White had been persuaded that keeping a small force in the north, at Dundee, under Penn Symons was merited for reasons mentioned earlier. Penn Symons was confident that he could defeat the Boers despite the disparity in numbers.[28] He gravely underestimated them. After an advanced party took Elandslaagte on 19 October, the Transvaal General, Lukas Meyer, positioned his commando on the high ground above Dundee and proceeded to bombard the garrison on 20 October. Penn Symons, who had done little to interrupt Meyer's movements, ordered an assault on the heights and the Battle of Talana Hill, the first battle of the South African War, commenced. Boer commandos failed to cooperate and British forces were able to seize the hill, but not without suffering significant casualties including Penn Symons, who was mortally wounded. Penn Symons's second in command, Major-General James Yule, did not have his mounted troops pursue the retreating Boers. Although Major-General John French followed up this event with a victory at Elandslaagte the next day, White was concerned about the safety of his outstretched forces and ordered French and Yule to retire to Ladysmith. When his forces were defeated with significant casualties at Nicholson's Nek and Modder Spruit on 30 October, White became convinced that there was little else he could do but pull back to Ladysmith and await reinforcements. Ladysmith had to be held at all costs, he believed. Its loss would threaten the town's civilian population, the Boers would gain valuable military supplies and resources, and the impact of Ladysmith's fall would have chilling moral consequences on Great Britain and its colonies.[29] On 2 November, the Boers laid siege to the town, filled with over 20,000 British troops, townspeople, refugees, and wounded. White's attempts to disrupt Boer operations, such as Major-General Sir Archibald Hunter's successful attack on Gun Hill 8 December, were few but his defences managed to keep the Boers at bay. Limited Boer attempts to assault Ladysmith, such as the attacks on Caesar's Camp and Wagon Hill on 6 January, were unsuccessful.

While the bulk of his men remained near Ladysmith, Commandant-General Piet Joubert advanced with a small force. He conducted

---

[28] Kenneth Griffith, *Thank God We Kept the Flag Flying* (New York: Viking Press, 1974), 31.
[29] Alfred T. Mahan, *The Story of the War in South Africa*, 3rd ed. (London: Sampson Low, Marston and Company, 1901), 179–81.

operations as far south as Estcourt before returning to the northern bank of the Tugela River and preparing its defences to halt a British crossing. He had opted for a cautious strategy.[30] He could have pressed on towards the lightly-defended Pietermaritzburg, just 100 miles away from Ladysmith, as war planners in September had advocated. Instead, he believed the moral and materiel advantages in taking Ladysmith were too significant to pass up. The siege lasted until 28 February. Joubert's strategy failed.

Those trapped in Ladysmith eagerly awaited Buller's advance. 'Buller, they tell us one day, is at Bloemfontein; next day he is coming round to Durban; the next he is a prisoner in Pretoria', wrote G. W. Steevens, the prominent journalist, who did not survive the siege.[31] Although officials back in London knew where Buller was, they also wondered what he was doing. Buller had amassed a force in Frere in mid-November, safely behind the Tugela River, and was considering possible approaches to Ladysmith, none of which was without its risks. He had last settled on crossing the Tugela at Potgeiter's Drift and then driving across the relatively open country across the enemy's flank. His plans were interrupted however, when the news arrived of a British defeat in the Cape Colony on 10 December at Stormberg. The next day, British forces suffered a second decisive defeat in the Cape Colony at Magersfontein (see 'Anatomy of the Battle: Magersfontein' section). Buller later wrote, 'With an enemy disheartened by failure I thought myself justified, in the peculiar circumstance, in risking a flank march of fifty miles with an enormous wagon-train, even though it might involve the uncovering of my communications. With an enemy elated by success this was no longer justified. I therefore determined to try to force the direct road to Ladysmith'.[32] Buller's decision to attack the Boers at Colenso on 15 December proved disastrous. Plagued by lack of intelligence and poor maps, Buller was unaware of the Boer defences and the significance of Hlangwane Hill. The 5th Brigade failed to locate its point of crossing, Bridle Drift, and got caught in a salient loop of the river. Defying Buller's orders, Colonel Charles Long pushed his artillery too far forward and into the enemy zone of fire, where the gunners were struck down. Attempts to rescue the guns led to the tragic death of Roberts's only son, Freddie, and six others. Despite having significant reserves who had yet to enter the battle, Buller called off the attack and ordered a retreat.

---

[30] Pretorius, *Anglo-Boer War 1899–1902*, 15.
[31] G. W. Steevens, *From Capetown to Ladysmith: An Unfinished Record of the South African War* (Edinburgh, London: Wm. Blackwood and Sons, 1900), 125.
[32] WO 132/24 p. 29, TNA.

The British suffered over 1,100 casualties while Boers losses were only thirty-eight.[33] General Louis Botha's victory at Colenso was complete. Buller would not try to force Boer positions on the Tugela again until late January.

The first of the three defeats in early December which the British press labelled as "Black Week" resulted from Major-General Sir William Gatacre's attempt to quiet the activity of Boers in the Cape Colony and drive the Orange Free State commando under General Jan Olivier back across the border. The Battle of Stormberg did not go as intended. Hoping to catch the Boers off guard, Gatacre conducted a night march, got lost, and advanced directly into the Boer line of fire. Although his forces did their best, they were tired and disorganized and Gatacre eventually ordered them to retire. Amazingly, however, only later did he realize that over 600 of his men had been left behind, unaware of his orders.[34]

When Buller elected to divide his forces and personally conduct the relief of Ladysmith, Lieutenant-General Lord Methuen, in command of the 1st Division at Orange River Station in the western Cape Colony, was given the task of relieving Kimberley. With limited transport and a lack of mounted troops, and with orders to secure the safety of the civilians once the siege of Kimberley lifted, Methuen believed his only viable route was to advance cautiously along the course of the Western Railway. General J. H. de la Rey anticipated his actions and convinced General Piet Cronjé, Assistant Commandant-General conducting operations along the western front, to interrupt the advance. First, at Belmont and then again at Graspan/Enslin and Modder River in late November, Methuen drove the Boer forces back but his successes were tempered by greater casualties and an inability to pursue the retiring enemy. Methuen struck at Magersfontein on 11 December (see the 'Anatomoy of the Battle: Magersfontein' section) but was unable to dislodge the defenders from their trenches. Operations in the western Cape came to a screeching halt. Leo Amery who would edit the *Times History of the War in South Africa* wrote, 'We let the existence of the railroad completely paralyze our movements ... It is so simple and obvious to stick to it – to improvise other transport requires thinking out afresh as it was not in the original programme and so it isn't done'.[35]

---

[33] Fransjohan Pretorius, *Historical Dictionary of the Anglo-Boer War* (Lanham: The Scarecrow Press, 2009), 92.
[34] Thomas Pakenham, *The Boer War* (New York: Random House, 1979), 223.
[35] L. Amery to V. Chirol, in John Barnes and David Nicholson (eds.), *The Leo Amery Diaries* (London: Hutchinson, 1980), entry dated 19 December 1899.

Black Week shook the British government from its complacency and dispelled any overconfidence which might have remained among its officers. Lansdowne's friend and India colleague, Roberts, was ordered to South Africa to take over the conduct of the war. The younger Lord Kitchener, the recent hero of Omdurman (see Chapter 13), would serve as his Chief of Staff and would later succeed him as Commander-in-Chief. In addition, the Sixth Division was sent out by year's end and the Seventh Division was mobilized. In order to counter the superior mobility of the Boers, the War Office asked for mounted troops. The government responded by raising a force of Imperial Yeomanry and accepting offers from its settler colonies for additional manpower. These and other reinforcements gave the British a huge numerical superiority over the Boers and allowed Roberts to conduct operations to relieve Ladysmith, Kimberley, and Mafeking, and simultaneously drive into the Orange Free State.

The second phase of the South African War began in the new year. While Roberts patiently assembled his forces at Modder River, Buller, supported by reinforcements, made two more attempts to gain the north bank of the Tugela. Returning to his earlier plan, he sent a force upstream, past Potgeiter's Drift to Trichardt's Drift, to conduct a wide-flanking movement around Boer defences on 17 January. Lieutenant-General Sir Charles Warren who had arrived with the 5th Division vacillated in his advance, giving time to Botha to regroup and strengthen Boer defences at Tabanyama. When he failed to dislodge the enemy a few days later, he asked Buller to choose a more direct approach and attack Spion Kop. Buller wrote, 'I debated with myself whether or not I should relieve Warren of his command', but in the end, puzzlingly, he supported Warren's plan.[36] The Battle of Spion Kop, 24 January 1900, was one of the worst British defeats in the war. Although he blamed Buller for the failure, Roberts gave him yet another try to break Boer resistance. The situation in Ladysmith was becoming more desperate. Death rates from enteric fever and dysentery were growing each day and rations had been significantly reduced – by February, horses were being slaughtered for food. White was not sure how long he could hold out. The Battle of Vaal Krantz, 5–7 February, however, did not bring the results for which Buller had hoped. The Ladysmith siege would continue.

Roberts arrived at Modder River Camp in early February and the British advance began shortly afterwards. He sent French on a wide-

---

[36] WO 132/24 p. 51, TNA.

flanking move to Kimberley with a large, mounted force. The strategy worked, despite heavy losses to the horses, and Kimberley was liberated on 15 February. After trapping Cronjé at Paardeberg on 17 February, Kitchener took over from the ailing Roberts and attacked the next day. He attempted to dislodge the Boer forces from a strongly entrenched position and his own men, especially those who attacked the front, suffered heavily and, some would argue, needlessly.[37] Nevertheless, after several more days of fighting, the British obtained a much-needed victory resulting in the capture of Cronjé and over 4,000 men. Boer morale was seriously rattled, not only in the Orange Free State, but in Natal where rumours flowed through Ladysmith that the Boers were heading home in despair.[38] On 27 February, the anniversary of Majuba, Buller finally broke through Boer lines at Pieter's Hill. The next day, soldiers and civilians welcomed Major Hubert Gough and a small detachment of British mounted troops into Ladysmith. The siege had been lifted.

After Paardeberg, Roberts did not allow the Boers an opportunity to regroup and pressed on towards Bloemfontein. Attempts at Poplar Grove, Driefontein, and Boshof delayed but failed to stop Roberts's drive. Boer forces were disorganized and unsure how stop the British. Bloemfontein fell on 13 March. After building up supplies and giving the men a much-needed rest, Roberts's drive continued in May. At Zand River on 10 May, the British defeated a combined force of Orange Free State and Transvaal burghers and Kroonstad was occupied the next day. While Roberts rested his men again, he received good news. The 217-day siege had been lifted at Mafeking. Roberts then pushed his forces onwards towards the Transvaal and, by the end of the month, Johannesburg had fallen. The Transvaal's capital, Pretoria, was occupied on 5 June.

Although a few more set-piece battles were to occur, notably at Bergendal in late August, and Roberts continued to view the war through a conventional lens, the third phase of the South African War, the guerrilla war, had begun in earnest. According to Bill Nasson and Fransjohan Pretorius, the Boers had reached a decision in the aftermath of the fall of Bloemfontein that they would continue the fight despite the setbacks. Well before the British, they realized that the type of war they were engaged in was transforming. Urged on by General Christiaan de Wet, they would abandon wagon laagers and adapt to even more mobile

---

[37] Howard Bailes, 'Military Aspects of the War', in Warwick (ed.), *The South African War*, 92.

[38] Henry Watkins-Pitchford, *Besieged in Ladysmith: A Letter to his Wife, Written in Ladysmith During the Siege* (Pietermaritzburg: Shuter & Shooter, 1964), 114–21.

strategy.[39] Another War Council held on 2 June confirmed the Boers' intent to wage a guerilla war. In the northern Orange Free State, now the annexed Orange River Colony, de Wet led his commando destroying rail and telegraph lines, blowing up bridges, and striking at isolated convoys and outposts.

To counter Boer efforts, Roberts did not alter his military policy fundamentally. He continued to believe that the British would win the war by occupying key towns and strategic points. He did, however, take administrative action via official proclamations to both threaten Boers who did not lay down their arms and those who provided comfort and aid to them as well as make overtures to those Boers who might work with him. He gave permission to his officers in the field, when there was evidence of local support, to raze homesteads and burn farmland near transportation and communication networks which were being harassed by armed burghers. In many cases, the evidence was manufactured.

The British drive through the Transvaal was interrupted by the first de Wet hunt in August 1900. Utilizing several mobile columns, Roberts attempted to cordon off de Wet's movements and then strike at the elusive Orange Free State general. The hunt, which pulled in more than 50,000 British soldiers, failed when 'Roberts left open Olifants Nek' in mid-August and de Wet escaped.[40] De Wet eluded a second 'hunt' later in the year. Roberts, however, did feel comfortable enough to annex the Transvaal on 1 September and, certain of victory, begin planning his departure. He left at the end of the year and Kitchener took over command.

Kitchener often felt constrained by Milner's civil administration but he was given a relatively free hand to craft his own war strategy. It was Kitchener who developed an overarching strategy for confronting the guerrilla campaign. In late 1901, he began erecting a blockhouse system in which thousands of small forts of stone, iron, and wood, were linked in a grid to limit the movement of Boer commandos. These were utilized in conjunction with nearly a hundred flying columns. He continued Roberts's policies of farm burning and property confiscation. He also instigated the use of concentration camps to remove civilians from the field preventing them producing for the war effort, and to cripple Boer morale. It was these last two tactics which led future British Prime

---

[39] Nasson, *The South African War 1899–1902*, 166–67; Pretorius, *Anglo-Boer War 1899–1902*, 24.
[40] Methuen held Roberts and Hamilton, who was supposed to remain at Oliphants Nek, responsible for de Wet's escape. Lord Methuen to M. E. Methuen, 23 August 1900, Wiltshire Records Office, Trowbridge, UK. (Now Wiltshire and Swindon History Centre, Chippenham, WSHC.)

Minister, Sir Henry Campbell-Bannerman, to accuse the government of carrying out the 'Methods of Barbarism'.[41]

The concentration camp system was the most devastating of Kitchener's counter-insurgency methods employed against the Boers. Although it had a significant impact on armed burghers in the field, the toll it took on the civilian population was even greater and cannot simply be reduced to the numbers who died in the camps, including 27,929 Boers and roughly 14,000 Africans.[42] Poor planning and neglect were the main reasons for the high death rates, especially among the women and children who made up the majority of the camp population. Many of the fifty-eight camps were situated far from the railway and reliable water sources. They were undersupplied with food, medicine, firewood, and coal. Sanitation was poorly maintained and, as a result, typhoid took the lives of many. Measles, smallpox, dysentery, and respiratory diseases also struck the camps very hard. Conditions improved late in the war after the reformer Emily Hobhouse returned from her tour of the camps and, through an active press campaign, put pressure on the British government to act. The legacy of the camps proved significant in the development of post-war Afrikaner nationalism.[43]

Despite the moral and military effect that the concentration camps and the scorched earth policy had on them, not to mention the growing number of British mounted infantry, Imperial Yeomanry, and irregular horse, the Boers continued to wage an effective guerrilla campaign through 1901 and into 1902. The number of incidents of British surrenders between June and September 1901, for example, averaged fifty-one a month and more than 1,000 soldiers were captured.[44] They continued to interrupt British communication and transportation, and, as the numbers reflect, enjoy victories against isolated detachments, blockhouses, and occasional careless companies, squadrons, and even columns. Smuts's September 1901 invasion of the Cape Colony met with qualified success. Also, in September, Botha defeated a sizeable

---

[41] H. C. G. Matthew, *The Liberal Imperialists: The Ideas and Politics of a Post-Gladstonian Elite* (London: Oxford University Press, 1973), 65, as cited in S. B. Spies, *Methods of Barbarism? Roberts and Kitchener and Civilians in the Boer Republics: January 1900–May 1902* (Cape Town: Human & Rousseau, 1977), 9.

[42] The number of Africans who died in the camps was probably much higher. Elizabeth van Heyningen, *The Concentration Camps of the Anglo-Boer War: A Social History* (Auckland Park: Jacana, 2013), 21, 169.

[43] Albert Grundlingh, 'The National Women's Monument', in Greg Cuthbertson, Albert Grundlingh, and Mary-Lynn Suttie (eds.), *Writing a Wider War: Rethinking Gender, Race, and Identity in the South African War, 1899–1902* (Athens: Ohio University Press, 2002), 19–21.

[44] Papers Relating to South African Surrenders, WO 108/372 pp. 94–124, TNA.

British force at Blood River Poort in Natal. And as late March 1902, de la Rey defeated Methuen at Tweebosch in the western Transvaal, capturing over 850 men including the wounded British general. But the resistance effort was not sustainable. Even though the Boers were making use of captured great coats, blankets, rifles, and ammunition, they were still running increasingly short on supplies.[45] Commandos in the field were also thinning. Numbers of men had accepted amnesty, others had been captured and sent to prison camps overseas, and some even switched sides, notably de Wet's younger brother, Piet. Although Steyn remained at large, Kruger had been forced over the border into Portuguese territory, fled to Holland, and attempted, in vain, to get international support for the Boer cause. In late March 1902, a number of high-profile Boer leaders, including Botha, de Wet, and de la Rey, agreed to meet in Klerksdorp to consider ending the war.

The road to peace was not straight forward as the Boer leaders continued to demand independence and Kitchener and Milner refused to discuss it. Nevertheless, by mid-May, there was some movement. Although the conditions in some districts were reasonably good, others were suffering heavily. The impact of the concentration camps also weighed heavily on the minds of many of the Boer delegates. Finally, there was growing fear of the armed black communities. It was de la Rey, who up to this point was one of the leading voices of the *bittereinders*, who, on 16 May, was willing to drop the demand for independence if a compromise peace could be reached.[46] His decision swayed many others. On 31 May 1902, Boer delegates at Vereeniging voted 54 to 6 to accept the British terms. Among those terms included provisions that Boers in the field would be granted amnesty once they agreed to take an oath of loyalty to the British crown. Prisoners of war would be allowed to return to South Africa pending the same condition. Boers could keep their weapons and were granted language and property rights. The British would aid in the reconstruction of the land and a promise of self-government was made. Some important issues, like the 'Native

---

[45] The Hague Convention forbade the improper use of captured enemy uniforms and insignia. There were certainly incidents in the war in which the Boers violated this custom. However, Boers often donned captured uniforms to simply stay warm as well as displayed insignia as trophies. See, for example Deneys Reitz, *Commando: A Boer Journal of the Boer War* (London: Faber and Faber, 1929), 198. The Boer Republics were not signatories of The Hague Convention.

[46] Fransjohan Pretorius, 'Confronted with the facts: Why the Boer delegates at Vereeniging accepted a humiliating peace to end the South African War, 31 May 1902', in Stephen M. Miller (ed.), *Soldiers and Settlers in Africa, 1850–1918* (Leiden: Brill, 2009), 199–200, 208, 209.

Franchise', were set aside for the time being.[47] The Treaty of Vereeniging was signed that night. The South African War was over.

Anatomy of a Battle: Magersfontein

After three successive victories in late November 1899, Methuen and the 1st Division stopped at the Modder River in the Cape Colony. The general was eager to move forward and relieve Kimberley but he felt that he and his men needed rest.[48] While he waited, he launched air balloons to survey the immediate vicinity and sent his only veteran scouts, Rimington's Guides, to gather information on Boer positions in the direction of Spytfontein. These actions revealed movement of the enemy but could neither discern their numbers nor the trenches which they were constructing in front of the base of Magersfontein Hill. On 10 December 1899, the 1st Division was reinforced by the 3rd Highland Brigade. Despite lacking good intelligence, a sufficient force of mounted troops, and adequate transport which bound him to the Western Railway, Methuen ordered the advance to continue towards Magersfontein, six miles north of the Modder River and fifteen miles south of Kimberley. Later that day, the British came into contact with Boer forces and the artillery was ordered to conduct a bombardment of the southwestern face of the hill, the site selected for the next day's assault. The firing lasted almost three hours and Methuen, believing in the destructive capability of the new British explosive, lyddite, was convinced that Boer defences had been adequately softened. Unable to outflank the enemy because of his lack of mounted troops, Methuen planned a frontal attack to begin early the next morning.

As Methuen was soon to discover, the artillery bombardment had done little to either interrupt Boer preparations or demoralize the enemy. One reason for this is that the value of lyddite was overestimated. Many generals like Methuen had never witnessed its use before and believed the hype that is often associated with new technology.[49] A second reason is that Methuen expected the Boers to return his fire and, by drawing them out, they would reveal their positions and would make for easier targets. The Boer artillery, however, remained silent. Finally, British artillery was ordered to fire on the heights where Methuen expected the Boers to be positioned. They were not. While the British remained at Modder River, de la Rey had his men construct deep, narrow, and well-

---

[47] Peter Warwick, 'Introduction' to Part III, in *The South African War*, 334.
[48] Methuen was wounded in the leg at the Battle of Modder River.
[49] Lord Methuen to F. Stephenson, 19 December 1899, Methuen Papers, WHSC.

hidden, adjoining trenches about 150-200 yards in front of the base of the hill. Constructed three to four feet deep and nearly perpendicular to the ground, the trenches provided full protection to the lower body from British infantry fire and their narrowness offered excellent cover from British artillery fire. Leo Amery wrote that de la Rey's fieldworks at Magersfontein were 'one of the boldest and most original conception[s] in the history of war'.[50] To make matters worse, the bombardment alerted the Boers to the impending attack and the delay caused by nightfall gave them ample time to prepare for it. Not only did it do little material damage to the Boers, the experience strengthened their resolve and trust in their commander was reinforced.[51]

A night march was designed to provide full cover for the advancing British troops. Methuen, Gatacre, and other British generals were aware of the dangers involved in these types of operations, especially when conducted over unfamiliar ground, but they believed that the advantages outweighed the risks. Fighting an enemy armed with breech-loading weapons was relatively new to them and British tacticians had yet to figure out the best course to counter the improved accuracy, faster rates of fire, and greater ranges the weapons offered. Major-General Ian Hamilton, who was serving with White at Ladysmith and later acted as Kitchener's Chief of Staff, had utilized extended formations on the North-West Frontier a few years earlier.[52] This proved effective in South Africa as well, but night marches required close order. At Magersfontein, one of Methuen's staff officers, Major George E. Benson conducted a successful night march and got the Highland Brigade into position. However, the brigade commander, Major-General Andrew Wauchope, unaware of the Boer trenches and concerned that his men were still too far from the base of the hill, where he thought the Boers were positioned, did not give the order to his men to extend but instead pushed on them on further.[53] The decision proved critical. As the sun began to rise, the Boers could see the Highlanders only 400 yards away, without cover, and still in close order. They laid down a devasting fire, which was only tempered by the fact that many of the Boers were only beginning to rouse from their night of sleep. Wauchope attempted to lead an assault on the trenches but was hit, fatally, in the first few

---

[50] L. S. Amery (ed.), *The Times History of The War in South Africa 1899–1902*, vol. 2 (London: Sampson Low, Marston and Co., LTD., 1907), 386.
[51] Stephen M. Miller, *Lord Methuen and the British Army: Failure and Redemption in South Africa* (London: Frank Cass, 1999), 131–32.
[52] Methuen observed Hamilton's tactics at Dargai, 20 November 1897.
[53] P. S. Methuen to General Officer Commanding, 10–11 December 1899, rewritten 15 February 1900, WO 32/7966, TNA.

minutes. With his death, as well as two of the battalion commanders, the Highlanders scrambled for what cover they could find. Most remained static for the rest of the day. Despite reinforcements and flank attacks, the British could not regain momentum. Troops began retiring by the late afternoon and firing ceased by the early evening. The next day, Methuen and Cronjé arranged for an armistice to allow for the care of the wounded and the removal of the dead. British casualties topped 900; Boers, between 200 and 275.[54] The march to Kimberley was halted until the arrival of Roberts and reinforcements, especially a much-needed mounted force.

The Role of the Royal Navy

Since the South African War was a land campaign, the Royal Navy played only a supporting role. To prevent the Boers from obtaining weapons and supplies, the Royal Navy conducted a blockade of southern Africa. Ships were routinely stopped and boarded, particularly near Lourenço Marques (Maputo) the main port of Portuguese East Africa, and, at times, cargoes were confiscated or destroyed. In addition, early in the war, the HMS *Penelope* served as a makeshift prison for Boers captured at Elandslaagte and, later, Royal Navy transport ships stationed off Simon's Town similarly served as temporary holding facilities.[55] On land, sailors, marines, and naval guns played a role in Methuen's advance toward Kimberley where the Naval Brigade suffered disproportionately at the Battle of Graspan.[56] It was at the siege of Ladysmith, however, that naval guns played a crucial role. On the Natal front, White recognized quickly that his guns were out-ranged by the Boer's 155 mm Creusot 'Long Toms' and asked if the Royal Navy could help. A Naval brigade, equipped with two long-range, 4.7-inch quick-firing guns, was readied and sent to Natal. It arrived in Ladysmith on Mournful Monday, 30 October 1899, two days before the siege began.[57] Although the bombardment of the city lasted throughout the siege and caused terrible

---

[54] General Officer Commanding to Secretary of State for War, 14 December 1899, No. 1816, List of Casualties at Magersfontein 10–12 December 1899, WO 108, South Africa Telegrams, TNA. Breytenbach pinpoints the number at 255. J. H. Breytenbach, *Die Geskiedenis van die Tweede Vryheidsoorlog in Suid-Afrika, 1899–1902*, vol. 2 (Pretoria: Staatsdrukker, 1971), 174.

[55] Darrell Hall, *The Hall Handbook of the Anglo-Boer War 1899–1902* (Pietermaritzburg: University of Natal Press, 1999), 115.

[56] T. T. Jeans (ed.), *Naval Brigades in the South African War, 1899–1900* (London: Sampson, Low, Marston and Co., 1901), 34.

[57] Gerald Sharp, *The Siege of Ladysmith* (London: Macdonald and Jane's, 1976), 22.

destruction to both men and buildings, the naval guns provided White with the necessary tools to defend the city.

Aftermath

The impact of the South African War was felt deeply in Great Britain and its empire and, of course, in South Africa as well. If many Britons approached the declaration of war with unease, Black Week stirred the patriotism of the country. Spontaneous celebrations erupting at the end of the 217-day siege of Mafeking on 17 May 1900 and the Conservative victory in the autumn 'Khaki' election seemed indicators of continued support for the war. But if the war was popular in 1900, by its end, many had lost interest. The charges that Campbell-Bannerman, Hobhouse, and others laid out in regards to the British prosecution of the war were damaging. Similarly, the steady reports of casualties presented to the public in the context of a hard-to-understand, counter-insurgency campaign soured opinions on the conflict.[58] Within just a few years, pro-Boers like Campbell-Bannerman and David Lloyd George would be leading a reinvigorated Liberal party into power.

The rejection of so many potential British volunteers for health reasons and the poor showing of others in the field was of great concern. Liberals and the Fabian Society called for a campaign to eradicate slums, establish a minimum wage, and reform housing and education. The military was also targeted. Lord Elgin's Royal Commission on the War in South Africa, although politicized, showed major weaknesses in planning, intelligence, leadership, and operations. In the next year, 1904, Lord Esher's 'Report of the War Office (Reconstitution) Committee' and the 'Report of the Duke of Norfolk's Commission on the Militia and Volunteers' continued to recommend substantial changes such as the creation of the Army Council and a General Staff, and the reorganization of Home Defences and the volunteer forces.[59]

Although the Boers failed to attract allies in the war, Great Britain did feel the pressure of fighting a conflict which was viewed unfavorably throughout Europe and in the United States. Although the South African War was not the only reason the British pulled out of their self-imposed isolation and signed a treaty with the Japanese in 1902 and later

---

[58] For a discussion of British sentiment and the war, see Stephen M. Miller, 'In support of the "Imperial Mission"? Volunteering for the South African War', *Journal of Military History* 69, 3 (2005): 691–713.

[59] Alan Ramsay Skelley, *The Victorian Army at Home* (Montreal: McGill-Queen's University Press, 1977), 301–03.

reached the entente with France, it did play a role.[60] The impact of the war on imperial cohesion is unclear. Although it may have brought Australia, New Zealand, and Canada closer to Great Britain, it also helped shape local nationalisms, and in the case of Canada, created new rifts between English and French speakers.[61]

In South Africa, Great Britain invested significant amounts in restoring farms and homesteads, getting the mines up and running, and promoting resettlement lands. The latter as well as proposed changes to education were part of the 'Milnerization' process, or Milner's unsuccessful attempt to anglicize the Boers but mostly successful strategy to hold South Africa firmly in the British industrial orbit. These actions as well as his decision to bring indentured Chinese labor into the mines did not help to heal the wounds of the war.[62] Afrikaner nationalism, which had been developing since the late 1870s, was given a major boost by the war. Milner's policies ensured that it would continue to thrive.

Nevertheless, the British and the Boers were able to find common ground and came closer together on racial issues, particularly after the crushing of the Bambatha or Zulu Rebellion of 1906. Self-government was restored to the Transvaal and the Orange River Colony the following year. And, on the eighth anniversary of the Treaty of Vereeniging, the South African colonies were united, and the Union of South Africa became a dominion of the British Empire.

Further Reading

Amery, L. S. (ed.) *The Times History of the War in South Africa 1899–1902*. 7 vols. London: Sampson Low, Marston and Co., LTD., 1907.
Breytenbach, J. H. *Die Geskiedenis van die Tweede Vryheidsoorlog in Suid-Afrika, 1899–1902*. 6 vols. Pretoria: Staatsdrukker, 1960–96.
Crawford, John and Ian McGibbon (eds.) *One Flag, One Queen, One Tongue: New Zealand, the British Empire and the South African War*. Auckland: Auckland University Press, 2003.
Grundlingh, Albert. *The Dynamics of Treason: Boer Collaboration in the South African War of 1899–1902*. Pretoria: Protea Book House, 2006.
Maurice, Frederick, and M. H. Grant. (Official) *History of the War in South Africa, 1899–1902*. 4 vols. London: Hurst and Blackwood, 1906–1910.

---

[60] David Omissi and Andrew S. Thompson, 'Introduction: Investigating the impact of the war', in *The Impact of the South African War*, 14.
[61] Donal Lowry, '"The Boers were the beginning of the end"?: The wider impact of the South African War', in Donal Lowry (ed.), *The South Africa War Reappraised* (Manchester: Manchester University Press, 2000), 226–27.
[62] G. H. L. Le May, *The Afrikaners: An Historical Interpretation* (Oxford: Blackwell Publishers, 1995), 130–32.

Miller, Carman. *Painting the Map Red: Canada and the South African War 1899–1902*. Montreal, Kingston: McGill-Queen's University Press, 1998.
Miller, Stephen M. *Lord Methuen and the British Army: Failure and Redemption in South Africa*. London: Frank Cass, 1999.
— *Volunteers on the Veld: Britain's Citizen-Soldiers and the South African War*. Norman: Oklahoma University Press, 2007.
— *George White and the Victorian Army in India and Africa: Serving the Empire*. London: Palgrave-Macmillan, 2020.
Nasson, Bill. *Abraham Esau's War: A Black South African War in the Cape, 1899–1902*. New York: Cambridge University Press, 1991.
— *The War for South Africa: The Anglo-Boer War 1899–1902*. Cape Town: Tafelberg, 2010.
Omissi, David and Andrew S. Thompson (eds.) *The Impact of the South African War*. New York: Palgrave, 2002.
Pakenham, Thomas. *The Boer War*. New York: Random House, 1979.
Porter, Andrew. *The Origins of the South African War: Joseph Chamberlain and the Diplomacy of Imperialism 1895–99*. Manchester: Manchester University Press, 1980.
Pretorius, Fransjohan. *Life on Commando During the Anglo-Boer War, 1899–1902*. Cape Town: Human & Rousseau, 1999.
Smith, Iain R. *The Origins of the South African War, 1899–1902*. New York: Longman, 1996.
Spies, S. B. *Methods of Barbarism? Roberts and Kitchener and Civilians in the Boer Republics, January 1900–May 1902*. Cape Town: Human & Rousseau, 1977.
Stanley, Liz. *Mourning Becomes ... Post/Memory, Commemoration and the Concentration Camps of the South African War*. Manchester: Manchester University Press, 2006.
Van Heyningen, Elizabeth. *The Concentration Camps of the Anglo-Boer War: A Social History*. Auckland Park: Jacana, 2013.
The War in South Africa, a German Official Account. Trans. W.H. Waters. New York: E.P. Dutton, 1904.
Warwick, Peter, and S. B. Spies (eds.) *The South African War: The Anglo-Boer War*. Harlow: Longman, 1980.
Wilcox, Craig. *Australia's Boer War: The War in South Africa 1899–1902*. New York: Oxford University Press, 2002.

15 Conclusion

Stephen M. Miller

Historians have long debated the causes for the British Empire's rapid expansion in the second half of the nineteenth century. They have put forth economic explanations emphasizing the importance of trade, areas of investment, cheap labor, and extensive connections of an emerging service sector. Strategic arguments have focused on the need to protect communication and transportation networks from both local and international threats, and European rivalry ranging from Russian intrigue in Central Asia to French attempts to re-establish themselves on the Nile River, and from Italian incursions into the horn of Africa to the assertion of German interest in southwest Africa, which challenged Great Britain's relationships with the Boer Republics of South Africa. Theories which elevate the role of social imperialism, the need to captivate a growing and more malleable population, or even to assist agents of religion or 'civilization' have also been advanced. Traditionally, the role of politicians and parties in this process has been highlighted, as has been the function and importance of 'men on the spot'. Whether there was an over-arching strategy in Britain's pursuit of empire or if it was acquired 'in a fit of absence of mind' remains unsettled.[1]

The role of the army in the pursuit and maintenance of empire is often overlooked by those historians looking at causation. For the most part, this is fair. After all, the War Office was controlled by civilians. Nevertheless, military actors had a great impact on how the empire was constructed in drawing up war plans, in conducting operations, and in negotiating or dictating peace settlements. And obviously, although again largely ignored, officers in the field played a significant role in shaping responses made at home through the collection of data and the transmission of information. The British Army did much more than simply enforce the will of its elected leaders overseas.

---

[1] J. R. Seeley, *The Expansion of England: Two Course Lectures* (London: Macmillan and Co., 1883, 2nd edition and Reprint, 1914), 10.

The type of conflict and its location could shape the army's role as could the personality of a military commander. The latter could have an important influence on how his policies were received at home. Commanding officers were often given a great deal of leeway in determining the best measures to obtain the political aims of the campaigns they conducted. A successful campaign, a supportive government, and an appreciative public could lead to a decision which might shape the region for years to come, as it did in Upper Burma. Equally, policy blunders or a change of government might generate a military response which seemed as incomplete or inchoate, as it did in the case of the First Anglo-Boer War and the attempt to relieve Gordon in Khartoum. In the wars waged to 'wipe out an insult and avenge a wrong' in China, Abyssinia, and Asanteland, the British were content to withdraw after their victories ensured their continued influence in those areas. The same became true in Afghanistan once the British secured a friendly buffer state, although, in that case, military decisions were more closely watched by the British Government of India. When a commanding officer was asked to 'suppress an insurrection or repress lawlessness', as in the Indian Rebellion or along the North-West Frontier, there was already a strong civilian presence in the region and therefore there was less room for the army to be the sole or most important arbiter of the conflict. Regardless of the political role it might play in a campaign, without the army, the empire could not have been extended, pacified, and maintained.

The thirteen small wars examined in this volume have explored the political decisions made by British Army officers. They also have discussed the context of those wars in terms of domestic politics. Above all, though, they have focused on military actions: those of officers and men on both sides of the conflict. They have addressed concerns of strategy, tactics, and logistics. They have examined, where appropriate, the impact of the growing technological gap and how, in some cases, that same gap began to shrink by the turn of the century. Although the Royal Navy did not always play a significant part in these campaigns, it did, at times, offer invaluable operational support, and its role has been detailed when necessary. In some of the campaigns, the British Army was supplemented by local levees or volunteers. In the case of the South African War, the government not only accepted auxiliaries recruited in the Cape Colony and Natal and raised Volunteers and Imperial Yeomanry at home, it was forced to out of both military and political exigency to accept Canadian, New Zealand, and Australian offers to send soldiers.

Although this book has been presented as a history of Victorian wars, and all thirteen chapters discussed British troops, British politics, and other British concerns like economics and grand strategy, it was vital for all of its contributors to present the Asian, African, and Australasian perspective with care and detail. Leadership, organizational structure, manpower, productive capacities, and technology are just some of the aspects that have been discussed and evaluated in these chapters. When possible, local sources have been accessed in order to provide a better understanding of both sides in each conflict. Great Britain's enemies in these small wars were never simply 'half-civilized' or 'savages', as sometimes portrayed by Charles Callwell in his *Small Wars*. They did not act instinctively and they were certainly not limited in their ability to react because they were somehow racially and culturally inferior to their European foe.[2] Nevertheless, their strategy and tactics could be limited by organization, tradition, agrarian cycles, marginal resources, and social institutions. That said, the British system could also be inflexible at times. One of the major differences in this period, compared with eighteenth-century imperial conflicts, was the inability of Britain's foes, with a few exceptions, to obtain support from continental European powers in terms of manpower and weaponry. In several of the Victorian campaigns discussed in this volume, Britain was effective in recruiting auxiliaries or hiring laborers, guides, and scouts from among rival indigenous factions to assist them in their war effort. In India, in particular, the British success can be explained in part by their utilization of Sikh and Gurkha troops against the Rebellion. Furthermore, it changed the way they came to attribute so-called martial traits with certain races, and this led, in turn, to a re-thinking of recruitment in the Presidency Armies in the second half of the century.[3]

This volume began by recognizing the contribution of Brian Bond's 1967 edited collection, *Victorian Military Campaigns*.[4] Just as the seven chapters in that book could not provide exhaustive coverage of the topic, neither could the thirteen chapters in this one. Nevertheless, the contributors to this volume believe that their essays have offered a more comprehensive approach than *Victorian Military Campaigns* and have provided a more solid foundation for a better understanding of Britian's imperial conflicts. They hope their work will stimulate interest, leading to further investigations into a host of topics ranging from political and military decision making to recruitment, training, organization,

---

[2] C. E. Callwell, *Small Wars: Their Principles and Practice*, 3rd ed. (London: HMSO, 1906; Reprint, Lincoln: University of Nebraska Press, 1996), 31–32.
[3] See, for example, Heather Streets, *Martial Races: The Military, Race and Masculinity in British Imperial Culture, 1857–1914* (Manchester: Manchester University Press, 2004).
[4] Brian Bond (ed.), *Victorian Military Campaigns* (London: Hutchinson & Co., 1967).

and technology. Although there is much more to be said, particularly on other campaigns as well as African, Asian, and Australian and New Zealand actors, we trust that *Queen Victoria's Wars: British Military Campaigns, 1857–1902* has significantly progressed the scholarship of the Victorian army and the history of nineteenth-century imperial conflict. Above all, it will have opened up new questions and debates.

Index

Ababda, 207
Abadieh, 270, 273
Abdallāhi, Ibn-Mohammed Al-Khalifa, 260–61, 264–65, 269–70, 275, 277, 279
Abrakampa, 117
Abu Hamed, 268–70, 277
Abu Klea, 187, 213, 217
Addiscombe, 69
Aden, 67–68, 184
Adowa (Adwa), Battle of, 80, 263
Afridis, 6, 240–43, 246–49, 251–55, 258
Ahmed Kel, 137, 142
Ahmed, Mohammed, 203
Akasha, 266–68
Akbar, Mullah Syed, 247, 253
Akwapim, 106
Akyem, 113–15, 117
Alambagh, 28
al-Din, Shaykh, 275–76
Alexander II, Tsar, 127, 130, 144
Alexandria, 191–93, 196–98, 200, 204
Ali II, Ras, 63
Ali, Mehmet, 188
Ali, Sher, 126–28, 130–34, 137–39, 144
Alison, Sir Archibald, 192, 196–97
Allahabad, 20, 23, 26–27
amabutho, 152, 155–58, 160–63
Amankwatia, 110–11, 117, 119, 121
Amarar, 207
Ambala, 32, 126
Ambigol Wells, 267
Amery, Leo, 284, 296, 303
Amoafo, 116, 118–19, 121
Anglo-Egyptian Army, 208, 263–64, 273, 275–76
Anglo-Sikh Wars, 69
Annesley Bay, 73
Ansar, 207–8, 213–15, 217
Anstruther, Philip R., 177
Antalo, 75
Arabi, Ahmet, 187, 190, 192–93, 196–98, 201–2, 204

Arakan, 221, 228
Argandeh Valley, 138
Army Council, 305
Arogee (Arogi), Battle of, 76
artillery
   Armstrong gun, 57, 59, 88, 98, 113, 120, 122
   Gardner gun, 213, 235
   Gatling gun, 113, 118, 122, 161–62, 164, 183–84, 195, 200–1
   Hale rocket tubes, 113, 122, 164, 184
   howitzers, 32, 56, 88, 194, 274
   Long Tom, 155mm Creusot, 304
   lyddite, 274, 302
   Maxim gun, 263–64, 267, 273–76, 279
   mortars, 29, 32–33, 70, 88
   rockets, 119, 161, 256, 272
Arzu, 137
Ashburnham, Thomas, 50
Assin, 106, 114
Assinie, 122
Assouan, 271
Atbara River, 208, 264–65, 270–71, 273
Auckland, 84, 91, 93–94, 100
Australia, 86–87, 90, 290, 306, 309, 311
Ava, 221
Awadh, Kingdom of, 12–13, 15–19, 22–25, 27, 29
Ayshal, 63
Azraq, Osman, 275

Badcock, F.F., 250
badmashes (bandits), 135
Baggara (Baqara), 208, 264, 275
Bagh, 253
Bahadur Shah, 25, 28, 33, 36
Bahr el-Ghazal, 203, 261, 265
Baker, Valentine, 202, 205
Bala Hissar, 132
Baluchistan, 140
Bambatha Rebellion, 306
Bapedi, 169
Bara Valley, 253

Index

Barbados, 110, 112
Bareilly, 12, 18, 31
Barkai, 254
Barton, F.J.H, 245
Bashar, King Mir, 247
Bastier chain pump, 79
Basutoland, 173, 178
Bay of Natal, 147
Bayuda Desert, 265, 268–69
Beach, Sir Michael Hicks, 264
Beatty, David R., 272, 278
Beijing, 40, 43–45, 47–54, 57–59
Bell, John, 65
Bellairs, Sir William, 171–73
Bengal Army, 6, 8, 13–17, 19, 24, 71
Beni-Amer, 207
Benin, 106
Benson, George E., 303
Berber, 207, 212–13, 216, 264–65, 269–71, 278
Bergin, James, 78
Bernard, Sir Charles, 225, 229, 235
Bezuidenhout, P.L., 172
Bihar, 15, 18, 29
Bishara, Muhammad wad, 264, 268
Bithor, 21
Black Week, 289–90, 296, 305
Bloemfontein, 298
Bloemfontein Conference, 282–84
Blood River (Ncome), 173, 301
Bolan, 133
Bolan Pass, 128, 134, 144
Bombay Army, 16, 69, 71
Bombay-Burma Trading Company, 224
Bonaparte, Prince Louis Napoleon, 147
Bonny River, 113
Bonsu, Mensa, 124
Botha, Louis, 296–97, 300–1
Bowdich, Thomas, 106–7
Bowring, Sir John, 45
Brand, Johannes, 179, 181
Bridle Drift, 295
Bromhead, Gonville, 158
Bronkhorstspruit, 177–78
Browne, Edward, 234
Browne, Sir Sam, 132, 134–35
Brownlow, Sir Charles, 229
Bruce, Frederick, 51
Buckle, R.N., 120
Bulgarian Atrocities, 136
Buller, Sir Redvers, 112, 119, 160, 162–63, 283–84, 287, 291–98
Burnes, Alexander, 134
Burn-Murdoch, John F., 267
Burrows, George, 139

Butler, Sir William, 112–13, 117, 171, 287, 291–93

Caesar's Camp, 294
Cairo, 6, 191–93, 196–97, 201, 203, 205, 266, 270–71
Calcutta, 9, 19–20, 23, 25, 38
Callwell, C.E., 2–4, 6–7, 167, 245–46, 253, 310
Cambridge, Prince George, Duke of, 74–75, 115, 123, 174
Cameron, Charles, 66–68
Cameron, Sir Duncan, 93–99, 103
Campbell, Colin, 1st Baron Clyde, 28–31
Campbell-Bannerman, Sir Henry, 300, 305
Canada, 149, 196, 210, 290, 306
Canning, Charles, 1st Earl, 13, 23, 29–31, 36, 45
Canton (Guangzhou), 40–41, 43, 46, 48–51, 57–58
Canton River, 40, 51, 58
Cape Coast Castle, 106–7, 110–13, 116–17, 122–23
Cape Town, 149, 170, 176, 288–89, 291, 293
Cardwell, Edward, 1st Viscount, 107, 112, 114–15, 123, 174
Carnarvon, Henry Howard Molyneux Herbert, 4th Earl of, 149
Cavagnari, Sir Pierre Louis Napoleon, 134–36, 138
Cetshwayo kaMpande, 157, 159–62, 165
Chamberlain, Joseph, 281–83
Chamberlain, Sir Neville, 130, 132
Chamkannis, 258
Chapman, E.F., 137, 140, 142
Charasiab, 135
Chard, John, 158
Chelmsford, Frederick Thesiger, 2nd Baron, 150–51, 153–66
Chin Field Force, 233
Chindwin, 225, 228
Chinese Navy, 43
Chin-Lushai Hills, 228, 234
Chittagong, 9, 234
Churchill, Lord Randolph, 224
Churchill, Winston, 261, 273
Chusan (Zhoushan), 48, 52
Chute, Trevor, 99
Clark, George, 16
Coercion Act, 179
Colenso, Battle of, 295
Colley, Sir George Pomeroy, 131–34, 138, 169, 171, 173, 175–76, 178–84

314　Index

Commissariat Transport Corps, 93, 158, 182, 283, 288
concentration camps, 285, 294, 299–302
Congress of Berlin, 130
Constantinople, 128
Consular Service, 55
Controller-General of Finance, 189
Cousin-Montauban, Charles, Comte de Palikao, 53
Cranbrook, Gathorne Gathorne-Hardy, 1st Earl of, 136
Crimean War, 10, 36, 60, 72, 107, 127, 153, 194, 196
Crispi, Francesco, 80
Cromer, Evelyn Baring, 1st Earl of, 263–64, 266–67, 271
Cronjé, Piet, 172–73, 291, 295, 298, 304
Crosthwaite, Sir Charles, 222, 235
Curzon, George, 1st Marquess Curzon of Kedleston, 258
Customs and Consolidation Act, 122

Dabarki, 62
Dabulamanzi kaMpande, Prince, 158–59, 161
Dakka, 134
Dalhousie, James Andrew Broun-Ramsay, 1st Marquess of, 18, 21, 37
Damietta, 192–93
Damot, 67
Dargai Heights, 251–52, 254–55, 257
Dartnell, John, 157, 163
Debarki, 76
Delhi, 19–34, 37
Denkyira, 106, 114
Derby, Edward Smith-Stanley, 14th Earl of, 67–68
Digna, Osman (Uthman Abu Bakr Diqna), 204–7, 270, 273, 275–76
Dilke, Sir Charles, 2nd Baronet, 136
Dinka, 208
Disraeli, Benjamin, Earl of Beaconsfield, 8, 70, 127–28, 167, 282
Doab, 9, 20
Dongola, 208, 212, 263–69, 277
Driefontein, 298
Dufferin, Frederick Temple Blackwood, 1st Marquess of, 222, 224, 229
Dum Dum bullet, 256, 273
Dundee, 292, 294
Durban (Port Natal), 164
Durnford, Anthony, 157, 163–64

Earle, William, 212–13

East India Company, 19–20, 36, 86, 173, 234
Eastern Crisis, 128, 131
Egyptian Army, 260–61, 263–64, 267
  bashbuzuq, 193
  cavalry, 205, 267, 274, 276
  engineers, 198
  officer corps, 190
El Obeid, 204
El Teb, 205–6
Elandslaagte, 294, 304
Elgin, James Bruce, 8th Earl of, 41–43, 48, 54–55, 60
Elgin, Victor Bruce, 9th Earl of, 245, 305
Elias, R., 142
Elmina, 110–11, 114, 116, 122–23
Elmslie, F.B., 274
Eshowe, 156, 159–62
Estcourt, 295
Ethiopia, 63, 80
Ewart, Sir John Spencer, 273

Fante, 106–7, 110–11, 113, 115–16, 118–20, 122, 124
Fashoda, 204, 208, 278
Fatshun River, 58
Ferozepur, 32
Ferreira, Joachim, 182
Festing, Francis, 110, 122
Firket (Firka), 264–67, 270
First Anglo-Afghan War, 126–27, 131
First Anglo-Asante War, 106
First Anglo-Burmese War, 221
First Italo-Ethiopian War, 80
Fitzclarence, Edward, 269
Flad, Martin, 67–69
Fomena, 123
Fort Ali Masjid, 134, 243
Fort Atbara, 273
Fort Gulistan, 245
Fort Lockhart, 245
Fort Maude, 243
Forward Policy, 240
Franco-Burmese Treaty, 222
Franks, George M., 272
Fremantle, Edmund, 110, 116, 122
French, Sir John, 294, 297
Frere, Sir Henry Bartle, 149–52, 154–55, 159, 165, 169

Gabri, Fitaurari, 76
Gandamak, 133–34
Ganges River, 9, 25
Gatacre, Sir William F., 237, 270–74, 296, 303

Index

General Enlistment Act, 17
George, David Lloyd, 305
German South West Africa (Namibia), 281, 291
Ghana. *See* Gold Coast
ghazis, 31–33, 139, 141
Ghazni, 137
Ghilzais, 131, 133, 137, 143
Gibraltar, 81, 184
Girouard, E. Percy C., 266, 268
Gladstone, William, 192–93, 202, 205, 217–18
  and the Transvaal Campaign, 170, 181, 185
  as Prime Minister, 112, 114, 144, 165, 174, 179, 191, 260
Gleichen, Count Edward, 214
Glover, John, 111, 113, 116–17, 119
Gold Coast, 107–14, 122–24, 292
Gold, C.E., 91
Gondar, 65
Goodenough, Sir William, 58, 287
Gordon, Charles, 7, 187–88, 203, 205, 207, 210–13, 215–18, 260–61, 272, 278, 309
Gough, Sir Charles, 136, 143, 232
Gough, Sir Hubert, 298
Gough, Sir Hugh, viii, 142
Graham, Sir Gerald, 43, 205–7
Grand Canal, 52, 57
Grant, Sir Hope, 48, 52–56
Graspan, Battle of, 296, 304
Grey, Sir George, 90, 93–94, 96, 99
Griffin, Lepel, 140
Grodekov, N.L., 131
guerilla warfare, 246, 251, 299
Gulf of Guinea, 106
Gulf of Pechili, 52, 57
Gun War, 178
Gurkhas, 5, 29, 36, 135, 231, 233, 251, 254–55
Gwalior, 30

Hadendoah, 205–8
Hague Conference, The, 290
Haig, Douglas, 1st Earl, 271, 276
Haines, Sir Frederick, 132, 140, 143–44
Hallengra, 207
Hamilton, Sir Ian, 303
Hamran, 207
Hanging Act, the, 24
Harley, R.W., 122
Harman, Sir George, 237
Hassania, 208
Hauhau, 98
Haumene, Te Ua, 98
Havelock, Sir Henry, 27–28

Hazaras, 143
Hazrat Mahal, Begum, 28–29
Heidelberg, 175
heliograph, 164
Hely-Hutchinson, Sir Walter, 292
Hensman, Howard, 135–36
Herat, 139, 144
Herbert, Sidney, 1st Baron Herbert of Lea, 48, 57
Hicks, William, 187, 204–5, 210
Hills, James, 138, 141
Hilu, Ali wad, 208
Hlangwane Hill, 295
Hlobane, battle of, 160–61
Hluttaw, 224–25
Hobhouse, Emily, 300, 305
Hodson, William, 33
Hong Kong, 40, 43–46, 48–49, 52, 57
Hood, Horace L.A., 278
Hooper, W.W., 229
Hope, Sir James, 52
Household Cavalry, 198
Hughes, R.J., 142
Huirangi, 92
Hunter, Sir Archibald, 261, 266–67, 269, 271, 273, 277, 294
Hutt Valley, 90

illness
  cholera, 132, 228, 267
  diarrhoea, 273
  dysentery, 228, 297, 300
  enteric fever, 273
  fever, 297
  malaria, 228
  measles, 300
  pneumonia, 132
  smallpox, 116, 300
  typhoid, 132, 300
India Council, 127
iNdlondlo, 158
iNdluyengwe, 158
Ingogo River, 179
Irrawaddy Flotilla Company, 234
Irrawaddy River, 227–28
iSandlwana, 7, 150–51, 156–65
Ismail, Pasha, 188, 203
Ismailia, 192, 197–98

Ja'alin, 208, 269–70
Jakdul Wells, 212
Jalalabad, 134
Jama Masjid, 30, 33
Jameson Raid, 281, 283
Jan, Mahomed, 133, 136

Jezailchi, 241
Jhansi, 25, 30, 32
Johannesburg, 281, 293, 298
Joubert, Frans, 177–78, 181
Joubert, Piet, 173, 291, 294
Judge, C.B., 255
Jumna River, 9, 30

Kabbabish, 208
Kabul, 128–40, 143
Kachins, 220, 226, 231, 233
Kafr el-Dauar, 192–93, 196–97
Kaiserbagh, 29
Kandahar, 128, 132–37, 139–44
kaNdlela Godide, 156
Kanhow, 236
Kanpur, 19, 21, 25–27, 32, 38
Kāpiti, 90
Karens, 220, 231
Karnal, 32
Kashgil, 204
Kassa. *See* Tewodros II
Kassala, 68, 263, 265
Kassassin, 198–99
Kaufman, Konstantin, 127, 130
Kawiti, Te Ruki, 84, 88–90
Kaye, J.W., 12, 15
Kempster, James, 251
Keppel, Colin R., 278
Kereri Hills, 275–76
Kerma, 268
Khalifa, *see* Abdallāhi
Khalil, Ibrahim al, 275
Khambula, 160–61
Khan, Aslam, 245
Khan, Ayub, 137, 139–40, 144
Khan, Faiz Mohammed, 130
Khan, Gholam Hussein, 137
Khan, Jemadar Imam, 232
Khan, Muhammed Bakht, 31
Khan, Sir Syed Ahmad, 15
Khan, Yakub, 126, 130, 133–35
Khartoum, 187–88, 203–5, 207, 210–13, 215–18, 260, 274, 278–79, 309
Khiva, 127
Khojak Pass, 140
Khojent, 127
Khusalgarh, 246, 249
Khyber Pass, 18, 130–35, 241, 243–49, 252, 258
Kimberley, 149, 179–80, 291–93, 296–98, 302, 304–5
Kimberley, John Wodehouse, 1st Earl of, 114–15, 122–23
King, L. White, 242, 247

Kīngitanga, 91–97
Kipling, Rudyard, 208, 220, 237
Kitchener, Horatio Herbert, 1st Earl of, 263–72, 274–79, 282, 297–301, 303
Kitchener, Sir Walter, 279
Klerksdorp, 301
Knollys, Henry, 42
Kofi Karikari, King, 110, 114, 124
Kohat, 241–42, 246, 249–50, 256
Kokand, 127
Kolkata. *See* Calcutta
Koomayli Pass, 73–74
Kordofan, 203–4, 208, 279
Kororāreka, 84, 88
Korti, 211–13, 216, 268
Kosheh, 267
Kroonstad, 298
Kruger, Paul, 169–70, 173, 180–81, 282–83, 287–88, 291, 301
Kumase (Coomassie), 110, 114, 118–19, 121, 123
Kurram, 130, 132–35, 246, 249
kwaGingindlovu, 161
Kwaku Dua Panin, 110

Ladysmith, 291–98, 303–4
Laing's Nek, 178, 180–83
Lake Waikare, 95–96
Landi Kotal, 243, 245
Lansdowne, Henry Charles Keith Petty-FitzMaurice, 5th Marquess of, 283–84, 297
Lanyon, Owen, 169, 172–73, 176
Lawrence, Henry, 13, 18, 27–28
Lawrence, John, 1st Baron, 126, 134
Lekse, 232
Lesseps, Ferdinand de, 193
Lewis, D.F., 272
Lockhart, Sir William, 237, 246, 248–50, 252–53, 258
London Convention, 290
Long, Charles, 295
Lourenço Marques (Maputo), 304
Low, Sir Robert, 237
Lower Burma, 221, 224–25, 227, 231–32, 234, 236
Lucknow, 10, 19–22, 25, 27–29, 32, 34–35, 37–38
Lydenburg, 172, 176–78
Lyttelton, Sir Neville, 274
Lytton, Robert Bulwer-Lytton, 1st Earl of, 127–38

Macdonald, Hector A., 272, 276
Macpherson, Sir Herbert, 230

Index

Madeira, 164
Madras (Chennai), 9, 16, 52, 143
Madras Army, 20, 58, 71, 78, 227, 230, 232
Mafeking, 291–93, 297–98, 305
Magdala, 63, 67–70, 73–78, 81
Magersfontein, 295–96, 302–3
Magfar, 198
Magner, Michael, 78
Mahmud Ahmad, Emir, 264–65, 269–73
Māhoetahi, 92
Maidan Valley, 252–53
Maiwand, 139–40, 142, 144
Majuba Hill, 171, 178, 180–83
Malakand, 246
Malwa Field Force, 54
Mandalay, 6, 220–22, 224, 227–31, 234, 236
Manifold, M.G.E., 269
Manipur, 221
Marabastad, 172, 176–78
Maratha Confederacy, 21–23
Marchand, Jean-Baptiste, 265, 278
Martin, R.H., 274, 276
Massawa, 65–70, 73, 80–81
Mastura Valley, 253
Mathias, H.H., 255
Mavumengwana, kaNdlela, 156
Maxse, Sir F. Ivor, 276
Maxwell, John G., 272
Mayo, Richard Bourke, 6th Earl of, 126
Mbilini waMswati, Prince, 159
McCarthy, Sir Charles, 107
Meerut, 15, 24–25, 32, 38
Meiklejohn, Ronald F., 271
Melik, 273
Menelik I, Emperor, 80
Meremere, 94–95
Merewether, William, 68–69, 73
Merowe, 268–69
Merv, 127
Metemma, 265, 269–70, 274
Meyer, Lukas, 294
Mhow, 30
Michel, Sir John, 54
Middelburg, 177
Mikha'il, Yusuf, 275
military units, British
  1st Bn. Dorset Regiment, 254–55
  1st Bn. Gordon Highlanders, 255
  1st Bn. King's Dragoon Guards, 162
  1st Bn. Lincolnshire Regiment of Foot, 263, 271–73, 277
  1st Bn. Northampton Regiment, 253
  1st Bn. (Prince of Wales's) North Staffordshire Regiment, 263, 266
  1st Bn. (Queen's Own) Royal West Kent Regiment, 197
  1st Bn. Royal Irish Fusiliers, 201
  1st Bn. Royal Welsh Fusiliers, 232
  1st Bn. York and Lancaster Regiment, 206
  1st King's Dragoon Guards, 165
  1st Royal Sussex Regiment, 213, 215
  2nd Bn. 24th (the 2nd Warwickshire) Regiment of Foot, 158, 272
  2nd Bn. King's Own Scottish Borderers, 251
  2nd Bn. Sherwood Foresters (Deryshire) Regiment, 255
  2nd Rifle Brigade, 112, 117, 120–21, 263, 274
  3rd (Prince of Wales's) Dragoon Guards, 71
  4th Dragoon Guards, 214
  4th (King's Own) Regiment of Foot, 75–76
  5th (Princess Charlotte of Wales's) Dragoon Guards, 214
  10th Company, Royal Engineers, 78
  10th (Prince of Wales's Own) Royal Hussars, 206
  17th (Duke of Cambridge's Own) Lancers, 162
  19th (Queen Alexandra's Own) Royal Hussars, 206, 213–14
  21st (Empress of India's) Lancers, 263, 274, 276
  23rd (Royal Welsh Fusiliers) Regiment of Foot, 112, 117, 120
  24th Regiment of Foot, 157, 163–64
  32nd Battery, R.A., 274–75
  32nd Regiment of Foot, 28
  33rd (First Yorkshire West Riding) Regiment of Foot, 75, 78
  37th Battery, R.A., 274–75
  40th (2nd Somersetshire) Regiment of Foot, 95
  42nd (Royal Highland) Regiment of Foot (Black Watch), 108, 112–13, 118, 120–22, 200
  43rd (Monmouthshire) Regiment of Foot, 98
  44th (East Essex) Regiment of Foot, 134
  45th (Nottinghamshire) (Sherwood Foresters) Regiment of Foot, 78
  58th (Rutlandshire) Regiment of Foot, 181
  59th (2nd Northamptonshire) Regiment of Foot, 142
  60th King's Royal Rifle Corps, 181–82

318 Index

military units, British (cont.)
  65th (Second Yorkshire, North Riding) Regiment of Foot, 95
  66th (Berkshire) Regiment of Foot, 139
  68th (Durham) Regiment of Foot, 97
  79th (Queen's Own) Cameron Highlanders, 263, 265, 271–74, 278
  80th (Staffordshire Volunteers) Regiment of Foot, 159
  92nd (Gordon Highlanders) Regiment of Foot, 142, 181–82
  City of London Imperial Volunteers, 289
  Corps of Guides, 131, 134
  Duke of Cornwall's Light Infantry, 200
  Grenadier Guards, 263
  Highland Light Infantry, 200
  Imperial Yeomanry, 289, 297, 300, 309
  Lancashire Fusiliers, 263
  mounted infantry, 174, 213, 230, 234–35, 300
  Northumberland Fusiliers, 263
  Rimington's Guides, 302
  Royal Engineers, 52, 54, 117–20, 158, 174–75, 196
  Royal Horse Artillery (RHA), 198, 267
  Royal Irish Constabulary, 100
  Royal Marines, 45, 52, 110, 122, 197, 202, 205
  Royal Scots Fusiliers, 234
  Scots Guards, 213
  Seaforth Highlanders, 263, 271–72
  Volunteer Service Corps, 289
military units, British Imperial
  1st West India Regiment, 110, 112, 115
  2nd Madras Lancers, 232
  2nd (Prince of Wales's Own) Gurkha Regiment, 142–43, 255
  2nd West India Regiment, 107, 112, 115
  3rd Bengal Light Cavalry, 24–25
  3rd Bombay Light Cavalry, 71
  3rd Gurkha Regiment, 251
  3rd Regiment of Scinde Horse, 71
  3rd Sikhs, 255
  7th Oudh Irregular Infantry, 27
  8th Bengal Irregular Cavalry, 12
  10th Bengal Lancers, 71
  11th Bengal Native Infantry, 24
  12th Bengal Lancers, 71
  19th Bengal Lancers, 142
  19th Bengal Native Infantry, 15
  20th Bengal Native Infantry, 24
  21st Madras Infantry, 232
  25th Mountain Battery, Bombay Army, 71
  29th Bengal Native Infantry, 131
  34th Bengal Native Infantry, 15
  36th Sikhs, 245
  47th Bengal Native Infantry, 16
  Bengal Artillery, 28
  Bengal Sappers and Miners (later Bengal Engineers), 69
  Camel Corps, 209, 212–13, 263, 267, 274, 276
  Coolie Corps, 52, 227, 234
  Kahar corps, 71
  Khyber Rifles, 258
  Madras Sappers and Miners, 52, 76, 78
  Manipur Cavalry, 227
  Natal Mounted Volunteers, 163
  Natal Native Contingent, 153
  New Zealand Armed Constabulary, 100
  Peshawar Valley Field Force, 132
  Rangoon Volunteer Rifles, 234
military units, Chinese
  Banner Brigade, 46–47
  Green Standard, 46–47
Milner, Sir Alfred, 282–83, 299, 301, 306
Milyutin, Dimitri, 127
Mindat, 225
Mindon Min, King, 221
Minhla, 220
Mnyamana Buthelezi, 155
Modder River, 296–98, 302–3
Modder Spruit, 294
Mogaung, 231, 233
Mohammed, Dost, 126
Mohmand, 246
Montagu-Stuart-Wortley, Hon. Edward, 274
Mount Prospect, 178, 183
Moylan, Edward, 229
Mughal, Mirza, 22, 25–26, 31, 36, 38
Muhammad Ahma bin Abdullah (the Mahdi), 187, 208, 218, 260
Muhammad Ra'uf, Pasha, 203
Mumford, 113
Musket Wars, 83
Mzinyathi River, 155

Nakheila, 265, 271
Napier, Sir Robert, 65, 69–78, 80–81
Natal Field Force (NFF), 178–80
Neill, James, 26–27
Nevill, H.L., 253
Nga Puhi, 85
Ngāruawāhia, 96
Nicholson's Nek, 294
Niens, 42
Nile River, 4, 192–94, 202–4, 207, 260, 263–67, 269–71, 273–74, 277–78, 308

Blue, 208–12, 214–16, 277–79
Delta, 192, 197
White, 215, 261, 278
Nimach, 31
Ninth Cape Frontier War, 150, 153
Norman, Sir Henry, 9–10, 32–33
Northbrook, Thomas Baring, 1st Earl of, 126, 128
Northern War, 84–87, 90
North-West Frontier Province, 126, 144, 240–42, 246–47, 258, 282, 303, 309
Norton tube wells, 79
Ntombe River, 159
Ntshingwayo kaMahole, 156
Nubian Desert, 264, 268
Nuer, 208
Nyezane River, 156
Nyun, Bo Ya, 236

O'Donnell, H., 233
Oda River, 118
Ōhaeawai, 90
Olivier, Jan, 296
Omdurman, 215–17, 261, 263–65, 270–74, 297
oNdini (Ulundi), 154–56, 162–63, 165
opium, 40–43, 60
Opium War, 46
Ōpotiki, 99
Orakzais, 6, 240–41, 244, 246, 248–49, 252–53, 257–58
Orange Free State, 7, 171, 179, 281, 283, 285, 287–88, 290, 292–93, 296–99
Ottama, U, 225, 236
Ottoman Empire, ix, 68, 72, 130, 188, 190–91
Outram, Sir James, 28–29
Oxus River, 127

Paardeberg, 293, 298
Paardekraal, 173
Pāi Mārire, 98–100
Palmer, A. Power, 251
Palmerston, Henry John Temple, 3rd Viscount, 41–42, 52, 60, 66–67, 107
Pāterangi, 96–97
Pearson, Charles, 155–56, 159–61
Peel Commission, 37
Peel, Jonathan, 107
Pehtang (Beitang) River, 53, 58
Peiho (Hai) River, 40, 45, 48–53, 55–58, 60
Pekin, 51
Persia, 20, 28, 45, 69, 144
Peshawar, 246, 249, 253–54
Phayre, Sir Robert, 63, 69, 73, 76, 140

Pietermaritzburg, 178, 184, 291, 295
Pieter's Hill, 298
Plowden, Walter, 65–66
Poki, Hone Heke, 84
Pondicherry, 9
Poplar Grove, 298
Port Elizabeth, 289, 291
Port Said, 197
Portuguese East Africa (Mozambique), 291, 304
Potchefstroom, 171–73, 175–77
Potgeiter's Drift, 295, 297
Poverty Bay, 101
Pra River, 106–7, 110, 116–18
Pratt, Sir Thomas, 92–93
Prendergast, Sir Harry, 220, 227, 229–30
Pretoria, 168–69, 172, 175–77, 292, 295, 298
Pretoria Convention, 181, 281
Prideaux, W.F., 67
Primrose, James, 137, 139–40
Pritchard, Harry L., 266
Puketutu, 85
Pukhtun, 240, 243, 247
Pulleine, Henry, 163–64
Punjab, 5, 16, 19–21, 23–24, 32, 52, 60, 76, 227, 240, 258

Quetta, 128, 134, 140–41

Rahama, Zobeir, 203
Rahman, Abdur, 126, 133, 137–40, 143–44
railway, 35, 56, 68, 74, 122, 164, 184, 197, 200, 209–11, 231, 236, 264, 266–70, 273, 277
  Cape-Cairo railroad, 268
  Western Railway, 296, 302
Rait, Arthur, 113, 116, 119–21
Rangiriri, 94–96
Rangoon, 36, 220–21, 224, 236
Rani of Jhansi, the, 18, 21–22, 30
Rassam, Hormuzd, 67, 77
Rawalpindi, 246
Rawlinson, Sir Henry, 1st Baron, viii, 127, 237, 273
Reade, Winwood, 107, 120
Red Sea, 66, 79–80, 205, 260
Rewi Maniapoto, 96–97
Rey, J.H. de la, 296, 301–2
Rhodes, Cecil, 268, 281–82
Richards, F.W., 183
rifles and carbines
  Callisher and Terry carbine, 88
  Enfield rifle, 13, 19, 27, 34, 71, 88
  flintlock musket, 70, 88, 111, 227

320   Index

rifles and carbines (cont.)
  Lee-Metford rifle, 247, 252, 258
  Martini-Henry rifle, 122, 132, 165, 184, 195, 227, 247, 258
  matchlock musket, 35, 70
  Remington rifle, 193
  shotgun, double-barrelled, 70, 88
  Snider-Enfield rifle, 71, 76, 132, 227
  Westley-Richards rifle, 184
Ripon, George Robinson, 1st Marquess of, 128, 138–40
Roberts, Frederick, 1st Earl, 128, 131–38, 140–44, 226, 228, 230, 237, 240, 293, 295–300, 304
Röntgen rays, 256
Roos, Stephanus, 182
Roos-Keppel, George, 258
Rorke's Drift, 150, 154–62
Rose, Hugh, 1st Baron Strathnairn, 30
Rosetta, 192
Royal Navy
  Boadicea, 184
  brigade, 87, 96, 113, 117, 119, 122, 153, 174–75, 181–84, 200, 304–5
  Calcutta, 57
  Dido, 184
  Furious, 51
  gunners, 28, 87
  Hong Kong, 58
  Penelope, 304
  rocket brigade, 76, 78
  trade vessels, 40, 49
Ruapekapeka, 85, 90
Rundle, Sir H.M. Leslie, 266
Russell, John, 1st Earl, 66–67
Russell, Sir Baker, 113, 116, 119
Russell, William Howard, 10, 27, 29–30
Russia, 126–34, 137–38, 140, 144, 149, 188, 240, 308
Rustenburg, 172, 177

Sabluka (Sabaluqa), 265
Sahib, Nana, 18, 21, 26, 38
Salisbury Plain, 289
Salisbury, Robert Gascoygne-Cecil, 3rd Marquess of, 130, 261, 264, 266, 281, 283, 287, 291
Salween, 228
Samana, 242, 245–46, 248
Samarkand, 126
Sampagha Pass, 251
Sand River Convention, 168
Saragarhi, 245
Saran Sar, 252
Schuinshoogte, 179

Second Anglo-Asante War, 106, 110
Second Anglo-Boer War, 170, 185, 285
Second Anglo-Burmese War, 221
Second Anglo-China War, 69
Second Anglo-Pedi War, 169
Senafe (Senafay), 74–75
Seymour, Sir Michael, 49–51, 191
Shaftesbury, Anthony Ashley Cooper, 7th Earl of, 42
Shaka kaSenzangakhona, King, 147
Shalez, 137
Shan States, 221, 226, 232–33
Shanghai, 41, 46, 48, 51
Shepstone, Sir Theophilius, 146–50, 154, 168–69
Sherif, Mohammed esh, 208
Sherpur, 135–36
Shilluk, 208
Shinawari, 249–50
Shinde of Gwalior, 22
Shukaria, 207
Sidney, H.M., 269
siege train, 32, 35, 194
Sierra Leone, 107, 113
Sihayo kaXongo, 151, 155, 163
Sikhs, 5, 19–20, 28, 36, 231, 245, 255
Simla, 135
Simon's Town, 184, 304
Sittang, 227–28
Slim, William, 1st Viscount, 227
Smit, Nicolaas, 179, 182–83
Smith, W.H., 229
Smuts, Jan, 283, 287, 300
Smyth, Sir Leicester, 170, 178
Somopho kaZikhale, 161
Spion Kop, Battle of, 297
Spytfontein, 302
Standerton, 172, 177
Staveley, Sir Charles, 75–76
Stearn, Rev. Henry, 66
Stedman, Edward, 231, 237
Steevens, G.W., 295
Stewart, Sir Donald, 128, 132–35, 141–44
Stewart, Sir Herbert, 201, 212–14
Steyn, M.T., 283, 287–88, 301
Stolietov, Nikolai, 130
Stormberg, Battle of, 295–96
Straits Settlement, 45
Suakin, 68, 187, 205, 207, 210, 260–61, 266, 268, 270
Suez Canal, 6, 72, 167, 188, 191–92, 196–97
Supayalat, Queen, 220–21
Susu, 113, 121
Swanzy F. & A., 123

Index

Swat, 240
Swe, Boh, 225
Sweetwater Canal, 193, 195, 198–99
Swinhoe, Robert, 54–56, 59
Symons, William Penn, 234–35, 237, 292, 294

Taiping, 42, 47, 203
Taiping Rebellion, 59
Taku (Dagu) forts, 45, 47, 51–55, 59–60
Talana Hill, Battle of, 294
Talien (Dalian), 48–49, 52
Talien Bay, 57
Tangku (Tanggu), 53, 55
Tantia Tope, 23, 30, 38
Taranaki War, 85–88, 91–94, 99–101
Tartars, 46, 52–55, 58, 60
Tashkent, 127
Tauranga Campaign, 86–87, 97–98, 101
Te Ahuahu, 90
Te Arei, 92
Te Ātiawa, 91–92
Te Kooti Arikirangi Te Turuki, 86, 100–2, 104
Te Ngutu o te Manu, 101
Te Ranga, 98
telegraph, 18, 35–36, 57, 79, 93, 122, 134, 164, 184, 207, 246, 248, 269, 277–78, 299
Tel el-Kebir, 202, 219, 229
Tel el-Kebir, Battle of, 195–99
Tenasserim, 221
Tewabech, 63
Tewfik, Khedive, 190, 192
Tewodros II, 6, 62–80
Teze, 232
Thayetmyo, 227
Thibaw, King, 220–24
Thomas Cook and Sons, 211
Thomsett, Richard, 254
Thukela (Tugela) River, 155, 161
Tientsin (Tianjin), 41, 45, 49–51, 53, 55–59
Tirah Expeditionary Force (TEF), 242–58
Titokowaru, 86, 104
Tofrek, 187
Tokar, 205, 261, 265
Toungoo, 227, 231, 236
traditional weapons, 194
    bayonet, 35, 76, 78, 113, 142, 178, 184, 193, 195, 200, 206, 214, 235
    bow, 227
    dagger, 131
    javelin, 209
    kaskaras, 209
    kourbash, 194

lance, 132
shield, 70, 152, 208
spear, 47, 56, 70, 131, 152, 206, 208–9, 227, 233, 275–76
sword, 47, 56, 70, 113, 131–32, 141–43, 208
tomahawk, 88
Transkei, 173, 178
Transvaal (South African Republic), 146, 148–50, 167–73, 175–82, 184–85, 218, 281–83, 285, 287–88, 293–94
    annexation, 298–99
    border, 151, 154, 160
    government, 165, 290, 306
    military forces, 7
Travers, Eaton, 255
Treaty of Fomena, 123
Treaty of Gandamak, 134
Treaty of Tientsin, 45, 51
Treaty of Vereeniging, 294, 302, 306
Treaty of Waitangi, 83–84
Trichardt's Drift, 297
Tuker, Sir Francis, 38
Turkmen, 127
Tweebosch, 301

U, Bo Hla, 225
uDloko, 158
Uitlanders, 281
uKhahlamba (Drakensberg), 147
Um Dibaykarat, 279
uMxhapho, 156
use of animals, 78–79, 81, 137, 140, 166, 196, 243, 246, 249, 251, 253–54, 256–57
    bullock, 72, 74, 79, 250, 256
    camel, 72, 79, 209–13, 256, 266–67, 269, 271, 277
    cattle, 13, 19, 55, 147, 160, 166
    donkey, 72, 79, 256
    elephant, 72, 75, 79, 227
    horse, 72, 79, 174, 183, 197, 206, 230, 234–35, 276, 290, 297–98
    mule, 72, 74, 79, 114, 235, 255–57
    pack animals, 70, 230, 250, 257
    pig, 13
    pony, 72, 227, 230, 234, 256
uThulwana, 158
Utrecht, 177
Uys, J., 183

Vaal Krantz, Battle of, 297
Victoria Cross, 78, 159, 276
Victoria Memorial, 38
Victoria, Queen, 30, 66–67, 123, 127, 210
Völkner, Carl, 99

volksraad, 173
Volta River, 111, 116
Voortrekkers, 153, 173

Wad Hamed, 274
Wade, Thomas, 46–47
Wadi Halfa, 211–12, 260, 267–69, 277
Wagentrieber, George, 34
Wagon Hill, 294
Waikato River, 87, 93–95
Waikato War, 86–88, 91, 93–97, 104
Waimate, 90
Waireka (Kaipopo), 85, 91
Wāka Nene, Tāmati, 85, 90
Wakkerstroom, 172, 176–77
Wardaks, 131
Warren, Sir Charles, 297
Wassaw, 113, 117
Watson, J.K., 275
Wauchope, Andrew, 276, 303
Waziristan, 240
Wellington, 87, 90
Wessel, Marthinius, 173
Westmacott, Richard, 251–52
Wet, Christiaan de, 298
Whanganui River, 99
Wheeler, Sir Hugh, 19, 25–26
White Mfolozi River, 162
White Mutiny, 36
White, Sir George, 227–29, 233–38, 292–94, 297, 303–4
Whitmore, George, 101–2

Wilhelm II, Kaiser, 281
Wilson, Sir Archdale, 32
Wilson, Sir Charles, 214–15, 217
Wilson, Sir Henry, 237
Wingate, Sir F. Reginald, 260–61, 266–67, 269–71, 279
Witwatersrand, 168
Wolseley, Garnet, 1st Viscount, 6, 111–24, 161, 165–66, 169–70, 187, 191–92, 196–99, 201–2, 210–13, 217–18, 283–84, 292
Wonderfontein, 168–69
Wood, Sir H. Evelyn, 113, 120–21, 155, 159–62, 179–81, 202
Wuntho Expedition, 226

Xhosa, 55, 150

Ye Men, Commissioner, 50
Yeatman-Biggs, H., 249, 254–55
Yejju, 63
Ye-u, 232
Yule, James, 294

Zagazig, 200–1
Zand River, 298
Zariba, 213–14, 272–73, 275
Zayn, Mohamed el, Emir, 269
Zeerust, 177
Zobeir, Pasha, 207
Zula, 73–74, 78–79
Zululand, 136, 146, 154, 161, 164–66